Characteristics of Tasks in the Domain of Accounting

Simone Reindl-Stütz

Characteristics of Tasks in the Domain of Accounting

Springer

Simone Reindl-Stütz
Hofkirchen an der Trattnach, Austria

Dissertation at the Faculty of Social Sciences and Economics of the Johannes Kepler University Linz, 2023

ISBN 978-3-658-48957-1 ISBN 978-3-658-48958-8 (eBook)
https://doi.org/10.1007/978-3-658-48958-8

This book is a translation of the original German edition "Charakteristika von Aufgaben in der Domäne Rechnungswesen" by Simone Stütz, published by Springer Fachmedien Wiesbaden GmbH in 2024. The translation was done with the help of an artificial intelligence machine translation tool. A subsequent human revision was done primarily in terms of content, so that the book will read stylistically differently from a conventional translation. Springer Nature works continuously to further the development of tools for the production of books and on the related technologies to support the authors.

This Springer imprint is published by the registered company Springer Fachmedien Wiesbaden GmbH, part of Springer Nature.
The registered company address is: Abraham-Lincoln-Str. 46, 65189 Wiesbaden, Germany

Preface

Writing a dissertation poses a significant challenge that can only be overcome with the support of many individuals. Therefore, upon successful completion of the project, it is time to thank all those people who have wonderfully supported me over the past few years and have thus significantly contributed to the success of this dissertation.

First and foremost, my special thanks go to my doctoral supervisor, Univ.-Prof. Mag. Dr. Georg Hans Neuweg. Thank you very much for the unconditional support over the past years, for the many appreciative feedbacks and the numerous opportunities to develop professionally and especially personally in the course of my work at the institute. I would also like to thank my second supervisor, Univ.-Prof. Dr. Florian Berding. Thank you for the constructive and educational collaboration in different projects and for the support in the preparation of the dissertation. I would also like to thank Univ.-Prof. Mag. Dr. Christoph Helm, who not only served as a mentor in a career mentoring program, but who has always been open to my concerns and questions over the past years. My special thanks also go to all former and current employees of the Institute for Business and Vocational Education, with whom I have had the pleasure to work over the past years. I would like to particularly mention Dragana Papić, Mag.ª Michaela Mitterlehner, Dr. Martin Steger and Mag. Ruben Kulcsar. Thank you for the always good cooperation and for the encouraging and motivating words in difficult situations. Special thanks go to Mag.ª Michaela Mitterlehner, who has discussed the category system with me in countless conversations and has always given me valuable suggestions for further development. I would also like to thank our student assistant and diploma candidate, Simone Breitenthaller, who has made codings in the course of her diploma thesis. I would also like to thank all the people who have critically, but always appreciatively, discussed my dissertation project in the context of conferences or informal conversations.

Special thanks go to my friends and my family, without whose support and backing I would never have managed the doctoral project. My parents, Christiane and Josef, are the most generous, loving, and selfless people I know. I thank them from the bottom of my heart for their unconditional and unrestricted support. I thank them for always standing behind me and their trust in me is unwavering. Without them, I would not be where I am today. This work is dedicated to them.

My greatest thanks go to my partner Christoph. His ambition, his discipline, and his motivation inspire me every day. I thank him for his moral support over the past years, for his encouraging words in challenging times, for his unconditional love, for his incomparable humor, and for his faith in me and my endeavor.

Linz
June 2023

Simone Stütz

Contents

List of Figures

List of Tables

Introduction 1

1.1 Problem Statement

Accounting forms the "core of the operational information system" (Preiß, 2000, p. 50). It provides economically relevant information within the company and fulfills important functions of documentation, planning, control, and monitoring. It thus primarily serves to support entrepreneurial decisions by providing a computationally sound basis for decision-making (Schierenbeck & Wöhle, 2016, p. 601). Central terms of operational accounting, such as assets and capital, receivables and liabilities, inflows and outflows, revenues and expenditures, earnings and expenses, services and costs, profit and loss, are therefore not only relevant for people who are directly involved in accounting. Rather, they represent "central categories of commercial thinking and action" (Preiß, 2015, p. 189). Various departments and the people working there within a company access accounting data and use it as a basis to independently make economically justified and rational decisions. Tramm and Preiß (1996, p. 5) therefore argue that accounting knowledge is necessary for any commercial activity. Furthermore, Schneider (2010, pp. 57–58) notes that every economically active person should have a basic understanding of how accounting works. He goes a step further and sees accounting knowledge as part of a general understanding of economics. Tramm (2003, p. 5) refers to accounting as the "key to economic thinking."

S. Reindl-Stütz, *Characteristics of Tasks in the Domain of Accounting*,
https://doi.org/10.1007/978-3-658-48958-8_1

Given the significant position of operational accounting as an information system in companies, it is obvious that accounting also occupies a central role in business vocational education.[1]

The importance of accounting and accounting instruction is also reflected in the didactic research efforts of recent years and decades. There are theoretical and empirical research contributions on the didactic design of accounting instruction (for an overview see Bouley, 2017), on learning difficulties in instruction (Pawlik, 1979, 1980; Schiller, 2004; Seifried & Wuttke, 2010; Tramm et al., 1996; Türling et al., 2011; Wuttke & Seifried, 2012), on teaching materials (e.g. Bloemen, 2011; Ernst, 2011, 2012a; Stütz et al., 2022; Thoma & Schumacher, 2018; Wuttke et al., 2022; Zhou, 2022) on the methodical design of instruction (e.g. Götzl & Jahn, 2014; Götzl et al., 2013; Jahn, 2020; Seifried, 2004b, 2006a, 2008; Seifried et al., 2006), on competence models for the domain of accounting (e.g. Guggemos, 2016; Guggemos & Schönlein, 2015; Preiß, 2005a) or on the professional competence of (prospective) accounting teachers (e.g. Berding, 2015; Berger, 2015; Findeisen, 2017; Helm & Mayer, 2016; Riebenbauer, 2015, 2021; Schopf & Zwischenbrugger, 2015). Developments in didactic research in recent years include, for example, the identification of basic ideas ("Grundvorstellungen") in accounting (Berding, 2019; Berding, Riebenbauer & Slepcevic-Zach, 2019; Berding et al., 2021), the transfer of the modeling cycle developed in mathematics didactics into the domain of accounting to describe processes in dealing with problems from accounting (e.g. Berding, 2019; Berding, Beckmann & Kürten, 2019) as well as the development of the "Linzer Ebenenmodell" (Neuweg, 2020) and other didactic approaches (e.g. the Learning Cockpit by Pargmann et al., 2022).

As far as the target dimension of accounting instruction is concerned, two guiding images, that of the "practical accountant" and that of the "thinking accountant," have long been opposed to each other (Reinisch, 1996, 2005).[2] In the didactic discussion, there is agreement that teaching should not only be about imparting booking and calculation skills, but rather, in the sense of promoting

---

[1] For example, at Austrian commercial academies, the subject of business accounting, together with the subject of business administration, forms the core of vocational subjects. The subject is allocated 14 weekly hours over five years (BMBF, 2014, p. 8). In Germany, too, accounting occupies a central position in the training regulations and framework curricula of commercial professions. An analysis of 55 business vocational training professions conducted by Brötz et al. (2015, p. 93) shows that around 38% of all contents of the learning field "Commercial Control and Monitoring" are specific to accounting.

[2] The terms "practical" and "thinking accountant" are considered as proper names for a target category and are therefore not gendered.

"thinking accountants," about building a basic understanding of how accounting works and its purpose. In addition, accounting should not only be understood in its function of documenting operational processes, but as an instrument for recording, monitoring, and controlling operational processes, and should be used accordingly in teaching (e.g. Neuweg, 2020; Preiß, 2015; Tramm, 2014; Tramm & Preiß, 1996). Closely linked to the demand for the training of "thinking accountants," the ability to model is introduced as a central target category for instruction in accounting, referring to the modeling cycle originating from mathematics didactics. Students should acquire in class the ability "to model real phenomena with concepts and methods of accounting" and experience accounting as an "effective tool or instrument for understanding and shaping concrete phenomena in reality" (Berding, Beckmann & Kürten, 2019, pp. 569–570).

Curricula and teaching practice, of course, follow much more the guiding image of the "practical accountant." In teaching, there is often a one-sided focus on acquiring (mostly manual) booking and calculation skills in the area of financial accounting and emphasizing the documentation function of accounting, while balance sheet policy considerations, legal foundations, and the control and monitoring functions of accounting are underrepresented (Neuweg, 2020; Preiß, 2005a; Reinisch, 1996; Seifried & Sembill, 2005a; Tramm & Preiß, 1996). However, it is also doubtful whether the training of "practical accountants" is successful at all, as teaching has now moved too far away from the requirements of the economy and the changes that have taken place there, especially in the light of digitization, have not been sufficiently taken into account (Preiß, 2015, p. 190).

The demand for a stronger orientation towards the guiding image of the "thinking accountant" therefore seems particularly relevant in view of the dramatically changed world of work and will become even more acute, especially with the availability and use of Artificial Intelligence (AI). Thus, through digitization and the use of RPA (Robotic Process Automation) and AI systems, a large number of standard tasks in accounting, such as the booking of invoices, are now automated by IT systems. Routine tasks, such as data entry, account assignment, and booking of business transactions, are therefore increasingly disappearing. More important, however, are competencies for checking, modifying, and interpreting data and for recognizing relationships and interactions between individual areas of accounting (Hmyzo & Muzzu, 2020, p. 103; Preiß, 2015, pp. 192–193; Riebenbauer et al., 2022, pp. 202–203).

In addition to the question of which goals to pursue in teaching, the question also arises as to how these goals can be achieved. The processing of tasks plays a central role in school learning processes, as they significantly contribute to achieving the teaching objectives pursued in class (Blömeke et al., 2006, p. 334;

Kleinknecht & Schmid-Kühn, 2020, p. 410). While some areas in accounting didactics have already been intensively empirically researched or are being researched[3] , there are so far only a few findings on the quality and characteristics of tasks in the domain of accounting. The existing research results on tasks in accounting teaching suggest that many of the tasks are cognitively not very demanding, have little connection to the learners' life world, aim at the reproduction of knowledge and are therefore to be classified at a low level in terms of learning objective taxonomy (Bloemen, 2011; Ernst, 2012a; Schalek, 2007; Thoma & Schumacher, 2018; Wuttke et al., 2022; Zhou, 2022). It is obvious that the tasks in accounting also poorly fulfill the objectives discussed in the current didactic discussion, such as the promotion of modeling skills or the training to become "thinking accountants", but systematic investigations from a *didactic* perspective are still lacking. Looking at the current state of task research in the domain of accounting, a central research desideratum can be identified first.

Desideratum 1: There is a lack of explicitly *didactic evaluation criteria* and a *didactic category system* for analyzing and evaluating tasks from the domain of accounting, which was developed based on the current state of didactic discussion. Thus, all existing studies either use general didactic evaluation criteria, which can be used equally in different domains, or for example the category system developed by Bloemen (2011), which primarily focuses on professional action competence and was also not specifically developed for accounting and does not establish any connections to the didactic discussion. Didactic differentiations in task analysis are therefore still a research desideratum (Thonhauser, 2020, p. 473).

The dissertation aims to contribute to closing this research gap by identifying didactic criteria for the analysis and evaluation of tasks in accounting based on literature and developing a comprehensive category system based on these criteria. The basis for the development of the classification system is the current didactic discussion, in particular the construct of the "thinking accountant", the modeling cycle originating from mathematics didactics, and the "Linzer Ebenenmodell", which was developed to overcome a narrow focus of accounting teaching on booking activities in financial accounting and to take other aspects (e.g. the importance of legal bases, the consideration of formal business objectives) into account (Neuweg, 2020). The present work is therefore also conceived as a

[3] It should be noted with all empirical research findings that these largely originate from Germany. The transferability to the full-time commercial vocational education system in Austria is certainly debatable.

method study. Method studies primarily serve the development or further development of new scales, test procedures or research designs and have the claim that the results of the studies can be used by many other researchers (Döring & Bortz, 2016, pp. 187–188). In this sense, the didactic category system developed in the course of the dissertation project should also be made accessible to other researchers and thus contribute to the further development of didactic research in the domain of accounting, especially task research.

Following the theory-guided development of the category system, it will be subjected to an initial trial and empirically explored whether and to what extent tasks in the domain of accounting meet the requirements in terms of the category scheme. This can address a second research desideratum.

Desideratum 2: So far, there is a lack of empirical findings on the characterization of tasks used in *Austrian* accounting teaching. With Thoma and Schumacher (2018), there is only one published study that explicitly looks at tasks for accounting from Austrian textbooks. Therefore, tasks contained in Austrian textbooks will be analyzed and evaluated using the didactic category system. This can not only expand the empirical research status on tasks in accounting in general, but also focus on tasks from Austrian textbooks, an area that has so far been little or not at all illuminated.

The textbook tasks for accounting teaching at *commercial colleges ("Handelsakademien")* are chosen as the subject of the investigation. The "Handelsakademie" is a higher vocational school at the secondary level II. Together with the Higher Institute for Economic Professions (HLW), it forms the "institutional framework for economic vocational education in Austria" (Aff & Greimel-Fuhrmann, 2018, p. 208).[4] The commercial academy is focused because it is a central school type in the field of higher commercial education in Austria. The "market share" of the commercial academy among all Higher Vocational Schools is about 26% (37,814 out of 144,074 students in the 2020/21 school year). In comparison, the share of the HLW is around 18% (Statistics Austria, 2022, p. 129). Aff and Greimel-Fuhrmann (2018, p. 205) also refer to the commercial academy as the "most important economic vocational training track". According to § 65 and § 74 para. 1

[4] A special feature of the Austrian education system is that full-time vocational schools, alongside the dual system, represent a central pillar of vocational education (Aff & Greimel-Fuhrmann, 2018, p. 206). In the 2020/21 school year, 144,074 students attended a Higher Vocational School, 116,759 a vocational school. Overall, the proportion of students in vocational education at the secondary level II is very high at around 80% (Statistics Austria, 2022, p. 129).

of the School Organization Act (SchOG), it serves the acquisition of higher commercial education for all branches of the economy. The curriculum also stipulates that the training is equally oriented towards employability (*employability*) and study ability (*studiability*) and therefore provides integrated commercial education and general education (BMBF, 2014, p. 1). Accounting is anchored in the commercial academy as a separate subject under the name "business accounting" and is allocated 14 weekly hours spread over five grades (BMBF, 2014, pp. 1–8).

In light of the previous explanations, the dissertation project pursues two interests in knowledge.

First interest in knowledge: What are meaningful criteria for evaluating tasks for the domain of accounting in light of the current didactic discussion? How should a didactic category system for analyzing and evaluating tasks from the domain of accounting be designed?

Second interest in knowledge: How is the potential of textbook tasks in the domain of accounting, specifically for the subject of business accounting at Austrian commercial academies, to be assessed in light of the didactic criteria?

1.2 Approach and Structure of the Work

The research questions of the dissertation are answered by presenting the current state of discussion on selected aspects in accounting didactics in Chap. 2. First, a brief academic classification of accounting is made (Sect. 2.1). In Sect. 2.2, different goal categories for accounting education are discussed, particularly the two opposing models of the "practical" and the "thinking accountant". Furthermore, it is examined how the working world in the accounting profession is changing due to digitization and the use of digital technologies, and what consequences this has for goal setting in teaching. In Sect. 2.3, different competence models for the domain of accounting are presented. Sect. 2.4 is dedicated to various didactic approaches, especially the balance sheet method and the economic-instrumental accounting. The conclusion of this chapter is Sect. 2.5, which deals with learning and comprehension difficulties in accounting and their potential causes.

Based on an approximation to the state of research in didactics, Chap. 3 first addresses the ability to model in accounting. For this purpose, the modeling cycle developed in mathematics didactics is presented (Sect. 3.1) and it is explained how and in what form this has already been transferred to the domain of accounting (Sect. 3.2). Building on this, Sect. 3.3 introduces the Linz Level Model as a key reference concept for the development of the category system, which addresses many of the current criticisms of "traditional" accounting education and aims to contribute to the development of "thinking accountants" in accounting education and promote the ability to model.

In Chap. 4, the importance of tasks for learning processes is first discussed (Sect. 4.1). Subsequently, existing cross-domain and domain-specific categories and classification systems for the analysis and evaluation of tasks are presented (Sect. 4.2) and current research findings on the quality of tasks in accounting and related domains are discussed (Sect. 4.3).

In Chap. 5, using the "Linzer Ebenenmodell", approaches from accounting didactics, and the modeling cycle, a category system for the analysis and evaluation of tasks for the domain of accounting is developed. The classification scheme is used to analyze and evaluate existing tasks from textbooks for the subject of corporate accounting.

In Chap. 6, the empirical survey is planned. For this purpose, the research questions are first concretized in Sect. 6.1. It is then explained which methods of data evaluation are used (Sect. 6.2). In Sect. 6.3, the methods of data collection are described and the sample is defined.

The results of the empirical explorations are detailed in Chap. 7. In Chap. 8, the results are discussed in the light of previous research findings (Sect. 8.1) and the didactic discourse (Sect. 8.2). The work concludes with implications (Sect. 8.3), limitations of the study (Sect. 8.4) and a final consideration (Sect. 8.5). Fig. 1.1 shows the structure of the dissertation.

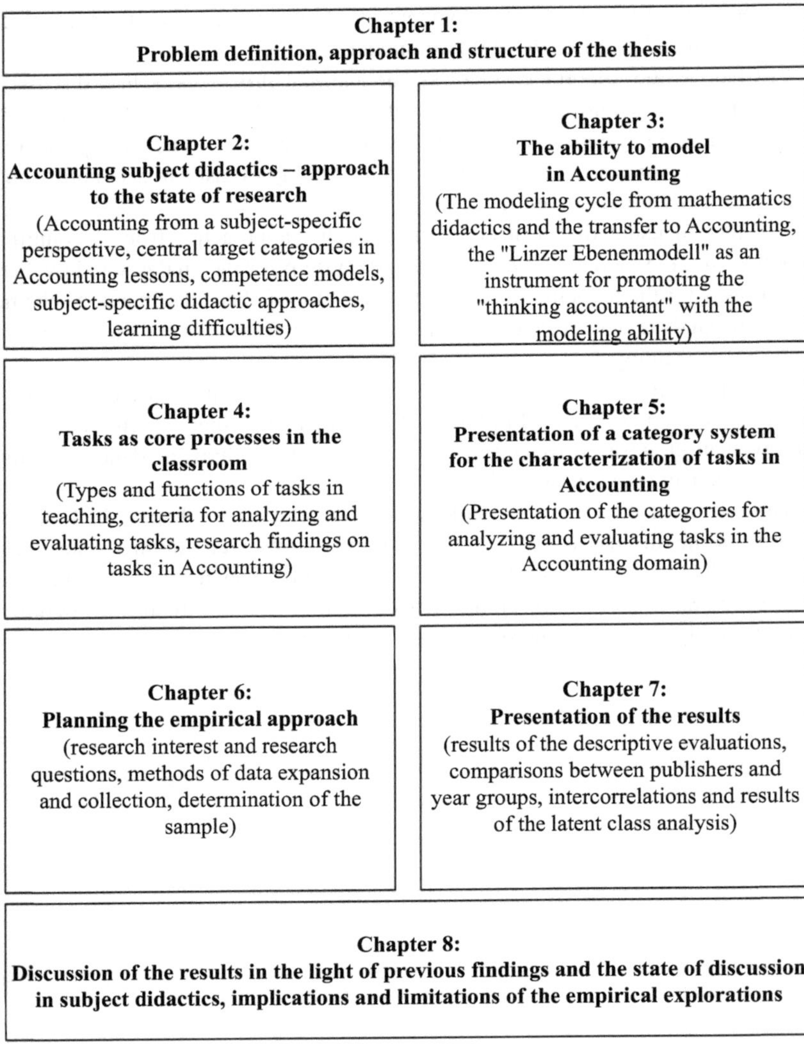

Fig. 1.1 Structure of the Dissertation

2 Didactics of Accounting—Approaching the State of Research

As already mentioned, there are numerous theoretical and empirical works on accounting didactics in the German-speaking area. For example, Helm (2016b) identified more than 370 contributions (including about 80 empirical works) on accounting didactics in a review. Thematically, the theoretical and empirical works can be assigned to different subject areas and deal with, for example,

- the historical development of accounting and accounting education (e.g., Dubs, 1996; Reinisch, 1994, 1996, 2005),
- objectives and guiding principles of accounting education (e.g., Achtenhagen, 1996; Preiß & Tramm, 1996; Reinisch, 1996, 2005; Schneider, 2000, 2005, 2010; Sloane, 1996; Tramm & Preiß, 1996),
- subject-didactic approaches, their advantages and disadvantages, and their effects on learning processes and learning success (e.g., Bouley, 2016, 2017; Burkhardt et al., 2014; Dolzsanksi, 2013b, 2014; Goldbach, 2012; Gross, 1990; Joost et al., 2007; Mathes, 2008; Minnameier & Link, 2010; Plinke, 2010, 2011a, 2011b, 2012, 2013, 2014a, 2014b, 2014c, 2015; Preiß, 1999, 2008, 2011; Preiß & Tramm, 1996; Rückwart, 2009, 2010; Seifried, 2004b; Sloane, 1996; Stommel, 2014a, 2014b; Tramm, 2005; Tramm & Preiß, 1996),
- learning difficulties and student errors (Deppe, 2017; Pawlik, 1979, 1980; Schiller, 2004; Tramm et al., 1996; Türling, 2014; Türling et al., 2011; Wuttke & Seifried, 2012),
- the development of competence models in accounting or in business vocational education (Beck et al., 2016; Guggemos, 2016; Guggemos & Schönlein, 2015; Helm, 2016a; Klotz & Winther, 2012; Lehmann & Seeber, 2007; Preiß, 2005a, 2005b; Weber et al., 2021; Weber, Wiethe-Körprich et al., 2016;

S. Reindl-Stütz, *Characteristics of Tasks in the Domain of Accounting*,
https://doi.org/10.1007/978-3-658-48958-8_2

Winther, 2010; Winther & Achtenhagen, 2008; Wuttke & Seifried, 2012; Wuttke et al., 2015),
- the learning success of learners and influencing factors on it, as well as motivational and emotional aspects of learners (e.g., Bouley, 2017; Fortmüller, 2012; Greimel-Fuhrmann, 2008, 2011; Helm, 2015, 2016c, 2016e, 2019; Helm & Stütz, 2020; Holtsch & Eberle, 2018; Kögler, 2015; Kögler & Wuttke, 2012; Schopf et al., 2018; Seifried, 2004a, 2004b, 2004d; Seifried & Klüber, 2006; Wuttke, 1999),
- epistemological beliefs and basic ideas of learners (Berding, 2015, 2016a, 2016b, 2018, 2019, 2020; Berding & Jahncke, 2020; Berding, Riebenbauer & Slepcevic-Zach, 2019; Berding et al., 2017; Berding et al., 2021),
- textbook and task analyses, e.g., the readability of textbooks, illustrations in textbooks, or the cognitive stimulation of textbook tasks (Bloemen, 2011; Ernst, 2011, 2012b, 2012c; Fritsch & Kopf, 2014; Kefer, 2013; Kombacher, 2016; Stock et al., 2011; Stütz et al., 2022; Thoma & Schumacher, 2018; Wuttke et al., 2022; Zhou, 2022),
- the professional competence of (prospective) teachers and influencing factors on it (e.g., Berding, 2015; Berding & Lamping, 2014; Berger, 2015; Bouley et al., 2015; Findeisen, 2017; Fortmüller & Grabowski, 2013; Helm & Mayer, 2016; Mindnich et al., 2013; Riebenbauer, 2015, 2020; Schopf & Zwischenbrugger, 2015; Seifried, 2006a, 2006b, 2009b, 2010; Stütz, 2021; Türling, 2014),
- the methodical design of teaching (e.g., Götzl & Jahn, 2014; Götzl et al., 2013; Jahn, 2020; Seifried, 2008; Seifried et al., 2006) as well as
- in recent years also with the changes in the accounting profession and the resulting need for adjustments in accounting education (e.g., Bieker, 2019; Hmyzo & Muzzu, 2020; Jordanski, 2020; Klein & Küst, 2020; Pargmann et al., 2022; Schröder, 2020)

Research on accounting didactics deals with many different focal points. A complete presentation and processing of the current state of research is therefore not possible within the scope of this work. Only an approximation to the current state of research with a focus on aspects relevant to the present study is possible. In the following, those contributions and empirical findings are presented and discussed that appear relevant for the theoretical foundation of the Linz level model, the modeling cycle, and subsequently the category system for the analysis and evaluation of tasks in accounting. This includes first a brief approach to accounting from a professional perspective (Sect. 2.1). From a subject-didactic perspective, the target categories and guiding principles of accounting education worked out in the subject-didactic discussion and their evaluation in the light of drastic changes in the labor market (Sect. 2.2) are relevant. Also relevant are the existing competence models for the domain of accounting (Sect. 2.3), the central subject-didactic approaches (Sect. 2.4) as well as learning difficulties in accounting and potential causes for them (Sect. 2.5).

2.1 Accounting from a Professional Perspective

Before looking at the domain of accounting from a subject-didactic perspective, a brief approach to accounting from a professional perspective should first be made.

Business accounting "includes all calculation systems for recording, documenting, analyzing, controlling, and monitoring the payment and performance flows occurring in the company" (Denk et al., 2016, p. 1). It thus represents the central information system of the company and fulfills, depending on the sub-area, different tasks and functions (Denk et al., 2016, p. 1; Schierenbeck & Wöhle, 2016, p. 601; Schneider et al., 2022, p. 17).

Firstly, a key task is to represent and document the company's processes in terms of value and quantity in the accounting system (documentation function). In addition to documenting operational processes, it is also about providing data or information for future processes and for business decisions, as well as preparing data for behavioral control (disposition function/control function). Thus, the operational accounting system provides a computational basis for corporate policy decision-making processes. Furthermore, it is the task of the operational accounting system to provide information for planning and subsequently to identify differences between planning and implementation. This refers to the planning and control function of accounting. The operational accounting system also fulfills central information functions for various internal and external stakeholders, e.g. for shareholders, creditors, the company management, employees, suppliers and customers, as well as the tax authorities (Bertl et al., 2022; Buchholz & Gerhards, 2016, p. 3; Denk et al., 2016, p. 1; Schierenbeck & Wöhle, 2016, p. 601; Schneider et al., 2022, p. 17; Töpfer, 2007, p. 1030–1031). The stakeholders differ in their information needs. While for creditors the central question is whether current and future liabilities can be serviced on time, shareholders are primarily interested in the current and future prospects of the company. For the tax authorities, the tax base and the amount of taxes to be paid are relevant (Wöhe et al., 2020, p. 630).

The operational accounting system is also based on a number of different calculation variables, the use of which is primarily oriented towards the information needs of the respective stakeholders and varies depending on the sub-area (Töpfer, 2007, p. 1032; Wöhe et al., 2020, p. 631). To classify the processes, four different pairs of terms are usually used: inflows and outflows, revenues and expenditures, income and expenses, services and costs. These are usually referred to as calculation or flow variables. Changes in the calculation variables (increases or decreases) subsequently lead to a change in the associated stock variable (Bertl et al., 2022, p. 6–7; Denk et al., 2016, p. 6; Schierenbeck & Wöhle, 2016, p. 617–618). Figure 2.1 shows calculation variables and stock variables and indicates in which sub-area of operational accounting these calculation and stock variables are used.

The terms inflows and outflows are primarily relevant for financial planning, where they refer to the inflow and outflow of liquid funds. In the context of financial planning, inflows and outflows are compared to ensure liquidity in the company in the short, medium, and long term and to identify any capital requirements. In the balance sheet, inflows and outflows are reflected in the liquid funds (Bertl et al., 2022, p. 6; Buchholz & Gerhards, 2016, p. 9–10; Denk et al., 2016, p. 6; Wöhe et al., 2020, p. 633).

Revenues and expenditures are to be distinguished from inflows and outflows, with these two pairs of terms overlapping. Revenues include inflows, in addition to which increases in receivables and decreases in liabilities also fall

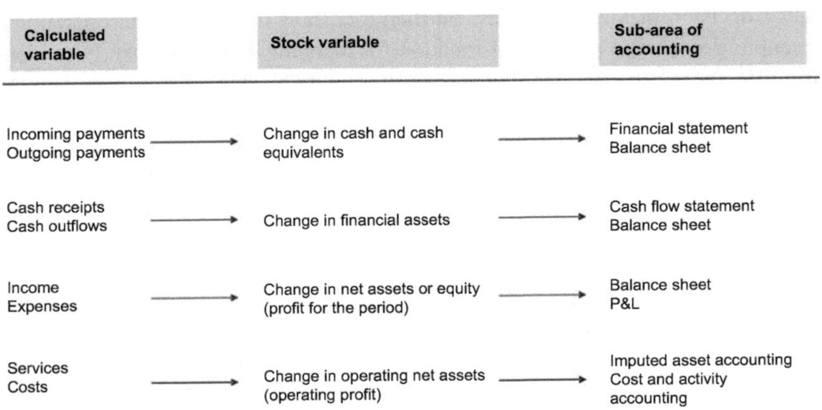

Fig. 2.1 Calculation and stock variables in accounting (Denk et al., 2016, p. 6)

under revenues. Analogously, expenditures include outflows on the one hand, and reductions in receivables and increases in liabilities on the other. Revenues and expenditures affect the stock variable “money assets”. In the balance sheet, a change in the money assets appears in the liquid funds as well as in the receivables and liabilities (Bertl et al., 2022, p. 6; Denk et al., 2016, p. 7; Wöhe et al., 2020, p. 633).

The pair of terms income and expenses is relevant for determining success in the context of the annual financial statements. Expense is understood as “the use of assets expressed in monetary units for a certain period. The use of assets is the total value consumption of the company, excluding changes in value serving the private purpose of the company” (Bertl et al., 2022, p. 6). Analogously, income represents remuneration valued in money for services rendered. The difference between income and expenses is the profit or loss, which in turn reduces or increases the net assets of the company. In the income statement, income and expenses are shown according to types of income (or types of expenses). In the balance sheet, the change in the equity position represents the success of the period (Bertl et al., 2022, p. 6; Buchholz & Gerhards, 2016, p. 11; Denk et al., 2016, p. 9; Schierenbeck & Wöhle, 2016, p. 618).

Services (revenues) and costs are terms of cost and performance accounting. A service is “a value increase valued in money, which is closely related to the operational service creation and utilization. Costs are the valued consumption of goods related to the objective of a billing period” (Denk et al., p. 12). The operational necessity (the objective reference) is thus an essential distinguishing criterion between services or costs and income or expenses. The difference between revenues and costs is the operating result (Wöhe et al., 2020, p. 636).

In connection with the different flow variables, the terms “pagatory” and “calculatory” should be mentioned and explained. The term “pagatory”[1] is a term of external accounting and means that only those processes that in some way relate to an actual payment flow are to be recorded in accounting. This does not mean that only cash payments are recorded in accounting, but that accounting processes must be linked to payments in order to be recorded. Calculatory costs, on the other hand, are not based on actual payment transactions, but can also be based on a fictitious, theoretical value consumption, which is taken into account in cost and performance accounting (e.g., a calculatory entrepreneur’s wage can be set in the context of a calculation, even though it is not a real expense in the company)

[1] Derived from the Latin word “pagare” = “to pay”.

(Buchholz & Gerhards, 2016, p. 21–23; Töpfer, 2007, p. 1070; Troßmann & Baumeister, 2015, p. 17–19).

When attempting to structure corporate accounting, it can initially be determined that the attempts at systematization are by no means uniform (Schierenbeck & Wöhle, 2016, pp. 601–602). A distinction that, however, appears in a large number of systematization proposals is the division into external and internal accounting (e.g. Buchholz & Gerhards, 2016, p. 6; Denk et al., 2016, pp. 2–4; Töpfer, 2007, p. 1031; Troßmann & Baumeister, 2015, p. 7; Wöhe et al., 2020, p. 629). Table 2.1 summarizes the comparison between external and internal accounting.

The primary objectives of external accounting are documentation and accountability, and it is intended to give external stakeholders an insight into a company's assets, financial situation, and earnings (Denk et al., 2016, p. 3). Thus, its task is to "inform external recipients [...] about the economic situation of the company" (Wöhe et al., 2020, p. 644). External accounting consists of financial accounting (for the documentation of all business transactions), which in turn forms the basis for the balance sheet (presentation of assets, liabilities and net assets) and

Table 2.1 Delineation of external and internal accounting (Denk et al., 2016, p. 2)

	External Accounting	Internal Accounting
Objective	Documentation and Accountability	Planning, control and monitoring of business processes
Substantive Reference Frame	Entire company	Subsidiaries, Business Areas, Profit Centers, Products
Temporal Reference Frame	Statements annually or quarterly	Evaluations within the year, shorter reporting cycles
Basis	Legal regulations	No legal regulations, aligned with business principles
Recipients	External information recipients of the company: Owners, employees, customers, suppliers, banks and other creditors, competitors, tax authorities, society/public	Internal information recipients of the company: Management, department heads, cost center managers, other internal recipients
Calculation Size	Cash basis	Accrual basis
Orientation	Rather past-oriented	Past and future-oriented

the income statement (presentation of sales, revenues and expenses) (Wöhe et al., 2020, p. 630). Since both the balance sheet and the income statement document business processes, external accounting is primarily a past-oriented calculation, although planning calculations are also possible or common here, usually for internal purposes (e.g. planned balance sheet, planned income statement) (Denk et al., 2016, p. 4; Prell-Leopoldseder, 2021, p. 14). Since external accounting primarily serves as a basis of information for external stakeholders, there are clear legal (e.g. UGB and EstG) guidelines for the preparation of the annual financial statements (Wöhe et al., 2020, p. 630). The instruments of external accounting usually cover the entire company (substantive reference frame) and are prepared annually or, in rare cases, quarterly (Denk et al., 2016, p. 3).

In contrast, internal accounting primarily fulfills planning, control, and monitoring functions within the company. It "is aimed at internal information recipients. Its task is to process numbers in such a way that they can provide solid support for operational planning, decision-making, and control processes. The structure and design are based on the problems of goods management. The methodology is to be justified by decision logic, not by recourse to calculation rules or external standards." (Troßmann & Baumeister, 2015, p. 3) Due to the internal recipients, there are no legal regulations for internal accounting and the evaluations concern, depending on the need, different areas of the company (e.g. different departments or products) and are often carried out within the year, as this is the only way to ensure that decision-relevant information can be provided (Denk et al., 2016, p. 3).

Key instruments of internal accounting include cost and performance accounting as well as financial accounting (Buchholz & Gerhards, 2016, p. 7; Troßmann & Baumeister, 2015, pp. 7–10). The main task of cost and performance accounting is to record the costs incurred in a company and to allocate them to the various positions or products of a company (Buchholz & Gerhards, 2016, p. 7). While cost and performance accounting records the costs in a company, financial accounting records all inflows and outflows in a company. It is important that these are not only recorded retrospectively (documented), but are planned in advance (planning function of accounting). Therefore, the financial plan is the central instrument for ensuring liquidity (Schneider & Schneider, 2019, p. 18).

Key (financial or success-economic) performance indicators of a company are profitability and liquidity. External accounting and cost and performance accounting primarily focus on profitability. Profitability sets a size (e.g. profit, sales) in relation to the capital employed. Accordingly, different profitability ratios can be distinguished. Financial accounting deals with liquidity, which can be understood as a positive cash balance, as a coverage ratio of assets for conversion back into money (liquidity) or of parts of assets to liabilities (liquidity grades), or as the ability of economic participants to meet payment obligations (Perridon et al., 2022, pp. 13–15; Schierenbeck & Wöhle, 2016, p. 76).

Following Schneider and Schneider (2019, pp. 13–16), corporate accounting answers four questions:

1. Does the company have sufficient liquid assets? If not, what needs to be done to cover all necessary payments? If yes, what happens with any potential financial surplus?
2. How wealthy is the company at a certain point in time?
3. Has the company made a profit or a loss during an accounting period?
4. What is the cost of the performance produced within the company?

While the first question is answered by financial accounting, the answers to questions two and three are central to financial bookkeeping. The question of costs within a company is answered by cost and performance accounting, from which further questions arise (e.g., pricing decision, product range decision, process decision, make-or-buy decision).

After a brief consideration of the accounting domain from a subject-specific perspective, the following sections will examine accounting from a didactic perspective, with a closer look at target categories in teaching (Sect. 2.2), existing competence models (Sect. 2.3), didactic approaches (Sect. 2.4), as well as learning difficulties and their causes (Sect. 2.5).

2.2 Central Target Categories in Accounting Education

2.2.1 Two Guiding Principles of Accounting Didactics

As explained in Sect. 2.1, corporate accounting fulfills different functions, e.g. the functions to document operational processes (documentation function), to control them (control function) and to inform stakeholders (information function). Derived from the different functions and objectives of corporate (external and internal) accounting, different intentions can also be pursued and different emphases can be set in accounting education.

Research on the didactics of accounting has been dealing for decades with the question of what the goal of accounting education should be. It is undisputed that accounting education, as vocational education, should qualify for executive activities and should therefore be practice-oriented. Almost all authors who comment on the objective emphasize the importance of the intellectual understanding of the subject matter, the dispositive aspect and the contribution of the teaching to the development of business understanding (Achtenhagen, 1996; Dubs, 1996; Neuweg, 2020; Schneider, 2010; Seifried, 2004b; Seifried & Sembill, 2005b; Sloane, 1996; Tramm & Preiß, 1996). For example, Dubs (1996, p. 136) argues that the teaching should be designed in such a way that all learners can "analyze and interpret the financial data of a company in order to understand the planning and control of financial events in a company and to analyze financial transactions." For this, the "main focus of the teaching is on understanding the larger context [...]" (Dubs, 1996, p. 127). He thus advocates highlighting particularly the control and planning function of accounting in teaching. For Schneider (2010, p. 66), the primary aim is to promote system understanding, as "every economically active person should be qualified as an intelligent conversation partner for those who actually book or prepare the annual financial statements [...]". For Tramm and Preiß (1996, p. 5), the guiding objective of accounting education is "understanding economic relationships through the penetration and mastery of commercial techniques".

Reinisch (1996, 2005) identified two guiding principles in the discussion about the "correct" objective in accounting education: the guiding principle of the "practical accountant" on the one hand, and the guiding principle of the "thinking accountant" on the other. In the guiding principle of the "practical accountant", "practice" initially forms the starting point and reference point for didactic decisions. Commercial activity is primarily seen as executive, not as dispositive activity. The focus is on the acquisition of skills that are directly usable in current business practice. The skills required in practice should be worked out in the classroom, and the corresponding content should be reflected in the curricula (representation strategy). As a didactic consequence for the design of the teaching, it can therefore be deduced that primarily "practice-oriented teaching methods" are used, for example, the consistent use of commercial accounting software. At the same time, if the professional qualification requirements change, these must also be followed by a change in the curricula (Reinisch, 1996, pp. 53–54). Accounting can therefore be depicted as a "bundle of functional qualification requirements that merchants must master" (Reinisch, 1996, p. 52). To avoid too narrow a definition of the concept of practice, it is emphasized that in addition to functional knowledge, work virtues are particularly needed for successful action in business practice. The focus is primarily on "the teaching of technical handling and procedural rules and basic work ethic attitudes that must be mastered to complete a work task" (Reinisch, 2005, p. 17). Virtues such as diligence, punctuality, thrift, caution, perseverance and accuracy are addressed. Accounting education in particular was seen as particularly suitable for training learners in work ethics. The enrichment of teaching with work ethic aspects is referred to as an addition strategy (Reinisch, 1996, p. 55).

The guiding principle of the "practical accountant" is contrasted with the guiding principle of the "thinking accountant". Also in the guiding principle of the "thinking accountant", professional practice forms an important reference point, but it is understood there as a "complex part of commercial professional practice" that "cannot be reduced to functional qualification requirements", but is seen as a sequence of complex economic decisions and actions. The aim of accounting education is therefore to train economic thinking (enrichment strategy). Practice is also expanded to include the life practice of all economic citizens. Accounting education is to be understood as part of general economic education, which overall aims to promote economic competence (expansion strategy) (Reinisch, 1996, p. 52). Since commercial action is seen as a permanent decision-making process, the focus should be on training economic thinking and expanding teaching to include dispositive elements (Reinisch, 1996, pp. 52–55).

It becomes clear that in the current scientific discussion, a teaching approach is favored that aims to promote "thinking accountants". Thus, a large part of the stated objectives of accounting education can be assigned to the guiding principle of the "thinking accountant", with understanding as well as operational security regularly being demanded in the sense of an integrative guiding principle (e.g. Seifried & Sembill, 2005a; Sloane, 1996; Tramm & Preiß, 1996).

However, it often remains unclear or insufficiently defined what exactly is meant by demands such as an "understanding of the larger context [...]" (Dubs, 1996, p. 127), an "understanding of the functioning and the significance of accounting" (Schneider, 2010, p. 57), an "understanding of economic relationships" (Tramm & Preiß, 1996, p. 5) or a "systematic intellectual understanding of the subject matter" and an "understanding of the systematics of double-entry bookkeeping" (Reinisch, 1996, p. 57). Schneider (2010, p. 57) also notes that "understanding [...] is difficult to operationalize comprehensively." When we speak of *understanding the accounting system* in the further course of the work, we mean that learners, in addition to the correct documentation of operational processes (i.e. the setting up of bookings), understand the logic of double-entry bookkeeping, can grasp the purpose of corporate (internal and external) accounting, can assess the effects of business transactions and their accounting representation, can use data from accounting (in the sense of the planning, control, and control functions of accounting) for decision support, and can estimate the influence of legal regulations and valuation leeway. This specifies and summarizes what many authors formulate in different emphases and clarity with the demands for the training of "thinking accountants" and for promoting understanding in accounting (e.g. Achtenhagen, 1996; Dubs, 1996; Neuweg, 2020; Schneider, 2010; Sloane, 1996; Tramm & Preiß, 1996).

However, it is questionable whether the demand for "thinking accountants" is met in current teaching practice. The few existing research results suggest that the guiding principle of the "practical accountant" still dominates in accounting education and there is a strong focus on the acquisition of calculation and booking techniques (Seifried, 2004b, p. 52). "The focus is on training and practicing calculation and booking skills; less importance is attached to a cognitively challenging, understanding-oriented teaching approach" (Seifried, 2004c, p. 328). However, it is also questionable whether the guiding principle of the "practical accountant" is adequately and contemporarily addressed in terms of preparation for professional practice. For example, Preiß (2015, p. 190) points out that accounting education has only inadequately adapted "to the technical and organizational changes in the economy and the resulting qualification requirements". The following discusses how the two guiding principles are to be assessed in light of the drastic changes in the world of work.

2.2.2 Practical and Thinking Accountant in the Light of Digitalization

The demands for a stronger emphasis on the "thinking accountant" or the claim for promoting comprehensive economic competence gain even more importance when considering the current developments and changes in the field of accounting. In recent years, several studies have dealt with how working conditions and resulting skill requirements are changing in the course of digitalization in accounting and what implications this has for a restructuring or reorientation of accounting education[2] (e.g. Berding et al., 2018; Bieker, 2019; Dengler & Matthes, 2015, 2018; Hmyzo & Muzzu, 2020; Jordanski, 2020; Klein & Küst, 2020; McKinney et al., 2017; Najderek, 2020; Pargmann et al., 2022; Pargmann et al., 2023; Riebenbauer et al., 2022; Schröder, 2020; Wilbers, 2019).

---

[2] In the anthology "Modern Accounting Education 2020" published by Berding, Jahncke and Slopinski in 2020 alone, there are five contributions dealing with digitalization in accounting and its consequences.

Technological change leads to drastic changes in the world of work and accordingly, in a "work world 4.0", the requirements for employees also change or some professions are no longer needed at all (Gössling et al., 2019, p. 547). For example, studies on the substitutability potential[3] of professions have shown that this is around 60% in the professional sector "commercial and business-related service professions" (Dengler & Matthes, 2021, p. 5). A study on the use of language models (*large language models*) such as *Generative Pre-trained Transformers* (GPTs) in different professional fields also shows that the area of "accounting and auditing" is particularly affected by the use of such GPTs and that there is considerable potential for time savings in almost all areas of activity (Eloundou et al., 2023).

The changes in the field of accounting are thus largely driven by technological innovations. In accounting, increasingly complex ERP systems (*Enterprise Resource Planning*), Big Data technologies and a variety of different automation technologies (e.g. RPA or AI) are being used (Hmyzo & Muzzu, 2020; Klein & Küst, 2020; Najderek, 2020; Pargmann et al., 2023). ERP systems are "integrated business software in the form of a comprehensive connecting system that can be used to control all production and business processes taking place in a company" (Jordanski, 2020, p. 59). The use of automation technologies, on the other hand, usually aims to increase the efficiency of processes, thereby saving costs and overall increasing quality and avoiding errors (Klein & Küst, 2020, p. 89). RPA systems, which are particularly suitable for simple, strongly rule-based and frequently recurring processes and automate these, are now being used particularly frequently. Together with the use of OCR (*Optical Character Recognition*), it can therefore be achieved that the processing of various processes (e.g. the posting of a bank document or an incoming invoice) is *completely* dark (so-called dark posting) and in *no* process step active intervention by an employee is required. An intervention by employees is therefore only necessary in the event of irregularities and errors. By linking RPA software solutions with AI, more complex processes and unstructured data can also be automated (Klein & Küst, 2020, p. 90; Langmann, 2020, p. 5; Svatopluk et al., 2018, pp. 11–16).

Diehm and Benzinger (2018, p. 842) sketch the analogous process of processing an incoming invoice without digitalization (Fig. 2.2). First, the invoice arrives at the company (e.g. in paper form or as an e-invoice). The invoice must

[3] The substitutability potential indicates to what extent professions are currently potentially replaceable by the use of computers or computer-controlled machines (Dengler & Matthes, 2018, p. 2).

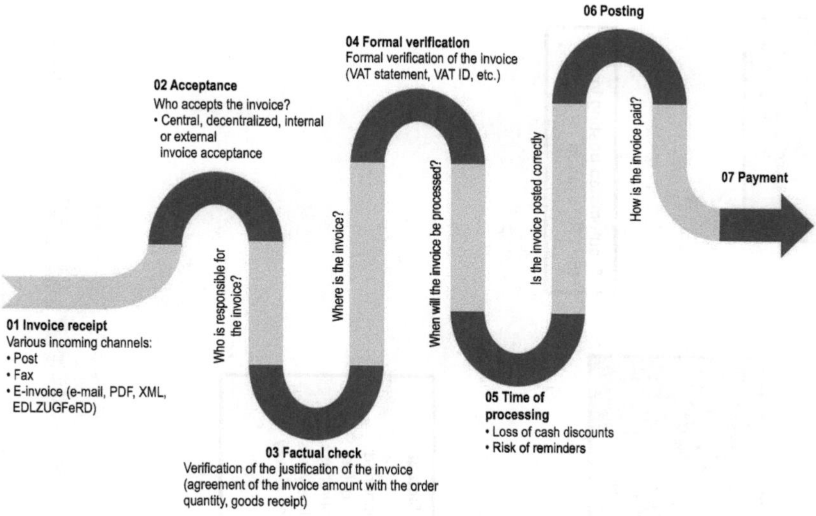

Fig. 2.2 Invoice processing without digitalization (Diehm & Benzinger, 2018, p. 842)

be accepted by the responsible party (or forwarded to it) and then checked for content (invoice amount with order with goods receipt) and form (VAT statement, VAT number). In the process, it usually passes through different departments and areas of responsibility. The invoice must then be processed, posted and paid, taking into account the correct timing (utilization of discounts or avoidance of the risk of reminders). All steps of the process are carried out manually by usually different people, which significantly increases the susceptibility to errors and takes more time.

The process is different in the case of a more automated and especially digitized processing of an incoming invoice (Fig. 2.3). First, invoices are imported into the system. If these are already in a structured form, a direct import is possible. If this is not the case, a transfer into the system using OCR is necessary. Following the transfer into the system, an automated evaluation of the invoice data takes place depending on the level of development. Ideally, a comparison with the master data of the supplier stored in the ERP system also takes place (e.g. to check for changes e.g. in bank data). The factual examination of the invoice for invoices with order reference is carried out via a *3-Way-Match*. So, the order (What was ordered?), delivery (What was delivered according to the delivery note or goods receipt?) and invoice (What was invoiced?) are automatically compared, taking

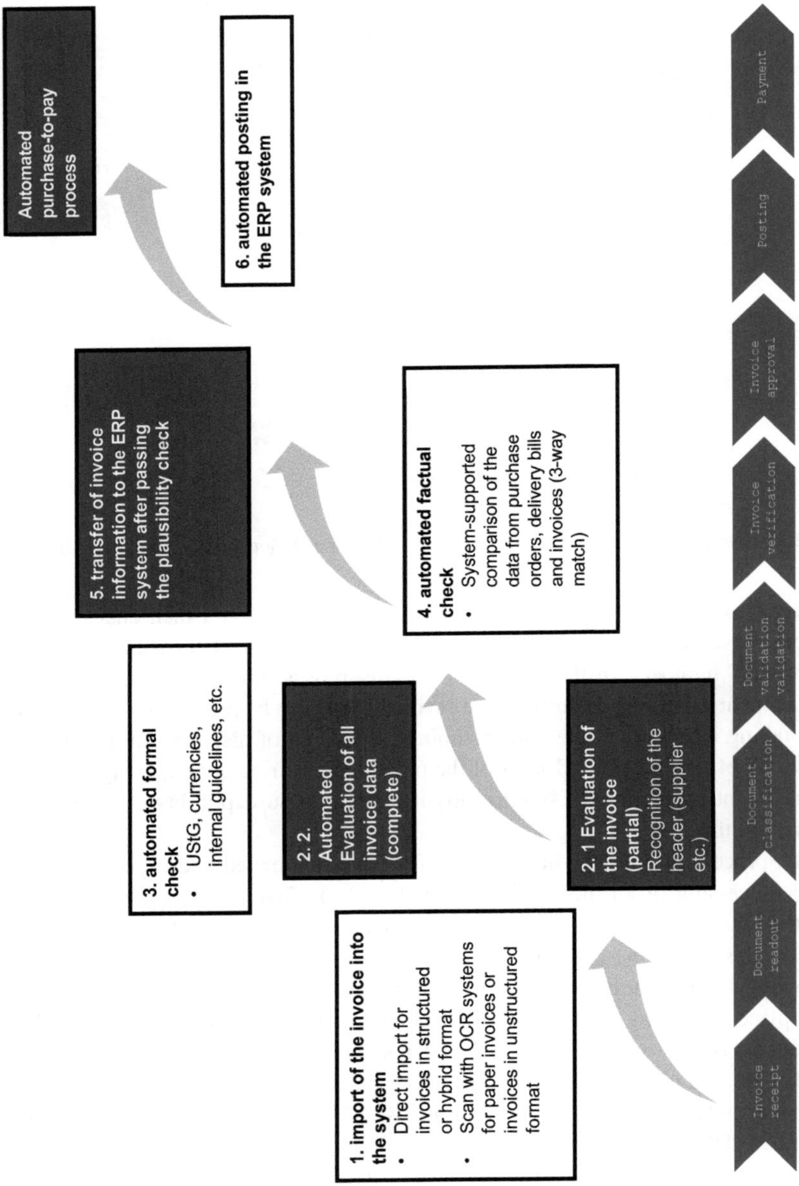

Fig. 2.3 Possibilities of digital invoice processing (Diehm & Benzinger, 2018, p. 843)

into account any price and quantity tolerances. Invoices with order reference can therefore be processed completely automatically. The booking in the ERP system is done without further visual control. This process is referred to as an automated *Purchase—to—Pay* process (Diehm & Benzinger, 2018, pp. 842–843).

The use of complex ERP systems, rule-based automation (e.g. bots, macros) and the use of RPA and AI essentially lead to many processes being automated and at the same time the availability and quality of data significantly increasing (Klein & Küst, 2020, pp. 88–90). This also results in changed requirements for employees working in accounting. Manual, highly repetitive activities for creating, capturing and preparing data will drastically decrease, while complex activities such as the plausibility check and verification of data or the evaluation and further development of the systems used themselves will increase (Hmyzo & Muzzu, 2020, p. 103; Klein & Küst, 2020, p. 92; Pargmann et al., 2022, p. 7; Pargmann et al., 2023, pp. 20–22). "In sum, merchants are increasingly required to cope with complex situations fraught with great uncertainty and to select and evaluate the necessary information" (Berding et al., 2018, p. 215).

Several implications can be derived for the training of future employees. It is clear that less focus than before should be placed on practicing booking and calculation techniques. Instead, more emphasis should be placed on a basic understanding that can be used to identify errors and validate data (Klein & Küst, 2020, p. 94). In addition, the focus should be on skills for identifying and solving problems, research and analysis skills, and a comprehensive understanding of data (Hmyzo & Muzzu, 2020, p. 111; Jordanski, 2020, p. 75). Riebenbauer et al. (2022) have dealt with the implications of increasing digitalization in accounting for educational processes at different levels (e.g., for the design of further and continuing education or for training in the higher education sector) in the course of a systematic literature review. They formulate, among other things, the focus on a holistic process understanding, a comprehensive orientation towards business processes, and the integrative teaching of specialist knowledge and IT skills as essential implications. The goal must be to provide learners with a basic education in the field of digitized finance and accounting in order to understand the processes of the available methods and to correctly interpret and classify their results against the respective economic background (Riebenbauer et al., 2022, p. 207).

In light of the previous explanations, it becomes clear in addition to the implications to be derived for employees in accounting and subsequently for training, that the dichotomous division into "practical accountants", who possess operational certainty, and "thinking accountants", who understand "the system", is becoming increasingly obsolete. The explanations on digitalization in accounting show that understanding is required for competent action in accounting due to technology, for example, to identify system errors and validate data. Activities usually performed by the "practical accountant", such as the booking of business transactions, are instead automated using RPA solutions and AI systems. In this context, the term "accountant" also seems outdated. Studies on the substitutability potential in different occupational fields (e.g., Dengler & Matthes, 2021) and findings on the use of generative language models (e.g., Eloundou et al., 2023) suggest that central tasks of the classic "accountant" are predominantly or almost completely replaced by digital technologies. In this sense, one could rather speak of the guiding principle of the "thinking controller". However, a one-sided focus on the "practical accountant" as the main target category of accounting teaching, where mastering booking and calculation techniques is in the foreground, is in any case no longer contemporary.

2.3 Competence Modeling and Measurement in the Accounting Domain

After defining the goals and competencies to be pursued in class, the question of competence measurement must also be answered. So far, two elaborated competence models exist for accounting itself. These are the competence model by Preiß (2005a) and the competence structure and competence level model[4] by Guggemos (2016), with only the model by Guggemos having been subjected to empirical testing. These are presented in more detail below (Sect. 2.3.1 and 2.3.2). Interesting and important sources of reference for the present work are also two models, which are not competence structure or level models in the strict sense, but were specifically developed for accounting and depict the thinking processes taking place in learners when working on tasks. While the model by Helm (2016d) was inductively developed from think-aloud protocols of learners, the model developed by Seifried et al. (2010) or Wuttke and Seifried (2012) follows a deductive approach and is strongly oriented towards works from the mathematical-scientific area. Both models are presented in more detail in Sect. 2.3.3.

In addition to works on the accounting domain, further research projects can be identified for the commercial vocational area in general, which focus on the modeling and measurement of commercial or economic or economic-citizen competence. Examples include the competence structure model for commercial

[4]Competence structure models distinguish and arrange individual competencies, competence level models capture levels of achievement in a competence (Neuweg, 2019, p. 59).

education by Winther and Achtenhagen (2008) (see also Winther, 2010; Winther & Achtenhagen, 2009), the works from the CoBALIT project[5] on the measurement of professional competence (especially intrapreneurship competence) in the commercial vocational domain of trainees in Switzerland and Germany (e.g., Bley & George, 2017; Eberle et al., 2016; Weber et al., 2021; Weber, Draxler et al., 2016; Weber, Wiethe-Körprich et al., 2016; Winther, Festner et al., 2016; Winther, Seeber et al., 2016), as well as the works in the course of the joint project DomPL-IK[6] on the modeling and measurement of domain-specific problem-solving competence in prospective industrial clerks in the field of controlling (Eigenmann et al., 2015; Rausch et al., 2016; Rausch & Wuttke, 2016; Seifried et al., 2016; Wuttke et al., 2015), both sub-projects of the research program ASCOT[7] (for an overview see Beck et al., 2016). Also worth mentioning are the works of the Leading House LINCA[8], in the course of which a competence structure model of economic competence was developed (for a summary see Rohr-Mentele, 2022) as well as the ULME studies (especially ULME III), in which subject-related performance tests were developed for different training occupations (e.g., office clerks) (Lehmann & Seeber, 2007; Nickolaus, 2008; Tramm & Seeber, 2006). Helm (2016c) presented two tests for measuring accounting competence (WBB 1 and 2; Knowledge Testing of Basic Accounting Knowledge), which, however, is strongly oriented towards textbook-type tasks (e.g., setting up booking entries and indicating profit impact) and also does not contain a developed competence model as the basis for test development (see also Helm & Wimmer, 2012).

2.3.1 Dimensions of Accounting Competence According to Preiß

Preiß (2005a) developed a competence model for the content area of accounting/controlling, based on the multidimensional PISA competence model for mathematics and using the economic-instrumental accounting as a didactic basis (see

[5] Competencies in the Field of Business and Administration, Learning, Instruction and Transition.

[6] Modeling and Measurement of Domain-Specific Problem-Solving Competence in Industrial Clerks.

[7] Technology-based Assessment of Skills and Competences in VET.

[8] Learning and Instruction for Commercial Apprentices.

also Sect. 2.4.2). He argues for the orientation towards mathematics by stating that the objectives of the instruction are comparable. Thus, in the PISA study, understanding of mathematics is described as follows: 1) Mathematical concepts are to be understood as tools for exploring the world. 2) The goals of mathematical education are therefore not (only) the acquisition of technical skills, but the understanding and functional use of mathematical tools. 3) To solve mathematical problems, the modeling of extra-mathematical and intra-mathematical problem situations is needed (Preiß, 2005a, p. 70, 2005b, p. 69). Preiß (2005a, p. 70) transfers this understanding, developed for the domain of mathematics, to business education and formulates:

- Accounting concepts are tools for exploring the "economic world".
- The goal of basic education in accounting is conceptual understanding and functional use of accounting, not merely technical skills.
- To solve typical tasks, the modeling of extra-instrumental and intra-instrumental problem situations is necessary.

Analogous to the approach to developing the PISA competence model for mathematics, Preiß (2005a, pp. 70–71, 2005b, p. 75) defines the annual financial statements, the accounts of the main ledger, the subsidiary ledgers, cost accounting, financial and liquidity planning, and investment calculation as relevant curricular areas of accounting. He includes both external and internal accounting. As overarching ideas, he formulates: 1) Actual value documentation and inventory-based updating, 2) Revaluation, settlement and accountability, 3) Comparison of actual values with plan, previous period and industry values, 4) Claim-related selection, restructuring and preparation of information and 5) Explanations of value constellations and measures for improvement. He adopts the process of "mathematizing" with the sub-steps of modeling, operating, interpreting and validating unchanged (see also the explanations on the modeling cycle in Chap. 3) (Fig. 2.4).

The starting and ending point of each process is a business case in the commercial working world. Business transactions are represented or processed in accounting and, taking into account norms, are recorded in accounting and mathematical terms. They are thus translated into the world of accounting and processed there. The results of these processes are checked for formal and material correctness. At the same time, the results are economically interpreted. There is a retranslation from the world of accounting into the real world. This results in new options for action and decisions, which in turn trigger new business cases (Preiß, 2005b, p. 73). Figure 2.5 visualizes the process.

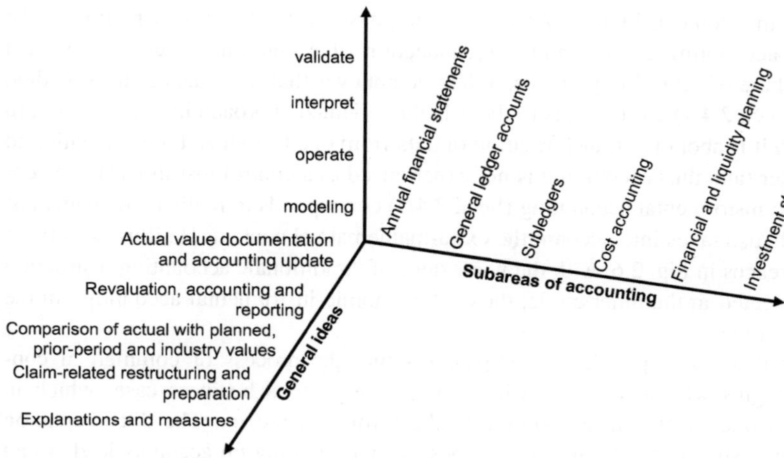

Fig. 2.4 Dimensions of Accounting Competence according to Preiß (2005a, p. 74)

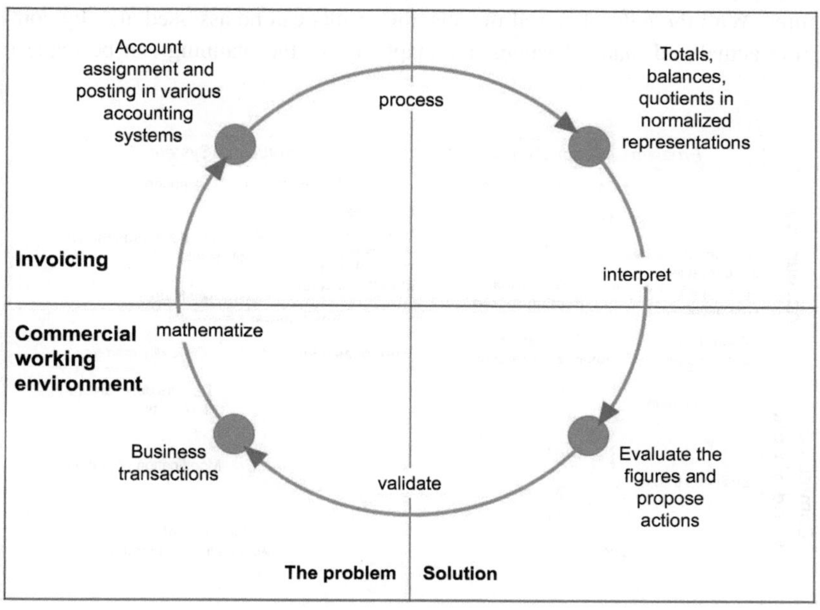

Fig. 2.5 Process of Instrumentalization in Accounting (Preiß, 2005b, p. 73)

In this context, Preiß (2005a, p. 71) emphasizes that the representation of the extra-accounting context and a reconnection of accounting results to the real world are of central importance. While he believes that the balance sheet method (see Sect. 2.4.1) corresponds to the calculus-oriented approach in mathematics, in which it is about the transformation of data from one formalized representation to another (and thus accounting is not experienced as a control instrument), the economic-instrumental accounting (Sect. 2.4.2) corresponds to realistic mathematics, which also takes into account the extra-mathematical context. He illustrates these differences in Fig. 2.6, with the work steps of "traditional" accounting instruction represented in the inner circle, those of economic-instrumental accounting in the outer circle.

Preiß (2005a, pp. 72–73) emphasizes that the process of commercial control begins with a decision, which in turn leads to a business case, which in turn is documented in accounting in the form of a receipt. The documentation of the business case in the form of posting and booking on accounts leads to an aggregation of individual cases and the determination of a new balance. These are then transferred into standardized representations, for example at the end of a billing period. Further evaluations are possible through the calculation of key figures. With the help of causal models, the results can be assessed and, by comparing actual and planned values, an adaptation of the planning can be made if

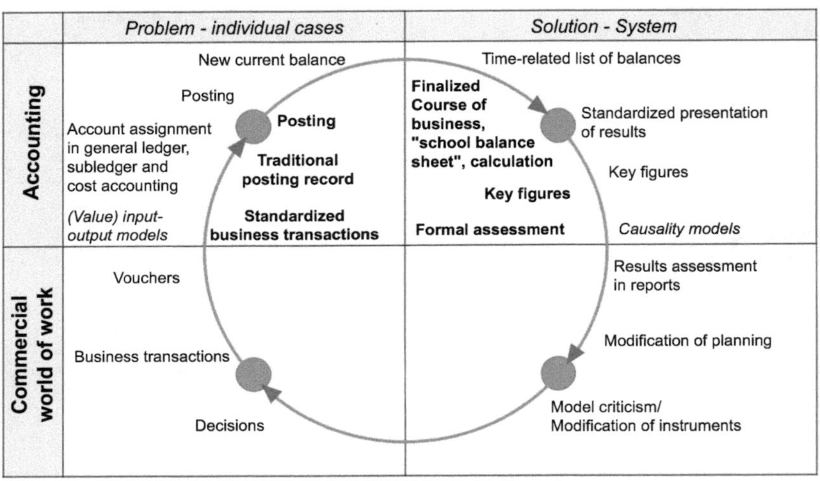

Fig. 2.6 Process of Commercial Control (Preiß, 2005a, p. 72)

necessary. The suitability of the tools used can be checked through the sub-step of validation.

In addition, Preiß (2005a, p. 73) defines the level of demand of a task as the fourth dimension. The difficulty of a task depends on the number of areas to be processed. Thus, "tasks with a low level of demand only affect one curricular sub-area, one overarching idea and one or a few sections of the control process. The more complex a task becomes, the more sections are affected in the respective dimensions".

2.3.2 Competence Structure and Competence Level Model for External Accounting according to Guggemos

Guggemos (2016) and Guggemos and Schönlein (2015) presented an elaborate competence model for external accounting, which focuses on the training profession of industrial clerk and consists of a competence structure model and a competence level model. In addition, test tasks for measuring competences in external accounting were developed and validated.

To explore competence structures and level gradations, a comprehensive domain analysis was conducted. This included the analysis of the framework curriculum for industrial clerks, the analysis of existing textbooks, the consultation of experts in interviews, the evaluation of existing final examinations, and the analysis of relevant job advertisements. With the five different domain approaches, different aspects of the competence model were to be worked out and covered (e.g., the analysis of the curriculum to ensure curricular validity, the survey of experts from accounting to identify typical activities). The core of the competence structure model is the value creation process, which is in turn represented (documented) using accounting, thus providing necessary information for planning, controlling and monitoring operational processes (Guggemos, 2016, pp. 73–77).

As a result, the content areas of external accounting (as a cross-sectional subject matter) were intertwined with relevant competence facets needed to handle accounting tasks. The relevant content areas defined were procurement, sales, basics of bookkeeping, annual financial statements, taxes, personnel, financing, and asset management. The relevant competence facets identified (mainly determined through expert interviews and analysis of job advertisements) were data collection, booking, making recognition and valuation decisions, controlling, and report creation (Guggemos, 2016, p. 98). As this is an inductive approach, the results were compared with the "overarching ideas" postulated by Preiß (2005a) and compared with the valid curriculum. In addition, they defined the two overarching

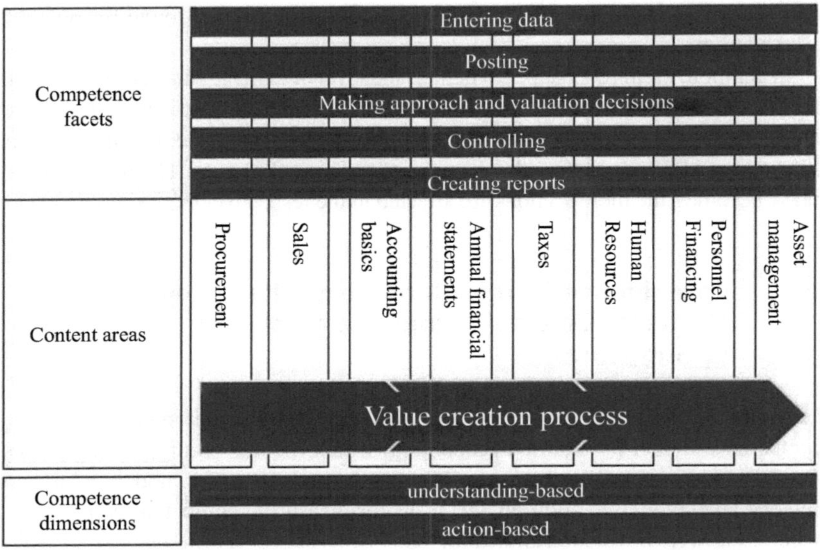

Fig. 2.7 Competence structure model according to Guggemos (2016, p. 98)

competence dimensions "understanding-based" and "action-based", as already introduced by Winther (2010, pp. 196–201). "Understanding-based" refers to the understanding of domain-specific ideas, while "action-based" addresses the purposeful execution of domain-specific tasks. This emphasizes the necessity of combining booking technical skills and economic understanding (Guggemos, 2016, p. 74). The competence structure model can be seen in Fig. 2.7.

To develop the competence level model, the level model developed by Winther (2010), which identifies the dimensions of functional modeling[9], content

[9] "In relation to a cognitive competence model, functional modeling means a) the availability of a processing model of the requirement situation and the ability to use adequate action and coping strategies based on knowledge or experience and b) the learners' access [...] to models of the given requirement situation and the activation of situation-appropriate processing models" (Winther, 2010, p. 100). The extent of functional modeling is, according to Winther (2010, pp. 102–103), crucially dependent on how open or structured a requirement situation is presented. Accordingly, she distinguishes four levels, from outstanding modeling performance (level 4, all decision levels such as problem formulation, specification of the target system, solution selection and testing, and decision-making are open), down to level 1, where no modeling is required, as, for example, solution methods are given.

complexity, and type of cognitive demand as difficulty-determining features, was linked with the business-instrumental accounting. From this, three difficulty-determining features were derived, each with four difficulty levels (see Fig. 2.8) (Guggemos, 2016, pp. 36–41; Guggemos & Schönlein, 2015, pp. 527–531).

The first difficulty-determining feature of an accounting task is modeling. This refers to the "transformation of a requirement situation into a processable model" (Guggemos & Schönlein, 2015, p. 527). To solve an accounting-specific problem, the initial situation must first be transformed into a model (modeling). This involves identifying the problems contained in a situation. The difficulty varies depending on the number of problems contained and the modeling aids provided. At the lowest level of difficulty, no modeling performance is required. At the second level, the problem must be identified, but a modeling aid is provided by limiting the content area (e.g., by marking a document as an incoming invoice). If the requirement situation includes several content areas or more than one problem, this is defined as the third level. The highest level of difficulty is given when several problems are included, which also cover several content areas (Guggemos, 2016, pp. 37–38; Guggemos & Schönlein, 2015, p. 528).

The second dimension of the level model represents information acquisition. In the phase of information acquisition, learners refer to documents and other sources or perform calculations to gain the information necessary for problem-solving. The particular importance of this dimension is emphasized, as document

Increase

Accounting competence

Modeling	Information acquisition	Cognitive processing
More than one problem across multiple domains	Independent information search and evaluation	Application/ Posting record with more than four accounts
One problem across multiple domains: alternatively: more than one problem	Multiple sources: alternatively: one source with complex calculations	Analysis/ Posting record with four accounts
One problem in delimited domain	One source incl. simple calculations	Understand/ Accounting record with three accounts
Problem given	No Information acquisition necessary	Reproduction/ Simple accounting record

Decrease

Fig. 2.8 Difficulty-determining features of accounting tasks (Guggemos, 2016, p. 41)

orientation is both curricularly required and documents reflect real, operational processes. The difficulty of a task is determined depending on how structured the information is given (e.g., a tabular presentation vs. a document), whether several sources have to be referred to, or whether these have to be obtained independently. At the lowest complexity level, all information is contained in a structured form, e.g., as a table. At the second level, a document is included from which information must be taken. This level also includes the generation of information through simple calculations (e.g., determination of the discount amount). The third level is present when more complex calculations have to be carried out (e.g., default interest) or information has to be taken from several different sources. The highest level of difficulty is reached with tasks that require an independent selection and use of sources, e.g., working with legal texts. The dimension of information acquisition is only relevant for action-based competence dimensions, as understanding-based tasks require the retrieval of information from long-term memory (Guggemos, 2016, pp. 38–29; Guggemos & Schönlein, 2015, pp. 528–529).

The third and last difficulty-determining dimension is defined as information processing, with this dimension explicitly distinguishing between understanding- and action-based competence. To describe the different difficulty levels of the understanding-based dimension, Guggemos and Schönlein (2015, pp. 529–530) refer back to the cognitive taxonomy table and distinguish, in ascending order of complexity, the levels of reproduction, understanding, analysis, and application. For action-based tasks, assignment to the taxonomy level is often difficult. Accordingly, they orient themselves in the action-based dimension on the assumption that the "complexity of a process increases with the number of steps to be carried out." For the domain of accounting, they therefore argue that an increasing number of accounts involved in the booking leads to a higher difficulty of the task (Guggemos & Schönlein, 2015, p. 529). Tasks that require the reproduction of knowledge (e.g., stating the retention period for invoices) are to be assigned to the lowest level of difficulty (understanding-based dimension). For action-oriented tasks, this level includes those tasks that require simple account assignments (e.g., one account each in debit and credit). At the next higher level, tasks are classified for the understanding-based dimension where understanding is required to solve the task (e.g., Why do we have to form depreciations?), for the action-oriented dimension bookings with three accounts. The third level includes bookings with four accounts (action-oriented) or tasks that require an analysis (understanding-oriented). The highest level includes complex booking structures involving more than four accounts. For the understanding-oriented dimension, the decision for a valuation method considering the company's objectives is given as an example (Guggemos, 2016, pp. 39–41; Guggemos & Schönlein, 2015, pp. 530–531). Figure 2.9 illustrates the problem-solving process for action-based tasks.

The competence level model was empirically tested using tasks from the professional examination “Commercial Control and Regulation”. The verification of the two-dimensional structure (understanding and action-oriented) was carried out using χ^2 tests (comparison of log-likelihood values). The two-dimensional model could be confirmed. The verification of task difficulty was carried out using a hierarchical regression model and a linear logistic test model (LLTM), with the difficulty-determining characteristics being included in the analysis as independent variables in the regression model. For this purpose, the difficulty level of the task was coded based on the characteristics shown above. The task difficulty (estimated using item response theory methods) was included in the regression model as a dependent variable. The findings on the validity of the model are not clear. While the model could be confirmed for tasks of the action-based dimension, the relationships between difficulty-determining characteristics and task difficulty could not be demonstrated for understanding-oriented requirement situations (Guggemos, 2016, pp. 42–58; Guggemos & Schönlein, 2015, pp. 531–545).

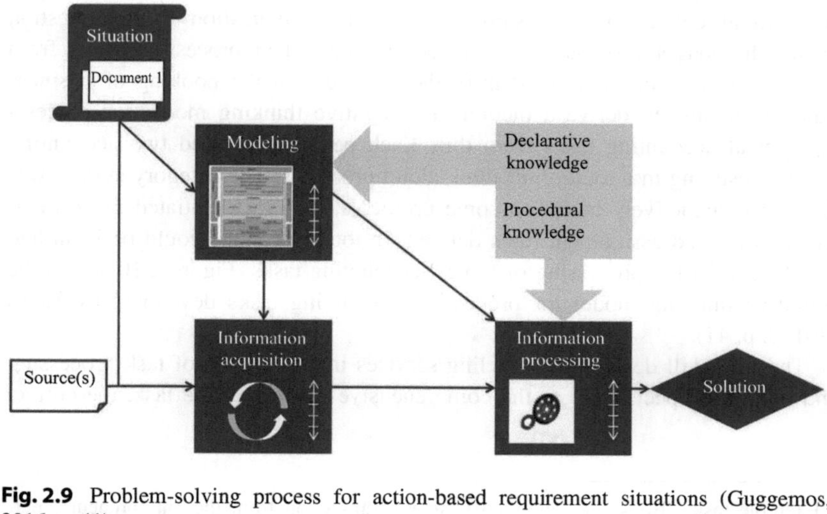

Fig. 2.9 Problem-solving process for action-based requirement situations (Guggemos, 2016, p. 41)

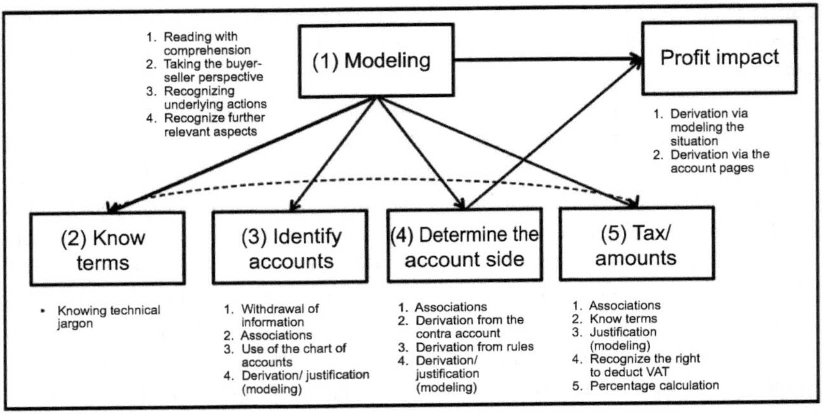

Fig. 2.10 Cognitive thinking model for processing accounting tasks (Helm, 2016, p. 41)

2.3.3 Models for Describing Thought Processes in the Processing of Accounting Tasks

Helm (2016d) dedicated a think-aloud study with ten students of a 2nd grade commercial college and 10 students of business education to the question of which thought processes learners go through when processing tasks from accounting. The aim was to identify thought steps in the booking of business transactions and to derive a theoretical, cognitive thinking model for processing typical accounting tasks from this. Each person processed two accounting tasks[10], resulting in a total of 40 think-aloud protocols. The category system was developed inductively based on some protocols, then differentiated in an iterative process and assignment rules defined. In total, six skills could be identified as relevant for the processing of typical accounting tasks. Figure 2.10 shows the cognitive thinking model for processing accounting tasks developed by Helm (2016d, p. 41).

The first skill deals with modeling services in the context of task processing and includes aspects such as the comprehensive reading of the task, the correct

[10]Example task: "Book the following business transaction from the entrepreneur's perspective and estimate the impact on profit! 1. You buy goods for your company on account (3300) for € 14,500,– + 20 % VAT" (Helm, 2016, p. 39).

assumption of perspective (Am I the buyer or the seller?), recognizing the real, operational processes (What actions have taken place?) as well as recognizing other relevant aspects for solving the tasks (e.g. Are these raw materials or commercial goods? What has already been booked?). Overall, it is mainly about correctly capturing the present business case and deriving further steps for processing from it. The first sub-competence can be understood as a basic competence, which is a prerequisite for the other skills. The second skill concerns the recognition and understanding of relevant technical terms (What does gross mean, what does net mean?). This skill also distinguishes itself from the aspect of "comprehensive reading", although a close connection to the first skill is recognizable. Skills three to five directly concern the (correct) setting up of a booking. The selection of the relevant accounts was identified as the third relevant skill. The learners proceed differently here. The selection of the accounts is either made via the task specification, via an account plan or via associations of certain operational processes with certain accounts or via a modeling service, in which, for example, a distinction is made between the buyer's and seller's perspective. After selecting the accounts, the correct account side (debit or credit) is determined in a fourth step, whereby different approaches are chosen here as well. A selection is again possible via associations ("input tax always in debit") or via the deduction from the counter account. Often the account side is also derived via formally learned "rules". Particularly indicative of this is the statement that the learner would have "remembered that it is in debit up to a certain class and from then on in credit" (Helm, 2016d, p. 40). The account side is much less frequently justified by value flows triggered by the business transaction (e.g. money flows into the company, therefore the bank account is in debit). The consideration of the tax amount was identified as the fifth step, whereby in this context skill two, the correct handling of technical terms, is central, as the learners must understand terms such as gross, net, inclusive or exclusive in order to correctly determine the tax amount. To estimate the impact on profit (skill six), the learners applied two different strategies, with the first variant being the far more prevalent strategy. The impact on profit was derived from the affected accounts and their position in the booking entry (e.g. "account class 4 is in credit, therefore increasing profit"). On the other hand, an attempt was made to derive the impact more through a modeling service and a reference to operational reality. The sub-steps also follow the order shown in the model, with the exception of the estimation of the impact on profit, as only sub-step 1 and 4 seem necessary for this (Helm, 2016d, pp. 39–41).

The developed cognitive thinking model was also used by Helm et al. (2022) as a theoretical basis to identify the skills mastered (or not mastered) by students using a cognitive diagnostic model and to work out skill profiles. For this purpose, tasks were selected from different textbooks and then evaluated as to how far the individual sub-skills are necessary to solve the task. These 34 tasks were presented to 773 students in the 9th grade (1st class of BHS) for processing. The quantitative evaluations have shown that the various sub-skills are not mutually compensable. So if a student cannot show a skill identified as relevant for the task, the probability of solving the task decreases. However, the hierarchical relationship or sequence of the sub-skills could not be confirmed.

Another model for characterizing sub-steps in the processing of tasks from accounting is that of Seifried et al. (2010) or Wuttke and Seifried (2012). Theoretical reference points were the works of Preiß (1999) on economic-instrumental accounting (see Sect. 2.4.2), approaches from mathematics education and the model of complete action. Thus, four ideal-typical steps of problem solving were developed, which are run through when processing a task and where errors can occur at each step. These four steps are 1) The capture of economic reality, 2) The representation or interpretation of economic reality, 3) The formalizing and mathematizing, and 4) The reflection and evaluation of the solution (Wuttke & Seifried, 2012, pp. 179–180). Figure 2.11 illustrates the four sub-steps.

The first level involves a basic understanding of economics, commercial knowledge, and the correct use of technical terms. In a second step, the present situation must be correctly encoded and thus interpreted. It is also central to adopt the correct perspective. The available information can either be in text form or in document form. After capturing and encoding the situation, the business case must be correctly recorded in accounting and mathematical terms. This involves selecting the correct accounts, determining whether they increase or decrease, and accordingly selecting the correct account side and making the booking. At this level, mathematical operations (e.g., the calculation of a VAT amount) are also required. The third step is followed by a phase of reflection. It is therefore necessary to determine whether the developed solution fits the task and how the overall result is to be assessed. Here too, a return to economic understanding is required. Furthermore, the consequences of the accounting operations are to be interpreted (Seifried et al., 2010, pp. 145–147; Türling, 2014, pp. 58–59; Wuttke & Seifried, 2012, p. 180).

While Türling used the model as a template for identifying and classifying student errors (see Sect. 2.5.1), Nobiling et al. (2020) used the substeps to classify the thought processes of learners when working on accounting tasks. The four substeps served as deductive categories[11] for classifying the verbal expressions

[11] Furthermore, types of knowledge (factual knowledge, conceptual knowledge, procedural knowledge, and metacognitive knowledge) and cognitive processes (remembering, understanding, applying, analyzing, evaluating, creating) were coded according to the taxonomy matrix of Anderson and Krathwohl (2001).

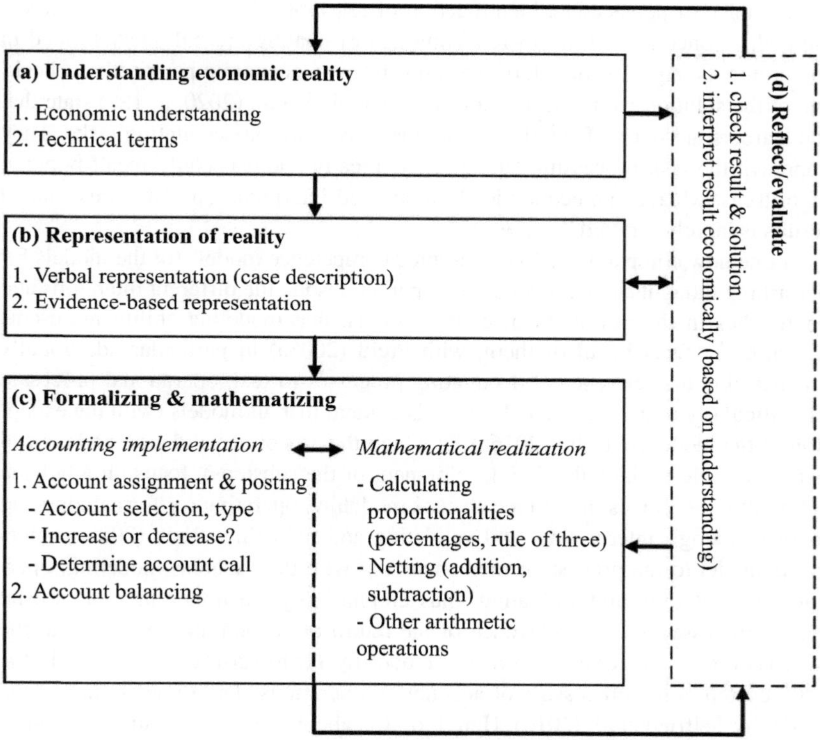

Fig. 2.11 Process of accounting modeling (Wuttke & Seifried, 2012, p. 179)

of the learners, which they made in the course of working on accounting tasks. For this purpose, a think-aloud study was designed, in which 21 people (students of business education) participated and in which the subjects worked on self-created tasks on different topics (e.g., purchase of commercial goods, offsetting of rental expenses). The evaluations of the think-aloud protocols show that the learners' statements very often refer to the level of formalizing and mathematizing. The learners therefore predominantly talk about which accounts they select, how they identify the correct account side, and how they calculate the correct amounts. There are significantly fewer statements about capturing the economic reality (What is the problem at all?) or about encoding the economic situation (e.g., choice of perspective, identification of relevant information). Also, expressions that concern the level of reflecting and evaluating are only very limited in the protocols (e.g., evaluation of the result from an economic perspective, checking of the solution path). As a conclusion, Nobiling et al. (2020, p. 129) state that the learners are not sufficiently able to correctly work on accounting tasks. They approach the task processing "quite schematically and especially recall booking algorithms, whereas an economically motivated interpretation of the determined results is largely omitted."

If one now compares the four presented competence models (or the models for describing thought steps), it becomes apparent despite the different intentions and approaches in the development of the models, that modeling ability represents a significant facet in all of them, with Preiß (2005a) in particular additionally emphasizing the reference of accounting processes to real, operational processes as particularly important. In addition, it is evident that all models (with the exception of the model by Helm (2016a), in which the aspect of validation and control is missing due to the inductive development of the substeps), focus on a holistic action process, consisting of the substeps modeling, operating (or formalizing and mathematizing), interpreting, and validating and reflecting. Preiß (2005a) refers in his model to the process of mathematizing with the subareas modeling, operating, interpreting, and validating, thus emphasizing the importance of holistic action processes and the relevance of the return of accounting operations to the real, economic situation. Also in the model by Helm (2016d), modeling is the first substep in the processing of accounting operations. The same applies to the model by Seifried et al. (2010). Here too, it is about a correct capture of the situation and an assessment of which activities are necessary. In Guggemos (2016) or Guggemos and Schönlein (2015), the modeling performance is a difficulty-determining feature. The gradation of the different difficulty levels or competence levels is done via the three features modeling, information acquisition, and information processing. Thus, the difficulty of action-oriented requirement situations varies depending on whether or how many problems are contained (modeling), whether independent information research is necessary (information acquisition), and how many different accounts are addressed (information processing). Table 2.2 attempts to classify the sub-competences addressed in the different models, with the model by Preiß (2005a) with the subfacets modeling, operating, interpreting, and validating serving as a reference source for classification.

Table 2.2 Comparison of the competence models according to different competence facets

Preiß (2005a)	Guggemos (2016) / Guggemos & Schönlein (2015)	Helm (2016d)	Seifried et al. (2010) / Wuttke & Seifried (2012)
Modeling	Difficulty-determining feature "Modeling"	Modeling, knowing terms	Capturing and encoding economic reality
Operating	Capturing data, booking	Identifying accounts, determining account side, tax/amounts	Formalizing/ Mathematizing
Interpreting	Making posting and valuation decisions	Impact on profit	Reflecting and Evaluating
Validating	Checking	–	

2.4 Balance Sheet Method and Economic Instrumental Approach—Two Central Didactic Approaches in Accounting

In addition to the question of what objectives should be pursued in accounting education and which competencies should be primarily promoted, there is also the question of how these objectives can be achieved and competencies appropriately promoted. In the research on the didactics of accounting, various didactic approaches have been developed and controversially discussed over the past decades, each making statements about content selection, sequencing, and methodological design in teaching, for example, the balance sheet method (Butze, 1936; Butze & Butze, 1932), the economic-instrumental accounting (Preiß & Tramm, 1988, 1996; Tramm, 2005), the pagatory approach (Gross, 1990), the account or combination method (Dauenhauer, 1977; Waltermann, 1976), the value and cash flow method (Rückwart, 2009), the function and benefit-oriented didactics (Plinke, 2013) as well as the problem, goal, and business process-oriented didactics (Dolzsanksi, 2013a, 2013b). The balance sheet method and the economic-instrumental accounting are of particular importance in the scientific discussion and in practice. Both approaches, their characteristics as well as advantages and disadvantages are controversially discussed in the scientific discourse (e.g. Burkhardt et al., 2014; Ernst, 2014; Goldbach, 2010, 2012; Mathes, 2008; Plinke, 2010, 2011a, 2011b, 2012, 2014a, 2014c; Preiß, 2008, 2011; Stommel, 2014a, 2014b). The balance sheet method and the economic-instrumental accounting are presented in basic terms below.

2.4.1 The Balance Sheet Method

The balance sheet method is considered the traditional and dominant approach in accounting education. Both the type of account and the corresponding booking can each be justified by the position of the account in the balance sheet. Initially, inventory and inventory list are worked out in the introductory lessons and condensed into a balance sheet (Mathes, 2006, p. 147; Sloane, 1996, p. 47). The sides of the balance sheet are named as the asset side (assets) and the liability side (liabilities), with the asset side indicating the use of funds (In what form are the funds tied up in the company?) and the liability side indicating the source of funds (Where do the funds come from?) (Schneider et al., 2022, p. 30; Wöhe et al., 2020, p. 649). After dealing with inventory and inventory list, the balance sheet accounts are derived from the balance sheet. For each balance sheet position, a T-account is set up. The opening balances of the balance sheet are transferred and from this the booking rules for neutral business transactions are derived. The booking rule can also be derived from the respective position of an account in the balance sheet (Dauenhauer, 1977, p. 197; Mathes, 2006, p. 147). The booking technique is often worked out in textbooks using the following questions: 1) Which accounts are affected? 2) Is it an active or passive inventory account? 3) Is there an increase or decrease on the respective account? 4) On which account side should therefore be booked? (Bouley, 2017, p. 13) All neutral transactions can be assigned to one of the following types: active exchange (an asset is increased, another is decreased), passive exchange (debt reduction by increasing other debts), balance sheet extension (increase of assets by increasing debts) and balance sheet reduction (reduction of assets and debts) (Bouley, 2017, p. 13; Schneider et al., 2022, p. 40). Equity is introduced into the balance sheet as a balancing item, as the balance sheet is considered a scale that can never be out of balance (Tramm, 2005, p. 104). Subsequently, profit-affecting business transactions are introduced, usually via a secondary service area, and the booking rules for profit accounts are developed. Expenses are considered value-reducing (equity is reduced), revenues as value-increasing (equity is increased) (Bensch, 2009, p. 198; Ernst, 2012a, p. 71; Mathes, 2006, p. 165; Seifried, 2004b, p. 29; Sloane, 1996, p. 47).

The balance sheet method is subject to comprehensive criticism, the differentiated and detailed presentation of which is not possible here. Therefore, essential points of criticism are addressed, which concern both scientific and learning psychological and methodological aspects.[12]

The criticism from a scientific point of view is diverse and first concerns the dissolution of the balance sheet into inventory accounts. This is problematic because no distinction is made between book and inventory values and the balance sheet (date-related account with actual values) and account system (target values) are mixed. The same applies to the transfer of the balances of the inventory accounts into the balance sheet. Here again, it is not taken into account that the balance sheet results from the inventory and is based on actual values, while the accounts show target values. This leads to the balance sheet being misinterpreted as a "collection basin of account balances" (Bensch, 2009, pp. 204–205; Ernst, 2012a, p. 70; Reinisch, 1996, p. 67; Seifried, 2004b, p. 29; Seifried & Sembill, 2005a, p. 1; Weller & Fischer, 1998, pp. 45–46). To avoid this inconsistency, the additions "The ending balances are actual balances" or "The closing balances on the accounts correspond to the inventory values" are often stated in the books (Bensch, 2009, p. 205; Bouley, 2017, p. 20; Ernst, 2012a, p. 70; Seifried, 2004b, p. 30). The transfer of the balances into the balance sheet leads to the creation of the balance sheet being seen as a mechanical process and design options as well as legal norms are not taken into account (Bouley, 2017, pp. 17–18; Reinisch, 1996, pp. 67–68; Seifried, 2004b, p. 31). The separate introduction of inventory and profit accounts is also viewed critically, as this initially does not take into account an important function of a company, namely the generation of profits (Bouley, 2017, p. 19; Preiß, 2000, p. 10). In connection with profit-affecting transactions, it is also critically noted that expenses are defined as reductions in equity, revenues as increases in equity. This can lead to students not considering expenses as a prerequisite for generating revenues and thus as necessary, but seeing expenses as a fundamentally negative size that should ideally be avoided. Overall, the approach strongly oriented towards booking logic runs the risk of misrecognizing the tasks and functions of the accounting information system, the information, control, and decision function (Bouley, 2017, p. 20; Seifried, 2004b, p. 32; Tramm, 2005, pp. 104–105).

From a methodological point of view, the strong orientation towards the balance sheet often (but not necessarily) goes hand in hand with the fact that the booking logic and technique are practiced using highly simplified business cases without reference to real operational processes. From a learning psychological

[12] For a more detailed presentation of the criticism of the balance sheet method, see the work by Bouley (2017, pp. 17–22).

perspective, the abstract approach to the topic is criticized. This is also reinforced by the fact that booking logic and economic interpretation are often not discussed together, but are temporally staggered and separated from each other. In addition, the large number of abstract terms (e.g. inventory, inventory list, assets, liabilities) and the insufficient connection to the learners' world of experience and prior knowledge are criticized. This also seems questionable from a motivational point of view (Bouley, 2017, p. 21; Reinisch, 1996, p. 67; Seifried, 2004b, p. 30).

It should be noted that the balance sheet method dominates in school accounting education. As Reinisch (1996, p. 67) already noted, "this 'balance sheet method' approach is so dominant in textbooks, curricula and probably also in teacher training that it is considered—outside the circle of its critics—as a 'natural' and therefore compelling sequence". However, recent studies on the use of the balance sheet method in accounting education are still lacking.

2.4.2 The Economic-Instrumental Accounting

Based on the criticism of traditional accounting education and the balance sheet method, Preiß and Tramm (1990) developed the economic-instrumental accounting as a didactic alternative to the common balance sheet method (see also Preiß, 1999; Preiß & Tramm, 1996 or Tramm, 2005). The aim of the economic-instrumental accounting, which is also known as the modeling method, is a stronger integration of accounting and business administration to promote "system thinking in economic contexts" (Preiß & Tramm, 1990, p. 27). The focus is not (only) on the immediate activity as an accountant, but on a "variety of clerical functions that involve a considerable amount of independent and cooperative decisions" (Preiß & Tramm, 1996, p. 228) as well as "the ability to cognitively orientate in economic areas of life, to understand contexts and thus to judge and actively co-design and co-determine economic processes and structures" (Preiß & Tramm, 1996, p. 226).

The focus is on the representation and interpretation of operational processes using accounting as a tool for managing the company. Therefore, from the beginning, it is important to work out the purpose and meaning of accounting operations and to clarify them to the learners (Preiß & Tramm, 1996, p. 238; Tramm, 2005, p. 103). Learners should understand accounting as the core of the company's information system and recognize that the company's performance processes are represented in condensed form in the accounting (Preiß & Tramm, 1990, pp. 30–31). In economic-instrumental accounting, the balance sheet is not the reference model for deriving bookings, but a general business model (see Fig. 2.12),

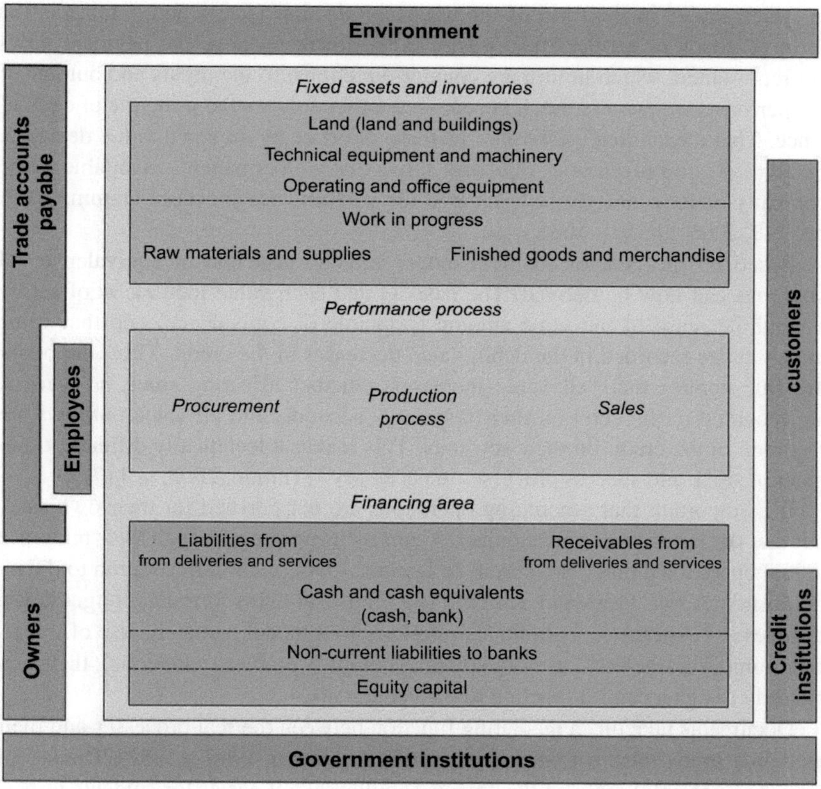

Fig. 2.12 General business model (Tramm, 2005, p. 107)

with which "the company's market relationships (real and nominal goods flows), its internal performance process and also the stocks can be represented and interpreted" (Tramm, 2005, p. 103). Business cases are therefore not interpreted for their impact on the balance sheet, but the cost and performance processes of the company are put in the center to derive accounting solutions from them (Tramm, 2003, p. 7). At the center of the general business model is the company itself, which in turn is surrounded by other systems ("surrounding systems" such as government institutions, customers, employees and suppliers). Goods and service flows between the company and various subsystems are visualized as inputs and outputs via arrows. In the company, the performance process forms the center, in which inputs in the form of the use of production factors and outputs in the form of goods or services take place. In the financing area, the payment flows are represented, which in turn are counter-directional to the inputs and outputs of the performance process. Each business case thus follows the principle of equivalence. This means that each value increase is offset by an equal value decrease. Fixed assets and inventories represent assets that are permanently available to the company or have not yet fully entered the performance process (Tramm, 2003, pp. 7–8, 2005, pp. 105–106).

Based on the general business model and the principle of equivalence, all bookings can now be derived. The basis is that each value increase is offset by a value decrease of the same amount (principle of equivalence) and that value increases are recorded in the debit, value decreases in the credit. Thus, the booking rule applies that "all value increases, whether affecting stock or success, are recorded in the debit on their respective accounts and all value outflows are recorded in the credit on their accounts. This makes a technically different treatment of stock and success processes unnecessary" (Tramm, 2005, p. 117).

It is important that accounting operations are not pursued for their own sake, but that the regulations and techniques gain their meaning through their reference to real operational processes (Preiß & Tramm, 1996, p. 247). In addition to didactic postulates that Preiß and Tramm (1996, pp. 244–254) formulate (e.g. clarity, openness to experience, continuous reference to a model company, use of a realistic number framework, use of authentic, complex problem situations), they particularly assign a central function to the documents.

Documents take on "a mediating function between the real processes and their modeling in the information system" (Preiß & Tramm, 1996, p. 252). The use of (as far as possible) realistic documents should make it easier for students to perform translation services between the real operational processes and the numerical work of accounting. In terms of content, teaching according to the modeling method begins with an introduction to the cash book, as it is assumed that this can better connect to the learners' previous experiences. The idea of the book-like updating of actual stocks and the comparison between actual and target stocks is worked out using the cash book as an example (Preiß & Tramm, 1990, p. 55).

Comprehensive criticism is also leveled at economic-instrumental accounting (see for example Minnameier & Link, 2010; Plinke, 2010, 2011a, 2011b, 2012, 2014a; Schneider, 2000 and reactions to the criticism at Burkhardt et al., 2014; Goldbach, 2010, 2012; Preiß, 2011; Seifried, 2004b). The booking rule based on the principle of equivalence is particularly criticized, as this leads to problematic interpretations (e.g. expenses as value increases, revenues as value decreases). This can lead to difficulties in understanding, as it probably contradicts the everyday understanding of the learners. On the other hand, this type of interpretation is not compatible with international accounting standards, according to which expenses are generally to be interpreted as reductions in equity. In addition, the consideration is not clearly determinable for all business cases (e.g. provisions) (Mathes, 2006, pp. 159–160; Plinke, 2010, pp. 172–173, 2013, p. 19, 2014c, p. 478). The designation of equity as the company's debt to the owners and thus as a negative value with a debt character is also criticized (Plinke, 2013, pp. 16–21, 2014c, p. 478). From a methodological point of view, the early and intensive use of a model company is particularly critically viewed, as this is too complex for learners without prior knowledge and requires a high degree of abstraction ability (Schneider, 2010, p. 63).

Empirical findings about the strengths and weaknesses of both didactic approaches, for example with regard to students' performance and motivation, are however hardly available. Although Seifried (2004b) examined the effectiveness of different didactic approaches, due to an intertwining with different teaching arrangements (self-organized vs. teacher-centered), the effect of the didactic approach cannot be clearly determined.

Bouley (2017, pp. 303–305) investigated the question of how students, who have been taught either according to the balance sheet method or the economic-instrumental accounting method, differ in terms of their competence acquisition (knowledge, motivation, interest, and attitude) at two business high schools in Baden-Württemberg with a sample of 43 students. The results show that the two groups do not differ in terms of their booking-specific knowledge. While both groups, as expected, recorded increases in booking-specific knowledge over time (significant time effect, $\eta^2 = .121$), significant group effects could not be identified (Bouley, 2017, p. 238). Both didactic approaches therefore seem to be equally suitable for building booking-specific knowledge. Looking at different content areas, it is evident that students who were taught according to the balance sheet method have strengths in the area of "tasks, importance and (legal) foundations of accounting"[13], while learners taught with the economic-instrumental method perform better in the content area "procurement and sales process". Significant group effects with medium to large effects were identified for both aspects ($\eta^2 = .099$ and .150 respectively) (Bouley, 2017, p. 248). In the case of

[13] This finding seems surprising in view of the problem situations of the balance sheet method, especially for the area of legal foundations. Bouley (2017, p. 250) explains this finding by the fact that the tasks mainly address the tasks and foundations of accounting, which are intensively dealt with at the beginning of balance sheet method teaching.

document-based accounting knowledge, learners of the economic-instrumental teaching achieve better values over all measurement points, which can also be attributed to group membership (significant group effect, $\eta^2 = .148$) (Bouley, 2017, p. 239). No difference between the groups could be determined with regard to motivational experiences in class. The same applies to the attitude towards accounting and accounting teaching.

2.5 Learning Difficulties in the Domain of Accounting and Their Causes

2.5.1 Learning Difficulties in the Domain of Accounting

The discussions about the "right" or preferable didactic approach to conveying content from accounting are largely fueled by the fact that accounting is generally considered a difficult and challenging subject matter, which often causes great problems for students (Seifried, 2004b, p. 46). It can be assumed that "learning difficulties occur to a greater extent in the subject of accounting than in other subjects" (Tramm et al., 1996, p. 173). A study by Neuweg and Pfatschbacher (2013, p. 23) also shows that the average grade in accounting is at the level of subjects such as mathematics and French and thus significantly worse than those of related business vocational subjects such as business administration or the practice firm.

The few empirical research findings suggest that some content areas within the domain of accounting are experienced as particularly difficult and challenging. In a study by Pawlik (1979, 1980), students were asked to rate the difficulty of various subject areas. The preparation of booking entries, the booking of inventory changes, and sales tax were rated as particularly error-prone and difficult. In addition, Pawlik found that there are correlations between difficulties with the learning content "preparation of booking entries" and subsequent subject areas such as the booking of inventory changes, depreciation, or the preparation of the balance sheet. She interprets this as an indication that understanding basic teaching content is of particular importance (Tramm et al., p. 164). In a survey conducted by Seifried (2004b, p. 49), students were asked to assess the difficulty level of various contents. The learners particularly rated the areas of accounting books, legal foundations and principles of proper accounting, as well as booking according to documents and booking of profit-affecting transactions as difficult. In a study by Tramm et al. (1996, pp. 180–188), not students, but subject leaders of Lower Saxony study seminars were surveyed. They named the content areas sales tax, goods accounts, balance sheet, the legal foundations, the booking of profit-affecting transactions, and the booking according to documents as particularly challenging. In addition to technical subject areas, the experts also stated that learners also have difficulties with the technical terms of accounting. Terms such as equity, receivables, liabilities, fixed assets, or current assets are particularly difficult for learners to understand.

In recent years, Seifried, Wuttke, and Türling have been particularly involved in identifying typical student errors (see Seifried et al., 2010; Seifried & Wuttke, 2010; Türling, 2014; Türling et al., 2012; Türling et al., 2011; Wuttke & Seifried, 2012). The research group used approaches from error research in mathematics didactics to develop a student error taxonomy for accounting teaching (see Sect. 2.3.3). According to Seifried et al. (2010, p. 147), accounting tasks are ideally processed in four steps. In a first step, the economic reality must be grasped. This requires a basic economic understanding (example: effect of depreciation) and the correct handling of technical terms (example: What are liabilities?). In a second step, learners have to encode the economic reality before they can perform mathematical and/or accounting operations in step 3. This is followed by the phase of result evaluation and reflection. Student errors can thus be located in one of the four steps of the problem-solving process.

Following the theoretical development of the error taxonomy, extensive empirical studies were conducted, which are characterized by the use of different methodological approaches (classroom observation, expert interviews, self-reports from students). The results of the empirical studies show that errors occur most frequently in steps 1 and 3, i.e., on the one hand in the perception of economic reality, and on the other hand in mathematical and/or accounting operations (e.g., in the account assignment and booking) (Türling, 2014, p. 159; Wuttke & Seifried, 2012, p. 188). In expert interviews with teachers and subject leaders of study seminars, the content areas inventory and success accounts, sales tax, and correction bookings were also identified as particularly error-prone areas. In addition, the experts state that students have problems across all content areas in forming booking entries (Türling, 2014, p. 156; Türling et al., 2011, p. 401).

Although the studies presented do not provide uniform findings due to the different research designs and are not directly comparable, the formation of booking entries can be identified as a difficult task in accounting teaching across all studies. Thus, learners seem to have particular difficulties with understanding the booking system (account and booking closure), with booking the sales tax, and with booking profit-affecting transactions. At the same time, it can be assumed that understanding the booking system and the purpose of bookings is a basic prerequisite for learning further subject areas (e.g., depreciation, preparation of the balance sheet, etc.). Therefore, understanding basic teaching content and fundamental terms of accounting is of particular importance (Tramm et al., 1996, p. 164). Especially in the subject of accounting, difficulties in understanding basic content often lead to students memorizing booking entries (Tramm et al., 1996, pp. 177–178).

2.5.2 Potential Causes for Learning Difficulties in Accounting

In addition to the realization that the domain of accounting in general and certain subject areas or activities in particular are experienced as challenging, it is also of interest to identify the causes of these learning difficulties. Some of the studies presented deal with (potential) causes for the frequently occurring learning difficulties in accounting education. In addition to individual learning prerequisites of the learners, which are mentioned in all studies as a cause for learning and comprehension difficulties, the following problem areas are discussed in particular (Schiller, 2004, pp. 343–360; Seifried, 2004b, pp. 46–50; Tramm et al., 1996, pp. 193–215; Türling, 2014, pp. 170–174; Türling et al., 2011, pp. 402–404):

- the neglect of business backgrounds,
- the content and methodological formalism,
- the reduction of accounting education to the technical-instrumental target dimension,
- the volume of material and too few practice opportunities, and
- the lack of practical experience of the learners.

As a cause for learning difficulties, Tramm et al. (1996, pp. 205–207) see the lack of reference of the accounting system to the associated business processes and procedures. Learners apparently find it difficult to "gain a vivid understanding of the underlying business processes from the numbers of accounting" (Tramm et al., 1996, p. 205). Accounting is not seen as a tool with which real business processes are documented, accompanied, evaluated or initiated, but as a mere abstract, formal system, the use and purpose of which often remains unrecognized. The learners lack "the problem awareness, why do I need this [...]" (Türling, 2014, p. 162).

Accounting also has "a very explicit formal character and shows a strongly axiomatized and partly against the everyday language intuition delimiting technical terminology" (Tramm et al., 1996, p. 172). It is not surprising that learners, due to their lack of practical experience, have difficulties understanding the real facts behind the accounting operations. At the same time, teachers apparently also fail to vividly convey this system, characterized by many formal and abstract terms, in class. Thus, a study by Findeisen (2017, p. 275) on the explanatory ability of students of business education shows that they have weaknesses in the domain of accounting with regard to the visualization of content and the availability of different explanation variants. In line with this are findings that show that even many active teachers believe that accounting is strongly characterized by a formalized character, that accounting thinking is determined by abstraction and that work in accounting consists mainly of the application of rules (formalism aspect, schema aspect). The application aspect of accounting (e.g., "knowledge in bookkeeping is important for the students' later life") is emphasized much less (Berding & Jahncke, 2020, p. 240; Seifried, 2010, p. 208).

Accounting education is also often characterized by a strongly teacher-centered teaching design, in which the questioning-developing classroom conversation is in the foreground. The individual lessons are usually identically structured and contain little varied practice phases in addition to a joint development of a new booking sentence (Jahn, 2020, pp. 14–15; Neuweg, 2020, p. 138; Seifried, 2004b, p. 41). Tasks in class are predominantly represented by short, abstract verbalizations, which in turn do not reveal any reference to real, business-related problem situations and thus represent accounting as an abstract system without recognizable purpose (Seifried, 2004b, p. 33).

The use of documents is also often omitted. Thus, a textbook analysis by Ernst (2012a, p. 127) shows that only 15% of all illustrations in German textbooks are realistic documents such as receipts. In the analysis of textbook tasks conducted by Stütz et al. (2022), it is shown that documents are used in only 3% of the tasks (for a detailed presentation of the research findings on the quality of tasks, see Sect. 4.3). In class, there is usually a strong focus on mastering the correct booking technique, while the teaching of business interrelationships is neglected (Tramm et al., 1996, p. 202).

The emphasis on the technical dimension of accounting is also evident when asking learners what activities they usually perform in class. Thus, students indicate that they set up bookings in most lessons, practice calculation skills and copy the teacher's records from the board. Never or almost never, however, do the learners have to analyze the development of a company over several years, apply bookkeeping to problems of business practice, or represent relationships (Seifried, 2004b, p. 43).

The findings on learning difficulties and their causes in the subject of accounting make it clear that it is not sufficient in class to practice and memorize bookings. More important, however, is to build an understanding of the booking logic in order to be able to derive bookings independently. In addition, it is important to work out the meaning and purpose of accounting illustrations and at the same time to establish stronger references to real business processes and business-related questions in order to facilitate the learning of central content from accounting for students. This also makes it clear that the promotion of "thinking accountants" in class is indicated, as this guiding principle explicitly overcomes the purely technical-formal target dimension and also takes into account the business backgrounds more strongly. The pressure for innovation increases when one considers the dominant focus on the model of the "practical accountant" in the light of increasing digitalization (see Sect. 2.2.2). Tramm et al. (1996, p. 216) also emphasize that learning and comprehension difficulties "do not affect a marginal area of the curriculum or a partial skill, but they threaten the basic understanding of economic interrelationships and thus the core of economic and business professional competence".

The following will therefore present a model that focuses on the promotion of "thinking accountants" in accounting education. To this end, modeling in accounting will first be discussed in more detail. First, the ability to model in the domain of mathematics is considered (Sect. 3.1), before the transfer of modeling ability to the domain of accounting is made in Sect. 3.2. Subsequently, the Linz Level Model (Neuweg, 2020) as a tool for promoting "thinking accountants" and modeling ability in accounting is presented in Sect. 3.3.

3 The Ability to Model in the Accounting Domain

3.1 Modeling in the Domain of Mathematics

International comparative studies such as TIMSS and PISA and the problems they have highlighted among many students in dealing with mathematical problems have led to a new discussion about the task culture in mathematics education. As a result, reality-related modeling tasks have moved more into focus as the core of a new task culture, although application and reality references in mathematics education have a long tradition (Böhm, 2013, p. 1; Maaß, 2005, p. 114; Schukajlow, 2011, p. 27).

Modeling tasks are characterized primarily by the fact that their solution requires a translation performance between the real world and the world of mathematics (Schukajlow, 2011, p. 28). Böhm (2013, p. 39) also emphasizes the importance of translation processes in modeling tasks and defines them as "tasks in which a reality-related situation is to be processed with mathematical means. This processing can have various purposes, but it requires a multi-step processing process, which in particular requires translation processes between the extra-mathematical situation and the mathematical model."

In mathematics didactics, mathematical modeling (and in this context also mathematical modeling competencies) has been intensively discussed for several years (Brand, 2020, p. 45). Mathematical modeling, a term that has only been used in this form for a few years, is today a "self-evident part" of mathematics education and is also defined as a general competence, for example, in the German KMK education standards for secondary level I (Böhm, 2013, p. 1; Greefrath & Maaß, 2020, p. 1–2). Although the term mathematical modeling was established relatively late, what is meant by it was already discussed much earlier in didactic discussion, for example, with the terms "application-oriented

S. Reindl-Stütz, *Characteristics of Tasks in the Domain of Accounting*, https://doi.org/10.1007/978-3-658-48958-8_3

mathematics education", "applications in mathematics education", "application references in mathematics education" or *applied problem solving* (Böhm, 2013, p. 35). Mathematical modeling involves "solving a real, extra-mathematical problem with the help of mathematics" (Brand, 2020, p. 46), with mathematics always being used as a "means to an end" (Böhm, 2013, p. 23). The starting point for such modeling processes is always a problem of reality that is to be solved with the help of the tools of mathematics (Hankeln, 2019, p. 10).

The focus is particularly on the question of which *sub-steps* are necessary to solve modeling tasks. Idealized and schematic representations are often used to describe such processing processes, which distinguish different steps of processing. In the German-speaking discourse, the term modeling cycle has been established for this, while in the English-speaking discussion the terms *applied problem solving process* or *mathematisation cycle* are used (Böhm, 2013, p. 25). However, it should be emphasized that modeling cycles can be used as models for analyzing solution activities when working on modeling tasks, but they do not represent the cognitive processes of learners when working on tasks. As Böhm (2013, p. 314) points out, there are now "numerous schematic representations that describe the processing process in an idealized way and name relevant stations for the modeling process that must be 'passed' in the processing process. However, they have little explanatory power for the emergence of cognitive processes during processing" (Böhm, 2013, p. 314). Greefrath and Maaß (2020, p. 2) also emphasize that modeling cycles must be understood as "idealized schemas" and these "do not represent the real cognitive processes of an individual when working on modeling problems."

In the didactic discussion, there are a multitude of different modeling cycles, which differ mainly in the number of steps to be completed and thus in the degree of detail, and whose concrete design also depends on the purpose of use and the respective theoretical reference concept (Brand, 2020, p. 46; Greefrath et al., 2013, p. 14; Greefrath & Maaß, 2020, p. 2; Kaiser et al., 2015, p. 364). For example, modeling cycles from applied mathematics, didactic modeling cycles, modeling cycles as a basis for the reconstruction of the situation model when using text tasks, and diagnostic modeling cycles can be distinguished according to the purpose of use (Böhm, 2013, p. 26). Greefrath et al. (2013, p. 16–18) distinguish cycles of direct mathematization (e.g., Ortlieb, 2004; Schupp, 1988), in which only one step from the situation to the mathematical model is used, cycles of two-step mathematization (e.g., Blum, 1985; Kaiser, 1995), in which an intermediate step is provided for the transition between the real world and the mathematical model, and cycles of three-step mathematization (e.g., modeling cycle of the

DISUM project[1], see e.g., Blum, 2011), which are characterized primarily by the introduction of a situation model as a mental representation of the situation.

A crucial distinguishing criterion besides the number (and designation) of sub-steps is particularly the distinction between real situation, real model, and situation model. While, for example, the modeling cycle according to Ortlieb (2004, p. 23) as a cycle of direct mathematization assumes a total of four sub-steps (modeling/mathematization, analysis/simulation, interpretation, and verification) in the processing of modeling tasks and goes directly from a real situation to a mathematical model, the cycle proposed by Blum (1985, p. 200) also comprises four sub-steps (simplifying/structuring/precising, mathematizing, mathematical work, re-interpretation), but explicitly distinguishes between the real situation and the real model and only in a next step of mathematization a mathematical model is developed. The transition from real situation to a real model is achieved by simplifying, structuring, and precising. The model of the DISUM project (see Blum, 2011, p. 18) is even more differentiated, with a situation model interposed between the real situation and the real model, which defines the mental representation of the initial situation by the learner as the first sub-step and was essentially shaped by research on text comprehension. The transition between real situation and situation model is captured over the sub-step of understanding.

A very well-known modeling cycle of two-step mathematization is that of Blum (1985, p. 200–204) (see Fig. 3.1). The starting point of the modeling process is a problematic situation. The learner must first "familiarize himself with the problem, make observations and formulate his guiding problem." To solve the problem, it is necessary to simplify, precisify, structure the initial situation and, if necessary, obtain further information. Based on these simplifications, structurings, and precisions, a real model is created, which largely reflects the real situation, but is largely simplified and structured. This is followed by a mathematization, i.e., a translation of the real model into mathematics. The result of this process is a mathematical model of the initial situation, which consists of objects (e.g., functions, vectors) and relationships between the objects. Subsequently, work is done within the mathematical model, which leads to mathematical results. It is essential that a retranslation of the results into reality takes place afterwards, i.e., the results are interpreted with a view to the real situation.

The seven-step modeling cycle developed as part of the DISUM project is shown in Fig. 3.2 (e.g., Blum, 2011; Greefrath et al., 2013). It essentially

[1] Didactic intervention forms for a self-reliance-oriented task-driven teaching using the example of mathematics.

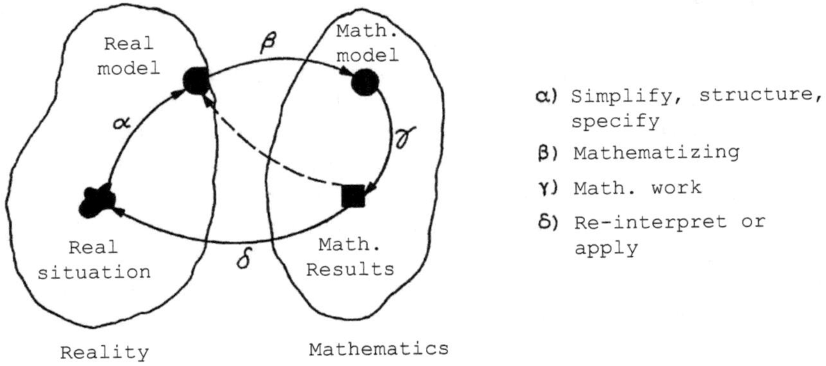

Fig. 3.1 Modeling cycle according to Blum (1985, p. 200)

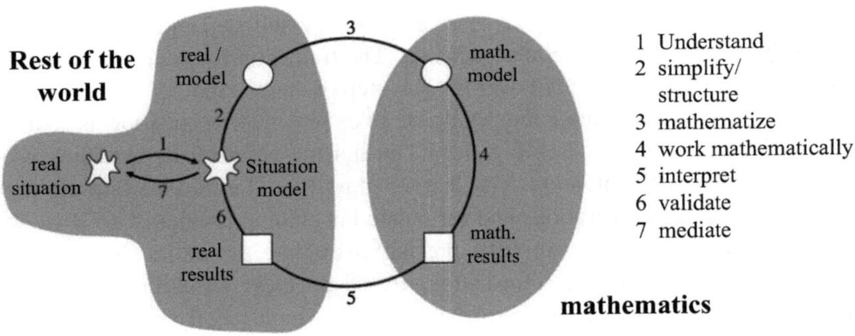

Fig. 3.2 Modeling cycle from the DISUM project (Schukajlow, 2011, p. 77)

coincides with the cycle already discussed, but makes differentiations and extensions. The first sub-step in processing modeling tasks in this cycle is understanding. The task description as a description of a reality-related situation must be read and understood by the learner, which means that a mental representation of the task must be formed. The basis for the construction of this mental representation is the text, available images of the situation, and the prior knowledge of the learners. In this step, the situation model is created (Schukajlow, 2011, p. 78). In a next step, a real model must be formed through simplification and structuring processes. Simplification and structuring essentially consist of distinguishing important from unimportant information, recognizing relationships between variables, making assumptions for simplification, and researching missing data. It is controversially discussed whether a distinction between the real situation and the situation model as a mental representation of the situation makes sense (Hankeln, 2019, p. 11; Hankeln & Beckschulte, 2020, p. 67; Schukajlow, 2011, p. 79).

The situation represented by the real model can be transferred into the world of mathematics through mathematization. This creates a mathematical model that is represented by mathematical objects or notations. After constructing the mathematical model, conclusions in the form of mathematical results must be drawn. This happens in the course of mathematical work, in which operations of different types, complexity, and number are carried out. However, the results found are of a mathematical nature and therefore require a retranslation into the real world. Therefore, to solve a real problem, an interpretation of the results is necessary, in which the results are related to the real-world problem and placed in the existing context. If the developed solution is checked (e.g., by recalculating and checking the calculation paths for errors) and critically reflected, this is referred to as validation. The last sub-step in the DISUM project's modeling cycle, communication, includes the documentation of the solution process (Blum, 2011, p. 18; Böhm, 2013, p. 27; Hankeln, 2019, p. 11; Hankeln & Beckschulte, 2020, pp. 67–68; Schukajlow, 2011, pp. 80–82).

Following the description of the ideal-typical sub-steps in processing modeling tasks, the question arises as to what competencies and abilities are required for this. Existing concepts for operationalizing modeling competence, for example for empirical studies, often use the modeling cycle as a basis for defining different sub-competencies, but a uniform definition does not exist (Böhm, 2013, pp. 50–51; Brand, 2020, p. 47; Kaiser et al., 2015, p. 369).

Brand (2020, p. 47) very generally states that modeling competencies include "the acquirable cognitive abilities and skills to adequately process and solve certain modeling problems as well as the willingness to use these abilities and skills in different modeling processes". In the German educational standards for mathematics for the general higher education entrance qualification, the ability to model is characterized as follows:

> This involves the transition between real situations and mathematical concepts, results, or methods. This includes both the construction of suitable mathematical models and the understanding or evaluation of given models. Typical sub-steps of modeling are the structuring and simplification of given real situations, the translation of real conditions into mathematical models, the interpretation of mathematical results in relation to real situations, and the checking of results for consistency and appropriateness in relation to the real situation. (Hankeln & Beckschulte, 2020, p. 66)

Based on the modeling cycle from the DISUM project, Greefrath and Maaß (2020, p. 4) define modeling competence over seven sub-competencies (see also Hankeln & Beckschulte, 2020, for example) (Table 3.1).

A very detailed operationalization of sub-competencies was developed by Kaiser et al. (2015, 369–370), who also orient themselves on the sub-steps of the modeling cycle and define a total of five sub-competencies (see also, for example, Hankeln, 2019, pp. 26–28; Maaß, 2005, p. 120). As the first sub-facet, they define *competencies for understanding a real problem and for setting up a real model* and distinguish abilities such as information research, the distinction between relevant and irrelevant information, the ability to make assumptions or the ability to "recognize variables influencing a situation" and "establish relationships between the variables" (Kaiser et al., 2015, pp. 369–370). The next sub-competency describes mathematization. This refers to *competencies for setting up a mathematical model from a real model.* Included are the abilities to translate facts into mathematical language, to simplify the number and complexity of relevant variables and their relationships, and to select appropriate mathematical notations (Hankeln, 2019, p. 27). In the context of mathematical work, *competencies for solving mathematical problems within a mathematical model* are mentioned, which essentially include abilities to apply heuristic strategies (e.g., dividing the problem into sub-problems, establishing relationships, varying the influencing

Table 3.1 Sub-competencies of modeling (Greefrath & Maaß, 2020, p. 4)

Sub-competency	Description
Understanding	The students construct their own mental model of a given problem situation and thus understand the question.
Simplifying	The students separate important and unimportant information about a real situation.
Mathematizing	The students translate simplified real situations into mathematical models (e.g., term, equation, figure, diagram, function).
Working mathematically	The students work with the mathematical model.
Interpreting	The students relate the results obtained in the model to the real situation and thus achieve real results.
Validating	The students check the real results for appropriateness. The students compare and evaluate different mathematical models for a real situation.
Communicating	The students relate the answers found in the situation model to the real situation and thus answer the question.

variables, etc.). As the fourth sub-area, *competencies for interpreting mathematical results in a real model* are defined. This sub-competency is differentiated by the ability to interpret mathematical results in non-mathematical situations, to generalize solutions, and to communicate problem solutions (Hankeln, 2019, p. 27; Kaiser et al., 2015, p. 370). As the last sub-competency, Kaiser et al. (2015, 370) formulate competencies for *questioning the solution and, if necessary, repeating the modeling process*.

All previous explanations show that the ability to translate between real situations and mathematics is particularly essential for mathematical modeling. Brand (2020, p. 47) also notes that the sub-competencies central to processing the individual sub-steps in the modeling process can be summarized into three sub-aspects and, in addition to the competency to work within mathematics, particularly include the transition between reality and mathematics on the one hand, and between mathematics and reality on the other. The following Sect. 3.2 will show how and in what form the modeling cycle from mathematics didactics was transferred to the subject didactic discourse of the accounting domain. To this end, Sect. 3.2 will first discuss a broad approach to the state of research, where points of connection can be identified, before Sect. 3.3 presents the "Linzer Ebenenmodell" (Neuweg, 2020) in more detail.

3.2 Transfer of the Modeling Cycle to the Accounting Domain

In the accounting domain, some explicit and implicit references to the modeling cycle of mathematics didactics or to mathematical modeling can be found. The connections and references to mathematics didactics are often justified by the fact that both systems (i.e., accounting and mathematics) consist of "abstract rules, procedures, and objects" and in both systems there is the claim that "this abstract system provides an effective tool or instrument for understanding and shaping concrete phenomena in reality" (Berding, Beckmann & Kürten, 2019, p. 570). Modeling processes therefore represent an "important component of successful action in accounting" and enable "the use of accounting as a tool for solving commercial problems" (Berding, 2019, p. 93).

Points of connection to the modeling cycle or to modeling ability as a central competency can be found in various works on accounting didactics, including the competency models of Guggemos (2016) and Guggemos and Schönlein (2015), Preiß (2005a), and Winther and Achtenhagen (2008) (see Sect. 2.3), in models for describing the thought steps of learners when working on accounting tasks (see

Helm, 2016d, Seifried et al., 2010 and Wuttke & Seifried, 2012 in Sect. 2.3.3) and at least implicitly also in economic instrumental accounting (e.g., Preiß & Tramm, 1996; Tramm, 2003, 2005, see Sect. 2.4.2) and in the "Linzer Ebenenmodell" according to Neuweg (2020).

Preiß (2005a, p. 70) explicitly refers to mathematics and bases the development of his competency model for accounting on the competency model of the PISA study, as he formulates, the "objectives of the lessons are comparable." According to his assessment, accounting is also to be understood as a tool for exploring the world and for solving tasks, especially extra- and intra-instrumental problem situations need to be modeled. Accordingly, he formulates the sub-steps of modeling, operating, interpreting, and validating as central to solving accounting-specific problems, based on the modeling cycle. In Guggemos (2016), the modeling performance, along with information acquisition and processing, is a difficulty-determining feature of a task from accounting. This refers to the "transformation of a requirement situation into a workable model" (Guggemos & Schönlein, 2015, p. 527). The difficulty of the modeling performance is primarily operationalized via the complexity and the number of problems to be solved.

In the cognitive thinking model of Helm (2016d) (see also Helm et al., 2022), modeling is the first sub-step in solving typical tasks from bookkeeping. The main focus is on correctly recognizing the situation described in the task (e.g., What action underlies the business transaction? From which perspective is the business case to be processed? What exactly needs to be done?). To develop an error taxonomy for the accounting domain, Seifried et al. (2010) (see also Wuttke & Seifried, 2012) also refer to mathematics didactics and formulate four levels of processing subject-specific tasks in accounting. The sub-steps of the modeling cycle are visible in the four defined levels. While the levels of capturing economic reality and representing reality correspond to the sub-steps of understanding, simplifying, and structuring, the level of formalizing and mathematizing represents the sub-steps of mathematizing and mathematical work. Reflecting and evaluating, i.e., checking the solution path or the economic interpretation of the result, corresponds to the sub-steps of interpreting and validating in the modeling cycle.

Jungwirth (2015, p. 34) transfers the approaches from mathematics didactics to the area of cost accounting and formulates as a target ability the competency to "recognize problems as such and to represent them in a model, which can be solved operationally using suitable instruments. The result would be to analyze, interpret, and communicate." At the same time, she also refers to the "Linzer Ebenenmodell" and gives as an example the break-even point analysis of a taxi company. The reference action field reveals goods or service flows (passenger transport from A to B) and cash flows (payment for the transport). The processes in the reference action field are documented in the factual action field (e.g., via a fuel receipt or a receipt for the transport). From a cost accounting perspective, it is particularly relevant how many taxi rides need to be completed (or how many kilometers need to be driven) to make a profit. So first, in the sense of the modeling cycle, the real situation needs to be captured and understood (transition between real situation and real model). The calculation of the critical quantity proves to be a suitable instrument for answering this question. The situation therefore needs to be transferred into a cost accounting or mathematical model (transition between real world and cost accounting). Operations are carried out within the models. However, the result must be economically interpreted in a further step. Based on the economic interpretation, entrepreneurial decisions can be made (retranslation from the cost accounting world to the operational reality).

In the discourse on accounting didactics, similar to mathematics didactics, the importance of switching between the real world and the accounting world is particularly emphasized. Florian Berding has dealt extensively with this transition in his work on basic concepts in accounting, which also ties in with work from mathematics didactics, especially the work on mathematical modeling (see, for example, Berding, 2019, 2020; Berding, Riebenbauer & Slepcevic-Zach, 2019; Berding et al., 2021). Basic concepts can be understood as "a person's content-related ideas of abstract objects, concepts, and procedures." At the same time, they are considered a prerequisite for "using abstract objects to solve real-world problems" (Berding, 2020, p. 135). Basic concepts have certain characteristics. They give abstract concepts a meaning (sense constitution) as they connect to already known "factual contexts or action concepts". Basic concepts also serve the mental representation of facts (representation) and thus enable the application of concepts to reality (application). Basic concepts usually do not stand isolated next to each other, but form a network (network structure). In addition, several different concepts are usually necessary to comprehensively cover a concept (diversity) (Berding, 2019, p. 149; Berding & Jahncke, 2020, p. 232; Berding, Riebenbauer & Slepcevic-Zach, 2019, p. 371; Berding et al., 2021, p. 566).

It can be assumed that basic concepts are particularly essential for translation performance, i.e., on the one hand for translating a real situation into the world of accounting and on the other hand for translating accounting results back into reality. Basic concepts "form the 'hinge' between phenomena in reality on the one hand and the numbers, symbols, and constructs of the formal accounting system on the other, i.e., they enable individuals to make flexible translations between these two levels" (Berding, 2019, p. 283). Figure 3.3 presents the model of basic concepts (Berding, Beckmann & Kürten, 2019, p. 571).

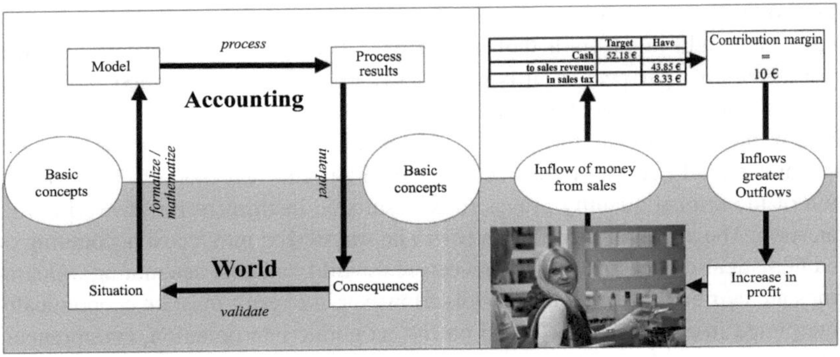

Fig. 3.3 Model of basic concepts in accounting (Berding, Beckmann & Kürten, 2019, p. 571)

The central point here is also, analogous to the modeling cycle, to translate a real situation (a real, economic phenomenon) into the world of accounting. For example, the real situation that money flows into the company through a cash sale is to be represented in accounting (formalizing and mathematizing). The representation of a real situation in the world of accounting usually takes place through the establishment of a booking (e.g., in this case a revenue booking with the cash register as the payment account). The booking sentence thus represents the translation performance. Subsequently, operations can be carried out *within* accounting (processing), which "provide merchants with profound insights for the design of real performance processes." For example, the contribution margin can be determined for the sale. In order for the information provided by accounting to be used for real purposes and decisions, it must be given a content-related meaning. Therefore, a retranslation from accounting into reality must be made (interpreting). The retranslation could mean that more cash inflows than cash outflows have occurred through the sales process and that the process has thus contributed to the success of the company. Basic concepts are used at the interfaces between the real world and accounting (i.e., in the steps of formalizing/mathematizing and interpreting) (Berding, Beckmann & Kürten, 2019, p. 572; Berding & Jahncke, 2020, p. 231–232; Berding, Riebenbauer & Slepcevic-Zach, 2019).[2]

For the domain of mathematics, there are already a large number of empirical findings that show that basic concepts influence learning processes. For example,

[2] For an example from cost and performance accounting, see Berding et al. (2021).

errors that occur when solving tasks can largely be traced back to missing or inappropriate basic concepts. The number or complexity of the basic concepts necessary for solving a task can also explain the difficulty of the task. In addition, it is assumed that the type, number, and complexity of basic concepts affect the learning strategies used and the motivation of the learners (for a summary, see Berding, 2019, pp. 100–112; Berding, Riebenbauer & Slepcevic-Zach, 2019, pp. 376–377). In the course of various projects, the basic concepts of learners on different concepts (e.g., expenditure and revenue, costs and services) of accounting were determined (Berding, 2019, 2020; Berding & Jahncke, 2020; Berding, Riebenbauer & Slepcevic-Zach, 2019; Berding et al., 2021). It was examined, on the one hand, which and how many basic concepts learners have, and on the other hand, how the number and type of basic concepts affect different variables, for example, on learning process variables such as motivation or in the sense of self-determination theory according to Deci and Ryan on autonomy support and competence experience as well as on learning success variables such as modeling ability and grades (for a summary of the previous findings, see Berding, 2020, p. 146).

In this context, the question of how the learners' modeling ability was assessed or measured is particularly interesting. To measure modeling ability, Berding, Beckmann, and Kürten (2019) developed a modeling test that focuses on success-relevant processes. The test consists of four different types of tasks that fully cover the modeling process and sufficiently consider documents, as the "representation of a process using a document represents the first abstraction step of a real process" (Berding, Beckmann & Kürten, 2019, p. 573). Therefore, working with and on documents is of particular importance. Tasks of the first category present photorealistic images of processes and situations related to success-relevant processes. In the sense of the model of basic concepts, these tasks present real situations that are to be translated into accounting. Figure 3.4 presents an example task from the modeling test according to Berding, Beckmann, and Kürten (2019, p. 574).

In tasks of type 2, an abstract object from accounting is given, for which a retranslation into reality must be made. For example, in a test task, booking sentences are given for which it must be determined whether they describe an expense for the company. In tasks of category 3, real processes are represented through photos and a selection of (non-)matching documents is presented. Learners then have to interpret the situation and the documents and correctly relate both areas (Which documents match which situation?). Tasks of the fourth category are based on the same principle, but here not documents, but booking sentences are given, which in turn are to be related to the real situation (Berding, Beckmann & Kürten, 2019, pp. 573–576). The measuring instrument was tested on a sample of 443 learners from 24 classes (consisting of classes from the technical college,

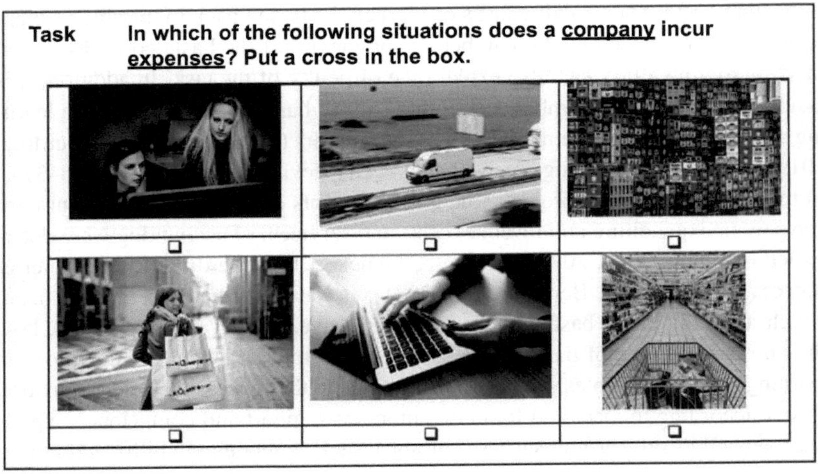

Fig. 3.4 Example task from the modeling test (Berding, Beckmann, and Kürten, 2019, p. 574)

the vocational high school, the vocational school, and dual training), checked for Rasch conformity, and revised several times or individual items were excluded. For the final version of the measuring instrument, consisting of ten tasks, a Rasch-conforming test can be assumed.

It is also interesting to question how and in what form the basic ideas of learners can be collected. To determine the basic ideas present in learners, diagnostic tasks are often used, in which two different strategies can be pursued based on the process of modeling. Thus, there is the possibility to define the subject level (i.e., a real situation) as the starting point and to demand from the learners to identify the corresponding mathematical (or accounting-specific) contents and procedures. These are tasks in the forward format. Tasks in the backward format, on the other hand, provide terms and procedures from accounting (e.g., booking entries, balance sheets, etc.) and require the learner to develop a corresponding economic situation (Berding, 2019, p. 145).[3] The basic ideas are then worked out content-analytically from the written and usually open answers of the learners. For exam-

[3] For examples of different diagnostic tasks, see Berding (2019, pp. 160–165).

ple, ten basic ideas could be identified for the term "expense" in Berding (2019, p. 194) through a deductive-inductive approach.[4]

The results of different studies show that basic ideas in accounting influence various variables. In the study conducted by Berding (2019, p. 255), it can be shown that basic ideas about the term expense explain about 29% of the variance in grades and about 10% of the variance in competence experience, with both positive and negative effects being observed depending on the content of the ideas. The results of the study by Berding, Riebenbauer and Slepcevic-Zach (2019, p. 390) also show that a higher number of basic ideas is associated with higher values in the three basic psychological needs (experience of autonomy, competence experience, and social inclusion). In the study by Berding and Jahncke (2020, p. 247), a multi-level structural equation model can show that a higher number of available basic ideas is associated with higher motivation, higher modeling ability, and better grades. As a didactic consequence, Berding, Riebenbauer and Slepcevic-Zach (2019, pp. 393–394) formulate that explicit work should be done in class on building a variety of viable basic ideas and that evidence, as "mediators between economic phenomena and their representation in accounting", and direct excerpts from economic reality should be used for this purpose. The connection of the different levels (i.e., reality and the world of accounting) is of particular importance.

Economic instrumental accounting also provides points of connection to the modeling cycle or mathematical modeling. Thus, economic instrumental accounting also focuses on the representation and interpretation of operational performance processes, in the sense of the modeling cycle, the translation of reality into the world of mathematics and the retranslation. Accounting is to be conveyed to the learners as an instrument or tool for controlling the company, with particular focus on translation services between real operational processes and the numerical work of accounting (Preiß & Tramm, 1996, p. 238; Tramm, 2005, p. 103). In describing the general business model, Preiß (1999, pp. 65–69) explicitly refers to mathematical modeling and adds economic modeling to the formal mathematical

[4]The basic ideas for the term "expense" were the procurement, input, consumption, destruction, transformation, cash outflow, inventory withdrawal, equity reduction, success reduction, and liquidity ideas. As examples: In the procurement idea, an expense is understood as the procurement of values. In the input idea, an expense is defined as a value that flows into the performance creation process. In the consumption idea, on the other hand, expenses are seen as consumption or consumption of values. In the cash outflow idea as outflow of funds (Berding, 2019, pp. 195–202).

modeling for the economic instrumental approach. Accounting includes the representation of a business case in the form of documents as well as economic models and terms and the mathematical rule system for booking and closing accounts. The economic models and the documents serve the transfer into the mathematical model as well as the supplement (beyond the mathematical work) for making economic decisions. The decisions can relate on the one hand to the design of reality and on the other hand to the exercise of balance sheet and valuation options when it comes to representing reality in the accounting system. Figure 3.5 illustrates the relationships and again shows, analogous to the modeling cycle, the partial steps of simplifying, mathematizing, mathematical working, and reinterpreting (Preiß, 1999, p. 66).

After the explanations on modeling ability in accounting, Sect. 3.3 introduces the Linz Level Model (Neuweg, 2020), where numerous references to the modeling cycle can also be made. Section 3.3.1 begins with a brief presentation of the compatibility of the Linz Level Model with the current didactic discussion, before Sect. 3.3.2 elaborates and describes the model in more detail.

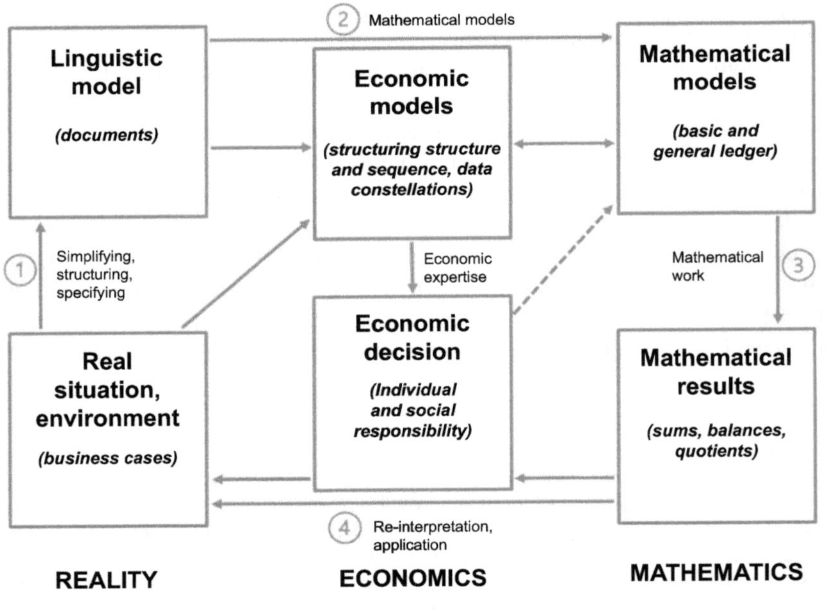

Fig. 3.5 Economic instrumental model building (Preiß, 1999, p. 66)

3.3 The "Linzer Ebenenmodell" as a Tool for Promoting the "Thinking Accountant" and Modeling Ability in Accounting

3.3.1 Criticism of Traditional Accounting Education as a Starting Point for the Development of the "Linzer Ebenenmodell"

In line with the current didactic discussion, Neuweg (2020, p. 135) also advocates for a stronger emphasis on the "thinking accountant" in accounting education, as only a small portion of graduates from commercial colleges actually work in the field of accounting and therefore need operational security when starting their careers. Moreover, even for those who work in the field of accounting, understanding the logic of booking, legal foundations, balance sheet policy objectives, and the purpose of accounting operations is more important than immediate operational capability, in light of the drastic changes in the working world (see Sect. 2.2.2). Many standard tasks in accounting are already fully automated through the use of RPA and AI systems (e.g., Hmyzo & Muzzu, 2020; Jordanski, 2020). Preiß (2015, p. 192) also notes that there are few data entry tasks left in financial accounting, and these are supported by document type assignments, account assignment suggestions, and help texts to minimize entry errors. More important than the ability to correctly record business transactions in accounting seems to be the ability to interpret and validate data and to detect errors (Neuweg, 2020, p. 135).

In his contribution, Neuweg (2020, pp. 136–138) identifies some problems with "traditional" accounting education that coincide with the problem situations and points of criticism discussed in the didactic discussion. He criticizes the lack of connection between accounting education and business education, which leads to accounting being primarily understood as a documentation system, not as a tool for planning, controlling, and monitoring business processes (see also, for example, Preiß, 2000, 2015). Thus, accounting operations are carried out (e.g., calculations are made and booking entries are formed). However, it remains invisible that these accounting operations 1) are expressions of business decisions and 2) result in new decisions and subsequently new business cases. There is a lack of process orientation, which makes it clear that other business processes have preceded business cases and further business cases will follow. In addition, there is a one-sided focus on documenting business processes, while the interpretation

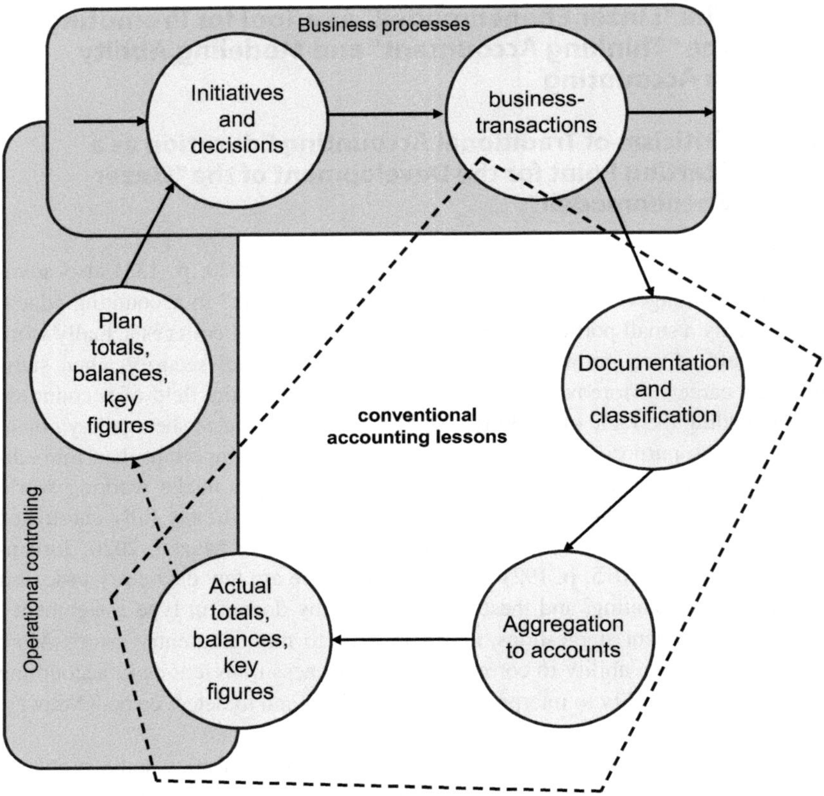

Fig. 3.6 Accounting and Business Process Orientation (Preiß, 2015, p. 191)

of documentation processes is often neglected.[5] This refers to the overemphasis on booking and calculation techniques, as also criticized in the discussion about the guiding images of the "practical" and "thinking accountant". The following graphic according to Preiß (2015, p. 191) illustrates this problem (Fig. 3.6).

[5] Booking entries are formed and calculations are made, but how these affect certain entrepreneurial variables (e.g., liquidity or profitability) is often overlooked.

> Traditional teaching presents business cases in a rudimentary and highly stylized manner. They are stripped of their temporality, i.e., their past and future reference, and are not made visible as expressions of business decisions. They lead to documentary operations, which ultimately result in account balances and, if at all, in actual key figures. And just as the business cases originally came "ex nihilo", they also end in nothing: it remains invisible that the actual data in the operational reality will now be compared with target data and that this comparison will trigger further initiatives and decisions that will lead to further business cases. (Neuweg, 2020, p. 137)

Neuweg (2020, p. 138) further criticizes the strongly teacher-centered teaching design and the lack of variation in teaching methods (e.g., Seifried, 2004b, 2004d; Seifried et al., 2006). In teaching, learners are often given little time for independent problem-solving, discussion, and interpretation, with the questioning-developing classroom conversation, in which the correct booking entry for an unknown business case is jointly developed and usually follows the same pattern, dominating.

> The question of how to book is attached to an unknown business case. In the questioning-developing classroom conversation, it is discussed which accounts are affected, what type of account it is, how the accounts change, and therefore on which side of the account to book. This is followed by practice. (Neuweg, 2020, p. 138)

Furthermore, Neuweg (2020, p. 136) views the balance sheet method as a critical concept in teaching. The balance sheet method usually leads to the creation of a balance sheet becoming a trivial, mechanical process in which the account balances are transferred to the balance sheet. It is not apparent that this is by no means a mechanical process, but that valuation processes, inventory data, legal norms, and balance sheet policy considerations play a significant role (see also, for example, Schneider, 2010, pp. 61–63; for criticism of the balance sheet method, see Sect. 2.4.1).

In this context, Neuweg (2020, pp. 136–137) addresses what he sees as central basic problems of accounting didactics. The strong orientation towards the balance sheet method leads to learners not understanding accounting processes as representations of real, operational processes, but as a "hermetic system in which 'information' leads to bookings, which in total relate to each other in a logically consistent system, but have no recognizable relationship to the 'real world'" (Neuweg, 2020, p. 136). In addition, booking entries are justified with the "logic of double-entry bookkeeping". In reality, however, they are usually expressions of corporate or tax law norms, which in turn pursue different objectives. It is also problematic that the operational reality is hardly taken into account in teaching. Learners therefore lack the reference to what is happening in the real world and how this relates to the operations they perform in accounting. Tasks are often formulated without context and without reference to real processes and procedures. In addition, hardly any documents are used, although they are the connection between the real world and the accounting world.

3.3.2 Presentation and Description of the "Linzer Ebenenmodell"

Based on the state of the didactic discussion, the criticism of "traditional" accounting education, and referring to the works of Resch (1988) and Tramm (2009, 2010, 2014), Neuweg (2020, p. 139) developed the "Linzer Ebenenmodell".[6]

The model deliberately overcomes a one-sided focus on booking and calculation operations by consistently establishing a relationship between the work of the accountant, the real operational processes, and the formal objectives of the company. At the same time, it shows that not only the "logic of double-entry bookkeeping" is relevant when forming booking entries, but especially legal norms. Thus, the model can be used to examine real operational processes using the different levels ("Ebenen"). It can support the teacher in their own professional training and in planning lessons (e.g., for designing or further developing tasks or for developing information inputs), and can also be made accessible to students in advanced lessons.

The model is initially defined over three levels or dimensions of economic professional activity. A person working in the economic professional field must

[6] According to Stachowiak (1973, pp. 131–134), models have three central properties. First, models are always "models of something", i.e., representations of natural or artificial originals (representation characteristic). Models also do not capture all properties of the original, but only those that the model creator has identified as significant (reduction characteristic). Models are also not uniquely assigned to their originals per se. They fulfill their replacement function a) for certain […] subjects, b) within certain time intervals, and c) with restriction to certain mental or actual operations. They are therefore purpose-bound (pragmatic characteristic). The Linz Level Model represents the operational reality in the form of business cases, their representation in accounting, and their reference back to the "real world" (representation characteristic). Not all properties of the original are captured. For example, the operational reality is represented by goods and service flows, cash flows, and social processes (reduction characteristic). The model serves the purpose of representing business cases and accounting topics on different levels and thus promoting understanding. It can be used by teachers for their own professional preparation and for planning lessons (pragmatic characteristic).

focus their attention on these three levels and ideally be able to switch flexibly between the three levels. Commercial activities are initially very much characterized by dealing with various documents, for example with letters or emails, with tables, with accounts, with different computer programs and input windows, etc. The first level is the level of information flows and is referred to as the *factual field of action*, as this is the level at which commercially active persons act and operate (Neuweg, 2018, p. 247, 2020, p. 139; Tramm, 2009, pp. 83–84, 2010, pp. 71–72, 2014, p. 100). For work in the factual field of action, it is central that it usually involves "symbolizing actions" (Tramm, 2014, p. 100) and that people on this level move "in a symbolically, especially linguistically and numerically, mediated reality" (Neuweg, 2018, p. 244).

The significance of actions in the factual field of action only arises from the fact that they prepare, accompany, document or evaluate actions on a second level, namely on the level of the *reference field of action* or the *real objective level*. Thus, the activities in the factual field of action are never an end in themselves, but always a means to an end. The documents that people in accounting deal with represent real operational processes, especially real goods flows, nominal goods flows, and formal and informal social transactions (Neuweg, 2018, p. 247, 2020, p. 139; Tramm, 2009, p. 84, 2010, p. 71, 2014, pp. 102–103).

Competent commercial action therefore requires not just being able to perform the immediate activities in the factual field of action. Rather, the focus must always be on the real processes—the objective level. This is also important because the merchant can only make interventions in the reference field of action indirectly.[7] It is therefore essential to become aware of these processes, which are "behind the documents and screen masks", and to model them in an abstract way (Tramm, 2009, p. 84, 2014, p. 101).

> Competent or 'non-partialized' action (cf. Volpert 1983) is demonstrated by the fact that the actor does not act solely on the basis of specific action rules of the factual field of action, but understands the functional connection of such rules to the reference field of action and can thus act intelligently and flexibly from the functional logic of the reference field of action. (Tramm, 2009, p. 84)

The activities in the reference field of action serve to achieve entrepreneurial objectives. Ultimately, however, they are not an end in themselves, but contribute

[7] As an example, Tramm (2014, p. 101) mentions the office clerk who orders delivery by mouse click, but does not himself work in the warehouse.

to the achievement of the company's formal objectives. The *formal objective level* as the third level defines the criteria towards which the company's performance processes are to be designed and evaluated (Neuweg, 2020, p. 139; Tramm, 2009, p. 85, 2014, p. 102).

According to Neuweg (2020, p. 139), the three levels are thus defined (see also Dolzsanksi, 2013b, p. 359; Neuweg, 2018, p. 247; Rückwart, 2009, p. 38; Tramm, 2009, p. 84, 2010, p. 72, 2014, p. 102):

- The level of information and data flows (documentation and data transformation level) as the factual field of action of the accountant. This is about initiating, accompanying and evaluating performance processes.
- The level of real and nominal goods flows or social processes as the level of the company's objectives or as the reference field of action of the accountant.
- The level of operational formal objectives, which controls the processes on the other two levels.

If the commercial worker succeeds in focusing his attention simultaneously on all three levels and switching flexibly between these levels, he becomes the "ideal operational overall actor" (Neuweg, 2018, p. 247; Tramm, 2009, p. 8, 2014, p. 103) and overcomes the "writing and counter perspective" (Reetz & Witt, 1974, p. 186).

In the didactic discussion, it is often said that the training of "thinking accountants" should be the target category of accounting instruction (see Sect. 2.2.1). Learners are to be trained as "interested, holistic system thinkers and independent working students with an enlightened economic basic understanding" (Seifried, 2004b, p. 52) and competent economic citizens (Schneider, 2010, p. 58) who have economic competence (Achtenhagen, 1996, pp. 27–28) and an understanding of economic interrelationships (Tramm & Preiß, 1996, p. 5). Based on the Linz level model, Neuweg (2020, p. 138) has defined the essential abilities of a "thinking accountant" from his point of view. "Understanding accounting" means that a person can not only form and independently derive booking entries, but also

1. understands which business processes have which accounting relevance and why,
2. can infer business processes and conditions from the financial accounting figures,
3. understands how accounting imaging processes are influenced by legal norms and what intentions are associated with the content of these legal norms,

4. understands the effects of booking processes on the balance sheet presentation of the asset and capital situation and on the profit and loss account,
5. can derive the associated effects on the external perception of the company by creditors, potential lenders and investors, and on the amount of tax,
6. can always and consistently view business processes and their representation in external accounting from the formal objective perspective, and can indicate which effects result on the (cost accounting and therefore "true") operating result and on the liquidity status of a company.

Figure 3.7 shows the "Linzer Ebenenmodell" according to Neuweg (2020, p. 140) with the three levels. The three levels are further differentiated and described below.

3.3.2.1 The Reference Field of Action as a Reflection of the Real World

The first level, *the reference field of action or the level of objective goals (fields 1 to 3)*, represents the real world, apart from accounting and the numerical representation that takes place there. The exchange processes of a company with its stakeholders are usually represented by nominal and real goods flows (Buchholz & Gerhards, 2016, p. 1–2; Neuweg, 2020, p. 139; Schierenbeck & Wöhle, 2016, p. 26). The company buys and sells goods and/or services (goods and service flows, field 1). The company receives and disburses funds (cash flows, field 2). Nominal and real goods flows are embedded in social processes (field 3),

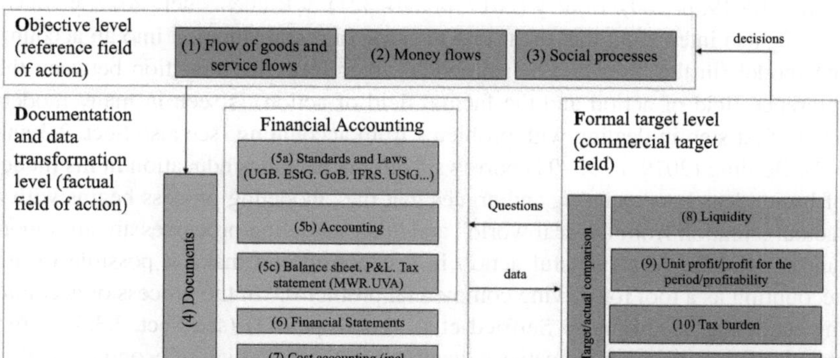

Fig. 3.7 The Linz level model according to Neuweg (2020, p. 140)

which take place both within the company and between the company and external stakeholders. At the level of the reference field of action, the company pursues its objective goals, which define the type, quantity, quality, location, and timing of production ("What should be produced?") (Neuweg, 2020, p. 139–140; Wöhe et al., 2020, p. 67).

In accounting education, the reference field of action, i.e., the operational reality, is usually obscured or highly stylized, making it unclear to learners what the accounting operations actually refer to and which processes in the "real world" lead to accounting activities and which do not (Neuweg, 2020, p. 140). The connection between operational reality and (abstract) accounting, however, seems to be of particular relevance and is repeatedly discussed in the didactic discussion. For example, Tramm et al. (1996, p. 192–193) discuss that learning difficulties arise precisely because of the abstractness of the content, the lack of practical references, and the lack of clarity (see also Sect. 2.5.2). Dolzsanksi (2014, p. 221) argues that more realism and a more realistic representation of operational processes are necessary in accounting education, and that the purpose of accounting needs to be emphasized more strongly. Preiß (2015, p. 189) advocates for a stronger link between observable processes in the real world and their representation in accounting. Sloane (1996, p. 55) also emphasizes that accounting needs to be more closely integrated into operational processes and understood as a tool for business decisions. Similar arguments for a more intensive examination of operational reality and a networking between the real world and the accounting world can also be found in older works by Dubs (1996, p. 130), Preiß (1999, p. 5–6), Preiß and Tramm (1996, p. 240) and in newer works by Berding, Beckmann and Kürten (2019, p. 569), Bouley (2017, p. 320–321) or Riebenbauer (2021, p. 154).

It is also interesting that the transformation of a real situation into an accounting model (in the "Linzer Ebenenmodell", therefore, the transition between the reference field of action and the factual field of action) is seen in many models as the first step in dealing with problems from accounting (see also Sect. 2.3 and 3.2). Berding (2019, p. 93–94) borrows from mathematics education in his model of basic ideas in accounting and argues that the "modeling process begins with a factual situation from the real world" and "that modeling processes are an important component of successful action in accounting and make it possible to use accounting as a tool for solving commercial problems." In the process of accounting modeling according to Seifried et al. (2010, p. 147) (see Sect. 2.3.3), reference is also made to mathematics education and the recording of economic reality is defined as the first step in accounting work. In the think-aloud study conducted by Helm (2016d), learners were asked to verbalize their thoughts when forming booking entries. In this context, modeling was identified as a basic competence in dealing with accounting tasks. Several student statements indicate that the first step in booking business transactions is a modeling performance.

This finding is by no means trivial, as the structure of textbook tasks often does not require such modeling, for example, when content areas (e.g., procurement of trading goods) and the required activities (e.g., document control) are given in the instructions (Helm, 2016d, p. 39) (see also Sect. 2.3.3). Jungwirth (2015) transfers the modeling process to the field of cost accounting and also emphasizes that in current teaching practice, no or hardly any modeling services are required on the part of the students, as the problem or task setting already starts at the operation, i.e., the (mathematical and/or accounting) execution. "Even in cost accounting, tasks usually start at the operation. The preliminary information is already given and the numbers just need to be put in the right order. Where the numbers come from is often not discussed" (Jungwirth, 2015, p. 35). Thus, she also addresses the missing connection between the real world (reference field of action) and accounting (factual field of action) (see also Sect. 3.2).

In the competence model of Guggemos (2016, p. 37) (see Sect. 2.3.2), modeling, i.e., the "transformation of a requirement situation into a workable model," is a difficulty-determining feature of an accounting task. In the competence model of Preiß (2005b, p. 75), who also refers to mathematics education, modeling is one of four cognitive operations. Also in the economic-instrumental accounting (Sect. 2.4.2), it is emphasized that students need to understand "the reciprocal relationship between the numerical system of accounting [...] and the real transformation processes" (Preiß & Tramm, 1996, p. 252).

These examples make it clear that a stronger connection between operational reality and the system of accounting is necessary. Preiß and Tramm (1996, p. 245) also argue that the "change of abstraction level between concrete objects and services in the company and their abstract equivalents in the numerical system of accounting is of considerable importance."

3.3.2.2 The Documentation and Data Transformation Level as a Factual Field of Action

The second level of the model forms the *factual field of action*, in which the businesswoman/businessman operates. However, the people working here do not directly work with goods, money, or people, but primarily with documents, data, receipts, or tables that form the interface between the real world and the world of accounting (Field 4) (Neuweg, 2020, p. 140). Preiß and Tramm (1996, p. 252) speak of a "mediating function of the document between the real processes and their modeling in the company's information system." The importance of documents is also emphasized in economic-instrumental accounting (see, for example,

Preiß, 1999, p. 64 Tramm, 2005, p. 110), where the "transfer of a complex life situation into a document is already the first step of reduction." At the same time, however, documents allow for easier reconstruction of the underlying real processes and are therefore preferable to text-based information (Preiß, 1999, p. 64). The importance of using as realistic documents and receipts as possible is almost undisputed in the didactic discussion (see, for example, Bensch, 2009, pp. 200–201, Berding, Beckmann & Kürten, 2019, p. 573, Mathes, 2006, p. 163, Tramm, 2003, p. 10, Seifried, 2004b, p. 291 or Seifried & Sembill, 2004, p. 378).

The documents are processed in financial accounting, which represents the central instrument of external accounting (Neuweg, 2020, pp. 140–141; Wöhe et al., 2020, pp. 629–630). In this process, bookings are made and any calculations are carried out (Field 5b). The rules for document processing result on the one hand from legal norms (Field 5a) and on the other hand from the rules of the double-entry system. A problem is also that too little attention is paid to the corporate and tax law foundations, although these have a significant influence on whether and how operational processes are depicted in financial accounting. These accounting activities become visible in the balance sheet and in the profit and loss account (Field 5c), which are the central components of the annual financial statements. The annual financial statements according to the Income Tax Act also form the basis for tax assessment (Neuweg, 2020, p. 141; Wöhe et al., 2020, p. 629). In addition to external accounting, however, internal accounting is also significant (see also Sect. 2.1). The financial statement (liquidity management) and cost accounting are defined as essential instruments of internal accounting (Buchholz & Gerhards, 2016, p. 7; Troßmann & Baumeister, 2015, pp. 7–10; Wöhe et al., 2020, p. 630). It is important that commercial operators also focus on internal accounting, as internal accounting provides essential information for the control, planning, and monitoring of business decisions and processes (Neuweg, 2020, p. 141). Preiß (2015, p. 190) also notes that traditional accounting teaching places a strong focus on conventional bookkeeping, while cost accounting and liquidity management are neglected.

3.3.2.3 Achieving Formal Goals as a Guiding Criterion for Action

Neither the activities at the objective level nor those in the factual field of action serve a purpose in themselves, but always serve the long-term achievement of certain formal goals. Therefore, it is crucial that commercial operators have the *commercial target field* in view, as this sets the criteria for action on the other two levels (Neuweg, 2018, pp. 247, 2020, p. 141; Tramm, 2014, p. 102). Formal goals determine the baseline of entrepreneurial action. Objective goals, on the other hand, have an instrumental character and, at least from a business perspective, serve to achieve the formal goals. Essential (economic) formal goals can be identified as cost goals (e.g., cost minimization), liquidity goals (ensuring financial equilibrium), and profitability and profit goals (e.g., profit maximization) (Perridon et al., 2022, pp. 13–15; Schierenbeck & Wöhle, 2016, p. 78; Töpfer, 2007, pp. 437–445; Wöhe et al., 2020, p. 67). According to Schneider and Schneider (2019, p. 13), the question of whether a company can manage with the funds available is particularly important, as one can "survive losses according to accounting" but not "insolvency". Accordingly, Neuweg (2020, p. 141) formulates liquidity as a formal goal (Field 8) alongside profitability (piece or period success, Field 9). Also relevant for the company is the tax burden (Field 10) and the external impact or external representation (Field 11).

For Neuweg (2020, p. 141), it is therefore important that

> in accounting teaching from the beginning, differences between the represented and the actual profit are discussed and not only later in cost accounting teaching. In addition to the profit effects, the aspects of liquidity, which are at least as important because monitoring liquidity is critical to survival, must also consistently be addressed. Therefore, liquidity and profitability emerge as important formal goals. The balance sheet and P&L must be considered, as they determine the tax burden and the external representation of the company.

If one now explicitly refers to the modeling cycle, then the reference field of action (Fields 1 to 3 of the "Linzer Ebenenmodell") can be seen as a *real model* (see, for example, Fig. 3.2). Reality is primarily represented through documents (*situation model*, Field 4 of the "Linzer Ebenenmodell"), which depict the processes of the real world. The task of a person working in accounting is to capture the operational reality (in the sense of the modeling cycle, therefore, to understand, simplify, and structure) and to transfer it into an accounting model (in the language of the modeling cycle: to mathematize). The translation of reality into an *accounting model* usually happens through the formation of booking sentences, which in turn are set up taking into account applicable norms and laws (Fields 5a and 5b). Within financial accounting (or also within the internal calculation circles of financial statements or cost accounting), accounting operations are carried out (in the modeling cycle, the mathematical work). As a result of these imaging and operation processes, the balance sheet is created in financial accounting as a computational comparison of the assets and liabilities of a company at a certain cut-off date (point-in-time accounting) as well as the profit and loss account as a period-related comparison of expenses and revenues (Field 5c) (Bertl et al., 2022, pp. 239–240). However, the accounting processes and the results of the operations must again be given a content-related meaning and the effects must be interpreted in the light of various formal goals (Fields 8 to 11). In the sense of the modeling cycle, a retranslation from the accounting world to the real world takes place. Based on these interpretation services, decisions are made, which in turn have consequences for reality.

After the didactic discussion status was worked out in the last sections and especially the modeling in accounting and the "Linzer Ebenenmodell" were examined more closely, Chap. 4 elaborates on the importance of tasks in teaching (Sect. 4.1). In Sect. 4.2, classification systems for evaluating tasks are presented and current research findings on task quality in accounting are discussed (Sect. 4.3).

The Completion of Tasks as a Core Process in Teaching

4

4.1 Tasks in the Classroom—A Definition

Tasks represent significant learning opportunities in the classroom and contribute significantly to enabling successful learning processes and achieving the teaching objectives pursued in the classroom (Blömeke et al., 2006, p. 334; Kleinknecht & Schmid-Kühn, 2020, p. 410). Tasks are therefore an important element of school learning and fulfill various functions (Thonhauser, 2020, p. 464). They generally serve to control performance, deepen and consolidate content, introduce new content, and practice certain procedures, methods, or techniques. Tasks thus significantly determine school instruction (A. Fischer & Gerdsmeier, 2007, p. 184). For Reusser (2014, p. 77), tasks are "carriers of learning opportunities" that represent the backbone of (subject) didactic learning arrangements and student-activating instruction as "activation and design tools". He refers to them as the "substrate of learning opportunities" and the "pivot of competence-oriented instruction" (Reusser, 2014, p. 80).

There are a multitude of definitions, terms, and classifications for tasks in the classroom. Pahl (1998, p. 13) defines tasks as "a request to learners to perform a certain action, answer a question, solve a problem, implement an instruction, realize a task, but also to make a decision and ask questions themselves that help to illuminate a problem area". For Gerdsmeier (2004, p. 23), tasks are "requests to learners to become cognitively active in a sometimes more, sometimes less predetermined path." Blömeke et al. (2006, p. 331) define tasks as "demands with which students are confronted in class by the teacher."

In the school context, the term task is usually associated with learning controls and exams on the one hand, and with exercises that are supposed to prepare for exams on the other hand. Thus, tasks for competence acquisition (learning tasks)

S. Reindl-Stütz, *Characteristics of Tasks in the Domain of Accounting*,
https://doi.org/10.1007/978-3-658-48958-8_4

and tasks for competence assessment (exam tasks) are distinguished (Thonhauser, 2008, p. 13). However, tasks can also fulfill other functions. Tasks can initially serve to define or concretize learning objectives by exemplarily showing which situations learners should be able to cope with at the end of the learning process. In this context, a distinction is made between performance (concrete action in a task solution) and competence (underlying, not directly observable disposition) (Thonhauser, 2020, p. 464–465). Tasks can also be used to assess the prerequisites of learners in order to appropriately consider the individual prior experiences of learners. Tasks as *learning* tasks primarily serve to stimulate learning by presenting situations or problems to learners that are currently (still) not manageable for them. Tasks as *practice* tasks, on the other hand, primarily serve to develop routines, i.e., the ability to cope with a situation quickly and safely. Tasks are also used for evaluation to check how fruitful and successful previous learning processes were. This is followed by planning for future learning processes. In addition to evaluation, tasks also serve for selection, by distinguishing learners with sufficient competence from those with insufficient competence (Thonhauser, 2020, p. 465–466).

A similar classification is made by Flechsig (2008, p. 241–242), who distinguishes depending on the purpose of use 1) tasks for the acquisition of competences (*learning* tasks), 2) tasks for the application of already acquired competences (*work* and *application* tasks), 3) tasks for checking existing competences (*control* or *test* tasks) and 4) tasks for maintaining or perfecting already existing competences (*practice* tasks). *Learning* tasks as tasks for the acquisition of competences differ from pure *application* tasks, where existing competences are used, from *control* tasks, where competences are checked, and from *practice* tasks, where competences are secured against “forgetting” or perfected. Learning tasks in the sense of acquisition tasks are therefore at the beginning of learning processes, while practice and application tasks are in the middle and control tasks are at the end of learning processes.

Since in the present study only tasks from different textbooks are analyzed and evaluated, and all types of tasks probably occur in textbooks (with the exception, of course, of exam tasks, which are used in the context of performance assessment), only the term *task* is used here. A more precise differentiation of the tasks, i.e., whether they are used at the beginning, during, or at the end of the learning process and whether they are therefore learning tasks, application tasks, practice tasks, or control tasks, is not made, as this also depends significantly on the specific use by the teacher.

The question is also which sources or resources teachers use for the design or selection of tasks. Textbooks in particular play a significant role in the planning and implementation of lessons and are among the most frequently used teaching materials (Bloemen, 2011, p. 11; Geissler, 2021, p. 67; Tramm & Goldbach, 2005, p. 203). For business vocational instruction, Tramm and Goldbach (2005, p. 203) state that the textbook "shapes instructional practice in many functions", "it serves teachers for professional as well as didactic-methodical preparation, it is used as a learning book in class and in post-class preparation and finally serves as a repetitorium in exam preparation." Textbooks fulfill different functions, such as structuring and preparing the content contained in the curriculum (structuring function). Through questions and work instructions, impulses are also given for the design of lessons (control function), by providing learning tasks that vary methodically and in complexity, the learned should be applied and made transferable (control and result assurance function) (Bloemen, 2011, p. 12–13; Fuchs et al., 2014, p. 10; Imhof, 1993, p. 24).

Although the intensity of textbook use certainly varies by subject or individually between different teachers and students, empirical studies suggest that textbooks are intensively used by both teachers and students (e.g., for the subject of political education see Oberle & Tatje, 2017; for mathematics, the use of textbooks was also surveyed as part of the TIMSS study, see Mullis et al., 2012, p. 391–395). Assuming first, that the processing of tasks is of essential importance for learning processes and second, that textbooks are a central resource for such tasks, it is worth taking a closer look at the characteristics, features, and quality of the tasks contained in textbooks.

4.2 Domain-Independent and Domain-Specific Criteria for the Analysis and Evaluation of Tasks

If one wants to evaluate tasks, evaluation standards or criteria are necessary that allow an assessment of the tasks. At the same time, a function of criteria or classification systems is that they sensitize for relevant characteristics, help to focus on important aspects and reveal blind spots and potential for improvement (Arndt, 2014, p. 222). In this sense, the evaluation criteria are not only seen as a standard for assessing tasks, but equally as criteria for designing and developing tasks.

The "Linzer Ebenenmodell" (Sect. 3.3) and the Modeling Cycle (Sect. 3.2) primarily serve as theoretical reference concepts for the development of criteria for assessing tasks in textbooks (see Chap. 5), with both concepts being compatible with the current didactic discourse (Chap. 2) and corresponding references being established. At the same time, it is worthwhile to focus on existing criteria or catalogs of criteria or systems to derive recommendations or suggestions for development work. For the analysis and evaluation of tasks, a number of domain-independent but also domain-specific criteria can be identified (for an overview, see also Berding & Lamping, 2014, pp. 47–48; Bloemen, 2011, pp. 21–30 or Berding, 2019, pp. 137–138), which are based on different theoretical approaches.

For example, Reusser (2014, p. 81) states that "good" learning tasks represent professional core ideas, stimulate learning processes that involve deep understanding and problem solving, arouse curiosity and promote motivation through action and everyday relevance, vividness and authenticity, allow multiple approaches, are formulated in a way that is appropriate for the learning group, enable individual and cooperative learning, promote professional and interdisciplinary competences, and allow participation and co-design in learning content and paths. Luthinger et al. (2014, p. 58) define the following ten learning-relevant characteristics of competence-oriented tasks: 1) Competence image (Does the task cover the entire competence or only individual aspects?), 2) Relevance to life, 3) Work on (pre-)concepts (Does the task take into account existing ideas of the learners?), 4) Type of knowledge, 5) Cognitive process (Type of cognitive performance), 6) Structuring of the task, 7) Diversity of representation forms, 8) Openness of the task (How clear or open is information about the initial and target state?), 9) Learning support (Offer of help in the tasks 10), Diversity of learning paths (Consideration of individual learning and processing paths as well as performance levels).

Bloemen (2011, pp. 28–30) also condenses frequently discussed demands in the literature and thus outlines seven construction and learning promotion criteria for tasks:

- In vocational education, learning tasks primarily serve to promote professional action competence and should therefore promote the *independence* and *self-control* of learners. Independence and self-control can be supported by high degrees of freedom and scope for design and decision-making.
- Closely linked to the promotion of independence and self-control is the demand for *openness*. For example, learners should be given the opportunity to independently select the problem-solving strategy suitable for solving the task, to work on different solution paths and to identify the underlying problem themselves.
- Learning tasks should also promote *social interaction, communication and cooperation*, which can be achieved through partner or group work. This should also train the learners' ability to handle conflicts and reach consensus.

- In preparation for professional practice, complex, problem-laden learning tasks that involve a *variety of demands or different activities* should be offered. This can be achieved by poorly structured, diffuse problem situations. On the other hand, overly simple situation descriptions should be avoided.
- In order for the learning tasks to actually promote professional action competence, they must show a *situatedness* in terms of content and methodology by relating to the world of work or life. This means that "the relevance of the knowledge acquired in the learning process for concrete situations in life must be recognizable and a transfer to comparable situations must be possible" (Bloemen, 2011, p. 30).
- The tasks should also be oriented towards the *complete action* (planning, execution, control). In this context, it is also important to give learners comprehensive insights into the process steps of professional action.
- Sufficient *information* and *feedback* are also necessary for action reflection and, if necessary, for adjusting actions.

A frequently used general didactic category system for assessing the cognitive demand content of tasks is that of the project group around Uwe Maier and Marc Kleinknecht (e.g. Kleinknecht et al., 2011; Maier et al., 2010). It was obtained from the review and content-analytical evaluation of general didactic and subject didactic task analysis criteria. The evaluation grid includes seven domain-independent analysis dimensions with three to five categories each and has been used in many different domains (e.g. German, Mathematics, Physics, History, Art or Sports, for an overview see Kleinknecht et al., 2013). For the domain of accounting, it was used by Ernst (2012a) and Thoma and Schumacher (2018) with adaptations or reductions (for the results see Sect. 4.3). For business education, it was applied exemplarily by Arndt (2013), critically evaluated and checked for completeness. Figure 4.1 shows the category system.

At the center of the grid is the analysis and evaluation of the cognitive activation potential of a task with the categories *Type of knowledge* and *cognitive process*. They use the taxonomy matrix of Anderson and Krathwohl (2001). Originally developed for the formulation or classification of teaching objectives as well as for the coordination of teaching objectives, instruction and examination (*curriculum alignment*), the taxonomy matrix is also often used for the analysis and evaluation of tasks. This matrix cross-references cognitive processes (remember, understand, apply, analyze, evaluate, create) and types of knowledge (factual knowledge, conceptual knowledge, procedural knowledge, metacognitive knowledge).

Dimension	Characteristics			
Type of knowledge	Facts	Procedures	Concepts	Metacognition
Cognitive process	Reproduction	Near transfer	Far transfer	Problem solving
Knowledge units (KU)	One KU	Up to 4 KU	More than 4 KU	
Openness	Defined/convergent	Defined/divergent	Vague/divergent	
Relevance to life	None	Constructed	Authentic	Real
Linguistic complexity	Low	Medium	High	
Forms of representation	One	Integration	Transformation	

Fig. 4.1 General didactic category system for analyzing the cognitive potential of tasks according to Maier et al. (2010, p. 90)

The dimension of type of knowledge is taken over unchanged into the category system, while a condensation to four manifestations is made in the dimension of cognitive processes. The term "understanding", which is operationalized with key terms such as interpret, exemplify, classify, summarize, infer, compare or explain, is omitted (Maier et al., 2013, pp. 31–32). Instead, a distinction is initially made between reproduction tasks and transfer tasks. While reproduction tasks require a memory performance, near transfer tasks require a small transfer performance, with the task situation differing only slightly from already known situations. Near transfer tasks are characterized by giving hints about which knowledge is required for the task solution and which actions are to be performed. Tasks with wide transfer, on the other hand, require the application of knowledge in new and unknown situations in which it is also not clear which knowledge should be applied in which form. Creative problem solving is defined as the fourth stage. In these tasks, unlike reproduction or near and wide transfer, new knowledge must first be generated for the task solution (Maier et al., 2013, pp. 32–33; Maier et al., 2010, p. 87).

The dimension *knowledge units* is seen as a sub-facet of task complexity. The central question is what knowledge is absolutely necessary to solve the task. A knowledge unit always represents the highest hierarchical level. This dimension distinguishes three manifestations. *Tasks with one knowledge unit*, for example, ask for a designation, a fact, or a date. At the level of conceptual knowledge, for example, a technical term needs to be explained. *Tasks with up to four knowledge units* combine, for example, conceptual knowledge and factual knowledge or require different aspects within one type of knowledge (e.g., different mathematical operations). *Tasks with more than four knowledge units* can in turn demand several knowledge units within one type of knowledge (e.g., many dates for certain historical events) or combine knowledge of different types (Kleinknecht et al., 2011, p. 333–334; Maier et al., 2013, p. 33–34; Maier et al., 2010, p. 87–88).

Drawing on the problem definition of cognitive psychology, the dimension *openness* of the task is established in the category system. Tasks can therefore be classified according to how clearly or openly the initial and target state and the transformation between the initial situation and the target are formulated. The dimension of openness includes three manifestations. *Defined and convergent* tasks are characterized by a clearly defined initial (What needs to be done?) and target state (What does the solution look like?). The work order is therefore clear and there is also only one correct solution. *Defined and divergent* tasks, on the other hand, have a clearly identifiable question, but different solutions are conceivable. In the case of *vaguely defined* and *divergent* tasks, both the work order and the target state are unclear. A problem or situation is described, but the situation itself does not result in a clearly defined question. Accordingly, different solution paths are also possible (Kleinknecht et al., 2011, p. 335; Maier et al., 2013, p. 35–36; Maier et al., 2010, p. 88).

The dimension *relevance to life* responds to the demand to link school content more closely to the life experiences of learners and distinguishes four different manifestations. While in *tasks without relevance to life* no connection is made to the learners' life reality, in *tasks with constructed relevance to life* a link is made between subject content and learners' experiences. However, the reference seems "contrived" and overall not very authentic. On the third level, *tasks with constructed, but authentic relevance to life* are classified. In these tasks, the reference to the learners' world of experience seems meaningful and authentic. *Tasks with real relevance to life* resolve the difference between the task and the learners' world of experience, as learners deal with real problems and solve them (e.g., organizing a class trip, drafting a job application for an internship) (Kleinknecht et al., 2011, p. 335; Maier et al., 2013, p. 36–37; Maier et al., 2010, p. 88–89).

The dimension of *linguistic-logical complexity* takes into account the manner of linguistic information presentation and the convergence between task text and processing steps. *Tasks with simple linguistic-logical complexity* contain little text and the order of the sentences corresponds to the order of task processing. In *tasks with medium linguistic-logical complexity*, the order of sentences and the steps of processing are not always identical. In addition, there are text passages with irrelevant information and complex sentence structures. *Tasks with high linguistic-logical complexity* are characterized by divergence of sentence order and processing steps as well as by confusing formulations and complex sentence structures (e.g., double negations, if-then connections) (Kleinknecht et al., 2011, p. 335–336; Maier et al., 2013, p. 37–38; Maier et al., 2010, p. 89).

The category *forms of knowledge representation* is based on findings from the field of cognitive psychology and takes into account the different forms of knowledge representation (e.g., verbal/propositional and pictorial/concrete). It involves two questions: 1) In what form is the knowledge required for task processing represented in the task? (e.g., texts, symbolic representations, auditory information, iconic representations), 2) In what form must the knowledge be processed or the solution created? In *tasks with one form of representation*, both the task information and the task solution are contained or to be developed in *one* form of representation. Tasks that *integrate* different forms of representation provide knowledge in various forms that learners need to integrate to develop the solution (e.g., information from textual representation and from a graphic). In a *transformation* into another form of representation, the knowledge needs to be transformed into a new form of representation, which is not specified by the task (e.g., creation of a graphic based on text information) (Kleinknecht et al., 2011, p. 336; Maier et al., 2013, p. 38–40; Maier et al., 2010, p. 90).

Blömeke et al. (2006, pp. 335–337) presented another domain-unspecific model for analyzing the quality of tasks. They base their approach on a cognitive-theoretical learning model and formulate nine requirements for tasks: 1) Exemplary exploration of a socially relevant educational content, 2) Addressing a need of the students, 3) Promotion of general intellectual abilities, 4) Novelty value in relation to the domain-specific knowledge and experience level, 5) Chance of coping, 6) Potential for internal differentiation, 7) Representation of an authentic situation, 8) Promotion of problem-solving ability, and 9) Requirement of social interactions. A task is initially characterized by the fact that it exemplarily explores a content identified as relevant by *society*. They refer to the distinction used by Klafki between educational *content* and educational *value* (cf. Klafki, 1963). A task must also always address a *need* of the learners. This can be the need to resolve a "cognitive conflict" or, for example, the needs for coping, appreciation, or self-realization. The *cognitive demand* of a task should be just above the already existing abilities ("zone of proximal development"). The taxonomy matrix by Anderson and Krathwohl (2001) is used as an indicator to determine which cognitive demands a task contains, distinguishing between cognitive processes and forms of knowledge. A task must also have a certain *novelty value*, i.e., go beyond already known content and/or methods. Only in this way can professional knowledge, skills, and abilities be expanded. Although the task should be challenging and have novelty value, it must still be *manageable* by the learners. If a task is seen as having no chance of coping, it is expected that the task will not be tackled. It is also important that the task is *understandable*, i.e., it is linguistically and content-wise understood by the learners. The chance of coping with the task also implies that opportunities for *internal differentiation* are offered, allowing for work at different levels or to different extents. It is also important that the knowledge, skills, and abilities acquired in the context of the task can be applied and transferred to new situations. A transfer to new situations can be facilitated by complex, authentic situations. The *complexity of the necessary modeling* and the *range of situation* are used as indicators for this requirement. The task should also promote the *problem-solving ability* of the learners as another requirement. This characteristic is defined in reference to the problem-solving process by the openness of the task, the number of possible solution paths, and the openness of the target state. The *social interaction* is defined as the ninth relevant characteristic. Tasks should therefore encourage social interactions through group work or other forms of exchange.

Leuders (2014, pp. 34–35) notes that "general didactic task categorizations across subjects and research approaches are usually too unspecific for subject-specific research—even though they certainly provide constructive impulses for interdisciplinary theory networking and method development". For this reason, the focus should therefore be on domain-specific classification systems and task characteristics. It can be noted that these are predominantly available for the mathematical-natural science area (e.g., for physics H. E. Fischer & Draxler, 2006; Leutner et al., 2008; for mathematics e.g., Büchter & Leuders, 2006; Jordan et al., 2006; Maaß, 2010; M. Neubrand et al., 2013). For the present study, mathematics education seems to be a relevant reference discipline, as mathematics is attributed a similar formal structure as the accounting domain (e.g., Thoma & Schumacher, 2018, p. 1) and as shown in Chap. 3 there are already some points of connection and reference between the two domains. According to Leuders (2014, p. 35), "task categorizations in mathematics education are as diverse as the intentions associated with them." In mathematics education research, criteria or characteristics for tasks are discussed that can also be found in other domains or in domain-unspecific category systems, e.g., the complexity of a task, the authenticity, the relevance for the learners, the cognitive demand level, and the openness (for a summary see e.g., Greefrath & Maaß, 2020, pp. 9–10).

Particularly interesting in this context are classification systems that specifically focus on modeling tasks or the modeling cycle (see also Sect. 3.1). Referring to the modeling cycle and considering already existing mathematical-didactic classification systems, Maaß (2010) developed a category system for analyzing and evaluating modeling tasks. The classification scheme comprises nine dimensions with a varying number of characteristics, with many subfacets being evaluated as present or not present. Figure 4.2 presents the category system according to Maaß (2010, p. 296). The first six categories have been specifically developed for modeling tasks, while the remaining three criteria do not explicitly refer to modeling tasks. For the present study, some criteria seem particularly

	Name of the classification[a]	Categories of the classification						
Classifications for modelling tasks	I Focus of modeling activity[a]	Whole process (no/yes)	Understanding the situation (no/yes)	Setting up the real model (no/yes)	Mathematizing (no/yes)	Working within mathematics (no/yes)	Interpreting (no/yes)	Validating (no/yes)
	II Data[a]	Superfluous (no/yes)	Missing (no/yes)	Superfluous and missing (no/yes)	Inconsistent (no/yes)	Matching (no/yes)		
	III Nature of relationship to reality[a]	Authentic (no/yes)	Close to reality (no/yes)	Embedded (no/yes)	Intentionally artificial (no/yes)	Fantasy (no/yes)		
	IV Situation[a]	Personal situation (no/yes)	Occupational situation (no/yes)	Public situation	Scientific situation (no/yes)			
	V Type of model used[a]	Descriptive (no/yes)	Normative (no/yes)					
	VI Type of representation[a]	Text (no/yes)	Picture (no/yes)	Text and picture (no/yes)	Material (no/yes)	Situation (no/yes)		
General classifications	VII Openness of a task[a]	Solved example (no/yes)	Ascertaining task (no/yes)	Reversal task (no/yes)	Complex problem (no/yes)	Complex reversal problem (no/yes)	Finding a situation (no/yes)	Open problem (no/yes)
	VIII Cognitive demand[b]	Extra-mathematical modelling	Inner-mathematical working	Basic pre positions	Dealing with texts containing mathematics	Reasoning mathematically	Dealing with mathematical representations	
	IX Mathematical content[b]	Mathematical area	School level					

[a]Choose one category in each classification

[b]Choose in each subcategory

Fig. 4.2 Classification scheme for modeling tasks according to Maaß (2010, p. 296)

relevant. Thus, the first category *Focus on modeling activity* asks whether the entire modeling cycle has to be completed or which substeps are necessary to solve the task (e.g., understanding, translating, mathematical working, interpreting, validating). The dimension *Data* considers whether tasks contain information that is not needed to solve the task or whether additional information needs to be researched in order to correctly solve the task. The category *Nature of the relationship to reality* assesses the authenticity of a task, while the category *Situation* indicates, in reference to the PISA classification, from which environment (e.g., personal, professional) the task originates. As with domain-wide classification systems, there are also categories for the openness of a task (e.g., *open problems* where neither the initial or target state nor solution paths are given), for the form of representation (textual representation, iconic representation), and for the cognitive demand level (e.g., the more basic ideas are needed, the more demanding a task is; see also Sect. 3.2) (Maaß, 2010, pp. 296–301).

The analyses of tasks within the framework of the COACTIV study are particularly well-known. The category system developed for this purpose (see in particular Jordan et al., 2006) includes not only the subject area (e.g., arithmetic, geometry, etc.), the type of knowledge, the basic ideas, the linguistic-logical complexity, and the form of representation (see also the classification scheme by Maier et al., 2010 or Kleinknecht et al., 2011 for the last two categories) but also the type of mathematical activity. Reference is made to the modeling cycle and it is assessed whether or at what level a task requires extra-mathematical modeling (translation between reality and mathematics and retranslation through interpretation and validation) and/or intra-mathematical modeling (translation processes within mathematics) (Jordan et al., 2008, p. 88–89; Jordan et al., 2006, p. 31–40). The categories "solution process" and "result" are also interesting, which deal, among other things, with the direction in which the task is processed (similar to the forward and backward format, see Berding, 2019, p. 145), how large the number of necessary solution steps is, and whether there is a correct solution or whether there can be several different solutions (Jordan et al., 2008, p. 90; Jordan et al., 2006, p. 59–66).

Turning to the business vocational domain, it becomes apparent that different, often non-specific criteria have been used for the analysis and evaluation of tasks in existing task analyses. For example, Thoma and Schumacher (2018) used the classification scheme by Maier et al. (2010), Zhou (2022) assessed, among other things, the content complexity, the openness, and the cognitive demand level of the tasks, Ernst (2012a) the cognitive demand level and the relevance to life, Wuttke et al. (2022) the problem content of the tasks, and Schalek (2007) the action orientation and also the cognitive demand level. At the same time, however, there are also a number of criteria that are more strongly didactic and domain-specific, such as the required modeling performance in Zhou (2022) with references to the models of Seifried et al. (2010) and Winther (2010) (see also Sect. 2.3.2 and 2.3.3), the proximity to professional problem-solving processes in Wuttke et al. (2022), the use of IT or documents in Ernst (2012a) or the business process orientation in Bloemen (2011).

Specifically for the assessment and design of business studies tasks, Bloemen (2011) developed a category system that is oriented towards the current development lines of vocational education defined by Rebmann and Tenfelde (2008). These include the development from qualification orientation to competence orientation, from instruction orientation to construction orientation, and from function orientation to business process orientation. Derived from the development from qualification orientation to competence orientation, Bloemen (2011, p. 85–86) formulates *professional action competence* as the first analysis dimension. Analogous to the competence structure model, the areas of technical competence, methodological competence, design competence, moral-ethical competence, social competence, and abstraction competence are defined as facets of this dimension. The tasks are assessed on a five-level scale, with the level gradations being justified in terms of learning theory. For technical competence, for example, it is distinguished whether no technical competence is required (level 0), whether technical content is to be remembered (level 1), linked (e.g., with prior knowledge, level 2), applied (level 3), or reflected (level 4). From the demand for construction orientation, Bloemen (2011, p. 98–103) derives the dimension *openness*, which consists of the sub-facets *problem openness*, *solution path openness*, and *result openness*. The *problem openness* is recorded on a four-level scale and indicates whether a task contains a problem (characterized by an undesired initial state, a desired target state, and barriers in the transformation) or how completely the problem description is formulated in the task. The *solution path openness* describes on a four-level scale how detailed the methods and/or procedures used to solve the task are already specified or whether these have to be identified by the learners themselves. The *result openness* as the third sub-facet of the dimension of openness deals with the question of how open a task is in terms of results, i.e., whether several different solution alternatives are possible or whether there is exactly one clear (and correct) result for the task.

With the category *everyday relevance*, Bloemen (2011, p. 103–104) captures whether or how strongly the tasks are relatable to the learners' experience. A distinction is made between tasks where there is no everyday relevance (level 0), tasks where an everyday relevance can be indirectly constructed (level 1), tasks that explicitly encourage an everyday relevance (level 2), and tasks that demand the processing of one's own experiences (level 3).

Particularly interesting for the present research project seems to be the dimension *business process orientation*, which is derived from the shift from function orientation to business process orientation that has taken place in business administration. This dimension is also recorded on a four-level scale. On the lowest level, tasks are classified that have no reference to work activities and thus no business process orientation is present (e.g., the task refers to the private sphere of the learners). On level 1, tasks are recorded that focus on an isolated consideration of individual activities, but do not have cross-sectional references. On level 2, tasks are included that consider the effects of operational activities on other business areas or on the entire company (e.g., the effects of poor quality of work on downstream business processes). On the highest level, tasks are recorded that have a comprehensive business process orientation. Such tasks "include upstream and/or downstream business processes, encourage the modeling of internal and external networking, or refer to the importance of action for the overall success of the company" (Bloemen, 2011, p. 106).

In summary, three criteria or characteristics have emerged in particular that appear in (almost) all both cross-domain and subject-specific classification systems:

- Dimensions or criteria that capture the *cognitive level* of tasks in different forms and with various level gradations, i.e., whether the solution to a task requires, for example, the reproduction of knowledge (remembering), the application, or an independent development performance in the sense of, for example, the taxonomy matrix according to Anderson and Krathwohl (2001) (e.g., Blömeke et al., 2006; Luthinger et al., 2014; Maaß, 2010; Maier et al., 2010; Reusser, 2014).
- Characteristics that capture the *everyday relevance*, the *proximity to everyday life*, the *concreteness*, the *relevance to life*, or the *relevance to the world of life* of a task, i.e., whether a task ties in with the learners' world of experience (e.g., Bloemen, 2011; Maaß, 2010; Maier et al., 2010; Reusser, 2014).
- Criteria that focus on the *openness* of a task, i.e., how concretely the problem is described, whether solution paths are outlined, and whether there are clear solutions or multiple results are conceivable (e.g., Bloemen, 2011; Blömeke et al., 2006; Jordan et al., 2006; Kleinknecht et al., 2011; Maaß, 2010; Reusser, 2014).

4.3 Research Findings on Tasks in the Accounting Domain and Related Domains

While there are already many empirical findings on the characteristics, features, and quality of tasks for the general education sector (for mathematics, for example, Blömeke et al., 2006; Drüke-Noe & Merk, 2013; Jordan et al., 2008; J. Neubrand, 2002), there are significantly fewer findings for the vocational, business-related sector, especially for the subject of accounting. Kleinknecht and Schmid-Kühn (2020, p. 412) also note that research on classroom tasks has so far focused on the mathematical and scientific sector. Findings from the business-related sector, especially from the domain of accounting, will be presented in the following. Table 4.1 shows a summary of the relevant studies, sorted in descending order by year of publication, focusing on findings particularly relevant to the present study.

Four aspects should be pointed out in advance. First, the studies were not collected based on a systematic literature review and are limited to findings from the German-speaking area (Germany and Austria). Findings from the Anglo-American area (e.g., USA) are not explicitly addressed, as German-speaking research on accounting didactics has so far made little reference to Anglo-American research, and the comparability and transferability of the findings are questionable. However, a search and review of relevant studies show that there are also few studies overall there, and when findings are available, the tasks generally do not meet the requirements well (e.g., Arek-Bawa & Dhunpath, 2017; Blix et al., 2021; Davidson, 2005; Davidson & Baldwin, 2005). The analyses from the Anglo-American area focus on the taxonomic level of the tasks. Second, the studies presented here do not exclusively focus on the domain of accounting, but very often on general business-related content (e.g., tasks from textbooks for the subject of business studies). In connection with this, third, the majority of the analyzed tasks come from Germany. For Austria, there is so far only one published study by Thoma and Schumacher (2018) that deals with task quality in the subject of business accounting. Fourth, not only studies that analyze tasks (from textbooks) were included, but also studies that evaluate examination tasks (e.g., from final exams for commercial training professions). The results of the various studies will be reported below.

Using AI for automated coding of textbook tasks, Stütz et al. (2022) analyzed 3361 tasks from a total of 14 different German textbooks for various training professions. Categories were used that are essentially based on the category system developed in this dissertation. The basis for the categories is the "Linzer

Table 4.1 Descriptive research findings on the quality of tasks in the accounting domain and related areas

Authors	Object of study	Country	N	Measured Construct(s)	Used Tools	Central findings
Stütz, Berding, Reincke and Scheper (2022)	Tasks from 14 textbooks for different commercial training professions	DE	3361	Process orientation, problem orientation, modeling cycle	Own development or testing of selected categories of the category system presented in this dissertation	– 57% of the tasks do not have a process orientation, 27% have a limited process orientation – In about 80% of the tasks, no realistic goods or money flows or social processes are represented – 3% of the tasks use documents – In 68% of the tasks, there is no problem, about 45% of the tasks require the research of additional information – The tasks mainly focus on operating within the accounting system (62%), while translating (15%), interpreting (27%) and validating (0%) occur much less frequently

(continued)

Table 4.1 (continued)

Authors	Object of study	Country	N	Measured Construct(s)	Used Tools	Central findings
Zhou (2022)	Year-end closing tasks from four text-books for advanced vocational schools	CHN	215	Content complexity, cognitive demand level, functional modeling and openness of solutions summarized as *cognitive requirements*	Own development among others based on the taxonomy matrix of Anderson & Krathwohl and the model of the steps of task processing in Accounting by Seifried/Türling/Wuttke (2010)	– 32.6% of the tasks require reproduction services, 67% of the tasks require application services – 0.5% of the tasks require the evaluation/reflection of the worked out solution – In 46.5% of the tasks, the task is clearly formulated, in 32.6% no hints are given – The tasks focus on the sub-steps "Encode economic reality" and "Mathematize/Formalize" – No task requires the complete run through all four sub-steps

(continued)

Table 4.1 (continued)

Authors	Object of study	Country	N	Measured Construct(s)	Used Tools	Central findings
Wuttke, Seeber, Geiser and Turhan (2022)	Tasks from commercial final and intermediate examinations for the training professions industrial clerk and office management clerk	DE	1454	Problem content of the tasks, proximity to professional problem-solving processes (authenticity, professional relevance)	Own development	– The tasks can overall be described as not very problematic – In 85% of the tasks, the current state is clearly defined and not to be determined by the learners themselves – In almost all tasks, it is clearly defined what the target state should look like – In 0.6% of the tasks, extensive information is to be researched and evaluated – 1.5% of the tasks are formulated open to solutions

(continued)

Table 4.1 (continued)

Authors	Object of study	Country	N	Measured Construct(s)	Used Tools	Central findings
Thoma and Schumacher (2018)	Tasks on difficult subject areas from four accounting textbooks for commercial colleges	AT	302	Cognitive activation potential	Shortened and adapted general didactic category system according to Maier et al. (2010)	– The tasks almost exclusively require reproduction or near transfer services – More than 85% of the tasks have no or only a constructed reference to the life world – Over 90% of the tasks have a low degree of openness (problem known and only one correct solution possible) – None of the examined tasks require the independent procurement of information – The tasks do not contain real problem situations and are characterized by small-step solution processes

(continued)

Table 4.1 (continued)

Authors	Object of study	Country	N	Measured Construct(s)	Used Tools	Central findings
Kombacher (2016)	Tasks related to ERP from textbooks for business vocational education at commercial colleges	AT	1193	Professional competence, openness, relevance to everyday life, business process orientation	Tool developed by Bloemen (2011)	– In about 60% of the tasks, the problem is described and does not need to be recognized by the learners themselves – In about 80% of the tasks, there is no reference to business processes or only individual activities are considered in isolation – Approximately 16% of the tasks have no or a constructed everyday relevance
Ernst (2012)	Tasks on various topics from six accounting textbooks	DE/USA	4795	Cognitive demand level, relevance to life, other aspects (e.g. use of IT, ethical aspects)	Abbreviated and adapted general didactic category system according to Maier et al. (2010), own development of further criteria (e.g. use of IT, ethical aspects)	– Around 90% of the tasks are reproduction or close transfer tasks – 13% of the tasks have a high relevance to life – 2.7% of the tasks use documents

(continued)

Table 4.1 (continued)

Authors	Object of study	Country	N	Measured Construct(s)	Used Tools	Central findings
Stock et al. (2011)	School leaving examinations from the 2008/09 school year, used at commercial colleges	AT	174	Content-related (e.g. topicality, practical relevance, networking), formal (e.g. compliance with standards) and IT dimension (e.g. software use)	Own development	– In about 8% of the final exams, the tasks are set in a process-oriented manner (independent problem recognition, independent solution paths) – In about 20% of the exams, there is a connection between accounting and business administration – About 88% of the tasks use documents

(continued)

Table 4.1 (continued)

Authors	Object of study	Country	N	Measured Construct(s)	Used Tools	Central findings
Bloemen (2011)	Tasks from the best-selling textbook for the learning field “Business Processes” for the training profession Industrial Clerk	DE	1328	Professional competence, openness, relevance to everyday life, business process orientation	Own development	– About 70% of the tasks require the reproduction of technical content (factual knowledge or booking operations) – In more than half of the tasks, no problem reference is recognizable – About 75% of the tasks have either no reference to business processes or only consider individual activities within a business process – 5.7% of the tasks have a complete business process orientation

(continued)

Table 4.1 (continued)

Authors	Object of study	Country	N	Measured Construct(s)	Used Tools	Central findings
Schalek (2007)	Tasks from a business teaching book for the training profession Industrial Clerk and a textbook for the training program “Trade, Service and Administration”	DE/ SWE	1095	Cognitive demand level	Learning objective taxonomy according to Bloom	– 90% of the tasks from the German textbook can be assigned to the lower three taxonomy levels of knowledge, understanding and application – 9% of the tasks can be classified in the category analysis, 1% of the tasks in the category evaluation

Note: AT = Austria; CHN = China; DE = Germany; SWE = Sweden

Ebenenmodell" (Neuweg, 2020) and the modeling cycle adopted from mathematics didactics (e.g., Berding, 2019; Berding, Beckmann & Kürten, 2019; Blum, 2011). The extent of process orientation, the detail of the description of operational reality, the use of documents, and the processing of different sub-steps of the modeling cycle in task processing were examined. The results of the descriptive evaluations show that the textbook tasks are overall little or limited in process orientation and only 16% of the tasks have a comprehensive process orientation. The operational reality (represented by the description of goods and service flows, cash flows, and social processes) is usually described in little detail, and documents are used in only 3% of the tasks. Regarding the sub-steps of the modeling cycle, the evaluations show that accounting operations (forming booking sentences) are in focus (required in 62% of the tasks), while the other sub-steps are addressed much less frequently. For example, 27% of the tasks require an interpretation and two tasks require a validation. In about 45% of the tasks, information is to be researched within or outside the task. However, a distinction between relevant and irrelevant information is never required. In addition, about 68% of the tasks do not contain a problem. A latent class analysis carried out could not identify different types of tasks, which is plausible due to the high concentration of codings and the correspondingly low variability in the data.

Wuttke et al. (2022) examined 1454 tasks from written final exams for two training professions in Germany (industrial clerk and office management clerk) with regard to their problem content and their proximity to real professional problem-solving processes. The basis for the analysis were the various steps in the context of problem-solving processes to determine the problem content of a task. These include the analysis and evaluation of the initial situation, the formulation of a desired target state, the research and processing of information, the development of a solution, and the reflection or action control. The proximity to real professional problem-solving processes was captured via the subcategories professional reference (Is the formulated requirement also relevant in professional reality?) and authenticity (Can the formulated requirement occur in a similar form in professional practice?). Evaluation was based on a two-stage (dichotomous) or three-stage evaluation scale. The results of the descriptive evaluations show that the problem content of the tasks can overall be assessed as low. For example, in about 85% of the tasks, the current state is already clearly defined, and in almost all tasks, it is also indicated which target state is to be achieved. In addition, extensive information from external sources is to be researched and evaluated in about 0.6% of the tasks. Irrelevant information for task processing is found in about 21% of the tasks. 1.5% of the tasks are designed to be open to solutions, thus allowing more than one correct solution. Looking at the criterion of proximity to real professional problem-solving processes, although all tasks have a professional reference, they are hardly formulated authentically, as only 18% of the tasks were classified as authentic (Wuttke et al., 2022, pp. 41–43).

In a study by Zhou (2022), 215 tasks from four different Chinese accounting textbooks were analyzed. The evaluation criteria used were content complexity (*content complexity*), taxonomic level (*cognitive taxonomy*), openness (*openness*), and required modeling performance (*functional modeling*). Content complexity was evaluated based on how many different concepts or knowledge units are needed to solve the task. To measure the taxonomic level, an ordinal scale with three levels was used, distinguishing between reproduction performances (*identify, remember, recall*), application performances (*apply, analyze, calculate, elaborate*), and evaluation or reflection performances (*evaluate, reflective assess*). In the category of modeling, a subcategory was initially used that shows whether the task offers supporting information that facilitates the solution of the task (*clear hints, partly hints, no hints*). In addition, the model by Seifried et al. (2010) or Wuttke and Seifried (2012) was used in this category, which distinguishes different substeps in the processing of tasks from the accounting domain (capturing economic reality, encoding, mathematizing, and interpreting and reflecting). In the category of openness, it was differentiated, based on already existing category systems, how clearly the current state is described in a task and how open a task is to solutions. The results of the descriptive evaluations show that the majority of tasks (67%) are application-oriented, while 32.6% of tasks aim at the reproduction of knowledge. Only 0.5% of the tasks require reflection or evaluation of a solution. As for the provision of assistance in solving the task, 46.5% of the tasks were classified in the category *clear hints*. It is therefore clear to the learners in what form the tasks are to be solved. In 32.6% of the tasks, no assistance is given in solving the task. Approximately 20% of the tasks can be classified as defined and divergent, thus allowing different solutions. Looking at the different substeps in the processing of accounting tasks, it becomes apparent that the majority of tasks (71.6%) focus on the substeps "encoding economic reality" and "formalizing and mathematizing". In no task are all four substeps to be completed, in 28.4% of the tasks the substep "capturing economic reality" is additionally required for task solution. In an analysis to identify task types (cluster analysis), the three classes *technical tasks* (n = 97), *modeling tasks* (n = 56), and *problem-related tasks* (n = 62) were identified, which differ in cognitive demand level (expressed by the sum of the four categories content complexity, taxonomic level, openness, and modeling performance). While the *technical tasks* have the lowest cognitive demand level (with sum values from 5 to 10), the *problem-related tasks* have the highest demand level.

In a preliminary study for a cross-national project conducted by Thoma and Schumacher (2018), tasks from Austrian accounting textbooks for commercial colleges were analyzed with regard to their cognitive activation potential. Thematically, the focus was on the evaluation of tasks from potentially difficult learning areas (the areas of sales tax, profit accounts, inventory accounts). To evaluate the tasks, the cross-disciplinary category system developed by Maier et al. (2010) was used, which was shortened and slightly adapted.[1] The analyses by Thoma and Schumacher (2018) show that the tasks mainly require reproduction and near transfer performances. To cope with the tasks, it is usually sufficient to transfer the knowledge from previously processed teaching examples to the exercise examples, to remember factual knowledge, or to form simple booking sentences. In addition, most tasks have a low degree of openness. Both the specific task and the steps of processing are known and predetermined. Overall, learners are given little freedom in task processing and solution finding. It is also striking that the majority of tasks are formulated without context. Thus, there is a complete lack of reference to operational reality. The focus of the tasks is therefore more on a step-by-step practice of knowledge and algorithms. "Metacognitive performances, creative problem solving, vaguely formulated, more complex tasks, as well as real-life references are completely missing" (Thoma & Schumacher, 2018, p. 15).

Ernst (2012a) presented a comprehensive study on the quality of German and US-American textbooks for accounting education at the secondary level II. As part of his analysis, he evaluated, using the criteria of cognitive demand and relevance to life[2], some of the tasks contained in the textbooks. In addition, he used criteria such as the use of IT, the answer format, or the openness of the solution path for evaluation. The tasks came from the subject areas of accounting, annual financial statements, and cost and performance accounting and were determined by random selection. The results of Ernst (2012a, pp. 105–107) show a similar picture to the evaluations of Thoma and Schumacher (2018). Overall, the majority of tasks can be classified as reproduction or near transfer tasks. Thus, the books mainly contain structurally identical or similar tasks that focus on practicing booking and calculation skills. Furthermore, only 10% of the tasks have a reference to real operational processes or the learners' life world, and in only 2.7% of the tasks are documents used.

[1] The final category system includes the six dimensions: type of knowledge, cognitive process, openness, relevance to life, linguistic-logical complexity, and material breadth.

[2] The category system according to Maier et al. (2010) also served as the basis for the analysis.

An analysis of commercial final examinations was carried out by Stock et al. (2011) on behalf of the Federal Ministry of Education, Art and Culture. They analyzed all 174 final examinations used in the 2008/2009 school year at Austrian commercial colleges. For this purpose, they created a catalog of criteria, consisting of content, formal, and IT-related requirement criteria. Particularly relevant for the present work is the content dimension. Overall, the tasks are well evaluated[3], but some weaknesses are evident. The results show that learners are usually not encouraged to independently obtain information from several sources and process it. In addition, the tasks hardly offer the opportunity to independently identify problems and develop solutions on their own (Stock et al., 2011, p. 18).

The other known studies do not explicitly deal with accounting, but focus on tasks from the field of business studies (Bloemen, 2011; Schalek, 2007) or the business vocational area in general (Kombacher, 2016). However, these come to very similar results. Thus, the study by Bloemen (2011) also shows that the vast majority of tasks focus on the reproduction of factual knowledge or simple booking operations, the tasks are overall little problematic, and the majority of tasks only consider isolated clerical activities, while the overall entrepreneurial perspective in the sense of a comprehensive business process orientation is left out. Learners are also given little freedom, as both the solution path is predetermined and the instruments, methods, and procedures needed to process the tasks are given.

Looking at the previous results on tasks in the business vocational domain, a quite coherent picture emerges, even though different evaluation criteria were used in part. However, the findings overall suggest that the tasks are only limited in their ability to enable cognitively demanding learning processes. Many of the tasks are cognitively not very stimulating, aim at reproduction or routine application of knowledge, and are classified at a low level in terms of learning objective taxonomy. Overall, there are few tasks that address higher cognitive processes or go beyond operating in the sense of the modeling cycle and also require interpretation or validation services. In addition, the tasks usually have no or only a constructed reference to the learners' life world, are not very process-oriented, not very authentic, overall not very problematically formulated and only rarely simulate authentic professional action situations (Bloemen, 2011; Ernst, 2012a; Kombacher, 2016; Schalek, 2007; Stütz et al., 2022; Thoma & Schumacher, 2018; Wuttke et al., 2022; Zhou, 2022).

[3] For example, documents were used in approximately 90% of the final examinations.

5 Presentation of the Category System for the Analysis and Evaluation of Tasks in the Accounting Domain

5.1 Task Requirements in the Accounting Domain Based on Previous Explorations

Based on the previous theoretical explorations, especially in light of the changes in the working world due to increasing digitalization (Sect. 2.2), existing competence models (Sect. 2.3), different didactic approaches, especially the economic-instrumental accounting (Sect. 2.4.2), learning difficulties and their causes in accounting (Sect. 2.5) as well as in light of the "Linzer Ebenenmodell" and mathematical modeling (Chap. 3), some requirements on tasks for the accounting domain can be formulated, which will be further specified and operationalized in the form of a comprehensive category system in a next step. At this point, a brief conclusion will be drawn, presenting the central requirements for accounting tasks:

- **Representation of the reality and process orientation:** Tasks in accounting should represent the *reality* in a realistic, detailed, and process-related manner. This is intended to facilitate the connection between the real world and its representation in the accounting systems for learners, thereby making it clear that real processes underlie the accounting representation, which in turn are embedded in a chain of events. Learners should be aware during the processing of different business cases that other processes have preceded these business cases and further business cases will follow. This demand primarily arises from the "Linzer Ebenenmodell" (Neuweg, 2020) and the economic-instrumental accounting (Preiß & Tramm, 1996; Tramm, 2005; Tramm & Preiß, 1996). At the same time, this demand also arises from the findings on learning

S. Reindl-Stütz, *Characteristics of Tasks in the Domain of Accounting*,
https://doi.org/10.1007/978-3-658-48958-8_5

difficulties in accounting, as it can be assumed that the lack of representation of the reality and the abstractness of the content are major causes of learning difficulties (Tramm et al., 1996; Türling, 2014). In addition, in the sense of the modeling cycle, the real world is the starting point for modeling services in accounting (Berding, Beckmann & Kürten, 2019; Seifried et al., 2010). Therefore, it seems significant to represent this appropriately in the task assignments. An orientation towards operational processes can also be argued from a subject-specific perspective, as process management as a "cross-sectional organizational concept" is attributed significant importance, for example, to optimize company processes and increase customer benefit (Vahs, 2019, pp. 207–208).

- **Use of documents:** In this context, the use of *documents* in accounting task assignments is of essential importance. Documents form the bridge between operational reality and accounting on the one hand, and on the other hand, they represent the first step of abstraction in the processing and solving of accounting tasks (e.g. Bensch, 2009; Berding, Beckmann & Kürten, 2019; Neuweg, 2020; Tramm, 2005).
- **Orientation towards legal norms:** Furthermore, it seems essential to justify representation processes in financial accounting through *corporate and tax law norms and guidelines*, as external accounting is significantly influenced by legal requirements (e.g. Neuweg, 2020; Preiß, 2015; Schneider, 2010).
- **From (simple) booking activities to more complex skills:** In light of the dramatic changes in the working world in the accounting profession due to increasing digitalization, tasks should overall place *little focus on the formation of booking entries*, as these are already being automated now and will be even more so in the future. In addition to adapting more closely to operational practice in order to ensure employability, tasks should also aim more at promoting the abilities for *plausibility checking* and *control* of *data*, for the *interpretation* of operational processes, for solving complex problems, and for using data for *decision-making* (e.g. Hmyzo & Muzzu, 2020; Jordanski, 2020; Klein & Küst, 2020; Neuweg, 2020; Preiß, 2015; Riebenbauer et al., 2022).
- **Ability to model:** Closely linked to this is the demand that tasks in the sense of the modeling cycle should not merely focus on the translation into accounting and working within the system (e.g. setting up bookings, balance sheets, etc.), but should consider all *substeps* of *understanding*, *formalizing*, *operating* within accounting as well as *interpreting* and *validating*. Interpretation services are primarily to be performed in light of the company's formal objectives. To solve accounting-specific problems, a comprehensive modeling ability is required, which should therefore be promoted by appropriate task

assignments (e.g. Berding, Beckmann & Kürten, 2019; Neuweg, 2020; Preiß, 2005a, 2015).

- **Connections and references to internal accounting and business administration:** Given the importance of *internal accounting* (especially cost and performance accounting and liquidity management), tasks should increasingly illuminate the subareas of internal accounting or establish connections between these areas. The same applies to a connection with business administration content. This demand is reinforced when considering the objectives to be pursued with accounting instruction, for example, the goal of building economic competence or a comprehensive economic understanding of economic interrelationships (e.g. Neuweg, 2020; Preiß, 2015).

Of course, one can (rightly) note that a number of other characteristics, especially those discussed in Sect. 4.2, appear relevant for tasks in accounting and should therefore be used as criteria for analyzing and evaluating the tasks (e.g. linguistic complexity, relevance to everyday life, type of knowledge and cognitive processes, independence, novelty value, comprehensibility, internal differentiation possibilities). Thus, the list of characteristics to be used for evaluation could probably be significantly extended (and differentiated). While it would be desirable on the one hand to use as many (and many different) criteria for evaluation as possible in order to be able to assess the quality and characteristics of the tasks very broadly, on the other hand, this would also obscure the view of the essentials. Moreover, the present work is intended to be a more *didactic* analysis and evaluation of the tasks. Therefore, it was deliberately decided not to include criteria such as cognitive level, type of knowledge, or everyday relevance of the tasks in the classification scheme.

A number of requirements can be defined for the development and compilation of the category system, which need to be taken into account:

- The categories should provide insights for answering the research questions and at the same time the category system must be complete, i.e., cover all aspects identified as relevant. This applies to the category system as a whole, but also to the individual categories and their characteristics (Atteslander, 2010, p. 204; Kuckartz & Rädiker, 2022, p. 63; Scheufele & Engelmann, 2009, p. 174). However, this does not mean that the category system must cover *all* potentially relevant criteria (for the present study, for example, all potentially important quality characteristics for accounting tasks), but always means *selective* completeness, i.e., complete with regard to the research interest (Scheufele & Engelmann, 2009, p. 174).

- The categories should be sharply defined. On the one hand, the categories must be clearly distinguishable from each other, on the other hand, there must be a clear demarcation between the different characteristics within a category. Especially with evaluative categories, care must be taken with the different characteristics to ensure that they do not overlap (Kuckartz & Rädiker, 2022, p. 64; Scheufele & Engelmann, 2009, p. 174).

The categories should be as uniform, clear, understandable and comprehensible as possible. Equivalent (sub)categories should also be similar in terms of their level of abstraction. The formulated subcategories should be dimensions, characteristics or subcategories of the main categories (Kuckartz & Rädiker, 2022, p. 64–65).

The final category system for evaluating the tasks has emerged in a process that has now lasted several years, with multiple revisions, expansions, extensive feedback and trials. The development of a demanding and at the same time practical category system posed a major challenge. Therefore, many opportunities were taken to discuss the category system and to obtain feedback from knowledgeable individuals in the field of accounting didactics. For example, the category system was discussed at the conference of the Section for Vocational and Business Education of the DGfE in Hamburg (2020), Bamberg (2021) and Freiburg (2022), at the Business Education Congress in Graz (2021), at the ÖFEB conference in Linz (2020) and at the dissertation colloquia at the JKU. The category system was discussed in more detail with the dissertation supervisors and, among others, with Assoc. Prof. Mag. Dr. Elisabeth Riebenbauer, Univ.-Prof. Mag. Dr. Christoph Helm and Junior Professor Dr. Josef Guggemos.[1]

The individual categories are explained below and the level of grading is explained. A short version of the category system can also be found in this section (Table 5.1). The long version with anchor examples and exact coding rules can be viewed in the appendix in the electronic supplementary material. Figure 5.1 visualizes the category system.

---

[1]At this point, I would like to thank all participants for their support and constructive and appreciative feedback.

Table 5.1 Summary presentation of the category system

Designation	Guiding questions/Description	Characteristics
Process orientation **Subcategories:** *Process orientation* *Process orientation of task processing*	***Process orientation:*** Is the relevant business case part of an event chain? Is it clear that another real business case preceded the business case and/or another real business case follows? ***Process orientation of task processing:*** Are several substeps of a real process to be processed within *one* task? (e.g. obtaining an offer, purchasing, depreciation, sale)	***Process orientation:*** 0 = no reference to previous or subsequent business cases 1 = reference to a previous *or* a subsequent business case 2 = reference to several previous, several subsequent *or* previous *and* subsequent business cases ***Process orientation of task processing:*** 0 = no process orientation of task processing 1 = limited process orientation of task processing 2 = comprehensive process orientation of task processing
Description of reality *Description of the flows of goods and services, cash flows and social processes*	How detailed/realistic are the flows of goods and services, cash flows and social processes represented? Subcategories for: flows of goods and services, cash flows and social processes	0 = goods or service flows or cash flows or social processes do not occur 1 = goods or service flows or cash flows or social processes are represented abstractly 2 = goods or service flows or cash flows or social processes are described in detail
Document use *Use of documents and other written materials*	Is a document used in the analysis unit? Subcategories for: receipts, balance lists, balance sheets, account presentations, profit and loss statements, asset directories, pictures/photographs, account plans, tables and other documents (e.g. mails, memos, etc.)	0 = respective document is not used 1 = respective document is used

(continued)

Table 5.1 (continued)

Designation	Guiding questions/Description	Characteristics
Modeling cycle: Orientation *Recognize Activity* *obtain information* *evaluate information*	***Recognize activity:*** Does the analysis unit prompt the learners to recognize the activity to be performed themselves or is the activity already clearly formulated? Is the solution unambiguous or are there different solution possibilities? ***Obtain information:*** Does the analysis unit prompt to independently research information or are all relevant information already contained in the task in textual form? ***Evaluate information:*** Does the analysis unit prompt to distinguish relevant from irrelevant information?	***Recognize activity:*** 0 = activity clearly indicated, solution (goal) unambiguous 1= activity narrowed down, but not precisely defined; solution (goal) unambiguous 2 = activity and/or solution open ***Obtain information:*** 0 = all information contained in the running text 1 = information is to be researched within the task 2 = information is to be researched from external or from several sources within the task ***Evaluate information:*** 0 = no distinction between relevant and irrelevant information required 1 = distinction between relevant and irrelevant information due to *unconscious* information surplus 2 = distinction between relevant and irrelevant information due to *conscious* information surplus
Modeling Cycle: Translate *Translate real events into the world of accounting*	Does the analysis unit require learners to translate a real-world business case into the world of accounting? Subcategories for: Translation through other work (e.g., application of technical terms) and translation through the creation of booking entries	0 = no translation of the real world into the world of accounting necessary 1 = translation of the real world into the world of accounting required

(continued)

Table 5.1 (continued)

Designation	Guiding questions/Description	Characteristics
Modeling Cycle: Internal Accounting Operations (Operating) *Perform internal accounting operations*	Does the analysis unit require learners to operate within the accounting system? Subcategories for: internal booking, balance sheet preparation, income statement preparation, MWR preparation, other internal accounting operations (e.g., managing fixed assets, preparing VAT returns)	0 = no operations within the accounting system required 1 = operations within the accounting system required
Modeling Cycle: Mathematical Operations	Does the analysis unit require learners to perform mathematical operations?	0 = no mathematical operations required 1 = mathematical operations required
Modeling Cycle: Interpret *Interpret solutions with regard to their impact on formal objectives*	Does the analysis unit ask to interpret a result in terms of its impact on a certain size (e.g., a formal objective)? Subcategories for: profitability/unit or period success; liquidity, balance sheet (positions), tax burden, external representation and other interpretations	0 = no interpretation required 1 = interpretation required
Modeling Cycle: Validate *Check solutions for correctness/plausibility*	Does the analysis unit require to check the plausibility of one's own solution or an existing solution (e.g., by recalculating, applying alternative solution paths for control, etc.) or to justify the solution/approach?	0 = no review or justification of the solution necessary 1 = review or justification of one's own solution or an existing solution necessary
Legal Norm Orientation *Explicitly apply legal norms or justify something about a norm*	Does the analysis unit require learners to justify an activity or a solution with regard to legal norms or standards?	0 = no justification of bookings/activities/decisions with reference to a legal norm 1 = justification of bookings/activities/decisions with reference to a legal norm or explicit work with a legal norm/application of a legal norm

(continued)

Table 5.1 (continued)

Designation	Guiding questions/Description	Characteristics
Decide *Make business decisions*	Does the analysis unit require to independently make business decisions that have effects on processes in the real world?	0 = no decisions to be made 1 = decisions to be made
Connections *Establish connections to internal accounting or to business administration*	Does the analysis unit require the connection to cost accounting, financial accounting or to business administration topics or is a connection established in the analysis unit? Subcategories for: cost accounting, financial statements and business administration	0 = no connection to be established 1 = connection to be established

5.2 Categories for Representing Business Reality and Process Orientation

The demand for tasks that are as vivid, practice-oriented, realistic, concrete and adapted to the experiences and living environment of the learners can be found not only in accounting didactics, but represents an almost universally valid claim to tasks (see e.g. Bloemen, 2011; Blömeke et al., 2006; Luthinger et al., 2014; Maier et al., 2010; Reusser, 2014).

In accounting didactics, it is particularly often discussed (and criticized) that tasks need to be more closely linked to real business processes and procedures, as "the real basis from which the business cases to be booked arise in practice is not visible in the classroom" (Neuweg, 2020, p. 136). The missing link between the real world and the world of accounting is often seen as a cause of learning difficulties, as learners find it difficult to "gain a vivid understanding of the underlying business processes from the figures of accounting" (Tramm et al., 1996, p. 205). Therefore, a realistic and detailed representation of business processes seems to be an essential criterion for task assignments in accounting. For example, Pargmann et al. (2022, p. 20) state that learning environments in accounting must incorporate real processes, as only in this way is "a conscious translation from real processes to accounting and back" possible. In business instrumental accounting (see Sect. 2.4.2), the continuous reference to business processes

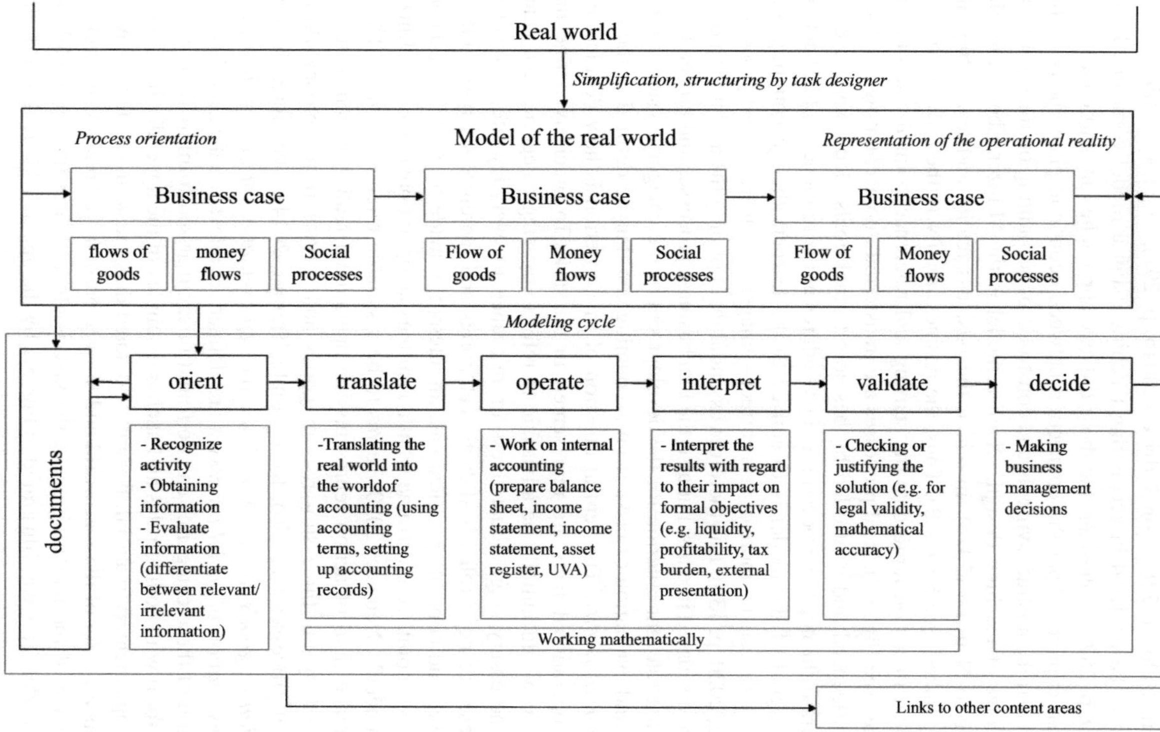

Fig. 5.1 Visualization of the category system for the analysis and evaluation of tasks from accounting

(ideally using a continuous model company) is also an important criterion (Preiß & Tramm, 1996, p. 246). For Seifried (2004b, p. 291), real and nominal goods flows are to be depicted in accounting teaching using a model company. Berding (2019, p. 287) emphasizes that those didactic approaches are particularly beneficial that explicitly "put the connection between economic phenomena on the one hand and the abstract symbols and constructs of accounting on the other hand at the center of teaching design." Such a model is the "Linzer Ebenenmodell" according to Neuweg (2020), in which the business reality and accounting are explicitly linked (see Sect. 3.3). Thus, the business reality in the form of the reference field of action represents the starting and reference point for accounting operations (see Fig. 3.7). Real processes are transferred into accounting via documents. Influenced and controlled by business formal goals, decisions are made that in turn influence the processes and procedures in the reference field of action. The main goal of the model is to convey to the learners that "accounting processes [...] represent—more or less correct—images of real stocks and processes" (Neuweg, 2020, p. 136). It is therefore essential that not only the accounting operations are discussed in class, but also the real business processes and procedures.

The first relevant criterion for the development of the category system for the analysis and evaluation of tasks from accounting can thus be defined as the *representation of reality*. The central question of this criterion is how detailed and realistic operational facts are represented in the task. To precisely define this category, it would initially be advisable to refer to existing categories and adapt them if necessary (e.g., situatedness or relevance to everyday life). However, since these are not explicitly didactic categories and therefore set partly different focuses and content specifications, an attempt is made to establish a didactic reference point. To determine what constitutes an operational fact, the "Linzer Ebenenmodell" (Neuweg, 2020) seems to be a suitable reference source. There, the reference field of action represents the operational reality, which in turn is represented by the three sub-areas of goods and service flows, money flows, and social processes (see also, for example, Tramm, 2014). Therefore, the *representation of goods and service flows*, the *representation of money flows*, and the *representation of social processes* are defined as relevant subcategories. The description of these categories can be found in summarized form in Table 5.1, in detailed form with coding rules and anchor examples in the appendix in the electronic supplementary material. It should be noted that a task in a textbook always represents a model of the real world and never represents the real world itself. In the language of the modeling cycle, the task is already the situation model, not the real model. This was illustrated in Fig. 5.1 by the upper field "real world" and the transition to the model of the real world through simplification and structuring processes by the task constructor.

Evaluative categories usually use dichotomous (e.g., not present—present) or ordinal scale levels (e.g., not pronounced—slightly pronounced—strongly pronounced) (Kuckartz & Rädiker, 2022, p. 56). For coding, an ordinal scale with three levels is chosen. This is intended to ensure sufficient variability and accuracy in the recording, while also making the assignment of tasks to a level and the differentiation between the levels manageable. At level 0, tasks are coded in which (depending on the subcategory) goods and service flows, money flows, or social processes do not occur at all. At the next higher level, tasks are classified that address goods and service flows, money flows, or social processes, but describe these in little detail and rather abstractly. So, for example, if a task refers to the purchase of a production machine but does not elaborate on it, coding at level 1 is performed. At the highest level (level 2), tasks are found that provide descriptions in detailed form and thus give learners a detailed insight into operational reality. A detailed description is given when, for example, flows are described in detail in textual form (e.g., What is the name of the production machine, why was it chosen, and for what purposes is it used?) or when, for example, illustrations are used.

In addition to a detailed representation of operational reality, it can be deduced from the "Linzer Ebenenmodell" that tasks in accounting should have a process orientation or a process orientation. In teaching, it often remains unclear that business transactions (which are then processed and processed in accounting lessons in the form of bookings) do not take place isolated, but are embedded in a series of business transactions and business processes (see Fig. 3.6 in Sect. 3.3.1). Neuweg (2020, p. 137) notes that the highly stylized representation strips business transactions of their "temporality, i.e., their reference to the past and future". Therefore, it is important for learners to see and understand that individual business transactions occur in a sequence of business transactions and business processes and are thus embedded in a process chain.

In a similar direction, but to be distinguished from the process orientation presented here, is the demand for a business process orientation, as formulated by Bloemen (2011), Dolzsanksi (2013b) or Tramm (2009), for example. There, too, the focus is on orientation towards operational business processes, but more as a contrast to a view oriented towards functions and departments. Bloemen (2011, p. 105) formulates the business process orientation as an evaluation criterion in the category system and means by this "the departure from an isolated, little networked understanding of economics and instead an orientation towards customer satisfaction, thinking in value chains and towards open, broader cross-departmental work activities". He defines as level stages tasks without a business process orientation, tasks with an isolated view of activities, tasks with cross-interface business processes, and tasks with a complete business process orientation. Tramm (2009, p. 82) formulates the process idea as a "thinking in process chains" instead of in functions and departments. However, the process orientation meant in this work refers to whether the business case dealt with in the task can be understood as part of an extensive chain of events, or whether it is presented in isolation and without reference to previous or subsequent business cases. Therefore, the relevant category *process orientation* is introduced, which focuses on the question of whether learners clearly understand that a business case was preceded by another real business case and/or further business cases will follow. So, for example, if the task deals with the depreciation of a machine, it would be in the sense of a process orientation to refer to the previous purchase of the machine. In Fig. 5.1, the process orientation is represented by the arrow connection between the individual business cases. However, this also makes it clear that the category process orientation means and measures something different than existing categories for business process orientation.

The category process orientation is also captured via an ordinal scale with three expressions. Tasks at level 0 are those that *have no reference to previous or subsequent business cases* (Fig. 5.2, line with round dots). It is therefore not clear that business transactions are expressions of decisions, but the focus is only on the present business case. Tasks of this level stage therefore do not offer learners the opportunity to gain insight into operational processes and to understand which activities/processes have led to the business case presented in the task or how the business case is to be further treated. Level 1 includes tasks that have a *limited process orientation* (Fig. 5.2, line with long dash). So a reference is made to *one* previous or to *one* subsequent business case (e.g., payment refers to the previous purchase; purchase refers to the solicitation of offers). They thus provide at least partial insight into which processes have taken place in reality or will take place in the future. At the highest level, tasks are classified that have a

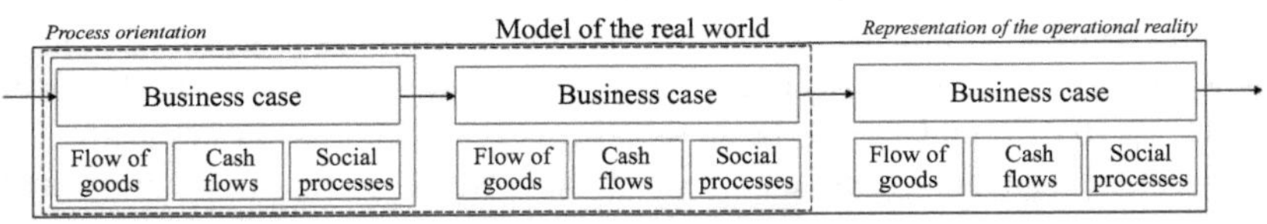

Fig. 5.2 Visualization of the category process orientation

comprehensive process orientation (Fig. 5.2, continuous line). This refers to tasks that represent a result chain, i.e., refer to several previous and/or subsequent business cases (e.g., solicitation of offers, purchase, payment, etc.). It is important to emphasize that the process orientation always refers to processes in the real world and not (merely) to processes within accounting itself. For example, the purchase of a machine with reference to a later payment (or with reference to the previous solicitation of offers) would represent a process orientation, but not the booking of the machine purchase and, for example, the closing of the relevant accounts or the indication of the impact on business success. In Table 5.1, there is an overview of the category, in the appendix in the electronic supplementary material a detailed description with anchor examples and coding rules.

The category *Process orientation of task processing* additionally collects whether multiple sub-steps need to be processed by the learners within a task (if there is a process orientation). So if a task addresses both the purchase and payment of a production machine, this category asks whether both sub-steps also need to be processed by the learner (i.e., for example, both purchase and payment need to be booked) or whether only a reference to the learners is made in the task, but this does not lead to an action on the part of the learners. The summary of this category can also be found in Table 5.1. Anchor examples and coding rules can be seen in the codebook in the appendix in the electronic supplementary material.

5.3 Category for the Use of Documents

Closely linked to the demand for as realistic, vivid and process-oriented representation of reality as possible is the demand for working with documents. The importance of receipts and documents for work in accounting and thus also for accounting teaching has already been presented in this work (see, for example, Bensch, 2009, 200–201; Berding, Beckmann & Kürten, 2019, p. 573; Mathes, 2006, p. 163; Seifried, 2004b, p. 291; Tramm, 2003, p. 10). For example, Preiß and Tramm (1996, p. 252) assume that the use of realistic documents in class plays a special role, as these represent business transactions and students should be enabled in class to perform translation services between the real processes and accounting. Preiß (1999, p. 64) further argues that documents have a higher complexity than the mostly text-based business cases in textbooks and therefore documents "facilitate the reconstruction of the underlying complex facts". In the "Linzer Ebenenmodell", the documents represent a separate field and form the "bridge between the reference field of action and the actual field of action" (Neuweg, 2020, p. 140). Riebenbauer (2021, p. 155) also notes that "the use of documents should be consistently promoted". This can make business problems and processes in the company more practical. Seifried and Sembill (2004, p. 378) formulate the "document-based representation of business facts" as a recommendation for accounting teaching. Bensch (2009, 201) notes that the "importance of documents in financial accounting must be given a wide space". The importance of documents is also emphasized in the curriculum, when it is formulated as a learning outcome that learners can record ongoing business cases based on original documents in accounting (BMBF, 2014, p. 3). In connection with learning and understanding difficulties, it is often argued that the use of documents can make teaching more vivid and can contribute to preventing or eliminating learning and understanding difficulties (e.g. Tramm et al., 1996, p. 201). Pargmann et al. (2022, p. 19–20) formulate the use of authentic documents as one of five elements for the design of learning environments in accounting.

In connection with modeling ability, documents also play a significant role, as they have an "intermediate step character" (Berding, Beckmann & Kürten, 2019, p. 573) and stand in the sense of the modeling cycle between real situation and real model. Therefore, documents abstract a real process and already make a first reduction to relevant aspects. Documents document and condense a process and in turn form the basis for further abstraction and condensation processes. Also with Seifried et al. (2010, p. 147), the document-based representation of a fact stands between the level of reality and mathematical and accounting model building. The representation of a real fact using a document therefore represents the first step of abstraction. Further formalizations are then made on this basis. As to whether the use of documents or documents reduces or increases the task difficulty, however, contradictory findings exist (e.g. Berding, Beckmann & Kürten, 2019, p. 590). Berding, Beckmann and Kürten (2019, p. 596) conclude from this that documents, on the one hand, have an important didactic function, but these must be "introduced into the classroom as carefully as booking entries, balance sheets, calculation methods, etc."

The *use of documents* is therefore defined as a relevant category for the analysis and evaluation of tasks. The documents are seen as the interface between reality (or the model of reality) and the world of accounting, which form the starting point for the learners' modeling services. The central question is whether a document is used in the task. To distinguish *which* documents are used in the tasks, different subcategories have been defined. The following were determined as relevant document types: receipt, balance list, balance sheet, account representation (e.g. T-account), profit and loss statement, asset directory, photograph/picture, chart of accounts, table, other document (e.g. contract, rate sheet, note, OP list, email, terms and conditions, etc.). A similar classification is also made by Ernst (2012a, p. 230–231).

The tasks are coded with 0 (document not present) if the corresponding document does not appear in the task or if the document is present, but it is not needed to solve the task. An exception here is the subcategory "Photography/Pictures". This is coded if the business case or fact is illustrated by the picture. Also coded with 0 is when the corresponding document (e.g. balance sheet, P&L) is to be created by the learner himself. The category Documents is presented in an overview in Table 5.1, in the appendix in the electronic supplementary material in detail.

5.4 Categories for the Modeling Cycle

The importance of modeling ability for solving accounting-specific problems was already worked out in Chap. 3. In order for merchants to be able to use accounting as a tool to solve problems, "they must be able to model real economic phenomena with accounting" (Berding, Beckmann & Kürten, 2019, p. 567). The importance of modeling ability is also evident in the competence models according to Guggemos (2016) and Preiß (2005a) as well as in the models for describing thinking steps when working on tasks from accounting according to Helm (2016d) and Seifried et al. (2010) or Wuttke and Seifried (2012). Also in the Linz level model according to Neuweg (2020) and in the economic instrumental accounting (e.g. Preiß, 1999; Tramm & Preiß, 1996) reference points to modeling ability can be identified. Accordingly, tasks in accounting should be designed in such a way that the learners' modeling ability is promoted. To analyze the different sub-steps in the processing of modeling tasks, so-called modeling cycles have established themselves (e.g. the modeling cycle of two-step mathematizing according to Blum, 1985). These will now be used to determine which sub-steps of the modeling cycle need to be completed in the course of processing tasks from accounting, in order to develop criteria for the analysis and evaluation of tasks on this basis.

The sub-step "Orienting"

Although the different modeling cycles differ in the number of sub-steps, in their differentiation and their theoretical connection as well as in the description and naming of the individual sub-steps, an *orientation performance* seems initially central for the processing of modeling tasks, which requires the learners to identify the problem contained in the task, to structure and simplify the problem by identifying the relevant aspects and to research new information if necessary.

In the modeling cycle according to Blum (1985, p. 200–204), for example, the starting point of the modeling process is a situation that initially needs to be simplified, specified, and structured by the learner. If necessary, additional information needs to be obtained. He refers to this first sub-step as "simplifying, structuring, and specifying". The seven-step modeling cycle developed in the course of the DISUM project (e.g., Blum, 2011; Greefrath et al., 2013) identifies understanding as well as simplifying and structuring as the first sub-steps, whereby relevant and irrelevant information needs to be differentiated, assumptions for simplification need to be made, and missing data needs to be researched during the simplification and structuring processes (Hankeln, 2019, p. 11; Hankeln & Beckschulte, 2020, p. 67; Schukajlow, 2011, p. 79). In reference to the modeling cycle from the DISUM project, Greefrath and Maaß (2020, p. 4) define modeling competence through seven sub-competences. The first sub-competence is defined as understanding, which they understand as the ability to "construct one's own mental model for a given problem situation and thus understand the question". This is followed by the ability to simplify, in which learners can distinguish relevant from irrelevant information. Kaiser et al. (2015, 369–370) also define competences for understanding a real problem as the first sub-facet and distinguish abilities such as information research, the distinction of relevant and irrelevant information, and the ability to make assumptions or the ability to "recognize variables influencing a situation" and "establish relationships between the variables". In the cognitive thinking model for typical thinking steps of students when working on accounting tasks according to Helm (2016d), the first sub-step is essentially an orientation performance when it comes to identifying the problem contained in the task (e.g., through comprehensive reading, adopting a perspective, recognizing the action, etc.). In the levels of processing subject-specific problems according to Seifried et al. (2010), the first two steps also involve correctly capturing economic reality and encoding it (e.g., choosing the correct perspective, identifying relevant information). Guggemos and Schönlein (2015, p. 527) name modeling as the difficulty-determining dimension in their competence level model and formulate the identification and delimitation of the problem to be solved as the first sub-step.

Based on this, an orientation performance seems essential in the first sub-step when working on tasks, which is mainly about identifying and understanding the problem contained in the task, distinguishing relevant and irrelevant information, and researching new information if necessary. For this reason, the main category *Orientation* is defined for the analysis and evaluation of tasks from accounting, which is differentiated into the three subcategories *Recognizing activity, Obtaining information* and *Evaluating information* (see field "Orientation" in Fig. 5.1).

A summary description of this category can be found in Table 5.1. Connections of this category can also be established to existing categories, for example, to the category of openness (defined for example via problem, solution path, and result openness) at Bloemen (2011), Maier et al. (2010), Maaß (2010) or Zhou (2022), to the category of problem-solving ability at Blömeke et al. (2006) or Wuttke et al. (2022) or to the category *Data* at Maaß (2010). In all cases, it is about whether learners have to recognize the problem contained in the task themselves (initial state), how clearly solutions and solution paths are given (target state), and whether independent information research and evaluation is required.

The category *Recognizing the activity* therefore first asks how delimited or open the initial state (What is the problem? What is the activity to be performed?) and the target state (What should the solution look like?) are defined. The category is ordinally scaled and distinguishes three levels. At level 0, tasks are coded in which the activity that learners must perform is clearly stated and the target state (solution) is clearly specified (e.g., "Form a provision on account 3060 in the amount of 3000 euros.", "Name the legal components of an invoice."). At level 1, tasks are assigned in which the activity is not exactly specified, but a delimitation has already been made (e.g., "Form the booking entries for the following business cases"). The task thus already makes a first delimitation for the learners and thus facilitates orientation, but the exact activity (e.g., On which accounts is which amount to be booked?) has to be identified by the learner himself. Also at the highest level, tasks are assigned in which the initial and/or target state are undefined (e.g., "Take all necessary steps.").

As the second subcategory, *Information research* is defined, also in ordinal scaling with three manifestations. This is about the question of whether a task prompts to independently research new information necessary for the solution of the task, or whether all relevant information is contained in the task. At level 0, tasks are coded in which all information needed to solve the task is contained in the task in textual form. At the next higher level, tasks are assigned that require information research from documents *within* the task (e.g., from an invoice, a balance list, a contract, an email, etc.). At the highest level (level 2), information research from *multiple sources within* the task or from *external* sources (e.g., a legal text, a website, etc.) is required. A similar level classification can be found, for example, at Guggemos and Schönlein (2015, p. 531).

As the third sub-facet of the orientation performance, the *Information evaluation* is defined, i.e., whether learners need to distinguish relevant and irrelevant information. This category is also ordinally scaled and defines tasks at level 0 that do not require information evaluation. So all information contained in the task is needed to solve the task. However, introductory information and context information are not taken into account. At level 1, tasks are assigned in which relevant and irrelevant information must be distinguished. The tasks thus contain an information surplus. However, this information surplus is not a conscious one, but results from the use of documents. For example, an invoice necessarily contains components that are not needed for the correct booking of the invoice. Also, if a balance list with different accounts is given, usually not the balances of all accounts are needed to solve a specific task. For this reason, tasks are assigned to level 2 in which a conscious information surplus is contained, for example, by specifying different prices or different depreciation amounts. So in this case too, learners need to distinguish between relevant and irrelevant information.

The sub-step "Translating"

Following the capture of the problem, a real, operational fact must be translated into the world of accounting. In the light of the "Linzer Ebenenmodell" according to Neuweg (2020), this step represents the transition between the reference field of action and the actual field of action. In the model of basic ideas according to Berding (2019, p. 94), this is the transition from a situation from the real world into a model of mathematics or accounting and is referred to as "mathematizing". In the model by Seifried et al. (2010, p. 146), the translation of a real, economic phenomenon into accounting is referred to as "formalizing and mathematizing", which involves correctly implementing the economic situation "in terms of content and accounting as well as mathematically". This includes the selection of accounts and posting, especially the setting up of the correct booking entry. In the language of mathematics didactics, this step is usually also referred to as formalizing and mathematizing (e.g., in the modeling cycle according to Blum, 1985). As an important competence of this sub-step, Greefrath and Maaß (2020, p. 4) formulate the ability to translate simplified real situations into mathematical models (e.g., equations, deadlines, or functions).

The translation of a fact into accounting (at least into financial accounting) usually takes place via the booking, i.e., the creation of a booking entry (in the "Linzer Ebenenmodell", field 5b booking). Therefore, a category is introduced for the classification system that asks whether a task requires the translation of a real fact into the world of accounting (*Translation*). For the main category, the term translation is used instead of formalizing and mathematizing to clarify the transition between the real world and the world of accounting. The category is dichotomously designed and also distinguishes two subcategories. First, a translation service may be required by setting up a booking entry. Here it is differentiated whether a booking has to be set up as part of a task (1) or not (0). The number and complexity of bookings (e.g., defined by the number of accounts involved) are not taken into account. Furthermore, it is also possible that a translation of a real fact into the world of accounting has to be made, but not by setting up a booking, but rather by other accounting activities or the use of technical terms, e.g., by classifying a business case as to whether it is fixed assets or current assets or by stating in which account class a business case is to be booked. Here again, a coding is made at level 0 (no translation required) or 1 (translation required). A summary of this category can be seen in Table 5.1 (for a detailed description see the appendix in the electronic supplementary material).

The sub-step "Internal Accounting Operations"

While the separation between mathematizing (e.g., from a problem statement the equation 2x + 3x = ?) and mathematical work (e.g., solving the equation, 2x + 3x = 5x) in mathematics is easy to understand, this clear separation for the domain of accounting is somewhat more difficult. Mathematizing (i.e., translating) represents the transfer of a real situation into the world of accounting by setting up a booking. However, there is no clear equivalent in accounting for mathematical work, as a booking in this sense (as is the case with mathematical equations) cannot be "solved". Instead, further operations can be carried out within the system following the translation of a business case into the world of accounting (Berding, Beckmann & Kürten, 2019, p. 572). Wuttke and Seifried (2012, pp. 179–180) capture the step of operating within accounting in the sub-step of formalizing and mathematizing, thus strictly speaking not distinguishing between the translation into accounting and the work within the system. In contrast, Preiß (2005a, p. 74) sees the operation within accounting as a separate sub-step. However, he does not define what these operations consist of and how they are to be delimited from the previous sub-step. Similarly, Berding (2019, p. 94) makes a distinction. He refers to the transition between model and result as "processing", but here too the boundary between translation (formalizing and mathematizing) and work within the system is not clear and it remains unclear which activities fall into which sub-step. In the modeling cycles of mathematics didactics, this sub-step is usually defined with the term "mathematical work" (Blum, 1985, 2011; Greefrath et al., 2013). Greefrath and Maaß (2020, p. 4) define mathematical work as the ability to work with mathematical models. In reference to the "Linzer Ebenenmodell", internal accounting operations most closely correspond to field 5c ("Balance Sheet, P&L, MWR, VAT return"), as the translation processes into financial accounting "create a model of the reference field of action". "The result of this modeling becomes visible in the balance sheet and P&L (field 5c)" (Neuweg, 2020, p. 141).

As a further category for the analysis and evaluation of tasks from accounting, the category *internal accounting work or operations* is therefore defined, although in previous works on modeling ability in accounting the distinction between translation (setting up bookings) and working in the accounting system has largely been omitted. The category of internal accounting operations focuses on the question of whether a task requires operations within the accounting system. The criterion for distinguishing between a translation service and work within the accounting system is the connection to a process in operational reality. While translations transfer a business fact into the world of accounting (e.g., the purchase of a company car is transferred to financial accounting by a booking), internal accounting work (e.g., opening an account, closing an account, creating a balance sheet, making offsetting bookings) strictly speaking has no equivalent in the real world, but these are processes within accounting that may have already been transferred into accounting through previous translation processes. In reference to the Linz level model and with reference to the preliminary work on the technical approach to the domain of accounting (see Sect. 2.1), the following are defined as internal accounting operations: setting up internal accounting bookings (e.g., opening accounts, closing accounts, making offsetting bookings, activating production costs, etc.), creating a balance sheet, creating a profit and loss account, creating a more-less calculation, and other internal accounting operations (e.g., creating a VAT return). Each subcategory is dichotomously designed. Therefore, it is only differentiated whether the sub-step has to be completed (1) or not (0). The detailed description with examples and coding rules can be found in the appendix in the electronic supplementary material.

The sub-step "Interpreting"

Interpreting is an essential sub-step in the modeling cycle and represents the transition between the world of accounting and the real world. Blum (1985, p. 204) refers to this sub-step for mathematics as "reinterpreting" and emphasizes that a retranslation of the results into reality is essential. In the modeling cycle of the DISUM project, interpreting is also an important sub-step (Greefrath et al., 2013, p. 18). Seifried et al. (2010, p. 146) capture the interpretation of accounting operations in the sub-step "Reflecting and Evaluating", while both Berding, Beckmann and Kürten (2019, p. 571) and Berding (2019, p. 94) and Preiß (2005a, p. 74) each provide for a separate sub-step. Regardless of this, however, it becomes clear that a retranslation into the real world is essential, as only in this way can "the information created in accounting be used for real purposes" (Berding, Beckmann & Kürten, 2019, p. 572). In the course of interpretation, the result is "again given content meaning" and "consequences for reality" are derived (Berding, Riebenbauer & Slepcevic-Zach, 2019, p. 370). To assess what consequences arise, the formal goals listed in the "Linzer Ebenenmodell" are suitable, as they control both the processes in the reference field of action and in the actual field of action. The formal goal level is thus the level that "provides the criteria towards which office action should shape or judge the processes in the reference field of action" (Neuweg, 2020, p. 139). In the "Linzer Ebenenmodell", liquidity, profitability, tax burden, and external presentation are defined as formal goals (Neuweg, 2020, p. 140).

On this basis, the main category *Interpreting* is introduced. This means whether learners are asked to interpret a result in light of the effects on one or more formal goals. In reference to the "Linzer Ebenenmodell", the impact on *liquidity*, *profitability* (or per-unit or period success), *tax burden*, and *external presentation* are defined as relevant subcategories. In addition, a subcategory with *other interpretations* (e.g., interpreting key figures or performing target-actual comparisons) is introduced. All subcategories are again dichotomously designed and therefore only distinguish whether an interpretation is required (1) or not (0).

The sub-step "Validating"

In some modeling cycles, a validation phase follows the interpretation phase. This refers to the examination of the developed solution for plausibility or correctness. Greefrath and Maaß (2020, p. 4) define essential sub-competencies of this phase as students "checking the real results for appropriateness" or "comparing or evaluating different mathematical models for a real situation". Typical activities within the scope of validation services include the critical examination of the solution or the checking of calculation paths for errors, for example by recalculating or by calculating alternative calculation and solution paths (Hankeln & Beckschulte, 2020, pp. 67–68). In the competence model according to Preiß (2005a, p. 74) and in the model of basic concepts according to Berding (2019, p. 94), validation represents the last sub-step. Seifried et al. (2010, p. 147) define the last level of processing subject-specific tasks in accounting as reflecting and evaluating, and include the review of the result and the solution path in addition to the interpretation.

Therefore, the category *Validation* is included in the classification system. The central question is whether a task requires checking one's own solution or an existing solution for plausibility or correctness. In the domain of accounting, this could involve activities such as checking an invoice for correctness, checking and possibly correcting booking entries, checking balance sheets or profit and loss accounts for correctness, or checking calculations. In addition, this category captures whether a chosen approach needs to be explicitly justified. This could be the case, for example, when justifying why a booking entry was made in a certain way, or when justifying why a purchased good was immediately recorded as an expense as a low-value economic good. The category of validation is again dichotomously recorded. So it is only distinguished whether a validation service is required (1) or not (0).

Legal Norm Orientation

In this context, another category seems relevant. External accounting, unlike internal accounting, is significantly shaped by legal requirements and standards (Bertl et al., 2022, p. 9; Denk et al., 2016, p. 2). The processes in financial accounting are therefore subject to legal requirements. This also means that the representations in external accounting do not necessarily correspond to reality, but are influenced by standards and laws. It therefore seems obvious and important that these legal standards are also addressed and processed in accounting lessons. At the same time, this means that the legal foundations should also be taken into account in tasks. For example, Neuweg (2020, p. 136) identifies as a basic problem of accounting didactics that "booking processes merely appear as an expression of the 'logic of double-entry bookkeeping', that they essentially also go back to legal norms, behind which intentions stand, often remains unclear." For this reason, legal norms form a separate field in the "Linzer Ebenenmodell" "The rules of document processing in accounting are largely derived from legal norms" (Neuweg, 2020, p. 140). Schneider (2010, p. 58) emphasizes that "from the perspective of general economic understanding, it can also be demanded that the citizen understands that the result of annual financial statements is massively influenced by rules (UGB, IFRS) and valuation freedoms." To build this understanding, however, knowledge of the legal foundations is important. Interestingly, the importance of legal norms has so far hardly found its way into didactic models of accounting, for example in the existing competence models. Neuweg (2020, p. 136) notes that even in the typology of student errors in accounting lessons proposed by Wuttke and Seifried (2012), "the commercial and tax law level is left out."

Therefore, the category Legal *Norm Orientation* is included in the category system. This category is about the question of whether a task requires the justification of an activity, a solution, a decision through a legal norm. This category cannot therefore be assigned to a single sub-step of the modeling cycle, but rather cuts across the different sub-steps. For example, a justification through a legal norm may be required at different points in the modeling cycle, for example during orientation (Is this business case relevant for accounting at all?), during translation (e.g. Am I allowed to record the relevant good as a low-value economic good immediately?), during internal accounting operations (e.g. Are offsetting bookings mandatory for the relevant business case?) or during validation (e.g. Does the invoice contain all legal invoice components? Was the provision correctly formed?). It is important to emphasize here that a coding with 1 (justification via legal norm necessary) is only made if the task explicitly asks to justify an activity or a solution via a norm. So if, for example, a provision for legal and consulting expenses is formed in the course of a business case, learners must at least implicitly consider the legal foundations (in this case in particular § 198 UGB). However, if the task only asks to form the provision (e.g. "Form a provision for legal and consulting expenses amounting to 3000 euros"), but not to decide for oneself (e.g. "May a provision be formed in the present case?") or to justify afterwards (e.g. "Was the formation of the provision permissible in the present case? If yes, why? If no, why not?"), no coding with 1 is to be made, but with 0. The category is again dichotomously designed.

The Sub-step "Deciding"

Accounting as a business information system is not only an instrument for documenting business processes, but it also serves to control and support business decisions by providing a mathematically founded basis for decision-making (Denk et al., 2016, p. 1; Schierenbeck & Wöhle, 2016, p. 601; Schneider et al., 2022, p. 17). As a rule, therefore, the representation (documentation) of business processes in accounting leads to interpretation services and, subsequently, business decisions are made on this basis, which in turn lead to new business cases (see also Fig. 3.7 in Sect. 3.3.1 on the Linz level model). In the language of the "Linzer Ebenenmodell", interpretations regarding formal goals lead to decisions that have effects on the reference field of action, i.e. the real world. From the target specifications, new business transactions are brought about through actions or decisions (Preiß, 2015, p. 189).

The last sub-step of a modeling cycle in the domain of accounting is therefore defined as *Deciding*. This sub-step does not occur in the modeling cycles from mathematics didactics, but seems sensible for accounting. Essentially, this category is about the question of whether a business decision needs to be made in the course of task processing, which in turn triggers new activities in the reference field of action. The category is dichotomously designed and therefore distinguishes whether a business decision needs to be made (1) or whether no decision is required (0). Relevant in this context is that only decisions are recorded that have an impact on processes in the real world (i.e. in the reference field of action). This is the case, for example, when deciding whether to include a product in the range or not, when deciding whether to buy machine A or B, or whether to continue the business or not. If learners have to make decisions that concern the accounting area or the accounting recording (e.g. May a provision be formed in the present case? Which depreciation rate may/should be used?), no coding with 1 is to be made. These decisions are recorded, for example, in the orientation or translation service.

Mathematical Work

A final category, similar to legal norm orientation, which cuts across the modeling cycle and can therefore occur at different points, represents mathematical work. In the modeling cycles of mathematics didactics, mathematical work forms the transition between the mathematical model and the mathematical result. Thus, mathematical work only takes place in the world of mathematics (Blum, 1985, p. 200, 2011, p. 18; Greefrath et al., 2013, pp. 17–18). This sub-step involves performing calculations that subsequently lead to mathematical results (Blum, 1985, p. 204). Greefrath and Maaß (2020, p. 4) include under this the ability to work with mathematical models. In the present modeling cycle, mathematical work would correspond to internal accounting work. There, too, operations are only carried out in the world of accounting.

For the domain of accounting, it can be assumed that mathematical work is linked to other steps of the modeling cycle. For example, mathematical work may be necessary when translating a real situation into the world of accounting, for example when calculating gross, net or tax amounts for bookings. Mathematical work can also be necessary for internal accounting activities (e.g. determining balances), when interpreting (e.g. to what extent the company's liquid assets are changing) or when validating (e.g. recalculating). For this reason, the category system also includes whether it is necessary to *work mathematically* during task processing. However, it is not recorded at which point in the modeling cycle it is necessary to operate mathematically. Mathematical work is recorded dichotomously. So it is differentiated whether mathematical work is necessary (1) or not (0). The complexity of the performance to be provided is also not taken into account.

For the different sub-steps of the modeling cycle, it can also be noted that many of them are also addressed in the curriculum. For example, as professional learning outcomes in the Entrepreneurship—Business and Management cluster for the area of corporate accounting, it is stipulated among other things that learners can book ongoing business cases in double-entry bookkeeping (translation), can determine the profit or loss of companies and can prepare annual financial statements (internal accounting work), can interpret and assess these (interpreting and validating) and can make entrepreneurial decisions (deciding) (BMBF, 2014, p. 3).

5.5 Categories for Connections with Other Relevant Content Areas

Neuweg (2020, p. 141) argues in his explanations that not only financial accounting should be addressed in accounting lessons, but consistent references should be made to internal accounting, especially to financial statements, liquidity management and cost accounting. It must "by no means give the impression that double-entry bookkeeping is the most important component and not cost accounting or liquidity management". Tramm (2003, p. 5) also emphasizes that from a business perspective, "the function of internal accounting for control and controlling processes is increasingly coming to the fore". Preiß (2015, p. 190) notes that accounting is still often seen "as if traditional bookkeeping were the most important component and not the numerous subsidiary books [...] as well as cost accounting and liquidity management". Dolzsanksi (2013b, p. 356) formulates as a guideline for the further development of accounting didactics that a "widening of the didactic models, away from a narrow focus on the basics of financial accounting, towards all subject-related aspects of accounting" should be undertaken. The importance of internal accounting for planning, controlling and monitoring company processes was also worked out in Sect. 2.1. Internal accounting "is aimed at internal information recipients. Its task is to process numbers in such a way that they can provide solid support for operational planning, decision-making and control processes" (Troßmann & Baumeister, 2015, p. 3).

From these arguments, it could be derived on the one hand that the proportion of financial accounting in the curriculum as a whole should be reduced and that internal accounting (especially cost accounting and liquidity management) should be upgraded. However, if one looks at the currently valid curriculum of the commercial college, it is noticeable that a large part of the content in the curriculum relates to financial accounting, while for example cost accounting is taught as an "insert" in the 3rd year for one semester. Liquidity Management is not explicitly dealt with in the subject of corporate accounting (if at all, then most likely in the area of controlling in the 5th year) (BMBF, 2014, pp. 55–63). In the analysis and evaluation of tasks from textbooks, one could then determine what proportion of tasks deal with financial accounting, liquidity management/financial statements and cost accounting. However, the flexible level change mentioned by Neuweg (2020, p. 139) is more about the networking of the different sub-areas of internal and external accounting.[2] Therefore, a criterion is introduced that determines *whether tasks require references or connections to cost accounting and/or financial statements*. These categories are therefore about whether a connection to cost accounting and/or financial statements needs to be established in the task. It is differentiated whether a connection is necessary (1) or not (0). The type and complexity of the networking performance are not taken into account. A 1 is coded if learners need to establish a connection to internal accounting or if the task itself establishes a connection (e.g. reference to cost accounting data), without learners having to perform a networking performance themselves. The categories are again explained in more detail in Table 5.1 and in the appendix in the electronic supplementary material and provided with examples.

In addition to a stronger networking between external and internal accounting, the better integration with business content is also repeatedly discussed. This is evident, for example, in the objectives formulated for accounting lessons and also in the demands formulated in the sense of the guiding principle of the "thinking accountant". Thus, Achtenhagen (1996, pp. 27–28) sees the development of an economic competence as the highest goal of accounting lessons. According to Sloane (1996, p. 26), accounting lessons should be used to provide insight into operational processes and procedures. The subject becomes "a catalyst for a general expansion of business competence". For Tramm and Preiß (1996, p. 5), the guiding goal of accounting lessons is to "understand economic relationships through the penetration and mastery of commercial techniques". According to Seifried (2004b, p. 52), a cross-subject, cross-learning field teaching should replace an isolated, subject-scientific consideration of the subject of accounting.[3] The "Linzer Ebenenmodell" also makes it clear that a link between accounting and business administration is essential when Neuweg (2020, p. 138) speaks of "business-thinking accountants". In economic-instrumental accounting,

[2] The curriculum also includes in the general educational objectives that learners can use their "comprehensive and networked economic knowledge [...] in their professional field of action". In the learning outcomes of the "Entrepreneurship—Business and Management" cluster, networked thinking and working is also formulated as a target skill.

[3] In vocational education in Germany, the traditional subject structuring was abandoned in favor of an orientation towards professional situations when creating curricula according to the learning field concept (Zurstrassen, 2009).

an "explicit, content-related link between accounting lessons and other core economic subjects is also demanded" (Preiß & Tramm, 1996, p. 226). The curriculum of the commercial college also states that "as far as possible, a networking between the individual subjects should be aimed for, with business administration as the leading subject of education being of particular importance" (BMBF, 2014, p. 4).

As a further subcategory for the analysis and evaluation of tasks from accounting, it is introduced whether a *connection to business management topics and content* needs to be established in the course of the tasks. The distinction is made only whether a networking performance is required, but not the extent or complexity. Unlike the other two subcategories for networking, here it is only coded with 1 (present) if the learners themselves have to work on a business management content in the context of task processing. The currently valid curriculum of the commercial college serves as a demarcation of what falls under a business administration content. A reference of the task alone, without corresponding performance of the learner, is not sufficient. In the appendix in the electronic supplementary material, the exact coding rules and examples can be found. A connection would be present, for example, if an incoming invoice had to be booked in accounting and subsequently the reasons for granting discounts had to be discussed. Another example would be if the default of a receivable had to be booked in accounting and subsequently measures had to be developed on how the default of receivables could be better prevented in the future.

In the course of the coding process, in addition to the deductively formed categories already presented, three further categories were inductively determined and all existing tasks were evaluated according to them. In Sect. 7.1.6 the inductively gained categories are described, related to the current state of didactic discussion and the results are reported.

6 Planning of the Empirical Survey

6.1 Research Interest and Research Questions

As already presented in Sect. 1.1, this dissertation pursues two research interests. Firstly, a significant goal is to develop a subject-didactic category system for the analysis and evaluation of tasks from the accounting domain. For this purpose, the subject-didactic state of discussion was presented in Chap. 2 and 3, domain-overarching and domain-specific requirements for tasks were presented in Chap. 4, current research findings on the quality of tasks in the accounting domain were reported, and in Chap. 5 demands on tasks from accounting were elaborated.

In addition to the development of a subject-didactic category system, the assessment and characterization of textbook tasks from accounting in the light of the discussed demands on tasks represents the second research interest. Therefore, the research questions need to be specified in this chapter.

Firstly, it is necessary to determine how the tasks are to be assessed in terms of the identified relevant characteristics. This results in the following research questions:

- **RQ1:** How process-oriented are tasks from textbooks for the accounting domain designed?
- **RQ2:** How detailed is the business reality represented in the tasks?
- **RQ3:** To what extent are documents used in the tasks and which documents are predominantly used?
- **RQ4:** Which sub-steps of the modeling cycle (orienting, translating, operating, interpreting, validating, deciding) occur in what frequency in the textbook

S. Reindl-Stütz, *Characteristics of Tasks in the Domain of Accounting*,
https://doi.org/10.1007/978-3-658-48958-8_6

tasks? Are there sub-steps that are addressed comparatively frequently or can sub-steps be identified that are addressed comparatively infrequently?

- **RQ5:** Do the textbook tasks have a legal norm orientation? Do learners have to explicitly justify their activity or solution by applying a legal norm or standard?
- **RQ6:** Are connections to other subject areas, specifically to business administration, cost accounting, and liquidity management, established in the textbook tasks?

Although the curriculum of the respective subject forms the basis for all textbooks, it cannot be ruled out that books from different publishers (and thus different authors) differ, as different didactic concepts and content focuses are pursued depending on the publisher or author teams. This assumption is also suggested by the findings of Seifried (2009a, pp. 234–235), who was able to show that teachers differ in their views on accounting instruction.[1] A systematic examination of tasks from different publishers has so far been lacking in accounting didactics. Therefore, research question 7 (RQ7) takes a closer look at differences between publishers.

- **RQ7:** Do the tasks from different publishers and thus different author teams differ in terms of the above-mentioned characteristics?

It is conceivable and likely that the tasks differ depending on the grade level. For example, it is plausible to assume that with higher grade levels (and thus increasing experience and competence of the learners) more or more demanding sub-steps of the modeling cycle (e.g., interpreting, validating, and deciding) have to be completed. This would also be in line with the curriculum, which is designed as a spiral curriculum so that "central contents are repeated over the course of the five years with increasing detail and ascending complexity level" (BMBF, 2014, p. 4). For the representation of business reality, on the other hand, it could be assumed that this is particularly pronounced in the lower grades, as it is particularly important there to establish the connection to the real world for the still inexperienced learners. Conversely, it can also be assumed that based on the dominating balance sheet method, the "practice", i.e., the business reality, is only

[1] Thus, Seifried (2009a, p. 235) was able to identify different types of teachers (constructivist-oriented teachers, instructional-oriented teachers, and a systematic mixed type), who differ in terms of different criteria (e.g., goals pursued in teaching, elements of lesson planning, accounting worldviews).

introduced and extensively discussed later. Based on these considerations, the following research question 8 arises.

- **RQ8:** Do the tasks of different grade levels differ in terms of the various characteristics?

For the consolidation of the results and for a better characterization of the tasks, the determination of task types or task classes is suitable. By determining task types, the different task classes can be better characterized and it can be determined what is specific for a class and in which characteristics the classes differ. The aim is to group objects together based on their similarity to a class (intra-group homogeneity) and to achieve as high a heterogeneity as possible between the different classes (inter-group heterogeneity). The formation of task classes therefore facilitates orientation by condensing the results. It also offers further description and explanation possibilities (Backhaus et al., 2021, pp. 490–491; Geiser, 2010, p. 236; Kuckartz, 2010, p. 556). Therefore, two research questions arise for the determination of correlations between the various characteristics and for the identification of different task types:

- **RQ9:** How are the various task characteristics related to each other? Are certain characteristics often associated with each other?
- **RQ10:** Can different task types or task classes be identified?

In the following chapter, the methods of data evaluation are presented. In Sect. 6.2.1, the descriptive evaluations and the conducted tests for determining differences are reported (research questions 1 to 8). In Sect. 6.2.2, the statistical procedures for determining correlations between the characteristics and for identifying task types are explained (research questions 9 and 10).

6.2 Planning of Data Evaluation

6.2.1 Descriptive Statistics and Tests for Identifying Differences

To answer research questions 1 to 6, absolute and relative frequencies are reported in the form of frequency tables and graphically visualized using different diagrams. For ordinal-scaled characteristics, the median is reported as a measure of position (Döring & Bortz, 2016, p. 251; Kuckartz et al., 2013, pp. 36–39).

To answer research questions 7 and 8, the differences between tasks from different publishers or years need to be identified. A number of statistical methods are available for identifying differences between various groups. All data collected here and available for analysis are ordinal scale data or dichotomous levels (categorical data). Therefore, non-parametric methods are used, which do not require interval scaling of the data and no normal distribution (Rasch et al., 2010, p. 143).

In the present project, different methods are used to test for differences, as the data types of the category system differ. There are categories that are designed in the form of an ordinal scale (with three manifestations), a ranking of the gradations is possible (e.g. the category process orientation). Other categories, on the other hand, are dichotomously designed, so a distinction is made between "present" and "not present". The characteristics of publisher and year are nominal characteristics, with three (publisher 1, 2 and 3) or five manifestations (year 1 to 5). A ranking is not possible with these characteristics.

The Chi-square test (χ^2-Test) can be used to analyze differences in nominal data or dichotomous characteristics. The Chi-square test compares empirically observed and expected frequencies using cross-tabulations. The expected frequency can be determined for each table cell (i.j) using the following formula from the marginal frequencies (Kuckartz et al., 2013, pp. 92–93):

$$f_{e(i,j)} = \frac{\text{row total } i \, x \text{ column total } j}{n}$$

Subsequently, to determine the Chi-square value, the deviations between observed and expected values (so-called residuals) are calculated, squared, and divided by the respective expected frequency (Hartmann et al., 2022, p. 54). For the Chi-square value, it is assumed that this is 0 if the two characteristics are independent of each other and therefore expected and observed frequencies are identical. The χ^2-value is higher, the greater the deviation between observed and expected frequencies, i.e., the more the variables depend on each other (Rasch et al., 2010, pp. 190–191). For the present data, a Chi-square multi-field test is used, as the variables publisher and year each have more than two manifestations. The remaining variables each have exactly two manifestations. So, in general, these are cross-tabulations with 6 (3 × 2) or 10 (5 × 2) fields (Bruhn, 1986, p. 194; Kuckartz et al., 2013, p. 95). A prerequisite for calculating Chi-square is that a maximum of 20% of all cells in the table may have an expected frequency less than five, as the quotient quickly increases with small expected values due to the calculation method (expected frequencies in the denominator), which can distort the relationship between the variables (Bruhn, 1986, p. 195; Kuckartz et al., 2013, pp. 96–97).

However, the implementation of Chi-square tests also has disadvantages. First, it should be noted that for cross-tabulations with more than 4 fields (2 × 2), the Chi-square test only determines *whether* a statistically significant result exists, but not which differences (between the various) groups cause the significant result. The Chi-square test thus only tests *globally* whether significant differences exist between observed and expected values (so-called Omnibus test) (Rasch et al., 2010, p. 192; Sharpe, 2015). Beasley (1995) and Sharpe (2015) point out that conducting a Chi-square test alone is not sufficient and therefore post-hoc testing is necessary for a more detailed analysis of the differences. Various approaches and possibilities are available for this. Both suggest, among other things, the *Standardized Residual Method.* Here, the individual residuals (i.e., the difference between expected and observed frequencies) are subjected to a significance test. Since cells with the highest expected frequencies also have the largest residuals, standardized residual values (*adjusted, standardized residuals*) are calculated based on the residuals. After that, it is checked for each standardized residual value whether it is statistically significant. However, a significance value of 0.05 is not assumed, but to avoid an alpha error accumulation, a value reduced by the Bonferroni correction (calculated from the significance level divided by the number of individual tests; with a significance level of 0.05 and e.g. 10 tests, the corrected value is 0.005). The exact procedure for conducting the post-hoc tests follows the recommendations and the procedure described by Sharpe (2015) and can be read there. The Chi-square tests are carried out using the "Cross-tabulations" function in SPSS. The significance checks for the post-hoc tests are carried out in Excel using the function "CHISQU.DIST.RT(*x, degrees of freedom*)".[2]

A statistically significant result does not make any statements about the strength of the relationship or effect. For this reason, Cramer's V is additionally determined to calculate the effect size. Cramer's V represents a measure of association and shows the strength of the relationship on a value range between 0 and 1 (Kuckartz et al., 2013, pp. 98–99; Tausendpfund, 2022, p. 119). A value of $V = .10$ can be interpreted as a small effect, a value of $V = .30$ as a medium effect and a value of $V = .50$ as a large effect (Cohen, 1988, pp. 224–225; Döring & Bortz, 2016, p. 821).

The Kruskal-Wallis test is suitable for comparing ordinal-scaled characteristics in more than two groups. This is also a non-parametric method. The Kruskal-Wallis test (also called H-test) is an alternative to one-way analysis of variance

---

[2] A check of the significances is also possible in SPSS, but the implementation in Excel is simpler and more efficient.

(ANOVA) when the prerequisites for this are not given (e.g. the interval scaling of the dependent variable) (Rasch et al., 2010, p. 164). The Kruskal-Wallis test only provides information about *whether* groups differ significantly, but cannot say which groups differentiate in the case of more than two groups. Therefore, post-hoc tests are also necessary in this case for a detailed analysis of the differences. Therefore, post-hoc tests are subsequently carried out by pairwise comparisons. To avoid an alpha error accumulation, a Bonferroni correction is again made (Field, 2017, p. 419; Rasch et al., 2010, p. 164). Since there is no standardized procedure or measure for indicating the effect size when comparing the medians of more than two groups, Field (2017, pp. 431–432) recommends calculating the effect sizes for each of the pairwise comparisons. The formula $r = \frac{z}{\sqrt{N}}$ is used to calculate the effect size measure r, where z defines the standardized test statistic and N the sample size. Here, a value below $r = .30$ is considered a small effect, a value between $r = .30$ and .50 as medium and values greater than $r = .50$ as a large effect (Cohen, 1988, pp. 79–80; Field, 2017, p. 179).

6.2.2 Intercorrelation Matrix and Latent Class Analysis for Identifying Relationships and Task Classes

In addition to identifying differences between tasks from different publishers and different grade levels, research question 9 determines how the characteristics are interrelated. Correlations between the various variables are calculated and presented for this purpose. Kendall's Tau (τ) is suitable for representing relationships between ordinally scaled characteristics (Döring & Bortz, 2016, p. 681).

To answer research question 10, a latent class analysis (*Latent Class Analysis*, abbreviated: LCA) is used. The LCA is a multivariate method used to classify data (e.g., people, tasks) into homogeneous subgroups (so-called "latent classes"). The basis for classification is the observed response patterns of individuals (or the codings for tasks). The LCA is suitable for the analysis of categorical (i.e., nominal or ordinal) data. If metric data are analyzed, this is referred to as a (latent) profile analysis. The LCA can be used confirmatorily, for example, when an existing theory about typological differences between individuals or tasks is to be tested. Alternatively, an exploratory approach is possible, in which no assumptions are made about the typologization in advance (Bacher & Vermunt, 2010, p. 553; Geiser, 2013, pp. 232–233; McCutcheon, 1987, p. 8). The LCA should also be differentiated from cluster analysis, which can be applied to all types of data, but is inferior to the LCA, especially for categorical (or non-metric) data. It differs from the LCA in several areas. First, unlike cluster analysis, the LCA makes certain distribution assumptions regarding the classification characteristics within each class.[3] This leads to the availability of measures for determining the number of classes, which allow an assessment of the quality of the class solutions. Such measures are lacking for cluster analysis, so determining the "correct" number of clusters and assessing the quality of a class solution is a problem there. Furthermore, the LCA is a probabilistic method. Therefore, each person (or each task) is assigned to the classes with a certain probability. In cluster analysis, however, the allocation is deterministic. A person (or a task) is assigned to a cluster with a probability of 1 (Bacher & Vermunt, 2010, pp. 554–555; Bortz & Schuster, 2010, pp. 453–545; Rost, 2004, pp. 154–156, 2006, p. 278). In cluster analysis, the similarity (spatial proximity) between individuals must also be defined. On this basis, the assignment of individuals to certain clusters is then made. In addition, the distance of the clusters must be determined, on the basis of which the separation of the clusters is determined. For this purpose, so-called similarity and distance measures are used, which exist for different types of data (nominal, ordinal, or interval scaled) (Bortz & Schuster, 2010, pp. 454–458; Rost, 2004, p. 156, 2006, pp. 277–278). The LCA, on the other hand, does not start from pairwise similarity or distance comparisons, but "by maximizing a likelihood function, those persons are assigned to the same latent class who have the same response probabilities with regard to all items of the test" (Rost, 2004, p. 156). The parameter estimates of the LCA are usually determined using a maximum likelihood estimation method. The aim is to maximize the likelihood function, i.e., to identify the class solution with the highest log-likelihood value. This value is a measure "for the probability of the data under the model" and forms the basis for calculating many model fit indices (Geiser, 2013, pp. 237–238). While cluster analysis classifies individuals (or tasks) *only* according to their similarity, the LCA is a mixture distribution model in which the total population is "unmixed" into subgroups, so that a certain model applies in each class. The observed distribution of frequencies is therefore considered as a mixture of different distributions (Rost, 2006, p. 279).

The number of classes required to adequately represent the response patterns is not a parameter that is estimated in the model. Therefore, in the context of exploratory LCA, the number of classes is to be determined through model comparisons. For this purpose, LCAs with different numbers of classes are cal-

[3] For example, a multinomial distribution for nominal characteristics, a binomial distribution or a multinomial distribution for ordinal characteristics (Bacher & Vermunt, 2010, p. 556).

culated and the quality is indicated using absolute and relative model-fit indices. The class solution with the best data fit (i.e., the best fit values), which is also easily interpretable in terms of content, should be selected (Geiser, 2013, p. 234). A number of different key figures or statistical methods are available for assessing absolute and relative model fit (for an overview see Geiser, 2013, pp. 257–268).

In assessing the absolute model fit (*absolute model fit*), the question at the center is to what extent a certain class solution can adequately reproduce the data. The Likelihood-Ratio-Test and the Pearson-χ^2 statistic are available to check the absolute model fit. In both tests, the empirically observed frequencies of the response patterns (so-called *patterns*) are compared with the *pattern* predicted by the respective model. Accordingly, significant results of the two evaluations indicate a statistically significant deviation between observed and model-predicted responses and thus indicate a lack of model fit (Geiser, 2013, pp. 258–259; McCutcheon, 2002, pp. 66–67).[4]

In the case of relative model fit (*relative model fit*), the quality of a model is assessed in comparison to another model with more or fewer classes. For this purpose, the Bootstrap-Likelihood-Ratio-Difference Test (BLRT), the Vuong-Lo-Mendell-Rubin Test (VLMRT), and various information-theoretical measures (AIC, BIC, and *sample size adjusted* BIC) are available for assessing relative model fit (Bacher & Vermunt, 2010, pp. 557–558; Geiser, 2013, pp. 263–268; McCutcheon, 2002, pp. 66–73; Rost, 2004, p. 157).

In the Bootstrap-Likelihood-Ratio-Test, a model with G classes is tested against a model with G—1 classes. A significant result shows that the model with G classes represents the data more adequately than the model with G—1 classes. The VLMRT follows a similar principle to the Likelihood-Ratio-Test, where a significant result shows that the present model fits better than a model with one class less (Geiser, 2013, pp. 263–267).

The so-called information measures (*Information Criteria*, IC) are very often used to assess the relative model fit. These are descriptive indices for model comparison. The information measures take into account both the model fit (How well does a model fit the data?) and the model parsimony (How many parameters are estimated?). Model fit and model parsimony are in a tension with each other. The model fit usually increases with the number of classes. At the same time, more parameters are estimated with each additional class, which in turn has a negative effect on model parsimony. For different class solutions, the model with

[4]It should be noted that in practice, due to insufficiently large samples, the asymptotic conditions for the Likelihood-Ratio-Test and the Pearson-χ^2 statistic are usually not met (Geiser, 2010, p. 260).

the minimum information measures is best suited. Different information measures are the AIC (*Akaike's Information Criterion*), the BIC (*Bayesian Information Criterion*), and the aBIC (*sample size adjusted BIC*) (Bacher & Vermunt, 2010, p. 557; Geiser, 2013, p. 269; McCutcheon, 2002, p. 69; Rost, 2004, p. 157). The entropy (*entropy*) indicates how well or clearly the different classes are separated from each other, with values close to 1 indicating a good separation, while values close to 0 indicate a poor separation (Celeux & Soromenho, 1996, p. 6; Geiser, 2013, p. 247). Since in LCAs the individuals (or tasks) are assigned to a class with a certain probability, the average assignment probability (*average latent class probabilities*) is a relevant quality criterion of a class solution. This refers to the probability with which a person (or a task) of a certain class k is actually assigned to the class k. The average assignment probability should be at least 80% (Geiser, 2013, p. 248).

The implementation of the LCA is carried out using the program *MPlus* (Muthén & Muthén, 2017) and based on the approach suggested by Geiser (2013, pp. 232–270). The data from Excel is processed using the program *R* and the use of different packages or commands (*readxl, Mplusautomation, prepareMplusData*). The specification of LCA models is enabled in *MPlus* via the module for analyzing mixture distribution models (*analysis: type = mixture*). Included in the analysis are variables describing the operational reality (process orientation, representation of goods flows, cash flows, and social processes, as well as document use), which are ordinal-scaled features with three characteristics (except for document use, which was dichotomously coded). In addition, the variables of the modeling cycle (the sub-steps of orientation, translation, operation, interpretation, validation, and decision-making) are included in the analysis in a condensed form. The exact description of the included variables is given in the presentation of results in Sect. 7.3.2. All variables of the analysis are defined as categorical using the command *categorical*.

One difficulty that can occur when calculating LCAs is so-called local likelihood maxima. Here, due to an insufficiently large number of sets of parameter starting values, a suboptimal or local solution (*local solution*) is identified because the model estimation process ends at a local likelihood maximum. These local solutions often coincide with incorrect fit statistics and parameter estimates. With solutions with a higher number of classes, the risk of local likelihood maxima is significantly higher. To avoid local maxima, Geiser (2013, p. 240) formulates a series of recommendations:

- Firstly, attention should be paid to a sufficiently large set of random starting value sets in the first step of model optimization. In addition, the num-

ber of iterations should also be increased. This can be determined using the commands *starts* and *stiterations*, with 10 sets of starting values and 10 iterations in the first step set as the default setting in *MPlus*. For more complex models, it is recommended to define at least 500 sets of starting values and 50 iterations.
- In addition, the replicability of the best log-likelihood value should be checked by at least two different sets of starting values.
- Since local maxima occur much more frequently with solutions with many classes, a model with fewer classes should generally be preferred.

6.3 Planning of Data Collection and Specification of the Sample

6.3.1 The Evaluative Content Analysis as a Method of Data Collection

The aim of the research project is to develop a subject-didactic category system with which tasks from the accounting domain can be analyzed and evaluated. For this purpose, the category system presented in Chap. 5 will be used, by judging for each task whether and to what extent the given criteria are met. Thus, an assessment of the material based on predetermined categories is to be made. A suitable method for assessing material is evaluative content analysis. Evaluative content analysis belongs to the family of qualitative content analysis. This is understood as "the systematic and methodically controlled scientific analysis of texts, images, films, and other contents of communication. [...] The focus of qualitative analysis is on categories with which the entire material relevant to the research question(s) is coded. [...]" (Kuckartz & Rädiker, 2022, p. 39).

Evaluative content analysis is, alongside the structuring qualitative content analysis and the type-forming qualitative content analysis, the third variant of content analysis (Kuckartz & Rädiker, 2022). Mayring (2015), on the other hand, distinguishes four different types of content analysis: formal structuring, content structuring, typifying structuring, and scaling structuring. Evaluative content analysis and scaling structuring are similar in terms of process and essential objectives. Therefore, the term evaluative content analysis will be used in the following.

The main goal of evaluative content analysis is to "assess material or certain parts of material on a scale (usually ordinal scale)" (Mayring, 2015, p. 106). This distinguishes evaluative content analysis significantly from other forms of content analysis, which, for example, aim to work out structures in the material (formal structuring), summarize contents (content structuring content analysis), or work out typologies from the material (type-forming qualitative content analysis or typifying structuring). What all forms of content analysis have in common is that they work in a compressing, summarizing, and category-based manner. The focus of the evaluation is therefore on analytical categories that are applied to the material and subsequently summarize it and reduce its complexity. It is also essential that these are systematic, rule-guided procedures whose application can be described in detail and comprehensibly (Kuckartz & Rädiker, 2022, pp. 111–112; Mayring, 2015, p. 13).

The ideal-typical process of evaluative content analysis is presented below and transferred to the own research project. Figure 6.1 shows the ideal-typical process of evaluative content analysis (Mayring, 2015, p. 107).

Step 1: Determination of the Units of Analysis
Step one consists of determining the *analysis* units. This should be distinguished from the concept of selection units. *Selection* units (*sampling units*) "represent

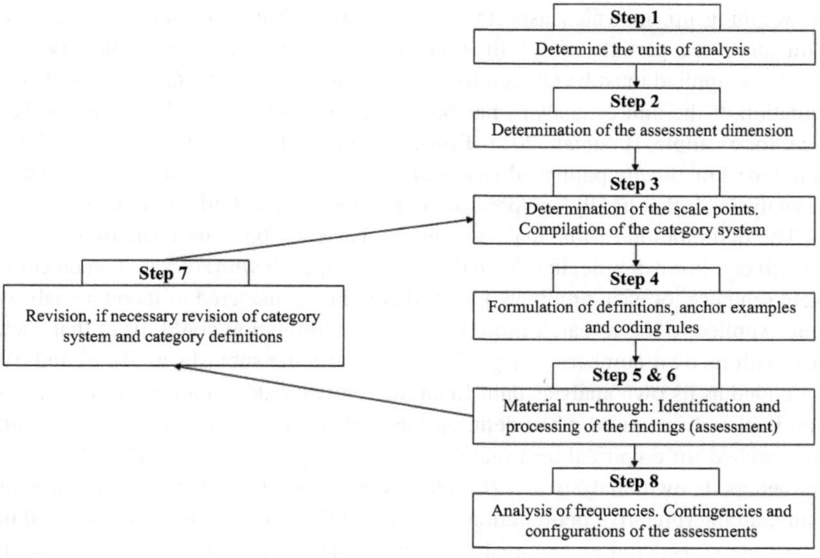

Fig. 6.1 Process of evaluative content analysis according to Mayring (2015, p. 107)

the basic unit of a content analysis and are selected from the total population (i.e., the set of all potential objects of study) for the content analysis according to a certain selection procedure" (Kuckartz, 2018, p. 30). A selection unit can, for example, be an issue of a newspaper or an interview. In the present project, the selection units are the tasks contained in the textbooks. These were determined using a stratified random selection from the total sample.

The unit of analysis (*unit of analysis* or *recording unit*) determines which units are analyzed and evaluated separately from each other. A selection unit can consist of several units of analysis (e.g., a newspaper consists of several articles, the newspaper represents the selection unit, the individual articles represent the units of analysis), but each unit of analysis is part of a selection unit (Kuckartz, 2018, pp. 30–31).

The determination of the units of analysis in the context of task analysis is a challenging task. For the present project, it is necessary to define whether a task consisting of several subtasks is defined as one unit of analysis, whether the subtasks represent separate units of analysis, or whether there are several units of analysis within the subtasks that need to be assessed separately from each other. Looking at previous task analyses, two problems emerge. First, there is no "rule of thumb" for determining the units of analysis. Rather, it is an iterative process of weighing up, in which aspects such as manageability, accuracy, the sample (full survey vs. partial survey), the objective of the project, and the category system to be applied must be taken into account. This leads to the fact that the determination of the unit of analysis has been handled very differently in past studies (see, for example, Bloemen, 2011; Ernst, 2012a; Stock et al., 2011). Second, little is reported in already published task analyses about the determination of the units of analysis, so that hardly any previous experience can be built upon here.

The delimitation of the analysis unit can basically be done formally or interpretatively. For example, in a formal delimitation, each word of a text, each complete sentence, or each article in a journal could be considered as its own analysis unit. Applied to the research project, a formal delimitation could mean that each task with its own numbering (e.g., Exercise 1 with the subtasks a), b), c) and d)) is defined as its own analysis unit. In an interpretative delimitation, an interpretation is already required when defining the analysis unit. For example, a text can be searched for empirical information, values, or specific topics and each can be defined as its own analysis unit (Lamnek & Krell, 2016, p. 465). For the present study, an interpretative delimitation could mean that related business cases within a task are considered as one analysis unit. In the present study, the delimitation was made both formally and interpretatively. The first aid was the already conducted study by Stütz et al. (2022), which already provided a sense of how to define analysis units. In addition, colleagues who already had experience with defining analysis units in the context of content analyses were consulted about this issue beforehand.

Three examples are used to illustrate the possibilities for defining an analysis unit and how the analysis unit was defined in the specific cases. An attempt was made to find a suitable balance in order not to define the analysis units too finely or too broadly, as the definition of the analysis unit subsequently influences the results. Figure 6.2 shows a task from a textbook relevant to the project on the topic of "Purchase of Fixed Assets".

If one follows a formal delimitation of the analysis unit, several options for definition arise. One option is that the entire task is considered as *one* analysis unit. Another option would be that tasks a) and b) are considered as two separate analysis units. One analysis unit would therefore represent the posting of the business cases, the second analysis unit the indication of the impact on corporate profit. However, if one looks at the task in terms of content, one sees that the business cases presented there are not related. Different goods are purchased (and depreciated), which each represent fixed assets or low-value economic goods. For each booking, it must then be indicated whether it is a neutral booking or whether it affects the profit of the company. In this (and structurally identical) tasks, it was therefore proceeded in such a way that each business case repre-

Ü 1.5 Recording the purchase of fixed assets, effect on profit or loss

Möbeltischlerei Christian Simhandl OG purchases the following assets:

15. 3.	K 313	Säge € 42,– + € 8,40 USt = € 50,40
16. 7.		Milling and drilling machine according to the adjacent invoice, immediate commissioning, useful life eight years, account number of the supplier Zgonc Handelsges.m.b.H. 33820
4.10.	E 865	Purchase of a desk for the office of Christian Simhandl € 1,890-+€ 378,- VAT = € 2,268- from Büroeinrichtungs-Gesellschaft mbH (33406)
25.10.	K 1172	Replacement battery for the hammer drill € 49,-+ € 9,80 USt = = € 58,80 from Maschinenhandels-Gesellschaft mbH against cash payment

Task: a) Set up the accounting records for these transactions. The low-value assets are posted to account 0480 Low-value machinery when purchased and fully depreciated on December 31 (U 34). C

b) Indicate whether the respective transaction increases (↑) or decreases (↓) equity, or whether it is a posting with no effect on income (Ø). D

Buchungstrainer
Ü 1.5

ZGONC
Mindestens 5 Jahre ZGONC GARANTIE
auf alle Artikel
E 624
ZGONC Handelsges.m.b.H.
1030 Wien, Modecenterstraße 3
Telefon: +43 1 740 60-0 Serie
FN 928135, Handelsgericht Wien
UID-Nummer: ATU16388102

Möbeltischlerei
Christian Simhandl OG
Gymnasiumstraße 12
2500 Baden
ATU52880994

Bon 232046 /112 16.07.20.. 11:08:41
1 EMCO Werkzeugfräs-Bohrmaschine Type FB-1 8.640,00A
Summe EUR 8.640,00
Summe EUR 8.640,00
A=Mwst 20 % 1.440,00A 7.200,00 Nt

Fig. 6.2 Example 1 for determining the analysis unit

sents its own analysis unit. The indication of the impact of the business case on the success of the company is always taken into account with the respective business case. The present task therefore consists of four analysis units. An analysis unit consists of the booking of the business case (as a fixed asset or low-value economic good) and the indication of the impact on success. Since the sample was drawn based on the analysis units and not based on the tasks, not each of the four analysis units is represented in the sample.

The second example (Fig. 6.3) shows a task on the topic of "Third Party Prepayments". If one makes a formal delimitation, the entire task can be considered as one analysis unit, as the subtasks are summarized under one task heading. On the other hand, based on the numbering, tasks 1 and 2 can each be seen as one analysis unit. A third option would be that within each subtask (e.g., Task 1 "Honigbienchen KG") each bullet point represents its own analysis unit (e.g., set up booking during the year, make adjustments, make bookings in the new year, indicate impact on success). In this and comparable cases, tasks 1 ("Honigbienchen KG") and 2 ("Live your Life GmbH") each represent separate analysis units, as they are not related business cases and the tasks concern different companies. However, no further differentiation is made within the subtasks, as all substeps concern one business case. The present task "Third Party Prepayments" therefore consists of two analysis units.

Tasks – "Third-party advance payments"

1. **Honigbienchen KG:** Honigbienchen KG has been asked by a customer to extend the original payment deadline (November 30) to January 30. The receivable due amounts to EUR 13,700.00 incl. 20% VAT and has already been booked. On December 1, corresponding deferral interest in the amount of EUR 30.00 is incurred. On January 14, the outstanding receivable is received in the bank account (SPK).

   - Make the postings during the year.
   - Then carry out the accrual/deferral on the balance sheet date.
   - What postings are made in the new year?
   - How do the posting records affect the company's success?

2. **Live your Life GmbH:** Live your Life GmbH rents out high-priced real estate to private and business customers. When renting a warehouse, the rental agreement stipulates that the rent is due quarterly on January 20, April 20, July 20 and October 20.

   EUR 18,000.00 incl. 20% VAT is received in the bank account on October 20 of the closing year.
   - Make the postings during the year.
   - Then carry out the accruals and deferrals on the balance sheet date.
   - What postings are made in the new year?
   - How do the posting records affect the company's success?

Fig. 6.3 Example 2 for determining the analysis unit

In addition to the delimitation of the sampling unit and the analysis unit (coding unit), the context unit (context unit) must also be taken into account. The context unit is defined as "the largest unit that may be consulted in order to understand and correctly categorize a coding unit" (Kuckartz, 2018, p. 44). Particularly relevant for the context unit in the context of task analysis are the introductory explanations for the tasks and the information texts in the textbook. This can better assess what expectations are placed on the learners. This will also be illustrated by an example. The following question is found in the sample (embedded in a larger example): "Are credit card payment expenses subject to sales tax? Justify your answer."

If the context unit is *not* taken into account in the analysis of the task (in this case the information texts in the book), one could argue that the task requires an explanation/solution to be justified using a legal norm. In this case, it would have to be stated that expenses for credit card payments are not subject to sales tax because they are tax-exempt according to § 6 para. 1 Z8 e UStG. The task would therefore be coded with 1 for norm orientation. If the information texts in the book are taken into account, then a few pages earlier it reads: "Expenses for credit card payments are not subject to sales tax". It is therefore plausible to assume that the task does *not* aim for the learners to argue using the relevant legal text, but rather it is a matter of reproduction performance. It is therefore coded with 0 for norm orientation.

The categories "Process Orientation" and "Process Orientation of Task Processing" occupy a special position, as they are about whether the learners realize that the respective business case is part of an event chain and whether the learners have to process several sub-steps of this event chain themselves (for a description of the categories see Sect. 5.2). The process orientation can either be given if the task itself refers to a previous sub-step (e.g. "We purchased a machine for production on May 2.") or if it indirectly emerges from the task that the business case is part of an event chain. If one looks at an example (Fig. 6.4), different business cases are dealt with in it (purchase of raw materials, sale to a customer, bank receipt for renting storage space, etc.). However, if one looks closer at the business cases, some business cases represent an event chain, which is however "interrupted" by other business cases that have no connection with these. Thus, the business cases of January 13 and January 20 are related (purchase of raw materials and subsequent payment), as are the business cases of January 23 and January 25 (sale of a fence and subsequent return). For simplification reasons, in such and similar cases (with sometimes significantly more business cases), each business case was considered as its own analysis unit. However, in the analysis of the process orientation, the other analysis units were considered as context units. For example,

3. **Metal construction Hummer:** There is a lot to do at the metal construction company Hummer based in Freistadt. The following business transactions still need to be properly recorded in the accounting system.

Date	Voucher	Business transaction
13. 1. 20..	ER 14	Purchase of steel (raw material) from the supplier Weber (33031) for 14,592.00 EUR + 20 % VAT For the delivery, a further 457.00 EUR including 20 % VAT will be charged for the delivery. The terms of payment are: net cash within 30 days.
15. 1. 20..	AR 3	Sale of a steel staircase worth EUR 5,765.00 excluding 20% VAT (payable within 14 days) to the customer Eder (20067).
18. 1. 20..	ER 15	The forwarding company Speedy GmbH (33859) charges the customer Eder EUR 259.00 gross for the transportation of the staircase.
19. 1. 20..	HY 23	For renting storage space to Mr. Brückl, the company receives the monthly rent of EUR 456.80 including 20% VAT transferred to the HYPO bank account.
20. 1. 20..	HY 24	Transfer of the ER 14.
22. 1. 20..	KA 34	Purchase of office supplies worth EUR 145.00 gross.
23. 1. 20..	AR 4	Sale of a fence for EUR 13,490.00 gross to the customer Berger (20107). The invoice is to be paid within 14 days without deduction.
25. 1. 20..	SO 1	Two fence elements are damaged and are returned by the customer Berger. A gross amount of EUR 860.00 is credited.
26. 1. 20..	KA 35	A customer orders spare parts (screws etc.). The products are sent by Post AG (parcel with approx. 1 kg). EUR 10.00 is paid in cash for the shipment.

Fig. 6.4 Example 3 for determining the analysis unit

if the business case of January 25 was included in the sample, then the coding of the process orientation (and the process orientation of task processing) took into account that the sale was previously discussed and had to be processed by the learner (both the process orientation and the process orientation of task processing were therefore coded with 1, as two sub-steps were dealt with *and* processed by the learner.)

In summary, the following rules were established and taken into account for determining the analysis or context units:

- If different business cases are dealt with within a task that are not related, then each business case represents its own analysis unit. The same applies to knowledge questions, which usually also each represent their own, separate analysis units.
- If a task contains a business case for which several tasks have to be completed, then this is usually to be coded as one analysis unit.
- The assessment of the impact on success (or other interpretations such as the impact of a business case on the balance sheet or the liquidity of the company) are never considered as a separate analysis unit, but are always taken into account with the business case that is to be interpreted.

- If task assignments allow for interpretation (e.g. "Justify your answer."), the information texts in the book should be considered as a context unit in order to better estimate what exactly the task assignment requires.
- Especially when evaluating the category of process orientation, the other analysis units within a task should be taken into account, even if they are not included in the sample.

Step 2: Determination of the assessment dimension
The most important task in a content analysis, however, is the development of categories. "The success or failure of content analysis depends on its categories, as the categories contain the substance of the research, a content analysis cannot be better than its category system" (Kuckartz & Rädiker, 2022, p. 53). For the present project, it was therefore necessary to find meaningful categories by which a task in accounting can be assessed. Reference points for category formation can be theoretical preliminary work on the one hand, and empirical evidence (i.e. the material at hand) on the other. In a-priori category formation (deductive category formation), the categories are developed independently of the material in advance, for example on the basis of a theory, a formulated hypothesis, an interview guide or an existing structure or the current state of research (Kuckartz & Rädiker, 2022, pp. 72–73; Scheufele & Engelmann, 2009, p. 164). If categories are developed in dealing with the material, then this is inductive category formation (Kuckartz, 2018, p. 72; Kuckartz & Rädiker, 2022, p. 82). For the development of categories for the analysis and evaluation of tasks from the domain of accounting, a deductive approach was initially and primarily chosen. The categories were derived a priori (deductively) from the theoretical preliminary work that was done in the previous sections. Reference concepts are the Linz Level Model (Neuweg, 2020), existing didactic approaches (e.g. the economic-instrumental accounting, Preiß & Tramm, 1996; Tramm, 2003, 2005), competence models from accounting (e.g. Guggemos, 2016; Guggemos & Schönlein, 2015; Preiß, 2005b), but also the modeling cycle from mathematics didactics, which have recently been transferred to accounting (Berding, Beckmann & Kürten, 2019; Blum, 1978, 2011).

When forming categories, a distinction can be made between different types of categories, e.g. among others between fact categories, thematic categories, evaluative categories, analytical categories or formal categories (Kuckartz & Rädiker, 2022, pp. 56–57; Scheufele & Engelmann, 2009, pp. 165–167). In the present project, evaluative categories are used, with which the evaluation of data is carried out on the basis of an evaluation scale.

Steps 3 and 4: Determination of manifestations, compilation of the category system, formulation of definitions, anchor examples and coding rules for the individual categories

Evaluative categories have a defined number of manifestations, on the basis of which the data are assessed. These are usually a dichotomous (e.g. not present—present) or ordinal scale level (e.g. not pronounced—little pronounced—strongly pronounced) (Kuckartz & Rädiker, 2022, p. 56). In the present project, either dichotomous or ordinal scale levels were used depending on the category. For some categories, a dichotomous scale is obvious (e.g. Is a document used or not?), for others an ordinal scaling seems sensible in order to keep the information content as high as possible. It should be noted that the more differentiated the ordinal scale, the more difficult and challenging it is to precisely delimit the manifestations and to classify the task into exactly one manifestation. For this reason, a maximum of three manifestations are defined for the ordinal scales.

The totality of all categories is referred to as the category system. In a category manual, all categories are to be described and defined in terms of content (category definition), coding rules are to be determined and anchor examples are to be established. Ideally, problem and doubt cases are also presented (Kuckartz & Rädiker, 2022, p. 61 ff.; Mayring, 2015, p. 124; Scheufele & Engelmann, 2009, p. 164). The development of the category system was detailed in Chap. 5.

Steps 5 to 7: Material run-through—processing of the findings, revision and revision of the category system and the category definitions

Following the compilation and development of the category system, the material run-through, i.e. the coding of the entire data material, is connected. In the course of the material run-through, new (inductive) categories may be formed and existing categories may be refined and revised.

The task coding was done in an Excel sheet, as the entries in Excel are clear and can be exported to all common statistical programs. In addition to the evaluation categories, the Excel file also contains general information, especially for the identification of tasks (running number of the analysis unit, number of the task, year and semester in which the task is used, textbook and page reference).

The first round of main codings took place from January 2022 to mid-March 2022 and was carried out by the author of the dissertation. Subsequently, some categories were slightly modified, specified, and refined or new categories were added. An adjustment of the analysis units was also made for some tasks. Following this, a cross-coding of all tasks for each category was carried out from March to July 2022. Several objectives were pursued with this. Firstly, a cross-coding should increase the comparability of the codings within a category, as there can be differences in the codings despite the detailed category system. Secondly, a second coding run was necessary anyway, as existing categories were modified on the one hand and new categories were added on the other. Thirdly, all codings should be checked again through the second coding run.

Step 8: Analysis of frequencies, contingencies, and configurations of assessments
In a final step, the codings serve as a basis for carrying out various evaluations. Kuckartz and Rädiker (2022, pp. 167–173) provide different analysis methods for evaluative content analysis. In the present project, the focus is initially on static-tabular evaluations at the level of individual categories or main categories in order to answer research questions 1 to 6. In particular, absolute and relative frequencies as well as measures of location are reported. In addition, Chi-square tests (for dichotomous characteristics) or Kruskal-Wallis tests (for ordinal-scaled characteristics) are carried out to answer research questions 7 and 8. To answer research questions 9 and 10, intercorrelations are reported and a latent class analysis is calculated. The statistical test procedures used were already described in detail in Sect. 6.2.

6.3.2 Definition of the Sample

As already explained in Sect. 1.1, tasks from textbooks are analyzed and evaluated in the present study, which are used in Austrian commercial colleges in the subject of accounting. The subject is found in the cluster "Entrepreneurship—Business and Management", which represents the most extensive cluster in terms of hours in the curriculum (54 out of 152 weekly hours in the core area).[5] In addition to accounting, business administration is the second central subject in this cluster. Both subjects are allocated 14 weekly hours spread over five grades (BMBF, 2014, p. 8).

In addition to the educational and teaching tasks and content for each subject, the curriculum also formulates general educational objectives, job-related learning outcomes for each of the five clusters, general didactic principles, and

[5] In the course of forming clusters, subjects with similar content are grouped and job-related learning outcomes are formulated for each cluster.

teaching principles[6]. The general didactic principles stipulate, among other things, that the curriculum is to be understood as a framework curriculum that should make it possible to take into account innovations and changes in, for example, economy, technology, or science. In addition, the curriculum is designed as a spiral curriculum in which central content is dealt with several times over the five grades, with the level of detail and complexity increasing (BMBF, 2014, p. 4).

In the general educational objectives, different competencies are formulated across clusters and subjects, which the learners should have after completing the commercial college.[7] The cluster "Entrepreneurship—Business and Management" stands for the development of practice-oriented business competence at a high level. Competencies to be promoted include solution and goal orientation, flexibility, communication skills, self-reflection, decision-making joy, teamwork, and customer orientation. Relevant working techniques include the procurement and evaluation of subject-specific information, networked thinking, project management, analytical thinking, and presentation and argumentation skills (BMBF, 2014, p. 3).

In the general educational objectives, the following job-related learning outcomes are stipulated for the subject of accounting:

> In the field of accounting, the students can book ongoing business cases on the basis of original documents in the income-expenditure accounting and double-entry bookkeeping, calculate company-relevant taxes and duties and handle their payment, determine the profit or loss of companies using the income-expenditure accounting, prepare annual financial statements, interpret and evaluate them, carry out cost and price calculations, determine contribution margins and make entrepreneurial decisions based on them, carry out a business settlement, analyze costs and assess their effects on prices and business results. (BMBF, 2014, p. 3)

For the subject of accounting, the didactic principles stipulate entrepreneurship education and the use of modern IT techniques to solve the tasks. In doing so, "practice-oriented tasks and competence-oriented teaching should lead

---

[6]Teaching principles are not assigned to individual subjects, but must be taken into account in the teaching of all subjects. Among other things, entrepreneurship education and economic education and consumer education are established as teaching principles (BMBF, 2014, pp. 6–7).

[7]For example: After completing the commercial academy, the students have the competence a) to use their comprehensive and networked economic knowledge as well as their practical experiences in their professional field of action and their life situation (BMBF, 2014, p. 1).

the students to logical, creative and networked thinking, to precise and persistent work, independently and in a team, as well as to responsible decision-making and action." If possible, connections should also be established between the various subjects, especially those of the cluster (BMBF, 2014, p. 55).

For the selection of textbooks from which the tasks should be taken, inclusion and exclusion criteria were defined in advance. Table 6.1 provides an overview of the general inclusion and exclusion criteria for the selection of textbooks.

Since the quality of tasks for the subject of accounting at Austrian commercial colleges is to be assessed, only textbooks used in commercial colleges and in the subject of accounting are included in the sample. Textbooks for other types of schools or for other subjects are not included in the sample. Furthermore, only textbooks that comply with § 14 SchUG para. 2 "in terms of content and form to the curriculum of the respective school level as well as the competence orientation [...] correspond" are considered for the analysis. According to § 14 para. 4 SchUG, a teacher may "only use teaching materials in class that, according to the result of his conscientious examination, meet the requirements of para. 2 or have been declared suitable for teaching use by the competent federal minister (para. 5)." The textbooks listed in the 2021/22 textbook list for Higher Commercial Schools (Code: 4600) of the BMBWF can be considered

Table 6.1 Inclusion and exclusion criteria for the selection of textbooks

Criterion	Inclusion	Exclusion
Type of school	Textbooks for use in commercial colleges	Textbooks for use in other types of schools
Subject matter	Textbooks for the subject of accounting	Textbooks for other subjects from the business and management cluster, e.g. business administration, business training, project management, practice firm and case studies
Approval/ Accreditation	Textbooks included in the textbook list for the 2021/2022 school year of the Federal Ministry of Education, Science and Research (BMBWF) (Code: 4600)	Textbooks not included in the textbook list for the 2021/2022 school year of the BMBWF (Code: 4600)
Curriculum	Textbooks for the currently valid curriculum	Textbooks for previous curricula
Grades	Textbooks for grades I. to V.	–

to meet this requirement, as they have been previously examined by the competent federal ministry (BMBWF, 2021). This also implies that the textbooks comply with the currently valid curriculum for the commercial college. For the subject of accounting, commercial colleges have textbooks from three different publishers available. Only the respective textbooks, but not any existing exercise books, are included in the sample.

In total, tasks from 15 different textbooks are available. The most recent edition at the time of evaluation was used in each case. The exact bibliographic details of the various books can be found in Table 6.2.

In a first step, the publishers were asked to provide the relevant textbooks. The 15 textbooks are available in hardcopy version. At the same time, all new textbooks contain a code for the e-book versions, which can be accessed via the *digi4school page* (www.digi4school.at). This is a publisher-independent platform where different textbooks can be unlocked using codes. In addition, the publishers offer their own websites where the e-books can be accessed (e.g., the digibox from Trauner (www.trauner-digibox.com) or the platform of Hölzel Verlag (www.lernenwillmehr.at). On these platforms, in addition to the online versions of the textbooks, additional learning materials such as interactive exercise examples, explanatory videos, or learning cards are usually available.

It also seems important from which content areas the tasks should be taken. Different approaches are conceivable here. For example, in previous task analyses, potentially particularly difficult subject areas (Thoma & Schumacher, 2018) or particularly important areas (e.g., learning fields for business processes at Bloemen, 2011) were used. In the present study, tasks are analyzed and evaluated that can be assigned to the area of external accounting, specifically the two major subject areas of *financial accounting* and *annual financial statements,*. This limitation is made for various reasons. Firstly, these two topics are those that are most intensively addressed in the curriculum. They are also dealt with over several years with varying intensity and level of detail (BMBF, 2014, pp. 55–63). In addition, external accounting is still the focus of didactic research, although this can certainly be viewed critically (e.g., Jungwirth, 2015, p. 34). Thus, both the competence model of Guggemos (2016) (see Sect. 2.3.2), the model for describing thought processes when working on accounting tasks by Helm (2016d) and the model for classifying student errors by Seifried et al. (2010) (see Sect. 2.3.3) explicitly or implicitly refer to external accounting. In the "Linzer Ebenenmodell" according to Neuweg (2020), the importance of internal accounting is emphasized, but a differentiation of different levels is again only made for external accounting. If the current state of didactic discussion now forms the starting

Table 6.2 Bibliographic details of the textbooks used

Year	Code	Bibliographic Details
I.	180.065	Dobrovits, I.; Gründl, C. M.; Tolic-Sapina, I.; Schneider, D.; Trinko, S./the accounting book. Corporate Accounting HAK I with digital additional package + E-Book/Verlag Jugend & Volk GmbH
	185.353	Haberl, K.-P.; Veidl, G.; Bauer, H.; Lechner, R./Accounting HAK I with digital additional package + E-Book/Hölzel Verlag GmbH
	170.442	Berlinger, R.; Ackerlauer, I.; Najand-Ellmer, M.; Klein, S.; Rammer, E.; Wilhelmstötter, M./Accounting I HAK incl. digital additional package + E-Book/Trauner Verlag + Buchservice GmbH
II.	180.066	Gründl, C. M.; Dobrovits, I.; Tolic-Sapina, I.; Schneider, D.; Trinko, S.; Stummvoll, K./the accounting book. Corporate Accounting HAK II with digital additional package + E-Book/Verlag Jugend & Volk GmbH
	190.415	Veidl, G.; Bauer, H.; Nitschinger, H.; Sachadonig, G./Accounting HAK II with digital additional package + E-Book/Hölzel Verlag GmbH
	170.775	Berlinger, R.; Ackerlauer, I.; Amon, M.; Najand-Ellmer, M.; Frei, J.; Rammer, E.; Schaur, E.; Wilhelmstötter, M./Accounting II HAK incl. digital additional package + E-Book/Trauner Verlag + Buchservice GmbH
III.	185.279	Gründl, C. M.; Dobrovits, I.; Tolic-Sapina, I.; Schneider, D.; Trinko, S./the accounting book. Corporate Accounting HAK III with digital additional package + E-Book/Verlag Jugend & Volk GmbH
	195.175	Veidl, G.; Bauer, H.; Nitschinger, H./Accounting HAK III with digital additional package + E-Book/Hölzel Verlag GmbH
	175.712	Berlinger, R.; Ackerlauer, I.; Najand-Ellmer, M.; Mayr, H.; Peterbauer, R.; Rammer, E.; Schaur, E.; Schmidhofer, R.; Winkler, A./Accounting III HAK incl. digital additional package + E-Book/Trauner Verlag + Buchservice GmbH
IV.	195.309	Dobrovits, I.; Tolic-Sapina, I.; Gründl, C. M.; Stummvoll, K.; Raso, A.; Schneider, D./the accounting book. Corporate Accounting HAK IV with digital additional package + E-Book
	200.207	Veidl, G.; Bauer, H.; Nitschinger, H./Accounting HAK IV with digital additional package + E-Book/Hölzel Verlag GmbH
	180.719	Berlinger, R.; Ackerlauer, I.; Najand-Ellmer, M.; Rammer, E.; Schaur, E.; Schmidhofer, R.; Wilhelmstötter, M./ Accounting IV HAK incl. digital additional package + E-Book/Trauner Verlag + Buchservice GmbH

(continued)

Table 6.2 (continued)

Year	Code	Bibliographic Details
V.	200.300	Dobrovits, I.; Tolic-Sapina, I.; Gründl, C. M.; Stummvoll, K.; Raso, A.; Schneider, D./the accounting book. Corporate Accounting HAK V with digital additional package + E-Book/Verlag Jugend & Volk GmbH
	185.614	Haberl, K.-P.; Veidl, G.; Bauer, H.; Lechner, R./Accounting HAK V with digital additional package. Annual financial statement analysis and criticism—Controlling—Case studies + E-Book/Hölzel Verlag GmbH
	185.609	Berlinger, R.; Ackerlauer, I.; Najand-Ellmer, M.; Schaur, E.; Schmidhofer, R.; Wilhelmstötter, M.; Peterbauer, R./Accounting V HAK incl. digital additional package + E-Book/Trauner Verlag + Buchservice GmbH

point for the development of the category system, it is obvious to focus on the topics that are centrally discussed in the didactic discussion in a first analysis.

The delimitation of the contents was made on the basis of the currently valid curriculum. The included areas cover ongoing, double-entry bookkeeping (e.g., booking of purchases, invoice settlement, foreign business) as well as year-end closing and balance sheet topics (e.g., provisions, accrual accounting, valuation of receivables, preparation of the balance sheet, etc.). Business arithmetic, income-expenditure accounting, payroll accounting, cost accounting, tax law, international accounting, and controlling are excluded from the analysis. In the 10th semester (5th year), no new subject areas are planned, but the repetition of the teaching material from the past years. These are relevant for the analysis, provided they concern the selected content areas. Table 6.3 shows the relevant chapters of the various textbooks. The chapter titles are given in parentheses.

After defining inclusion and exclusion criteria for the textbooks and a content limitation has been made, it is further necessary to define which types of tasks will be included in the sample. According to the broad definition of the task concept in Sect. 4.1, different types of tasks will be included in the analysis. These can be practice tasks, revision tasks, knowledge questions or case studies. The designation of the different types of tasks varies depending on the publisher. However, there are usually introductory demo examples with a sample solution at the beginning of each chapter, different practice tasks during the chapter, and revision tasks, summarizing examples, case studies, and knowledge questions at the end of a chapter. Excluded from the analysis are demo examples, as these are often not independently processed by the students and serve as an initial intro-

Table 6.3 Relevant chapters of the textbooks for the selection of tasks

Year	Trauner Verlag	Hölzel Verlag	Verlag Jugend & Volk
I.	Chap. 5 (Double-entry bookkeeping)	Chap. 5 (System of double-entry bookkeeping); Chap. 6 (Double-entry bookkeeping in practice); Chap. 7; (Business case studies)*; Appendix Practice*	Chap. 6 (Basics of double-entry bookkeeping I); Chap. 7 (Basics of double-entry bookkeeping II); Chap. 8 (Basics of double-entry bookkeeping III); Chap. 9 (Bookkeeping in practice I); Chap. 10 (Bookkeeping in practice II); Chap. 11 (Bookkeeping in practice III)
II.	Chap. 1 (Double-entry bookkeeping); Chap. 2 (Securities and Leasing—Investing and Financing); Chap. 3 (International Business Activity)	Chap. 1 (Double-entry bookkeeping in practice—Basics); Chap. 2 (Double-entry bookkeeping in practice—Advanced); Chap. 3 (Other Business Cases); Chap. 4 (Goods and Payment Transactions with Foreign Countries); Chap. 7 (Business Case Studies for the 3rd and 4th Semester)*; Appendix Practice*	Chap. 2 (Fixed Assets); Chap. 3 (Accounts Receivable Accounting); Chap. 4 (Accounts Payable Accounting); Chap. 5 (Invoice Settlement); Chap. 6 (Further Bookings from Business Practice); Chap. 7 (Sum and Balance Sheet); Chap. 8 (Other Business Cases); Chap. 9 (Goods and Payment Transactions with Foreign Countries)
III.	Chap. 6 (Annual Financial Statements); Chap. 7 (Case Study on the Annual Financial Statements)	Chap. 6 (Basics of the Annual Financial Statements); Chap. 7 (Asset Valuation); Chap. 8 (Goods and Material Valuation); Chap. 9 (Valuation of Unfinished and Finished Products); Chap. 10 (Business Case Studies for the 5th and 6th Semester)*; Appendix Practice*	Chap. 10 (Overview of the Annual Financial Statements); Chap. 11 (Valuation of Fixed Assets); Chap. 12 (Valuation of Inventories); Chap. 13 (Valuation of Unfinished and Finished Products)

(continued)

Table 6.3 (continued)

Year	Trauner Verlag	Hölzel Verlag	Verlag Jugend & Volk
IV.	Chap. 1 (Basics of Annual Financial Statement Preparation); Chap. 2 (Preparatory Work for the Annual Financial Statements); Chap. 3 (Case Study on the Preparatory Work for the Annual Financial Statements); Chap. 4 (Preparation of the Annual Financial Statements); Chap. 5 (Tax MWR)	Chap. 1 (Valuation of Receivables and Liabilities); Chap. 2 (Accrual Accounting); Chap. 3 (Provisions); Chap. 4 (Preparation of the Annual Financial Statements); Chap. 7 (Business Case Studies for the 7th and 8th Semester)*; Appendix Practice*	Chap. 1 (Annual Financial Statements); Chap. 2 (Current Assets: Receivables Valuation); Chap. 3 (Valuation of Receivables and Liabilities in Foreign Currency); Chap. 4 (Accruals); Chap. 5 (Provisions); Chap. 6 (Equity); Case Studies on Accounting—Comprehensive Exercises and Examples
V.	Chap. 1 (Annual Financial Statement Analysis and Critique); Chap. 3 (Fit for the Matura)*	Chap. 1 (Annual Financial Statement Analysis and Critique); Chap. 3 (Simple Business Case Studies)*; Chap. 4 (Task Formulations for the Preparation for the Written Exam "Business Special Exam")*	Chap. 1 (Annual Financial Statement Analysis: Ratios); Chap. 3 (Case Studies with Tasks from All Years)*

* if a relevant content area is concerned

duction to the topic. Also excluded are questions that are given, for example, in the form of a problem-oriented lesson introduction or in margins as thought impulses, as these usually do not serve the acquisition or application of competencies, but are dedicated to an initial examination of the topic and should provide an introduction to a topic. Only tasks that are printed in the textbook are included in the analysis. Tasks that are contained in additional materials or in the e-book are not included for reasons of clarity.

Table 6.4 provides an overview of the tasks contained in the relevant content areas per textbook. What constitutes *a* task and is counted as a task is initially defined purely *formally* to get a first overview of the number of tasks. What is counted as *a* task is what is summarized under a task heading. So if, for example, the heading is "Task—Maintenance of a facility" and this task is divided into sub-points a), b), c), then this is initially defined as *one* task in the first counting step. It is different with large tasks (e.g. case studies) that contain the processing of tasks from different companies. If, for example, the task is "The annual finan-

Table 6.4 Number of potential tasks by publisher and year

	Trauner	Hölzel	Jugend & Volk	
Year	Number of Tasks	Number of Tasks	Number of Tasks	Σ
I.	54 (3.9 %)	53 (3.8 %)	156 (11.2 %)	263
II.	105 (7.6 %)	106 (7.6 %)	168 (12.1 %)	379
III.	58 (4.2 %)	84 (6.0 %)	93 (6.7 %)	235
IV.	109 (7.8 %)	109 (7.8 %)	114 (8.2 %)	332
V.	52 (3.7 %)	78 (5.6 %)	51 (3.7 %)	181
Σ	**378 (27.2 %)**	**430 (30.9 %)**	**582 (41.9 %)**	
Σ total 1390				

Note: The table only contains the number of tasks from the relevant content areas and therefore does not correspond to the total number of tasks in the textbooks. The percentage share of the total number of tasks is given in brackets

cial statements of the small GmbH" and the task contains sub-points 1) Verena Kaar GmbH (with sub-points a to k), 2) Estermann GmbH (with sub-points a to i) and 3) Tiefbau Gramlinger GmbH (with sub-points a to r), then sub-points 1 to 3 are each counted as one task.

In total, 1390 tasks were identified as potentially relevant for the evaluation. As expected, the most relevant tasks can be found in years II and IV, as the selected content areas (double-entry bookkeeping and balance sheet accounting) are most intensively dealt with in these years. When dividing the tasks by publisher, it can be seen that the books of the publisher Jugend & Volk contain the most (as relevant identified) tasks, followed by Hölzel Publishing and Trauner Publishing. Especially in years I and II, the number of tasks at the publisher Jugend & Volk deviates significantly from the number of tasks at the other publishers. However, this does not mean that the total volume of tasks is more extensive, it could also be that the tasks are more detailed and therefore the number of tasks is higher.

Therefore, the number of tasks should be distinguished from the number of *analysis units* in a further step, as these later represent the characteristic carriers in the task evaluation. Thus, a task can comprise several analysis units if it contains (as in the above example) several, independent subtasks, all of which can be evaluated as individual analysis units. Often, but not always, this is also reflected in corresponding formal aspects, such as outlines (e.g., subdivision into 1., 2.,

Table 6.5 Number of potential analysis units by publisher and grade

	Trauner Publishing	Hölzel Publishing	Publisher Jugend & Volk	
Gr.	Number of Analysis Units	Number of Analysis Units	Number of Analysis Units	Σ
I.	471 (6.5 %)	396 (5.5 %)	722 (10.0 %)	1589
II.	850 (11.7 %)	660 (9.1 %)	766 (10.6 %)	2276
III.	302 (4.2 %)	341 (4.7 %)	305 (4.2 %)	948
IV.	651 (9.0 %)	524 (7.2 %)	421 (5.8 %)	1596
V.	358 (4.9 %)	340 (4.7 %)	137 (1.9 %)	835
Σ	**2632 (36.3 %)**	**2261 (31.2 %)**	**2351 (32.5 %)**	
Σ total 7244				

Note: The respective percentage share of the tasks in the total population is given in brackets

3., or a) b) c)). As a rule, therefore, the number of analysis units is considerably higher than the number of tasks. Thus, the 15 included textbooks contain 7244 relevant analysis units. Table 6.5 shows the number of analysis units per textbook and grade. It turns out that a task consists of an average of five analysis units. The largest number of analysis units was identified in the books of the Trauner publishing house, although these books contain the smallest number of tasks. This can be attributed primarily to the presence of knowledge questions in the books of the Trauner publishing house.[8] The decision of what to define as an analysis unit is a challenging and not unproblematic task and has been handled differently in previous task analyses or sometimes presented in a way that is not very comprehensible. The definition of the analysis units was described separately in Sect. 6.3.1 as part of the description of the evaluative content analysis and backed up with examples.

Since the number of analysis units is estimated to be too extensive for a full survey, a selection must be made. The basis for the sampling is the analysis units. The selection is made using a stratified random sample (*stratified random sam-*

[8] Each knowledge question within a "KnowledgeCheck" block represents its own analysis unit. In contrast, the textbooks of the other two publishers contain hardly any knowledge questions (in the books of the Hölzel publishing house, these are almost exclusively in the online supplementary material) or significantly fewer.

ple) (Döring & Bortz, 2016, pp. 312–313; Quatember, 2019, pp. 101–102). The advantage of the stratified random sample is, on the one hand, that a separate evaluation of the individual layers is possible. Furthermore, if the sample sizes within the layers are selected proportionally to the layer sizes of the total population, representativeness with respect to the respective layering characteristics can be ensured. The rule is that the layers should be chosen so that the characteristic carriers within a layer are as similar as possible, and as different as possible between the layers (Kauermann & Küchenhoff, 2011, pp. 138–144).

To answer research questions 7 and 8 (see Sect. 6.1), in this case, the *year of publication* (five variations) and the *textbook publisher* or the different author groups (three variations) serve as stratification characteristics. Potentially, other stratification characteristics could have been conceivable. The subject area was not used as a stratification characteristic because a precise assignment of topics (e.g., provisions, asset valuation, etc.) would have led to many variations. This would lead to limitations in the later data evaluation, as only a small number of tasks for each subject area are included in the sample. In addition, the different task areas (current, double-entry bookkeeping and balance sheet accounting) indirectly influence the sample selection through the proportional consideration of the layer sizes. The task type was also not used as a stratification characteristic, as the publishers work with different task types and some task types (e.g., knowledge questions) do not occur at all in some books, but in others after each chapter.

The sample sizes of the different strata are considered proportional to the layer sizes in the total population. Larger layers also receive a larger share in the sample. The determination of the *sample size* is primarily based on the evaluation methods to be used. In the sense of an a priori power analysis, depending on the set significance level, the effect size and the test power, "optimal" sample sizes can be determined (Döring & Bortz, 2016, p. 814). The sample size is not problematic for descriptive evaluations. For different significance tests, Döring and Bortz (2016, p. 843) give different sample sizes depending on effect sizes and significance levels. For the Chi-square test, sample sizes of 964 (df = 2) or 1194 (df = 4) are given at a significance level of.05 and small effect sizes, and 107 (df = 2) or 133 (df = 4) for medium effect sizes (Döring & Bortz, 2016, p. 843). Specifically for the Kruskal-Wallis test (H-test) as a non-parametric variance analysis, neither Döring and Bortz (2016) nor Cohen (1988) report optimal sample sizes. For the parametric counterpart, the one-way analysis of variance, sample sizes of 322 (df = 2) or 240 (df = 4) are given at a significance level of.05 and small effect sizes, and 52 (df = 2) or 39 (df = 4) for medium effect sizes. For bivariate correlations, the optimal sample sizes are 617 (small effect sizes) or 68 (medium effect sizes) (Döring & Bortz, 2016, p. 843). For the implementation of

Table 6.6 Sample composition according to stratified sample selection

	Trauner Publisher	Hölzel Publisher	Publisher Jugend & Volk	
Year	Number of Analysis units	Number of Analysis units	Number of Analysis units	Σ
I.	130 (6.5%)	109 (5.5%)	199 (10.0%)	438
II.	235 (11.7%)	182 (9.1%)	211 (10.6%)	628
III.	83 (4.2%)	94 (4.7%)	84 (4.2%)	261
IV.	180 (9.0%)	145 (7.2%)	116 (5.8%)	441
V.	99 (4.9%)	94 (4.7%)	39 (2.0%)	232
Σ	**727 (36.3%)**	**624 (31.2%)**	**649 (32.5%)**	
Σ total		**2000**		

an LCA, very large sample sizes are required (with inferential statistical assurance of the number of classes using the Likelihood-Ratio-Test). Thus, the sample should consist of at least as many people as there are possible response patterns. This leads to the fact that the required sample size, depending on the number of items and response categories, becomes very large (Gollwitzer, 2012, p. 307). This problem can be addressed by simulating the test distribution for small samples with a so-called *bootstrap procedure* or by using so-called information criteria to determine the number of classes (Geiser, 2010, pp. 260–261; Gollwitzer, 2012, p. 308).

Based on the recommendations for the lower limit of the sample size for different methods and considering the claim to analyze as many (yet realistic) tasks as possible, a sample size of 2000 analysis units is determined. This corresponds to approximately 27% of all potentially relevant analysis units. According to the proportional consideration of the number of analysis units per publisher and year, Table 6.6 shows the composition of the sample.

Within the individual stratification characteristics, a random selection is made. The random selection is carried out using the "Select Cases" function of the SPSS statistics program. In the course of the counting process, each analysis unit of a textbook was assigned a number. SPSS then outputs the numbers that were determined by random selection.

7 Presentation of the Results

7.1 Descriptive Results of the Evaluative Content Analysis and Comparisons of Publishers and School Years

The following chapter reports the descriptive findings of the evaluative content analysis. The analysis included 2000 analysis units from 15 different textbooks from three different publishers for the subject of accounting at Austrian commercial colleges.

Table 7.1 first provides an overview of all evaluated categories and presents the absolute and relative frequencies for the total sample. An initial overview of the results shows that many codings are at level 0 in almost all categories. This applies, for example, to the categories for references to business administration and internal accounting (cost accounting and liquidity management) as well as the characteristics inductively derived from the material. Many codings at level 0 also exist for the sub-steps of interpreting (e.g., indicating the impact on the tax burden or liquidity), validating, and deciding. Comparatively more codings at level 1 exist in the sub-step of translating and in different characteristics of the task stem (e.g., use of documents). Overall, the descriptive findings suggest that the tasks only inadequately meet the requirements set by the category system.

Table 7.2 provides an overview of the significant differences between tasks from different publishers or years. The test statistics of all tests conducted are also included in the appendix in the electronic supplementary material. To determine differences, subcategories were combined into main categories. Thus, a total of 15 characteristics were determined to see if differences exist between tasks from different publishers or years. The overview of the results shows that significant differences exist in almost all characteristics. For example, tasks from

S. Reindl-Stütz, *Characteristics of Tasks in the Domain of Accounting*,
https://doi.org/10.1007/978-3-658-48958-8_7

Table 7.1 Overview of the Descriptive Findings

			absolute and relative frequencies		
		Categories	**0**	**1**	**2**
	Task master	Process reference	1,097 (54.85 %)	643 (32.15 %)	260 (13.00 %)
		Goods and Service flows	996 (49.80 %)	988 (49.40 %)	16 (0.80 %)
		Cash flows	1,209 (60.45 %)	707 (35.35 %)	84 (4.20 %)
		Social processes	1,866 (93.30 %)	116 (5.80 %)	18 (0.90 %)
		Use of documents	1,056 (52.80 %)	944 (47.20 %)	
	Orientation	Recognize activity	263 (13.15 %)	1,659 (82.95 %)	78 (3.90 %)
		Information research	1,254 (62.70 %)	586 (29.30 %)	160 (8.00 %)
		Information evaluation	1,261 (63.05 %)	697 (34.85 %)	42 (2.10 %)
Modeling Cycle	*Translate*	Translation performance by Other work	1,787 (89.35 %)	213 (10.65 %)	
		Translation work by Postings	548 (27.40 %)	1,452 (72.60 %)	
	Operate	Intra-accounting Postings	1,787 (89.35 %)	213 (10.65 %)	
		Preparation of balance sheet	1,952 (97.60 %)	48 (2.40 %)	
		Prepare income statement	1,960 (98.00 %)	40 (2.00 %)	
		Prepare MWR	1,980 (99.00 %)	20 (1.00 %)	
		Other internal work Work	1,961 (98.05 %)	39 (1.95 %)	
		Mathematical work	800 (40.00 %)	1,200 (60.00 %)	
	Interpret	Profit impact	1,312 (65.60 %)	688 (34.40 %)	
		Liquidity impact	1,997 (99.85 %)	3 (0.15 %)	
		Impact on balance sheet	1,945 (97.25 %)	55 (2.75 %)	
		Effect on tax burden	1,994 (99.70 %)	6 (0.30 %)	
		Effect on External presentation	1,998 (99.90 %)	2 (0.10 %)	
		Other interpretations	1,972 (98.60 %)	28 (1.40 %)	
	Validate/ decide	Validate/justify	1,902 (95.10 %)	98 (4.90 %)	
		Standardization	1,983 (99.20 %)	17 (0.85 %)	
		Business management Making business decisions	1,992 (99.60 %)	8 (0.40 %)	
	Networking	KORE	1,981 (99.05 %)	19 (0.95 %)	
		FINRE	1,985 (99.25 %)	15 (0.75 %)	
		BW	1,959 (97.95 %)	41 (2.05 %)	
	Inductive	Reverse format	1,992 (99.60 %)	8 (0.40 %)	
		Target shape	1,956 (97.80 %)	44 (2.20 %)	
		Change of perspective	1,961 (98.05 %)	39 (1.95%)	

Abbreviations: KORE = Cost Accounting; FINRE = Financial Accounting; BW = Business Administration

different publishers differ in terms of process orientation, representation of operational reality, the need for information research and evaluation, and interpretation and validation services to be provided. Differences were also identified at the level of the years, for example, in the use of documents, the process orientation, or the representation of operational reality.

Table 7.2 Overview of Significant Differences between Publishers and/or Years

Category	Leveling	Procedure	Differences		Detailed Results
			Publisher	Year	
Process Orientation	ordinal	Kruskal-Wallis	yes	yes	• Significant differences between all three publishers (tasks of the Hölzel publisher with highest values, tasks of the Trauner publisher with lowest values) • Significant differences between the 1st year and the other years as well as between the 3rd year and the 4th or 5th year (tasks of the 1st year with the lowest values, tasks of the 3rd year with the highest values)
Representation of Reality	ordinal	Kruskal-Wallis	n. s.	yes	• Significant differences between 4th or 5th year and the other years (in the 4th and 5th year, an above-average number of tasks with no representation of operational reality)
Use of Documents	dichotomous	χ^2-Test	n. s.	yes	• 5th year significantly above expected value, 2nd year significantly below expected value
Activity Recognition	ordinal	Kruskal-Wallis	yes	yes	• Significant differences between the Hölzel publisher and the other publishers (tasks of the Hölzel publisher achieve higher values) • Significant differences between the 5th year and the other years (tasks of the 5th year achieve higher values)
Information research	ordinal	Kruskal-Wallis	yes	yes	• Significant differences between Trauner Verlag and Jugend & Volk Verlag (tasks from Jugend & Volk Verlag often require information gathering) • Significant differences between the 5th grade and the other grades (tasks from the 5th grade often require information gathering)
Evaluate information	ordinal	Kruskal-Wallis	yes	yes	• Significant differences between Trauner Verlag and Jugend & Volk Verlag (tasks from Jugend & Volk Verlag often require information evaluation) • Significant differences between the 5th grade and the other grades (tasks from the 5th grade often require information evaluation)
Translate	dichotomous	χ^2-Test	yes	yes	• Hölzel Verlag significantly above expected value, Jugend & Volk Verlag significantly below expected value • 2nd grade significantly above expected value

(continued)

Table 7.2 (continued)

Category	Leveling	Procedure	Differences		Detailed Results
			Publisher	Year	
Internal accounting operations	dichotomous	χ^2-Test	yes	yes	• Jugend & Volk Verlag significantly above expected value, Hölzel Verlag significantly below expected value • 1st and 4th grade significantly above expected value, 2nd grade significantly below expected value
Work mathematically	dichotomous	χ^2-Test	n. s.	yes	• 4th grade significantly above expected value, 1st and 2nd grade significantly below expected value
Interpret	dichotomous	χ^2-Test	yes	yes	• Hölzel Verlag significantly above expected value, Trauner Verlag significantly below expected value • 2nd grade significantly above expected value, 3rd grade significantly below expected value
Validate	dichotomous	χ^2-Test	yes	n. s.	• Jugend & Volk Verlag significantly above expected value, Hölzel Verlag significantly below expected value
Legal Norm orientation	dichotomous	χ^2-Test	yes	n. s.	• Jugend & Volk Verlag significantly above expected value
Connections to business content	dichotomous	χ^2-Test	yes	n. s.	• Jugend & Volk Verlag significantly above expected value, Trauner Verlag significantly below expected value
Specification of a formal goal	dichotomous	χ^2-Test	yes	yes	• Trauner Verlag significantly above expected value, Hölzel Verlag significantly below expected value • 4th and 5th grade significantly above expected value, 1st and 2nd grade significantly below expected value
Change of perspective	dichotomous	χ^2-Test	yes	yes	• Trauner Verlag significantly below expected value, Jugend & Volk Verlag significantly above expected value • 2nd grade significantly above expected value, 5th grade significantly below expected value

Note: Presentation of significant differences between publishers and/or grades; n. s. = not significant

The following Sect. 7.1 reports the detailed results for each category. The structure of the chapters follows this logic: First, the descriptive results for the total sample are graphically and/or tabularly presented and described. This is followed by examples for each level of the respective category. Subsequently, differences between tasks from different publishers and from different years are discussed. In Sect. 7.2, the results on the reliability of the content analysis are presented. In Sect. 7.3, the results of the correlation analyses (intercorrelation matrix) and the latent class analysis are reported. A discussion and critical examination of the results, as well as the integration with existing research findings, is provided in the following chapter (Chap. 8).

7.1.1 Results for the Process Orientation Category

Descriptive findings of the process orientation category

Looking at the results of the frequency analysis for the total sample (Fig. 7.1), it is evident that around 55% of the tasks do not have a process orientation. This corresponds to a total of 1097 tasks. A limited process orientation was found in 32.2% (n = 643) of the tasks. So, while reference was made to previous or subsequent business transactions, a comprehensive chain of events (multiple business transactions) was omitted. A comprehensive process orientation is given in 260

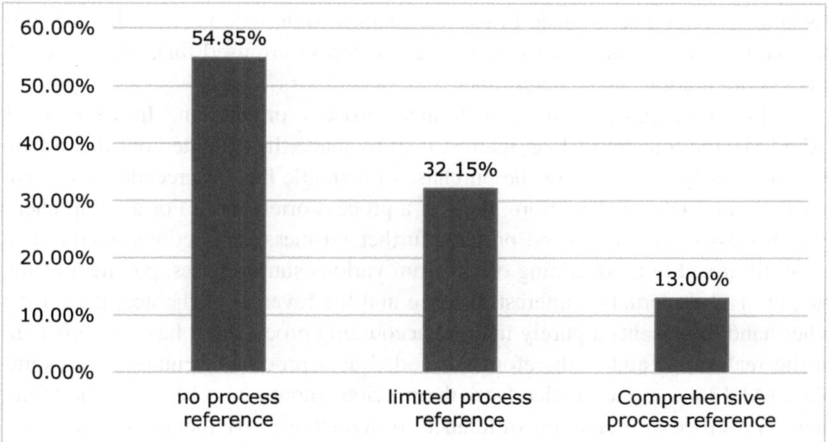

Fig. 7.1 Relative frequencies of the category process orientation

tasks (13.0%), as a chain of events was presented by referring to several previous and/or subsequent business transactions. The median is 0. The results thus show that the majority of the analyzed tasks *focus* on a single business transaction in isolation, and the reference to relevant upstream and downstream processes is often neglected. Nonetheless, many tasks at least refer to a previous or later business transaction. However, the representation of a comprehensive chain of events occurs significantly less frequently.

Examples of different levels of the category process orientation
Table 7.3 presents various examples for the category at individual levels. Tasks that have no process orientation are classified at level 0. In example 1 (AE29), the cash purchase of packaging material is discussed, previous or subsequent processes of reality that are related to the present business transaction are not represented. It should be noted for this type and structurally similar tasks (e.g., cash payment for office supplies or professional literature, cash payment of a fuel bill, payment of postage fees, etc.) that the connection to other relevant business transactions is not immediately apparent (because they often do not exist) and a reference to real processes appears less relevant than in other business transactions (e.g., purchase of a production machine or other fixed assets, sale of goods to customers, etc.). Example 2 (AE134) is a classic knowledge question. In this and similar tasks, there is no reference to a specific company, as these are usually formulated abstractly and without context. Therefore, no process orientation can be determined. In the context of AE 514 (example 3), a depreciation has to be booked, no reference is made to related business transactions (e.g., the previous purchase of the trucks or hints as to what the trucks are used for). Therefore, no process orientation can be determined.

Tasks of category 1 have a limited process orientation. In example 1 (AE1144), the transfer of loan interest is to be made. It is pointed out that a loan was previously taken out for the purchase of a shuttle bus (= preceding, relevant business transaction). Therefore, there is a process orientation. For a comprehensive process orientation to be present, further business transactions would have to be discussed (e.g., obtaining offers from various shuttle buses, payment of the bus, etc.) The accrual of interest expense and the reversal of the accrual, on the other hand, represents a purely internal accounting process that has no equivalent in the real world and is therefore not coded as a process orientation. In example 2 (AE1368), a due invoice from the previous month is to be paid. Therefore, there is a process orientation (reference to invoicing at payment). In example 3 (AE843) of level 1, there is also a limited process orientation. Both the purchase and the later complaint of the goods are dealt with. Thus, two content-related

Table 7.3 Example tasks at the different levels of the Process Orientation category

Category	Example tasks from the sample
No Process Orientation (0)	**Example 1 (AE29):** Book the following business cases: KA 86: On March 6, 20.. we buy packaging material for 36.40 EUR incl. 20% VAT. We pay in cash.
	Example 2 (AE134): Name the account class in which raw materials can be found.
	Example 3 (AE514, excerpt): The following facts must still be taken into account in the balance sheet work as of December 31, 2020. 4. The depreciation of the existing trucks amounts to 42,500.00 EUR.
Limited Process Orientation (1)	**Example 1 (AE1144):** The Hotel Heiligkreuz takes out a loan of € 30,000 from Express Credit for the purchase of a shuttle bus. The credit agreements include, among other things, that the loan interest must be paid in advance for half a year. August 23: B121 Transfer of € 900 in loan interest for half a year in advance to Express Credit. Booking on account 8290 Interest expense for loans. December 31: U 46 The interest expense is to be accrued. January 1, next year: U4 The accrual is to be reversed. a) Set up the booking sentences from the point of view of the Hotel Heiligkreuz for the old and the new year. b) Indicate whether the respective booking increases, decreases the equity or whether it is a neutral booking.
	Example 2 (AE1368, excerpt): Your tasks: a) Tick next to the account designations on the accounts whether it is an active or passive inventory account. b) Enter the business cases on the accounts. The accounts have already been opened. Don't forget to specify the counter account next to the date. c) Tick in the margin column the type of booking: Is it a balance sheet extension, a balance sheet reduction, an active exchange or a passive exchange? January 5, 20..: Valerie Weber goes to one of her suppliers to look at and test brand new fitness equipment. She pays a bill due from the previous month in cash: € 700.00.
	Example 3 (AE843, excerpt): In the sports shop Andreas Egger e. U. the following business cases arise in April, among others: April 10: E 348 The Lisa Lobnik OG delivers ten Arctic synthetic sleeping bags for € 400 + € 80 VAT = € 480 for later payment. April 13: The seams of the synthetic sleeping bags are often not properly set and sometimes not present at all. A return shipment of the entire delivery was agreed with the supplier Lisa Lobnik OG. The Lisa Lobnik OG issues a credit note for € 480. a) Set up the booking sentences. b) Indicate whether the respective booking increases, decreases the equity or whether it is a neutral booking.

(continued)

Table 7.3 (continued)

<table>
<tr><th>Category</th><th>Example tasks from the sample</th></tr>
<tr><td rowspan="2">Comprehensive Process Orientation (2)</td><td>Example 1 (AE1777):
On August 2, 2020, a new swivel chair for the entrepreneur is delivered by Toy Box. The invoice (date: August 2, 2020) for 1960 € + 20% VAT is transferred from the company bank account as agreed on September 2, 2020. The leather swivel chair is put into operation immediately after delivery. The useful life is ten years. On January 2, 2031, the chair breaks and is disposed of immediately.
a) Book the current business cases for 2020 in the form of booking sentences.
b) Provide all bookings as of December 31 in connection with the depreciation for the years 2020 to 2031 in the form of booking sentences. Depreciation is carried out using the direct method.
c) Present all accounts that are booked in 2020, 2030 and in 2031.</td></tr>
<tr><td>Example 2 (AE 478):
Make the necessary bookings and documents for the company Thomas Radler e.U.:
August 21, 20..: The Run & Relax GmbH, Wiener Straße 24, 4040 Linz, customer account number: 20044 orders four home trainers “Trimm-Max” from Thomas Radler at 289.00 EUR excl. 20% VAT each.
August 22, 20..: The invoice for the four delivered home trainers (AR 561) is created and sent to the Run & Relax GmbH. It shows the following picture:
<table>
<tr><th colspan="2">Invoice</th></tr>
<tr><td>4 pieces exercise bike "Trimm-Max" à 289,00 EUR</td><td>1,156.00 EUR</td></tr>
<tr><td>+ 20 % VAT</td><td>231.20 EUR</td></tr>
<tr><td>Invoice amount</td><td>1,387.20 EUR</td></tr>
</table>
Payable within 10 days with 2% discount or 30 days without deduction.
September 29, 20..: The Run & Relax GmbH has not yet paid the AR 561. Therefore, set up a polite payment reminder.
October 12, 20..: The Run & Relax GmbH has not responded to the reminder. Therefore, send a second reminder, asking your customer to settle the outstanding invoice by October 22, 20..
October 25, 20..: Despite your reminders, the Run & Relax GmbH has not responded. Therefore, send a third and final reminder and set a final payment deadline until November 4, 20...
November 6, 20..: Your customer has not responded to the third reminder. Therefore, you call your customer and learn that the company has applied for a restructuring procedure and will offer a quota of 30%.
November 13, 20..: You read in the newspaper that the restructuring procedure has been opened.
December 31, 20..: As part of the annual financial statements, you have to take into account that the restructuring procedure has been opened at your customer. The OP list shows the following picture (OP list depicted). You have properly registered your claim with the court. No value adjustment is shown on account 2080. You expect a quota of 20%.
May 12, next year: In the official gazette of the Wiener Zeitung, you read that the accepted payment plan has been confirmed and a quota of 50%, payable in three installments, has been decided. Make the necessary booking!
December 31, next year: There are neither dubious nor irrecoverable receivables. The value adjustment shown on account 2080 is therefore to be reversed.</td></tr>
</table>

business transactions are addressed. Tasks of the category with a comprehensive process orientation represent relevant business transactions as a chain of events by dealing with several consecutive processes. This allows learners to gain better insight into real operational processes and to view accounting processes in the light of real processes. In example 1 (AE1777), delivery, payment, ongoing wear and tear, and disposal of the swivel chair are addressed, which represents a comprehensive process orientation. The indication of the impact on profit, on the other hand, represents an interpretive performance that has no equivalent in the real world and is therefore not evaluated as a process orientation. Example 2 (AE478) represents a very comprehensive chain of events, covering almost all aspects from the order, invoicing, to the payment request, reminder, and treatment of the outstanding receivable in the course of the annual financial statements (depreciation of part of the receivable due to the restructuring process).

As a subcategory of process orientation, it was determined in a further step whether the business cases addressed in the task (if a process orientation exists) actually need to be processed by the learners, or whether they are merely hints in the task that, however, do not lead to any action for the learners. This category was named "Process Orientation of Task Processing" and can therefore only be coded if the process orientation was coded with at least 1 (limited process orientation).

643 tasks were coded as limited process-oriented (i.e., a reference is made to a previous or subsequent business case). However, only one business case had to be processed in 53% (n = 340) of the tasks. In analysis unit 1144 (see Table 7.3), reference is made to the previous loan taken out to purchase a shuttle bus. However, the learner only has to process the payment of the loan interest (but not, for example, the purchase of the bus or the taking out of the loan). The delimitation of the loan interest and the dissolution of the accruals represent a purely accounting process and are therefore taken into account in the intra-accounting operations, but do not represent a process orientation, as this always refers to real, operational processes. Analysis unit 1368 also provides an example of this level of grading. In the remaining 47% (n = 303), the business cases addressed in the task must also be processed by the learners. Analysis unit 843 (see Table 7.3) is an example of this classification. There is a process orientation (reference to incoming invoice and complaint) and both sub-steps have to be processed by the learners (booking of the incoming invoice and booking of the credit note). In 260 tasks (13% of the total sample), a comprehensive process orientation was coded (i.e., an event chain with more than two business cases is presented). However, only one business case of the event chain had to be processed in 7 tasks (2.7%), and in a further 37 tasks (14%) two business cases (e.g., reference is made to

Table 7.4 Cross table of process orientation and process orientation of task processing

		Process orientation of task processing			Total
		One BC to process	Two BCs to process	More than two BCs to process	
Process orientation	Limited process orientation	340	303	0	643
	Comprehensive process orientation	7	37	216	260
Total		347	340	216	903

Note: BC = Business case or business cases

order, purchase, and payment, but only the acquisition and payment have to be processed, not the order). In the remaining 216 tasks (83%), more than two sub-steps had to be processed. Analysis unit 487 (Table 7.3) is an example of this category of tasks. An event chain is presented and this has to be processed by the learners themselves. Table 7.4 summarizes the results in the form of a cross table.

Publisher and year comparisons for the category Process Orientation

Figure 7.2 shows the relative share of codings with "no process orientation", "limited process orientation" and "comprehensive process orientation" for the three different publishers. The evaluations separated by publishers show that the tasks of the different publishers differ in terms of their process orientation. Thus, 62.4% of the tasks of the Trauner publishing house, 45.2% of the tasks of the Hölzel publishing house and 55.6% of the tasks of the Jugend & Volk publishing house have no process orientation. 29.4% of the tasks of the Trauner publishing house, 37.8% of the tasks of the Hölzel publishing house and 29.7% of the tasks of Jugend & Volk are limited process-oriented. 17.0% of the tasks of the Hölzel publishing house are comprehensively process-oriented. For the Jugend & Volk publishing house, the value is 14.6%, for the Trauner publishing house it is 8.1% of the tasks. The median is 0 for the tasks from the Trauner publishing house and from the Jugend & Volk publishing house, and 1 for the tasks from the Hölzel publishing house. A Kruskal-Wallis test conducted shows that the differences in process orientation between the publishers are significant ($H(2) = 45.549$, $p = .001$). Since a Kruskal-Wallis test only shows whether groups differ significantly from each other, but not between which groups there are differences, pairwise comparisons were carried out subsequently. The pairwise post-hoc comparisons with Bonferroni correction show that all three groups differ significantly from each other. The effect sizes range between.086 (pairwise comparison

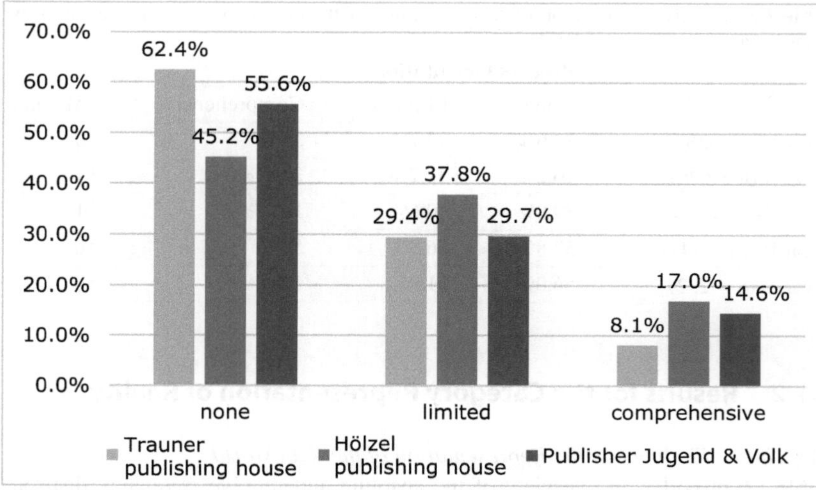

Fig. 7.2 Relative frequencies of the category Process Orientation by publisher

between Trauner publishing house and Jugend & Volk publishing house) and.184 (pairwise comparison between Trauner publishing house and Hölzel publishing house) and can therefore be assessed as weak (Cohen, 1988, pp. 79–80; Field, 2017, pp. 179).

Table 7.5 shows the distribution of level gradings separated by school years. Here too, there are sometimes significant differences between the years. For example, the proportion of tasks without process orientation varies from 39.8% (3rd school level) to 72.6% (1st school level). In the 1st grade, the proportion of tasks with a comprehensive process orientation is 3.7%, while in the 2nd and 3rd grade it is 22.1% and 19.5% respectively. Accordingly, the median for the tasks from the 2nd and 3rd grade is 1, while it is 0 for the other grades. The Kruskal-Wallis test also provides significant results, meaning that the process orientation differs significantly between the grades (H(4) = 126.397, p =.000). The pairwise comparisons between the grades show, as expected, that the tasks of the 1st school year differ significantly from the tasks of the other grades. The effect sizes range between.113 and.334 and can therefore be characterized as weak to medium effects (Cohen, 1988, p. 79–80; Field, 2017, p. 179). Significant differences were also identified between the 3rd and the 4th or 5th grade, as well as between the 2nd and the 4th and 5th school year.

Table 7.5 Relative distribution of level gradings of the categor y process orientation by school year

	Process Orientation			
	None	Limited	Comprehensive	Median
Year I (n = 438)	72.6%	23.7%	3.7%	0
Year II (n = 628)	46.2%	31.7%	22.1%	1
Year III (n = 261)	39.8%	40.6%	19.5%	1
Year IV (n = 441)	57.8%	36.3%	5.9%	0
Year V (n = 232)	56.0%	31.9%	12.1%	0

7.1.2 Results for the Category Representation of Reality

Descriptive Findings on the Representation of the Real World

Table 7.6 provides an overview of the absolute and relative frequency distribution as well as the median values for the subcategories "Representation of Goods and Service Flows", "Representation of Cash Flows" and "Representation of Social Processes".

In all three categories, it is striking that very few tasks achieve coding at the highest level. The detailed and realistic description of goods or service flows, cash flows, and social processes therefore only occasionally appears in the tasks. It is also striking that in 93.3% of the tasks, no social processes are addressed at all, which in turn makes it more difficult for learners to gain insights into operational processes and business reality. Goods and service flows and cash flows are not addressed at all in half or more than half of the tasks. When goods and service flows or cash flows are addressed, they are usually described in a rather abstract and not very concrete way. The comparatively high number of codings at the "detailed" level in the representation of cash flows can be justified by the use of realistic bank statements or bank receipts at this level. It should be noted

Table 7.6 Absolute and relative frequencies of the category Representation of Business Reality

	None	Abstract	Detailed	Median
Goods and Service Flows	996 (49.8%)	988 (49.4%)	16 (0.8%)	1
Cash Flows	1209 (60.5%)	707 (35.4%)	84 (4.2%)	0
Social Processes	1866 (93.3%)	116 (5.8%)	18 (0.9%)	0

that in codings at level 0, no distinction is made between whether the respective flows are not addressed but would basically be relevant for the present business case (e.g., when paying an invoice, it would basically be interesting to know which goods or service flows have flowed in advance that lead to this payment), or whether the nature of the respective business case does not result in any coding (e.g., when forming a provision, there is no cash flow, so it cannot sensibly be addressed; the same applies to the booking of a depreciation, the valuation of a receivable, or many other areas of the annual financial statements).

Examples of different level gradations of the categories for the representation of reality

Table 7.7 shows example tasks of the different level gradations. If we first look at the codings with 0 in the goods and service flows, we often find knowledge questions there (as in the other categories), as these are very often formulated out of context and therefore do not represent business reality. Example 2 and comparable tasks were also coded with "no representation" in the category of goods and service flows, as no goods or service flow takes place in the course of the business case (only a cash flow). In example 3, it is exactly the opposite—a goods or service flow takes place (delivery of the furniture), but the invoice is paid at

Table 7.7 Examples of different level gradations of the category Representation of Reality

Category	Example tasks from the sample
No Representation	<u>**Goods and Service Flows:**</u> **Example 1 (AE135):** State against which account inventory accounts are closed.
	Example 2 (AE736, excerpt): In the Third-Wave-Café "14 Steps", Heidi Grascher e.U., the following business cases occur in November among others: 7. Heidi Grascher withdraws € 1300 from the bank account and puts the money in the business cash register.
	<u>**Cash Flows:**</u> **Example 3 (AE854, excerpt):** 17.3. E260: The freight forwarder Gebrüder Weiss GmbH (33044) submits an invoice of € 325 + € 65 VAT = € 390 for the delivery of the furniture to Karl Frühbichler e.U. a) Formulate the booking entries. b) Indicate whether the respective business case increases, decreases the equity, or whether it is a neutral booking.
	Example 4 (AE1919): Doris Kremser forms for her company Let´s Golf e.U. for the first time this year a provision for anniversary payments (employees): € 3,000.00 (provision value was determined actuarially.) Book the initial formation of the personnel provision and indicate the effect on earnings. *In all the examples mentioned here, no social processes are also included.*

(continued)

Table 7.7 (continued)

Category	Example tasks from the sample
Abstract, less concrete representation (1)	**Goods and service flows:** **Example 5 (AE890, excerpt):** The following business transactions have occurred in the sole proprietorship Karl Müller e.U.: 14.4. E646 Acquisition of a small truck, VW Kasten TDI, purchase value € 18,400,- + € 3600,- VAT = 22,080,- from Hirsch GmbH (33701). a) Record the business transactions. Low-value assets should be recorded immediately upon purchase on account 7060 Depreciation of low-value assets. b) Indicate whether the respective business transaction increases, decreases the equity, or whether it is a neutral booking.
	Example 6 (AE513, excerpt): You must take into account the following facts in the balance sheet work as of 31.12.2020. Note the impact on success for each booking entry! 1. The software package shown on account 0120 Data Processing Program was purchased in January 2018 for 8,840.00 EUR net. The useful life is five years.
	Cash flows: **Example 7 (AE165, excerpt):** Record the business transactions from the perspective of the dishware specialist Mostic e.U. with today's date. SP55 Transfer of the business rent from the bank account at the Sparkasse in the amount of 620.00 EUR plus 20 % VAT.
	Example 8 (AE1572): Bernd buys the Asus monitor and pays for it with the debit card of Softbit GmbH. Enter the corresponding booking in the booking list (date: 30.7). Also indicate how the booking affects the company's success.
	Social processes: **Example 9 (AE1902):** A customer of Let's Golf e.U. is having payment difficulties. Doris Kremser grants him a longer payment term for the outstanding claim in the amount of 9,800.00 € incl. 20 % VAT, due on 02.11.2021, but agrees on default interest at the rate of 8 % p.a. for five months. The customer settles the entire outstanding claim incl. the default interest as agreed—the debit note is sent by email on 02.04.2022 and immediately transferred by the customer. The amount is credited to Doris' bank account on the same day. a) List all bookings for 2021 and 2022 related to the business transaction (accrual, payment—without opening and closing bookings). b) Indicate what type of accrual accounting is involved.
	Example 10 (AE1728, excerpt): Record the business transactions from the perspective of the youth hostel Dragon Backpackers on accounts and indicate the impact on success. 15.03 ER 83 Hotel supplies Tega (33021) delivers Dragon Backpackers 50 dish sets of the Armonia hard glass dish series, consisting of flat plates, coffee cups, etc. The goods are handed over packed in boxes on a pallet. The invoice amounts to 435.00 € + pallet deposit 20.00 € (excl. 20 % VAT). 17.03. S33 20 dish sets do not match the order (wrong color). Magdalena Fritz negotiates a discount of 35 % on the value of the goods for these. She receives the credit note by email.

(continued)

Table 7.7 (continued)

Category	Example tasks from the sample
Detailed representa-tion (2)	**Goods and service flows:**

Goods and service flows:

Example 11 (AE232):

The grocer Aloisia Brunner buys 200 chocolate bunnies from the company Mondelez Austria GmbH for the Easter business. According to the agreement in the purchase contract, Mrs. Brunner has to make a down payment for the delivery. Record the following business transactions from Mrs. Brunner's perspective and indicate what impact these bookings have on success.

26.2.20.. Advance invoice from Mondelez Austria GmbH (33451) for 200 chocolate bunnies in the amount of 150.00 EUR incl. 10 % VAT.
2.3.20.. HY29 Mrs. Brunner transfers the down payment of 150.00 EUR to the company.
10.3.20.. ER 29 Invoice for the delivery of 200 chocolate bunnies

Total net amount	500.00 EUR
– Net down payment	136.36 EUR
Remaining amount net	363.64 EUR
+ 10% VAT	36.36 EUR
Gross remaining amount	**400.00 EUR**

19.3.20.. HY36 Transfer of the remaining amount to the company Mondelez Austria GmbH to settle the incoming invoice of March 10, 20..

Example 12 (AE1870):

In the past fiscal year, all hair dryers (a total of 36 pieces) were replaced by the hair dryer Dry Curl in several branches.

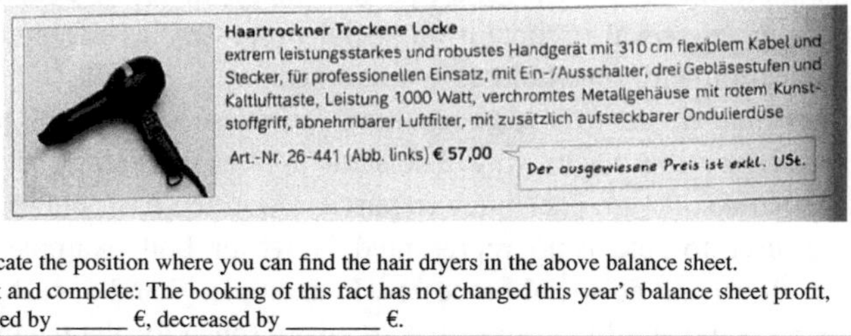

a) Indicate the position where you can find the hair dryers in the above balance sheet.
b) Tick and complete: The booking of this fact has not changed this year's balance sheet profit, increased by ______ €, decreased by _______ €.

Cash flows:

Example 13 (AE327):

Steiner e.U.: Mr. Steiner bought winter interest bonds this business year. At the time of purchase, he was charged accrued interest of 21.27 EUR. On December 31, 20.. he receives the following interest payment. Book the bank statement. *(Bank statement given)*

Social processes:

Example 14 (AE1557):

Finally, Peter Stern is the owner of a multimedia laptop. Unfortunately, a few things went wrong during the purchase: Peter picked up the laptop after a three-week delivery delay from a computer specialty store, initially owing the agreed €1,200.00 excl. VAT. The negotiated payment condition is "Payable within 30 days without deduction or within 8 days less 3% discount". He happily drove back to his business, turned on the laptop and saw—nothing. The screen remained black, only a few pixel errors could Peter recognize. He immediately packed the device back into the box and drove to the shop. However, the device was not broken, but no programs had been installed yet. The seller offered Peter to take over this for an additional cost of €95.00 incl. VAT. For the pixel errors, the two agreed on a price reduction of 5% on the purchase price. Peter paid the entire bill (laptop price and additional costs) minus the discount on the eighth day after the purchase less the agreed discount.

(continued)

Table 7.7 (continued)

Category	Example tasks from the sample
	Complete the following: 1. What are the acquisition costs for the laptop? *(Calculation scheme given)* 2. How much did the laptop actually cost Peter Stern?
	Example 15 (AE520, excerpt): The following facts must be taken into account in the balance sheet work as of December 31. In August of the closing year, the roof was covered at the Breitenfellner family's house. Obviously, the work was done poorly. Mrs. Breitenfellner has already complained several times that water penetrates in some places during heavy rain. The inspection by Mr. Josef Wenzl sen. has shown that the complaint was justified. The following protocol is sent by Mr. Wenzl sen. to the accounting department: Bruck an der Mur, am 29. Dezember 20.. Betrifft: Besichtigung des Daches Fam. Breitenfellner Die Behebung der leichten Baumängel bei Fam. Breitenfellner wird auf 2.000,00 EUR geschätzt. Die Behebung des Schadens wird im Frühjahr des nächsten Jahres erfolgen.

a later date and accordingly there is no cash flow (however, a possible later payment could be referred to). In example 4, a provision is formed. This is a business case that in turn does not trigger a cash flow and is therefore coded with 0. All the examples discussed also contain no social processes, as no internal or external communication with stakeholders is addressed.

In example 5, there is a goods flow (purchase of a small truck), but it is described in a rather vague way. The same applies to example 6. It is clear from the task that a software package was purchased in the past, but exactly what it is, what it is used for, etc. is not represented. However, both examples do not include any cash flows and no social processes. In examples 7 and 8, cash flows occur, as in both cases money flows out of the company (once for the payment of business rent, once for the payment of a computer monitor). In both examples, goods or service flows also occur (rental relationship as a service, computer monitor as a goods flow), but no social processes. However, social processes are included in examples 9 and 10, although these were not represented in great detail. For this reason, both tasks are examples of level 1 (abstract representation) of the "social processes" category. In example 9, it becomes clear that there has been a coordination between the buyer and the seller regarding the extension of the payment target. In addition, it is noted that the two parties have agreed on the payment of default interest. In example 10, the complaint and the negotiation of a discount form the social process, i.e. the communication between the buyer and the seller.

Tasks in which goods and service flows, cash flows and/or social processes are represented in detail are particularly interesting, as they make it easier for learners to gain insight into operational processes. In example 11, although the goods

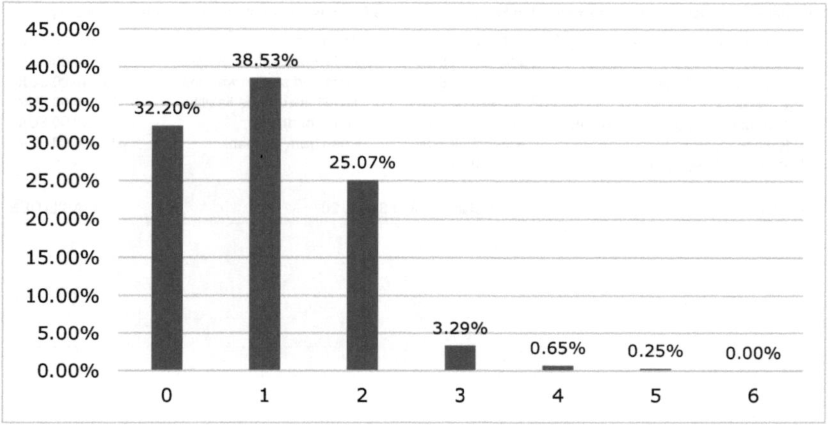

Fig. 7.3 Total values for the category Representation of reality

flows (chocolate Easter bunnies) are not described in detail, a picture is used to visualize the goods. In these and comparable cases, therefore, coding was done with 2 (detailed representation). In addition, in example 11, cash flows are also described in detail (several partial payments) and social processes are at least hinted at (agreement in the purchase contract). In example 12, the goods flow (hair dryer) is represented in detail through the use of a picture and the precise description of the product. Example 13 is an example of a detailed and realistic representation of a cash flow, because a bank statement is used. Examples 14 and 15 are tasks that were coded with level 2 in the representation of social processes. In both cases, communication processes between the company and external stakeholders are described in detail. For example, in example 15, the negotiation of payment targets and conditions, the price discount, and the repair or additional service are addressed. In example 15, the communication between the company and several external persons is also visible (representation of the complaint, inspection by an external expert, protocol of the expert).

If you now add up the values of the three subcategories to a total value for the main category, the following picture emerges (Fig. 7.3):

In total, a maximum value of 6 can be achieved if all three categories are coded at the highest level (i.e., both goods and service flows, cash flows, and social processes are detailed in the task). However, this is not achieved by any task. The median is 1, the mean is 1.02. In 32.2% of the tasks, neither goods or

1. prepare a balance sheet for the Yellow Inn Hotel based on the following information and calculate the equity:

■ Bank balance	27,410.00 EUR	Trade payables	39,300.00 EUR
■ Property	394,260.00 EUR	Receivables from guests	7,650.00 EUR
■ Tax office liabilities	18,930.00 EUR	Cars and station wagons	19,740.00 EUR
■ Cash desk	3,120.00 EUR	Health insurance liabilities	11,400.00 EUR
■ Operating and office equipment	173,610.00 EUR	Stock of drinks	10,230.00 EUR
■ Kitchen stock	6,550.00 EUR	Loan from the bank	221,000.00 EUR
■ Stock of cleaning materials	1,560.00 EUR		

ASSETS	Balance sheet 31.12. 20.	LIABILITIES
Total assets		**Total assets**

Fig. 7.4 Example task for the characteristic "no representation of operational reality"

service flows, cash flows, or social processes are addressed. These are usually pure knowledge questions (examples: "Explain the term equity.", "Explain what a POS terminal is.", "Explain the reason why the inventory accounts are reconciled with the consumption accounts at the end of the year.") In these, usually no reference is made to a company or to operational processes. On the other hand, these are often tasks where purely internal accounting work is to be done (e.g., opening and closing of existing accounts, preparation of a trial balance, calculation of key figures, etc.), and therefore it is also not looked at which processes in the real world lead to these internal accounting works. Figure 7.4 shows an example of this type of tasks.

Most frequently (in 38.5% of the tasks), *one* aspect is treated abstractly (e.g., goods or service flow, cash flow, or social process), in a further 25.07% either one aspect is described in detail (e.g., precise product description or representation of a cash flow using a bank statement) or two aspects are represented abstractly (e.g., abstract description of a product with simultaneous or subsequent payment). 4.2% of the tasks achieve a value of at least 3, which would mean that either all three subcategories are represented in at least an abstract form, or two subcategories are represented, one of which is detailed. If you combine the individual total values (0 to 6) into a scale with three characteristics (where the value

Dipl.-Ing. Regelhofer e.U., Vienna, concludes a contract with P.H. Peterson LLC, Boston, account number 33714, for the delivery of machines (merchandise) on October 20. 2.12.20.. E2588 Delivery of the machines; the invoice is for USD 139,400.00 Exchange rates: 1.1387/1.1287 10.12.20.. B201 USD 80,000.00 - USD 1,600.00 discount = USD 78,400.00 was transferred to P.H. Peterson LLC. Settled at the exchange rate of 1.1201 = € 69,993.75 + € 208 expenses = € 70,201.75 12.12.20.. E2599 The forwarding company Interlogistik GmbH (33864) charges € 2,500 for delivery costs. a) Set up the posting records. b) Indicate whether the respective posting record increases or decreases equity or whether it is a posting with no effect on income.

Fig. 7.5 Example task for the medium characteristic of the category Representation of operational reality

0 is rated as "no representation of reality", the values 1 to 3 as "limited, abstract representation of reality" and the values 4 to 6 as "detailed representation of reality"), then it can be said that 32.20% of the tasks do not represent reality at all, 66.89% of the tasks represent reality abstractly and 0.9% of the tasks provide a detailed description.

Figure 7.5 shows a task with a medium characteristic in the category "Representation of reality". Goods and service flows are represented by the delivery of the machines, cash flows by the payment of the goods and social processes by the reference to the contract conclusion. However, all three sub-aspects are treated in little detail.

Figure 7.6 contains a task that provides a comparatively detailed description of reality. The task describes what services the company Baugut GmbH provides for the restaurant Goldener Hahn (conversion work, insulation, winter garden element, tile arch, etc.). In addition, communication processes between the two parties become visible through the mention of the commissioning and the agreement of the payment conditions. Cash flows are detailed through the representation of partial payments and payment conditions.

Figure 7.7 also shows a task with a high degree of detail. The description of the purchase of the bicycles, their external condition (sprayed logo, dragon-like figures on the handlebars, etc.) as well as their purpose of use are described in detail. In addition, the communication between the owner of the youth hostel and the companies Dragon Backpackers and Wild OG is precisely depicted (sale, call from Mrs. Fritz, agreement on return, return of the dragon figures and credit note). The payment of the invoice includes cash flows in the task.

Restaurant Goldener Hahn: In January 2020, the restaurant owner commissions Baugut GmbH (33088) to build a conservatory. As part of the work, the restaurant owner also had the remaining façade of his building re-insulated and the interior of the original building repainted. Three partial payments of the same amount are agreed with the general contractor. These installments are paid by bank transfer. The first installment is due at the start of construction, the second installment on completion of the conservatory element and the remaining payment on completion of the conservatory. The net costs for the conservatory are made up of the following:

Umbauarbeiten (Wintergarten)	8.500,00 EUR
Isolierung des bestehenden Gebäudes	12.400,00 EUR
Wintergartenelement	21.000,00 EUR
Fliesenboden inklusive Verlegung im Wintergarten	10.000,00 EUR
Einrichtung des Wintergartens	12.000,00 EUR
Beleuchtung und Elektroinstallationen im Wintergarten	2.300,00 EUR
Innenverputz und Malerarbeiten im Wintergarten	2.500,00 EUR
Ausmalen des Restaurantbereiches	1.300,00 EUR
Nettobetrag	**70.000,00 EUR**

Due date of the installments (payment by bank transfer):
Partial payment January 15, 2020 EUR 23,333.33 + 20% VAT
Partial payment March 12, 2020 EUR 23,333.33 + 20% VAT
Partial payment March 31, 2020 EUR 23,333.33 + 20% VAT

Fig. 7.6 Example task 1 for a high characteristic of the category Representation of reality

Publisher and year comparisons for the categories representing business reality
For reasons of clarity, the three subcategories were combined into a scale by forming a sum value to determine differences between publishers or years. The maximum sum value is 6. The higher the value, the more detailed the reality is depicted in the task in the form of goods and service flows, cash flows, and social processes. Figure 7.8 shows the results. It is noticeable that the tasks from the Hölzel publishing house achieve a sum value of zero significantly less often than the tasks from the other two publishers. In addition, the tasks from the Hölzel publishing house more often achieve sum values of one and two. At the same time, the tasks from the Jugend & Volk publishing house more often achieve sum values of three to five. However, the median is 1 for all three publishers. A conducted Kruskal-Wallis test, however, does not yield a significant result ($H(2) = 5504$, $p =.064$).

The different distributions of the sum values separated by year can be taken from Table 7.8. It shows that the proportion of tasks that do not represent the operational reality at all (sum value 0) varies greatly by year. While the proportion in the 2nd year is 19.9%, it is 42.2% in the 5th year and 55.1% in the 4th year. Accordingly, the distributions also vary for the remaining values.

Sport Stern sells bikes and helmets (*invoice included*) to the Dragon Backpackers youth hostel. The youth hostel would like to make the bikes available to guests free of charge so that they can explore the city cheaply. On July 16, Franziska Fritz, managing director of the youth hostel, calls Peter Stern excitedly. Unfortunately, they have underestimated the amount of space required for the many bicycles. She politely requests that she be allowed to return four bikes and four helmets. Peter accepts the request and immediately issues a credit note. By July 20, the outstanding invoice amount has already been credited to Peter Stern's account. Franziska also wants to use the bikes remaining in the youth hostel as advertising for the youth hostel. For this reason, she has Wild OG spray-paint the youth hostel logo on all the bikes and mount dragon-like figures on the handlebars. The following invoice is issued by Wild Ride: (*invoice included*). But there are problems here too: With three edges, the kite figures break off immediately – as proof, Franziska sends the figures back to Wild Ride. Wild Ride issues a credit note on 04.08. in the amount of € 375.99 net, 20 % VAT. Franziska transfers the outstanding invoice amount on time at the end of the payment period.

a) Create the credit note for the youth hostel.
b) Post all business transactions to accounts. The youth hostel is assigned the customer number 20256.
c) […]

Fig. 7.7 Excerpt from Example Task 2 for high degree of representation of business reality

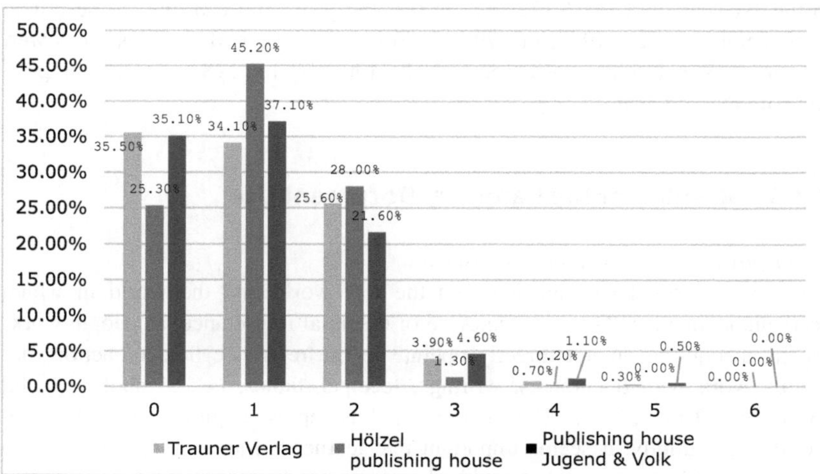

Fig. 7.8 Representation of reality by publisher

Table 7.8 Representation of operational reality by year

	0	1	2	3	4	5	6	Median
Year I (n = 438)	26.3 %	41.1 %	32.2 %	0.5 %	0.0 %	0.0 %	0.0 %	1
Year II (n = 628)	19.9 %	40.8 %	31.2 %	6.1 %	1.4 %	0.6 %	0.0 %	1
Year III (n = 261)	24.1 %	58.6 %	13.8 %	2.3 %	0.8 %	0.4 %	0.0 %	1
Year IV (n = 441)	55.1 %	25.4 %	16.8 %	2.7 %	0.0 %	0.0 %	0.0 %	0
Year V (n = 232)	42.2 %	30.2 %	23.3 %	3.4 %	0.9 %	0.0 %	0.0 %	1

The median value, however, is 1 for all years except the 4th. The results of the Kruskal-Wallis test are significant ($H(4) = 142.765$, $p = .000$). Therefore, statistically significant differences in the representation of operational between tasks of different school years can be identified. The pairwise comparisons show that primarily the tasks of the 4th and 5th years differ significantly from the tasks of the other school years. The effect sizes vary for the 4th year between.257 (difference to the 1st year) and.353 (difference to the 2nd year) and can thus be described as moderate (Cohen, 1988, pp. 79–80). For the 5th year, the values are lower, between.128 (pairwise comparison with the 4th year) and.198 (pairwise comparison with the 2nd year).

7.1.3 Results for the Category Document Use

Descriptive findings on document use

Documents form the bridge between the real world and the world in which accountants operate. They are therefore of essential importance, as people working in accounting do not directly operate in the reference field of action, but mainly work with documents, writings, receipts, tables, i.e., symbol-mediated (Neuweg, 2020, p. 139). The documents thus represent processes of the real world. Accordingly, it seems important that learners in accounting lessons also become familiar with working with documents and that tasks do not exhaust themselves in the verbal description of business cases. The category Document Use therefore checks whether and which documents are used in tasks from accounting. The category is dichotomous (0 = no document use, 1 = document

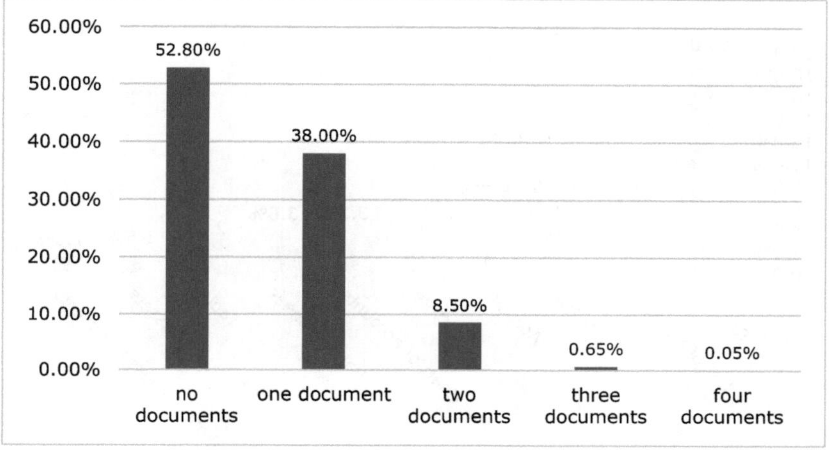

Fig. 7.9 Representation of document use

use) and is divided into several subcategories that distinguish different types of documents (e.g., receipt, balance list, balance sheet, account, P&L, asset directory, etc.) and are again dichotomous (respective document present or not present).

The evaluations of the absolute and relative frequencies show that in 52.8% of the tasks (n = 1056) no documents are used. In the remaining 47.2% (n = 944) of the tasks, at least one document (or type of document) is included. If the findings are differentiated further, it shows that of the 944 tasks that use documents, 760 tasks (81%) use one type of document, 170 tasks (18%) use two types of documents (e.g., receipt and balance list), another 13 tasks (1.4%) use three types of documents and one task uses four types of documents (0.4%). Figure 7.9 graphically represents the findings.

The most frequently used documents are receipts (in 19% of tasks), followed by balance lists (9.2%), other documents (6.2%), account presentations (5.7%), images (4.9%), chart of accounts (3.7%), balance sheets (3.6%), tables (2.3%), asset directories (1.5%) and profit and loss statements (1.3%). Figure 7.10 graphically represents the findings. Receipts are usually incoming invoices, outgoing invoices, bank or cash receipts. The other documents mainly include the following documents: documents from accounting or from accounting-related areas from the company (various statements, operational accounting sheets,

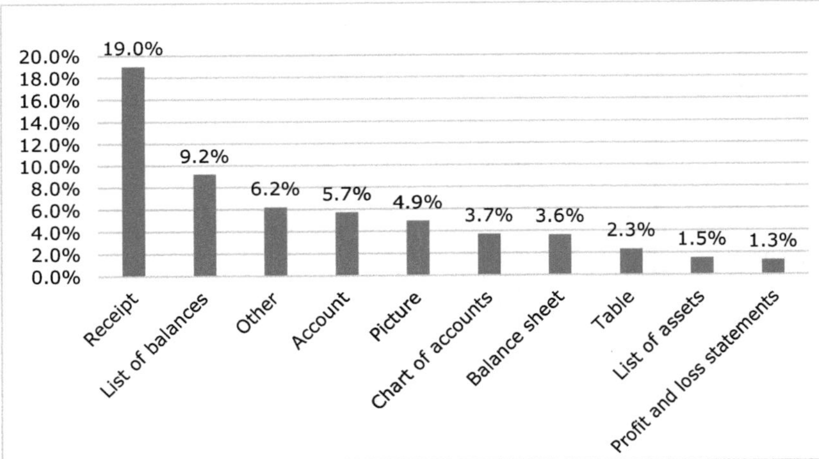

Fig. 7.10 Different types of documents in the tasks

extracts from accounting programs, foreign exchange rate sheets, open item lists, extracts from warehouse accounting, item lists, cost records, price lists, e-banking forms), legal documents from external stakeholders (excerpts from general terms and conditions, anonymous orders, notices, insurance policies, prepayments, announcements, legal texts, partnership agreements, leasing contracts, rental contracts, etc.) as well as documents of internal and external communication (e-mails, notes, post-its, SMS or speech bubbles). It should be noted that many documents only use excerpts or simplified representations. However, this is understandable and necessary considering the page limitations of textbooks.

Publisher and year comparisons for the category Document Use

At the publisher level, no significant differences between observed and expected values can be determined for the use of documents (χ^2 (2) = 5.75, p =.056). At the year level, significant differences can be determined (χ^2 (4) = 70.616, p =.001, V =.188). Figure 7.11 shows in what percentage of tasks in the respective year a document is used. While the use of documents in the 1st, 3rd and 4th year hardly differs from each other (with 42.5% to 49.4% each), the 2nd and 5th year deviate significantly from these values. In the second year, documents are used in 39.8% of tasks, in the 5th year, however, in 71.1%. Since a Chi-square

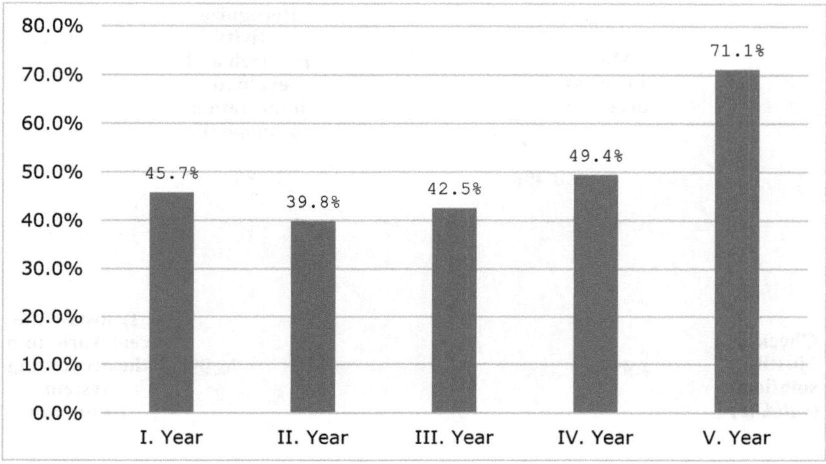

Fig. 7.11 Use of documents by year

test only makes a statement about whether the expected value and observed value differ significantly from each other (omnibus test), but not where exactly (so in this case in which years) the significant differences lie, post-hoc tests were carried out. To avoid an alpha error accumulation, a Bonferroni correction was made. In the present case, ten individual tests were carried out (five years with two possible characteristics each). The significance level was therefore reduced to 0.005 (0.05 divided by the number of individual tests). The post-hoc evaluations show what the descriptive evaluations already suggest. In the 2nd year, the observed value is significantly below the expected value, while in the 5th year it is significantly above the expected value. To determine the strength of the relationship, Cramer's V was calculated. With a value of.188, the relationship between year and document use can be described as weak (Cohen, 1988, pp. 224–225).

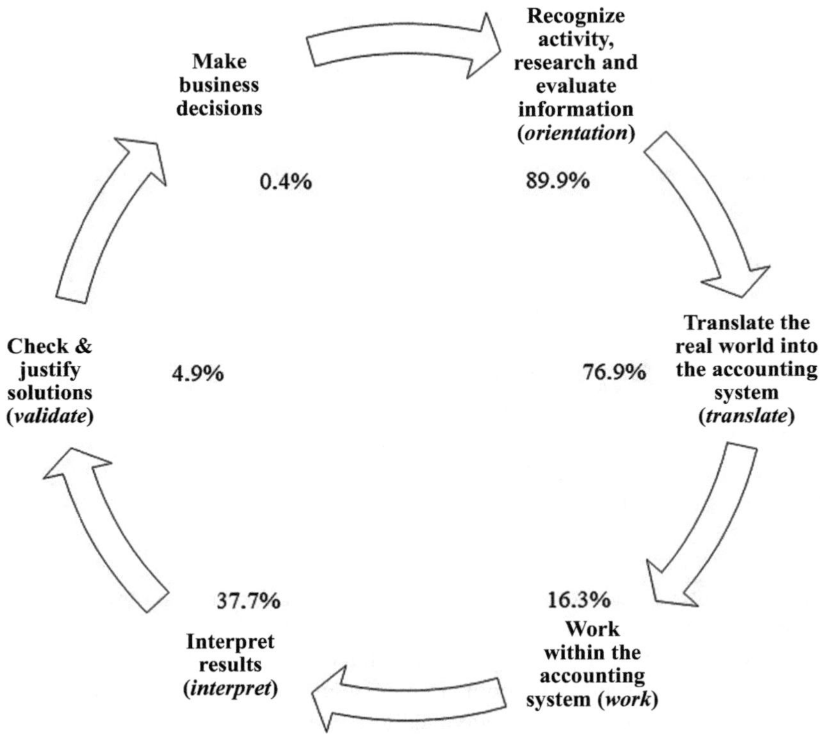

Fig. 7.12 Overview of descriptive findings on the modeling cycle

7.1.4 Results for the Category Modeling Cycle

In this section, the descriptive findings on the modeling cycle are reported. Before the detailed results for each subcategory are reported, a first overview of the main categories should be given for better orientation. Figure 7.12[1] provides a first overview of the findings. It is evident for each partial step in the modeling

[1] For a clearer representation, the subcategories were summarized. Thus, the partial step of orientation consists of three subcategories, which were summarized into one category for this representation. It was only differentiated whether the partial step has to be completed or not.

cycle, in what percentage of tasks the respective partial step has to be completed. Thus, in 89.9% of the tasks, an orientation performance is necessary (e.g., delimiting activity, researching information and/or distinguishing relevant from irrelevant information). In 76.9% of the tasks, a translation of the real world into the world of accounting is required (e.g., by forming booking entries), in 16.3% of the tasks, work is to be done within accounting (e.g., setting up a balance sheet or a profit and loss statement, performing internal accounting bookings). In 37.7% of the tasks, results are to be interpreted (e.g., with regard to their impact on business success). In 4.9% of the tasks, a developed or already existing solution must be checked or justified and in 0.4%, business decisions have to be made.

However, the graphic does not provide information about which sub-steps *within* a task must be processed together, but in what percentage of tasks the respective sub-step occurs. The following table (Table 7.9) therefore shows, in descending order of frequency, which sub-steps must be completed together. The first column indicates whether a sub-step occurs (1) or does not occur (0). For example, the code in line six means that in the tasks with this coding, the sub-steps of orientation, translation, and operation occur, but not the steps of interpretation, validation, and decision-making (111000). This results in different task profiles. For example, there are a total of 695 tasks (34.75%), in which the sub-steps of orientation and translation must be completed (110000). So, the activity to be performed must be recognized (and possibly information must be researched and evaluated) and then a real situation must be translated into the world of accounting. In a further 634 tasks (31.70%), the facts must also be interpreted (110100). In 7.4% of the tasks, an orientation performance is required and operation within the accounting system is necessary (101000). These three task profiles comprise 73.85% of all tasks. In 5.45% of the tasks, no sub-step has to be completed. These are usually knowledge questions that mostly require the reproduction of knowledge. In addition, there are many other combinations of sub-steps, which, however, occur much less frequently.

If one follows the ideal-typical process of the modeling cycle, it would be desirable that as many sub-steps as possible have to be completed in a task and that these also follow the sequence postulated in the modeling cycle. The evaluations show that the majority of tasks do not follow the ideal-typical process, but rather individual sub-steps are focused on and often sub-steps are addressed together that do not follow each other in the modeling cycle (e.g. the combinations 110110 or 101100). No task could be identified that requires going through all six sub-steps (111111) and only one task that requires the completion of the first five sub-steps (111110). In 14 tasks, the sub-steps of orientation, translation, operation, and interpretation must be completed (111100). Another 86 tasks require an orien-

Table 7.9 Task profile according to sub-steps in the modeling cycle

Sub-steps	Frequency	Percent	Cumulative Percent
110000	695	34.75%	34.75%
110100	634	31.70%	66.45%
101000	148	7.40%	73.85%
000000	109	5.45%	79.30%
111000	86	4.30%	83.60%
100000	70	3.50%	87.10%
010000	44	2.20%	89.30%
101100	38	1.90%	91.20%
110110	27	1.35%	92.55%
100100	22	1.10%	93.65%
110110	18	0.90%	94.55%
001000	17	0.85%	95.40%
100010	17	0.85%	96.25%
111100	14	0.70 %	96.95 %
000100	11	0.55 %	97.50 %
101010	8	0.40 %	97.90 %
000010	6	0.30 %	98.20 %
111010	5	0.25 %	98.45 %
010010	4	0.20 %	98.65 %
010100	4	0.2 %	98.85 %
100001	4	0.20 %	99.05 %
100110	4	0.20 %	99.25 %
011000	3	0.20 %	99.40 %
101110	3	0.20 %	99.55 %
100101	2	0.10 %	99.65 %
000110	1	0.05 %	99.70 %
001010	1	0.05 %	99.75 %
001100	1	0.05 %	99.80 %
011010	1	0.05 %	99.85 %
100011	1	0.05 %	99.90 %
110111	1	0.05 %	99.95 %
111110	1	0.05 %	100.00 %

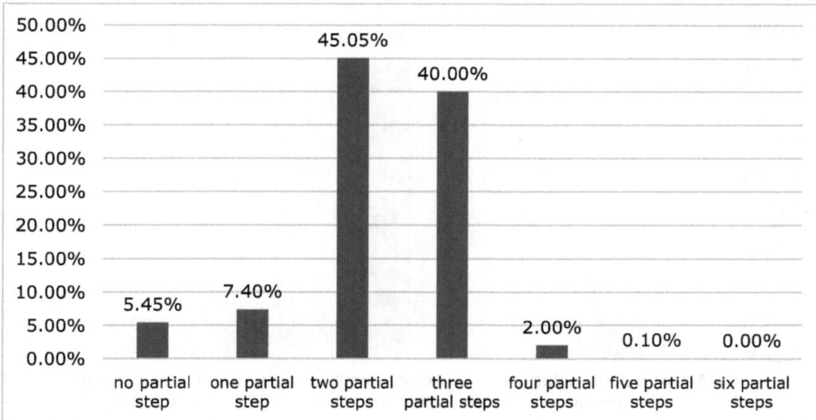

Fig. 7.13 Number of steps in the modeling cycle within a task

tation performance, a translation performance, and operation within the accounting system (111000). The results also show that there are very few tasks that require going through three or more sub-steps (Fig. 7.13). 45.05% of the tasks require the completion of two sub-steps, another 40.0% of three sub-steps.

7.1.4.1 Results for the Category "Orientation"

Descriptive Findings
Orientation (also referred to as understanding or simplifying in the modeling cycle of mathematics didactics) forms the first sub-step in the modeling cycle. To do this, the learners first need to understand the situation and determine which activities are required in the task. In addition, the information contained in the situation may need to be evaluated for relevance and possibly further information may need to be researched. Accordingly, the sub-step of orientation was differentiated using the three subcategories of recognizing activity, obtaining information, and evaluating information. All three subcategories are ordinally scaled (ranking possible), with three levels (0,1,2) being distinguished.

In the subcategory of recognizing the relevant activity, the central question is whether the task prompts the learners to recognize the activity to be performed themselves (initial state), or whether this is already clearly formulated in the task. In addition, the subcategory distinguishes whether the solution to the task is clear or whether there are different solution options (target state). The levels "activity

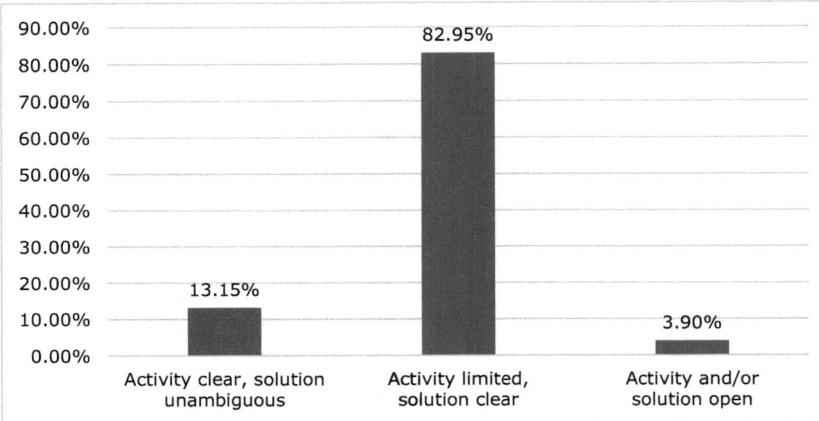

Fig. 7.14 Descriptive findings on the subcategory Recognizing Activity

clear, solution/target clear", "activity defined, solution/target clear" and "activity and/or target open" are distinguished.

The descriptive findings show (Table 7.1) that in 13.2% (n = 263) of the tasks, the activity to be performed is clear and the solution/target is also clear. In 1,659 (83%) tasks, the activity must be specified by the learner themselves, but the task provides hints on what to do without exactly prescribing the activity. However, the solution is clearly defined. So it is clear what the solution should look like. In 3.9% of the tasks (n = 78), either the activity (i.e., the learner does not know exactly what to do) or the solution path is open. The median is at a value of 1. Figure 7.14 graphically presents the findings.

For the category of obtaining information, it is distinguished whether all necessary information is *within* the task in *textual* form (in the running text) or whether learners need to research additional information within the task (e.g., from receipts, balance lists, and other documents) or outside the task (e.g., from a legal text, from an internet source). Three levels were defined, with 0 coded if all information is contained in textual form within the task, 1 was coded if information within the task is to be researched from *one* document (e.g., from a receipt, from a balance list, from a contract, from an email, etc.) and 2 was coded if either within the task information is to be obtained from *more than one* document (e.g., from a receipt and a balance list) or if information is to be obtained from an external source outside the task.

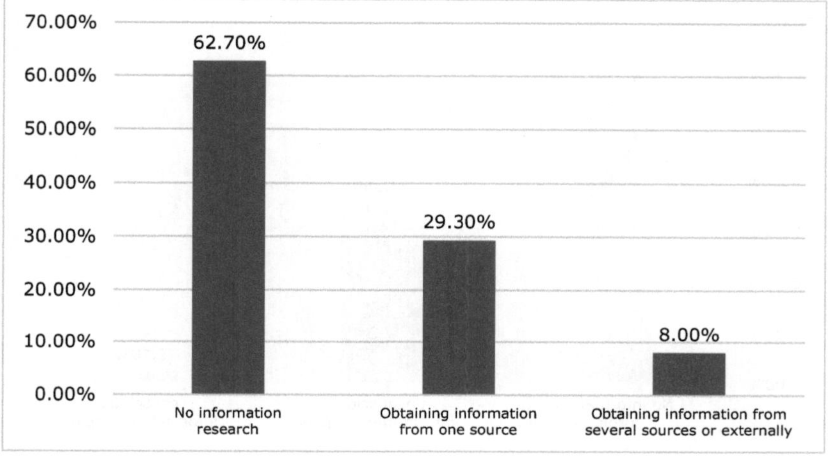

Fig. 7.15 Descriptive findings on the subcategory Obtaining Information

Figure 7.15 presents the descriptive findings in a bar chart and shows that in 62.7% of the tasks (n = 1254) all necessary information is contained in textual form within the task and therefore no additional information needs to be researched by the learners. In 29.3% of the tasks (n = 86), not all information is included and learners therefore need to research further information within the task from different documents. In 160 tasks (8%), multiple documents are to be used for information gathering or the information is to be obtained from external sources. The median value is 0.

While the subcategory of information research asks whether additional information needs to be researched, the category of information evaluation focuses on the question of whether learners need to distinguish between relevant and irrelevant information in the task, i.e., whether there is an information surplus in the task. The scale again distinguishes three levels. At level 0, tasks were coded in which *all* contained information is also relevant for the task (context information about the company's business activity, etc. was not considered). At level 1, tasks were coded in which learners need to distinguish between relevant and irrelevant information. The distinction, however, results from the type of documents used in the task. For example, a receipt always contains information that is not necessary for the immediate task (the same applies, for example, to a balance list that contains many different accounts, only one of which is needed for the task). The

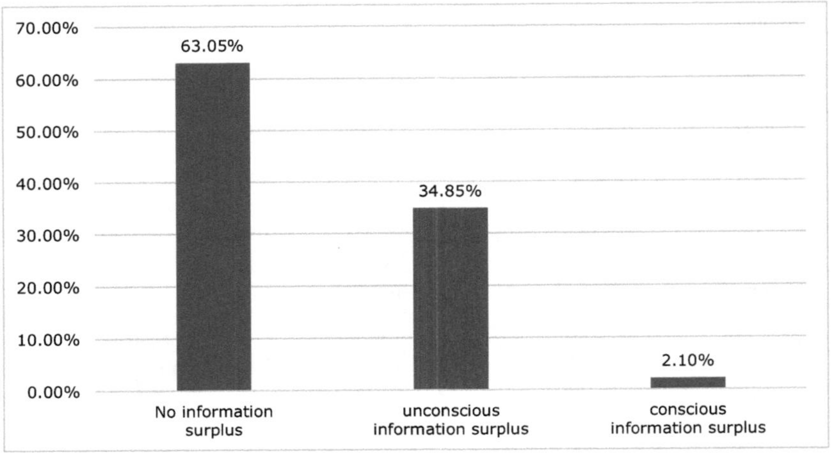

Fig. 7.16 Descriptive findings on the category Evaluating Information

information surplus is usually not deliberate (i.e., deliberately introduced by the task designers), but results from the type of documents. Therefore, in addition to the distinction between 0 (no distinction between relevant and irrelevant information) and 1 (distinction between relevant and irrelevant information), a third level was introduced in which tasks are coded in which there is an information surplus *and* it can be assumed that it was deliberately introduced by the task constructor (e.g., different depreciation rates, different exchange rates, different prices—purchase price, selling price, replacement price—for the valuation of a private withdrawal, etc.)

The evaluation of the codings shows (Table 7.1) that in 63.1% of the tasks (n = 1261) no distinction needs to be made between relevant and irrelevant information, as all contained information is relevant for the task. In 34.8% of the tasks (n = 697), a distinction is necessary because not all available information is needed for the task. In these tasks, the information surplus results from the type of documents. In 42 tasks (2.1%), it can be assumed that the information surplus was deliberately constructed to require an information selection (i.e., a distinction between relevant and irrelevant for the task). In total, a distinction between relevant and irrelevant information is required in 36.9% of the tasks (n = 739). The median value, like for information gathering, is at a value of 0. Figure 7.16 graphically presents the results.

Example tasks for the sub-step Orientation

Table 7.10 provides examples of the different level gradations of the subcategory "Recognizing Activity". Examples 1 to 3 are tasks in which both the activity to be performed is clearly stated and the solution is unambiguous. For example, in task 1, it is necessary to tick whether the respective statement is true or false (The activity is clear, the solution path is clear or there is *one* correct solution.) In example 2, different business cases need to be classified as fixed assets or expenses. Here too, the activity is clearly stated and the solution is unambiguous. Example 3 poses a knowledge question. Here too, both the activity and the solution are clear. Examples 4 and 5 are tasks in which the activity needs to be further narrowed down by the learners. In example 4, it is clear to the learners that they have to set up a booking. This is evident from the task itself and from the heading. Therefore, it does not initially need to be questioned whether the business case is relevant for accounting at all—this is made clear by the head-

Table 7.10 Example tasks for the subcategory "Recognizing Activity"

<table>
<tr><th>Category</th><th>Example tasks from the sample</th></tr>
<tr><td rowspan="3">Activity clearly stated, solution unambiguous</td><td>Example 1 (AE1):
Who has to keep double-entry bookkeeping?
<table>
<tr><th></th><th>Richtig</th><th>Falsch</th></tr>
<tr><td>Unternehmer/innen dürfen immer selbst entscheiden, wie sie ihre Bücher führen.</td><td></td><td></td></tr>
<tr><td>Kapitalgesellschaften (Aktiengesellschaften, GmbHs) müssen immer die doppelte Buchführung anwenden.</td><td></td><td></td></tr>
<tr><td>Unternehmen mit einem jährlichen Umsatz von mehr als 700.000,00 EUR in zwei aufeinanderfolgenden Jahren müssen ab dem folgenden Jahr die doppelte Buchhaltung führen.</td><td></td><td></td></tr>
<tr><td>Unternehmen mit einem Jahresumsatz von weniger als 700.000,00 EUR dürfen die doppelte Buchhaltung nicht anwenden.</td><td></td><td></td></tr>
<tr><td>Freie Berufe (Rechtsanwälte, Ärzte) müssen die doppelte Buchführung nicht betreiben.</td><td></td><td></td></tr>
</table></td></tr>
<tr><td>Example 2 (AE1465):
Your task: Tick whether the following items belong to fixed assets (i.e. need to be activated) or whether they are booked as expenses affecting earnings.
<table>
<tr><th>Nr.</th><th>Position</th><th>Anlagevermögen (Aktivierung)</th><th>Aufwand</th></tr>
<tr><td>1</td><td>Druckerpatronen: € 120,00 inkl. USt</td><td>☐</td><td>☐</td></tr>
<tr><td>2</td><td>Tische und Stühle: € 799,00 inkl. USt</td><td>☐</td><td>☐</td></tr>
<tr><td>3</td><td>CDs und DVDs: € 95,00 inkl. USt</td><td>☐</td><td>☐</td></tr>
<tr><td>4</td><td>Lizenzen für Programme und Betriebssysteme: € 599,00 inkl. USt</td><td>☐</td><td>☐</td></tr>
<tr><td>5</td><td>Werbeposter und Broschüren: € 910,00 inkl. USt</td><td>☐</td><td>☐</td></tr>
<tr><td>6</td><td>Ordner und Ablagesysteme: € 210,00 inkl. USt</td><td>☐</td><td>☐</td></tr>
<tr><td>7</td><td>Beamer und Multifunktionsdrucker: € 1.029,99 inkl. USt</td><td>☐</td><td>☐</td></tr>
</table></td></tr>
<tr><td>Example 3 (AE317):
Explain how the profit and loss accounts are closed at the end of the fiscal year.</td></tr>
</table>

(continued)

Table 7.10 (continued)

Category	Example tasks from the sample
Activity narrowed down, Solution unambiguous	**Example 4 (AE894, excerpt):** *Heading: Forming booking entries* In the wholesale company for sports articles MeinSport GmbH, the following business cases arise in October among others: […] 3.10. E1123 Purchase of fitness equipment from Kettler Austria GmbH (33038) for € 14,600.00. 5.10. E1131 The freight forwarder Gebrüder Weiss GmbH (33044) submits an invoice for € 620,- + 20 % VAT € _______ = € ______ for the delivery of the fitness equipment. 8.10. S625 Credit note from Kettler Austria GmbH (33038) € 279.60 (incl. 20 % VAT), as some fitness equipment has scratches. 24.10 *Receipt listed* […] Book the business cases.
	Example 5 (AE512): *Heading: Provisions* For Rasch Bau GmbH, the following facts arise at the end of the year. Carry out all necessary bookings and note the impact on earnings. […] The outstanding holiday entitlements as of 31 December of the current fiscal year amount to 11,270.00 EUR.
Activity and/or Solution open	**Example 6 (123, excerpt):** Your supervisor Ms. Demir has put some receipts on your desk. a) Assign the appropriate document types to the following receipts. If it is not a receipt, note this directly on the document. b) Then the receipts are to be booked. *Various receipts listed (including non-booking relevant documents)*
	Example 7 (AE3): Take the inventory result of your classroom and try to estimate the value of the items using the internet. *Note: The inventory is to be set up in the task before.*

ing and the task ("Book the business cases!"). However, the learners themselves need to determine which accounts are relevant, whether these should be booked in debit or credit, and to what extent. When purchasing the fitness equipment, for example, it needs to be determined whether it is merchandise or fixed assets that remain in the company. When booking the receipt (purchase of copier paper, payment with Mastercard), the type of receipt needs to be identified first and it needs to be defined to which account the copier paper should be booked (and subsequently on which side of the account to book and to what extent). In example 5, it is also clear that facts need to be booked and the heading ("Provisions") also narrows down the subject area. However, the learners themselves need to recognize what type of provision it is and on which account it should be booked. They also need to recognize that a provision has already been reported on the relevant account (shown in the balance list) and therefore an adjustment of the provision needs to be made. These and similar structured tasks were therefore usually coded with 1, as the activity is already narrowed down by the task (it is clear that a booking needs to be made), but further specifications need to be made by the task processor (account class, account type, account side, amounts, etc.). Examples 6 and 7 are tasks in which either the activity and/or the solution to be worked out are open. Example 6 was assigned to this level gradation because the learners need to recognize for each business case whether it is relevant for booking or not, as the task also contains business cases (e.g. an order confirmation) that are not to be booked. Only then is it necessary to determine for the booking-relevant business cases what type of document it is and how exactly to book. In example 7, the learners know that an inventory needs to be set up. *How* exactly this is to be done (What does the list look like? Where can information be found for estimating the prices and how is it estimated?) is however open. Accordingly, the solution to this task is also not unambiguous (there are different items on the list, the learners can use different sources to determine the values and determine the estimated values themselves, etc.).

For the subcategory of information gathering, tasks 1 to 3 represent examples of the level "no information gathering". No further information needs to be researched to solve the task. Examples 5 and 6 represent level 1 "researching information within the task", as research is required from *one* source within the task (for example 5, the information about the amount of the existing provision is to be taken from the balance list, in example 6, the information is to be taken from the document). Task 7 is an example of level 2, as information needs to be researched outside the task (in this case, the internet is the source of information).

Examples 1 to 3 also represent examples where no distinction needs to be made between relevant and irrelevant information, as there is no information surplus. In example 5, there is an information surplus (some accounts are listed in the balance list), but this results from the nature of the documents. The learner must therefore select the account relevant for task processing and identify the other accounts as irrelevant for the task. Accordingly, this task was coded with

1. Figure 7.17 shows a task that contains a deliberate information surplus. The specification of three different prices (cost price, replacement price, selling price) is deliberately chosen so that the learners themselves have to decide which price to choose.

Publisher and year comparisons for the category Orientation

For the category Recognizing Activity, Fig. 7.18 shows the relative distribution of levels separated by publisher. While the tasks from Trauner Verlag and Jugend & Volk Verlag show a similar distribution between the levels, the results of the tasks from Hölzel Verlag deviate more strongly. It is evident that significantly fewer tasks from Hölzel Verlag are assigned to category 0 (activity clear, solution clear). The value is 3.2%, while it is 16.9% and 18.5% for the tasks from Trauner Verlag and Jugend & Volk Verlag, respectively. There are also deviations at level 1 (activity defined, solution clear). While 77.9% and 77.8% of the tasks from Trauner Verlag and Jugend & Volk Verlag are assigned to this category, it is 94.2% for Hölzel Verlag. Accordingly, the proportion of tasks with the highest level (activity and/or solution open) is lowest at Hölzel Verlag at 2.6%. The median for the tasks of all three publishers is 1. A Kruskal-Wallis test used to determine differences provides significant results ($H(2) = 46.854$, $p = .001$). The pairwise post-hoc comparisons also show that there are significant differences between Hölzel Verlag and the other publishers, but not between Trauner Verlag and Jugend & Volk Verlag. The effect can be described as weak ($r = .144$ or.182) (Cohen, 1988, pp. 79–80; Field, 2017, pp. 179).

Differences were also observed between the school years (Table 7.11), with the distribution in the 5th year textbook deviating from the distributions in the other textbooks. While in the book for the 5th school year 5.6% of the tasks were classified in the lowest category, in the other textbooks it was between 12.3 and 17.5%. Another significant difference is seen at the highest level. There, in the 5th school year, 11.6% of the tasks are assigned, while in the remaining school years it is between 1.4 and 4.1%. However, the median value for all tasks is 1. The Kruskal-Wallis test conducted is significant ($H(4) = 38.322$, $p = .001$), with the post-hoc pair comparisons showing that the significant result is due to the differences between the tasks of the 5th school year and the remaining tasks, but not due to differences between the other tasks. The effect sizes range from.171 to.226 and can therefore be classified as weak to moderate (Cohen, 1988, p. 79–80; Field, 2017, p. 179).

AE1088:

Private withdrawal of two tennis rackets on October 17, 2021; cost price per item € 208, replacement price per item on October 17 € 195, sales price excl. VAT per item on October 17 € 310

Task: Determine the valuation and set up the accounting records.

Fig. 7.17 Task with deliberate information surplus

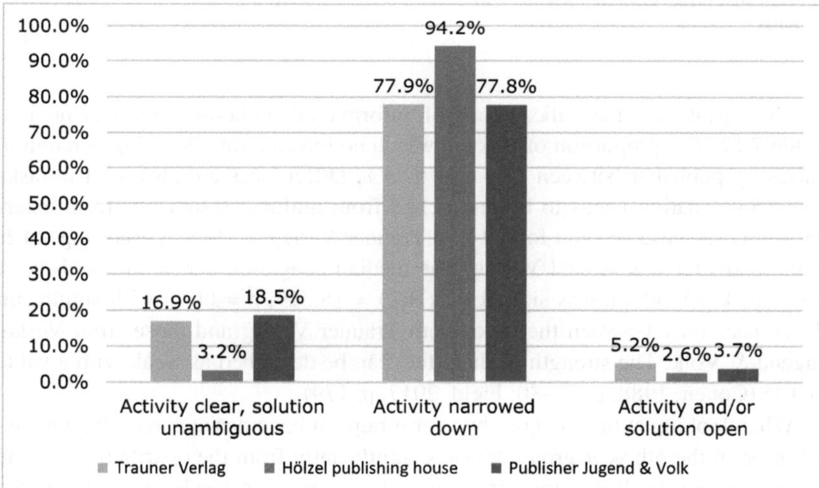

Fig. 7.18 Distribution of the category Recognizing Activity by publishers

Table 7.11 Distribution of the category Recognize Activity by years

	Activity clear, solution unambiguous (0)	Activity narrowed down, solution unambiguous (1)	Activity and/or solution open (2)	Median
Year I (n = 438)	13.00 %	85.60 %	1.40 %	1
Year II (n = 628)	13.40 %	83.10 %	3.50 %	1
Year III (n = 261)	12.30 %	85.80 %	1.90 %	1
Year IV (n = 441)	17.50 %	78.50 %	4.10 %	1
Year V (n = 232)	5.60 %	82.80 %	11.60 %	1

Table 7.12 Need for information gathering by publisher

	Information research			
	None	From one source	From multiple sources or external	Median
Trauner Verlag (n = 727)	67.3 %	27.6 %	5.1 %	0
Hölzel Verlag (n = 624)	61.9 %	30.0 %	8.2 %	0
Verlag Jugend & Volk (n = 649)	58.4 %	30.5 %	11.1 %	0

The results for the subcategory of information gathering are presented in Table 7.12. The proportion of tasks in which no information gathering is required varies by publisher between 58.4 and 67.3%. Differences are also seen in tasks where information needs to be researched from multiple sources or from external sources. These account for 5.1% at Trauner Verlag, 8.2% at Verlag Jugend & Volk, and 11.1% at Hölzel Verlag. The median is again 0 across the publishers. The Kruskal-Wallis test is significant ($H(2) = 15.529$, $p =.001$), with significant differences only between the tasks from Trauner Verlag and those from Verlag Jugend & Volk. The strength of the effect can be described as weak with a value of.105 (Cohen, 1988, p. 79–80; Field, 2017, p. 179).

When looking at the category by year groups, it becomes apparent that the distribution in the 5th year group deviates significantly from the distributions of the other year groups. While in years 1 to 4, no information needs to be researched in 61.9 to 69.6% of the tasks, the proportion in the 5th year group is 39.2%. Subsequently, the proportion of tasks in which information from multiple sources (or from external sources) needs to be researched in the 5th year group is 15.5%, while it is between 5.9 and 9.2% in the other year groups. Accordingly, the median for the tasks of the 5th year group is 1, while it is 0 for the tasks of the other year groups. The Kruskal-Wallis test conducted to determine differences between the year groups is significant ($H(4) = 68.662$, $p =.001$). However, the pairwise comparisons show that there are significant differences only between the 5th year group and the other year groups. The effect sizes range from.236 to.300 and can be described as weak to moderate (Fig. 7.19).

The third subcategory represents the evaluation of information. Table 7.13 shows the distribution of the different levels separated by publisher. It is evi-

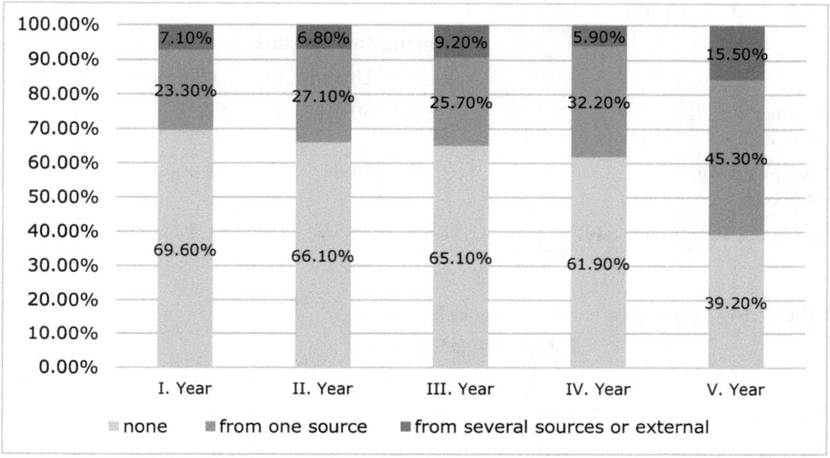

Fig. 7.19 Category Information Gathering by Year Groups

dent that the tasks of the publisher Jugend & Volk often contain an unconscious surplus of information. Conversely, it is less common for all the information contained in the task to be needed to solve the task, i.e., there is no surplus of information. In the highest category, the Hölzel Verlag has the highest value with 2.9% of the tasks at this level. The results of the Kruskal-Wallis test are again significant (H(2) = 14.690, p =.001), with the pairwise comparisons showing that a significant difference only exists between the tasks of the publisher Jugend & Volk and those of the Trauner Verlag. However, the effect is weak (r =.103) (Cohen, 1988, pp. 79–80).

Now, looking at the distribution of proficiency levels across the different grades (see Table 7.14), it becomes apparent again that the 5th grade contains comparatively fewer tasks in which no information evaluation is necessary and comparatively more tasks in which there is at least an unconscious information surplus (and therefore an information evaluation is required). While in grades 1 to 4, between 60.2 and 72.6% of the tasks do not require an information evaluation, this is the case for 42.7% of the tasks in the 5th grade. The 4th grade has the highest proportion of tasks with a conscious information surplus. The Kruskal-Wallis test is significant (H(4) = 57.043, p =.001) and therefore shows that there

Table 7.13 Evaluation of Information by Publisher

	Information Surplus			
	None	Unconscious	Conscious	Median
Trauner Verlag (n = 727)	67.8%	30.5%	1.7%	0
Hölzel Verlag (n = 624)	63.1%	34.0%	2.9%	0
Jugend & Verlag (n = 649)	57.6%	40.5%	1.8%	0

Table 7.14 Information surplus category by grades

	Information Surplus			
	None	Unconscious	Conscious	Median
Year I (n = 438)	72.6%	26.5%	0.9%	0
Year II (n = 628)	64.0%	33.8%	2.2%	0
Year III (n = 261)	60.2%	37.9%	1.9%	0
Year IV (n = 441)	64.6%	31.7%	3.6%	0
Year V (n = 232)	42.7%	56.0%	1.3%	1

are significant differences between the grades. The post-hoc pairwise comparisons show that there are only significant differences between the 5th grade and the other grades, but not between the other grades (with effect sizes between.173 and.288).

7.1.4.2 Results for the Translation Sub-step

Descriptive findings for the translation sub-step

Translating real, operational situations into the world of accounting is an important step in the modeling cycle. Learners are asked to describe real phenomena with accounting terms and to represent them in the accounting system. While in mathematics the translation performance consists, for example, in setting up an equation, in the domain of accounting, booking entries primarily represent the central translation performance. For this reason, the setup of a booking is not assigned to the operating sub-step, but to the translation sub-step.

The category "Setting up bookings" therefore asks whether learners have to transfer a real situation into the world of accounting by forming a booking.

The category is dichotomously designed (0 = no translation performance through bookings required; 1 = translation performance through bookings required). In addition to setting up bookings, however, there are other translation services that do *not* consist in forming a booking. Therefore, the category "Translation through other work" was introduced as a second subcategory of the main category. This refers to activities that also require a translation of real facts into accounting, but do not contain bookings or are required in addition to setting up booking entries. Examples include the classification of specific business transactions into liabilities or provisions, the classification of facts into fixed assets or expenses, evaluating receivables for collectability, indicating the relevant account class for a specific business transaction, etc. What these examples have in common is that in some form a translation from the real world into the world of accounting has to take place, for example by using accounting terms to describe or classify real facts. A dichotomous scale was also constructed for this category.

The descriptive findings (Table 7.1) show that in 72.6% of the tasks (n = 1452) booking entries have to be set up, while in 27.4% (n = 548) no bookings have to be made. For the category "Translation through other work", it is shown that this is explicitly required in 10.7% (n = 213) of the tasks, but not in the remaining 89.4% (n = 1787).[2] Overall, a translation performance is required in 76.9% of the tasks.

Example tasks for the translation category

Examples 1 to 4 represent tasks that require a translation service, although they are somewhat different. In examples 1 and 2, real facts are to be translated into accounting by assigning them accounting terms. Real phenomena are therefore categorized using the language of accounting (in these cases, for example, the classification according to the collectability of the receivable and the categorization into provision or liability). In example 3, real operational processes are also to be translated into accounting, as it is to be determined in which account class the business transactions are to be booked. A translation process therefore takes place again, but without the formation of a booking sentence. In example 4, although a real fact (purchase of a truck) is to be translated into accounting

[2] It should be noted that coding only takes place when the task explicitly asks for a translation performance. Of course, learners can also ask themselves whether the respective good is a fixed asset or is directly booked as an expense, whether it is a liability or a provision, but in the category "Translation through other work", coding only takes place when learners are *explicitly* prompted to make a classification.

by forming a booking sentence, the learners are also encouraged to consider in advance which accounts are affected, whether they are active and passive inventory accounts, whether the accounts increase or decrease and whether they are therefore in debit or credit. This also represents a translation service, which is provided here independently of the formation of a booking sentence. These and structurally similar tasks were therefore coded in the category "Translation through other work" and "Translation through formation of bookings".

Examples 5 and 6 represent "classic" accounting tasks, as they very often appear in textbooks. By forming booking sentences, business transactions from operational reality are translated into the world of accounting and documented there (Table 7.15).

Year and publisher comparisons for the sub-step of translation

The two subcategories were combined into one category for the determination of differences between publishers or years, which in turn also only distinguishes whether a translation service is to be performed or not. For this reason, a chi-square test is also to be applied here, as it is a dichotomous feature.

A significant result was found for the differences at the publisher level (χ^2 (2) = 88.216, p =.001, V =.210). The strength of the effect can be estimated as weak to medium with.210 (Cohen, 1988, p. 224–225). Table 7.16 shows the differences between observed and expected frequencies at the three different publishers. At Trauner Verlag, a translation is to be made in 75% of the tasks, at Hölzel Verlag in 89.1%, and at Verlag Jugend & Volk in 67.2%. Post-hoc tests show that at Hölzel Verlag the observed frequencies are significantly above the expected frequencies, while they are significantly below the expected values at Verlag Jugend & Volk.

At the grade level, significant but weak differences were also found (χ^2 (4) = 16,880, p =.002, V =.092) (Cohen, 1988, p. 224–225). However, the results of the post-hoc tests show that only in the 2nd grade the observed value is significantly above the expected value. Figure 7.20 shows in what percentage of tasks a translation performance is to be provided.

7.1.4.3 Results on internal accounting operations and mathematical operations

Internal Accounting Operations

Descriptive findings on internal accounting operations

Table 7.15 Example tasks for the sub-step of translation

<table>
<tr><th>Category</th><th>Example tasks from the sample</th></tr>
<tr><td>Translation through other work</td><td>
Example 1 (AE1119):
Karl Hofer e.U., against whom we have a delivery claim of €12,000 (€10,000 + €2,000 VAT), is experiencing payment difficulties. Reorganization proceedings with self-administration have been initiated, a rate of 30% is expected.
Analyze whether the receivable is fully recoverable, doubtful or irrecoverable.
Example 2 (AE501):
Provision or liability? Put a cross in the box:
<table>
<tr><th>Incident</th><th>Provision</th><th>Liability</th></tr>
<tr><td>Mr. Radler buys bicycles on target from a supplier.</td><td></td><td></td></tr>
<tr><td>Mr. Radler expects warranty losses of approx. 1.5% of sales this year.</td><td></td><td></td></tr>
<tr><td>Mr. Radler fears that a competitor will sue him for damages because he is using one of his product names.</td><td></td><td></td></tr>
<tr><td>Mr. Radler takes out a loan from his bank.</td><td></td><td></td></tr>
</table>
Example 3 (AE75):
For which of the following business transactions is an expense account posted in class 7 or 8? Put a cross in the box and write down the account number:
<table>
<tr><th>Geschäftsfall</th><th>Klasse 7</th><th>Klasse 8</th><th>Weder noch</th><th>Konto-Nr.</th></tr>
<tr><td>Wir kaufen Handelswaren ein.</td><td></td><td></td><td></td><td></td></tr>
<tr><td>Wir bezahlen die Betriebshaftpflichtversicherung.</td><td></td><td></td><td></td><td></td></tr>
<tr><td>Wir kaufen Büromaterial.</td><td></td><td></td><td></td><td></td></tr>
<tr><td>Wir werden mit Mahnspesen belastet.</td><td></td><td></td><td></td><td></td></tr>
<tr><td>Wir erhalten die Telefonrechnung für den letzten Monat.</td><td></td><td></td><td></td><td></td></tr>
<tr><td>Wir kaufen Rohstoffe für die Produktion.</td><td></td><td></td><td></td><td></td></tr>
<tr><td>Wir erhalten die Stromrechnung für den letzten Monat.</td><td></td><td></td><td></td><td></td></tr>
<tr><td>Wir bezahlen die monatliche Miete.</td><td></td><td></td><td></td><td></td></tr>
<tr><td>Unser Bankkonto wird wegen des Darlehens mit Zinsen belastet.</td><td></td><td></td><td></td><td></td></tr>
<tr><td>Weil wir eine Rechnung nicht zeitgerecht beglichen haben, werden uns Verzugszinsen verrechnet.</td><td></td><td></td><td></td><td></td></tr>
<tr><td>Wir kaufen einen neuen Computermonitor.</td><td></td><td></td><td></td><td></td></tr>
<tr><td>Wir kaufen Kugelschreiber für das Büro.</td><td></td><td></td><td></td><td></td></tr>
<tr><td>Wir verbuchen die Rechnung des Steuerberaters für die monatliche Buchhaltung.</td><td></td><td></td><td></td><td></td></tr>
<tr><td>Wir schaffen einen neuen Pkw an.</td><td></td><td></td><td></td><td></td></tr>
</table>
Example 4 (AE735):
In the Third-Wave-Cafe "14 Steps", Heidi Grascher e.U., the following business transactions, among others, occur in November:
Heidi Grascher buys a transporter (truck) for € 30.800,- against later payment.
<table>
<tr><th>1</th><th>2</th><th>3</th><th>4</th></tr>
<tr><td>Welche Konten sind beteiligt?</td><td>Aktives oder passives Bestandskonto?</td><td>Vermehrung (+) oder Verminderung (-)?</td><td>Soll oder Haben?</td></tr>
<tr><td></td><td></td><td></td><td></td></tr>
<tr><td></td><td></td><td></td><td></td></tr>
</table>
<table><tr><td>Buchungssatz:</td></tr></table>
</td></tr>
</table>

(continued)

Table 7.15 (continued)

Translation by setting up posting records	**Example 5 (AE54, excerpt):** Help Ms. Klim to post the following business transactions. Also consider whether the postings are relevant to profit or loss (increasing, decreasing or not affecting profit or loss). […] d) On 17.03.20... an incoming invoice in the amount of EUR 800.00 is settled y bank transfer (BK 24). Posting record: ______ e) On 19.03.20.. 24.80 EUR interest is credited to the bank account (BK 24). Posting record: ______ f) On 28.03.20.. Mrs. Klim pays parcel charges in the amount of EUR 13.40 in cash (KA 55) Posting record: ______ **Example 6 (AE849):** Carina Holzer GmbH, production of packaging material, wants to expand its vehicle fleet. This results in the following business transactions: 5.3. E138 Purchase of a small truck from Tim Steyr OG (33159) for € 75,000 (incl. 20% VAT) 20.3. transfer of € 75,000 to Tim Steyr OG to settle E138
	30.4. E256 A new company car is purchased from Autohaus Müller GmbH (33160) for € 33,000 (incl. 20% VAT and NOVA) for the sales representatives. 10.5. E279 An electric car is purchased from Julian Weiner GmbH (33161) for € 37,200 (incl. 20% VAT) for business trips by the management. a) Set up the accounting records. b) Indicate whether the respective transaction increases or decreases equity or whether it is a posting with no effect on income.

The category of internal accounting operations captures the extent to which learners must perform internal accounting tasks as part of the task. With internal accounting operations, there is no translation from the real world into the world of accounting, but operations are performed within the system. This includes activities such as opening accounts, closing accounts, making balancing entries, creating a balance sheet, preparing a profit and loss statement, performing a more-or-less calculation, etc. The distinguishing criterion to a translation service is that there is usually no correspondence in the real world for internal accounting operations—so processes from the real world are not directly represented. While a balance sheet also represents reality (in broad terms and neglecting the scope of balance sheet policy), the *translation* from the real world into the world of accounting is not directly done by the balance sheet, but by documenting business transactions during posting, by conducting the inventory and preparing the

Table 7.16 Differences in translation performance by publisher

			Translation Performance		Total
			No	Yes	
Publisher	Trauner Verlag	Number	182	545	727
		Expected Number	168.3	558.7	727
		% of Publisher	25.0 %	75.0 %	
	Hölzel Verlag	Number	68	556	624
		Expected Number	144.5	479.5	624
		% of Publisher	10.9 %	89.1 %	
	Verlag Jugend & Volk	Number	213	436	649
		Expected Number	150.2	498.8	649
		% of Publisher	32.8 %	67.2 %	
Total		Number	463	1537	2000
		Expected Number	463	1537	2000
		% of Publisher	23.2 %	76.9 %	

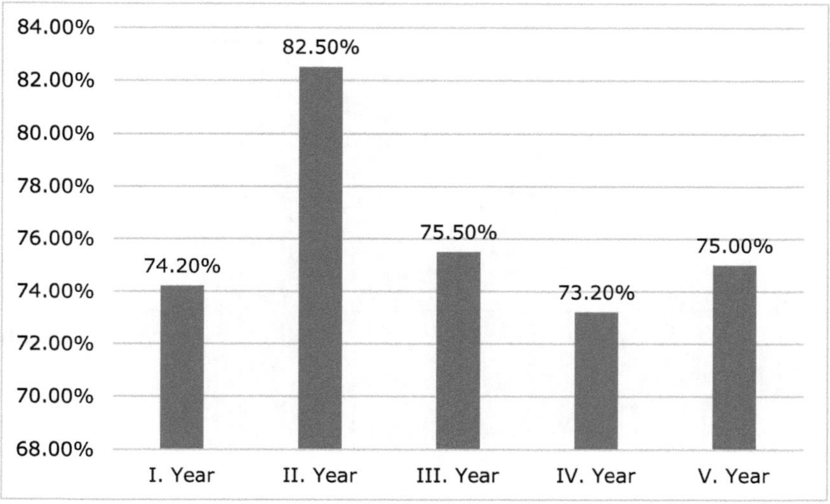

Fig. 7.20 Translation performance by grade

Table 7.17 Example tasks for the category of internal accounting operations

<table>
<tr><th>Category</th><th>Example tasks from the sample</th></tr>
<tr><td rowspan="3">Internal Accounting Operations: Bookings</td><td>Example 1 (AE783, excerpt):
Opening balance of the trading company Gerald Koller e.U., Hauptstraße 15, 9500 Villach (Opening balance shown).
Business cases:
8.1. E1 Purchase of goods from supplier Kolbitz Warenvertriebs-GmbH (33024) € 8160,- + € ________ VAT = € 9,792,-
[...]
31.1 U1 Transfer of the input tax account to VAT liability
31.1 U2 Transfer of the sales tax account to VAT liability
d) Set up the booking entries for the transfer of input tax and sales tax to VAT liability.</td></tr>
<tr><td>Example 2 (AE1904, excerpt):
Melanie Maxian, owner of Pimp my Car, is sitting with her tax advisor to discuss the provisions for this year. The following cases should still be recorded in the accounting:
1. Something apparently went wrong when installing new Japanese tuning tires of the brand Zsunamee. The two rear tires had come off—fortunately still when driving away in the garage—the customer is suing for damages of € 8000.
2. Melanie will be represented by a lawyer. She has already noted that she can expect about € 10,000 + 20% VAT for her consultation.
Your task:
Present the formation of these provisions on accounts and close them.</td></tr>
<tr><td>Example 3 (AE20):
Search for the following accounts from the chart of accounts and first consider in which account class you could find the account.
<table>
<tr><th>Kontenbezeichnung</th><th>Kontenklasse</th><th>Kontonummer</th></tr>
<tr><td>Werbeaufwand</td><td></td><td></td></tr>
<tr><td>Gebäude</td><td></td><td></td></tr>
<tr><td>Lieferforderungen</td><td></td><td></td></tr>
<tr><td>Lkw</td><td></td><td></td></tr>
<tr><td>Paketgebühren</td><td></td><td></td></tr>
<tr><td>Zinserträge aus Bankguthaben</td><td></td><td></td></tr>
<tr><td>Lieferverbindlichkeiten</td><td></td><td></td></tr>
<tr><td>Betriebs- und Geschäftsausstattung</td><td></td><td></td></tr>
<tr><td>Rohstoffvorrat</td><td></td><td></td></tr>
<tr><td>Mieterträge</td><td></td><td></td></tr>
<tr><td>Zinsaufwand für Darlehen</td><td></td><td></td></tr>
<tr><td>Datenverarbeitungsprogramme, Software</td><td></td><td></td></tr>
</table>
</td></tr>
</table>

(continued)

Table 7.17 (continued)

Category	Example tasks from the sample
Internal Accounting Operations: Preparing a balance sheet, Preparing an income statement preparing	**Example 4 (AE766, excerpt):** Opening of accounts based on the following balance sheet as of December 31 of the previous year of the trading company Martina Kaiser e.U.:*(Opening balance shown)* Business cases: 3.1. Payment for building repair by bank transfer € 9908,- 7.1. Purchase of goods on credit € 7870,- 11.1 Credit on the bank account € 2520,-; a customer has settled an invoice [...] a) Set up the booking entries for the ongoing business cases. b) Enter the balances from January 1 on the active and passive inventory accounts. c) Post the business cases on the listed accounts. d) Calculate the difference between the ending balance and the beginning balance of the trading goods and set up the corresponding booking entry. Close the private account against the capital account. Enter the two booking entries on the respective accounts. e) Create the summary and balance sheet. f) Prepare the income statement and the closing balance sheet.
	Example 5 (AE1858, excerpt): The balances of the accounts show the following picture for the Easy Living Hotel GmbH as of 31.12.:*(List of balances listed)* Your task: Prepare the balance sheet and the income statement according to UGB classification in the templates.
Internal Accounting Operations: Conducting MWR	**Example 6 (AE607, excerpt):** Franz Breitdorfer e.U.: The company Franz Breitdorfer e.U., agricultural machinery trade and repairs, Eugendorf, is a company registered in the commercial register, which is obliged to keep accounts under company law. For the year 20.. a balance sheet profit of 67,369.00 EUR was determined under company law. Determine the taxable and the final balance sheet success for the company Franz Breitdorfer e.U. for the year 20.. using the tax more-less calculation, taking into account the following information: [...] e) Donations: The company Franz Breitdorfer e.U. has made donations to the local football club of 860.00 EUR in the current financial year. He also donated 300.00 EUR to the Arche Noah association.
Internal Accounting Operations: Other tasks	**Example 7 (AE 396, excerpt):** Complete the missing elements in the present asset directory of the Cafeteria Lubinger (*Asset directory included).*
	Example 8 (AE113): Prepare the VAT advance notification for August 20.. for the watchmaker Maximilian Berger. Name: Uhren Berger e.U. Address: Uhrmacherweg 54, 4020 Linz Phone: + 43 732 3 78 55 Tax office number: 46 Tax number: 511/9980 • Total amount of the assessment bases for deliveries and other services (20%) 1870,- EUR • Total amount of input tax 420.00 EUR

Table 7.18 Differences in internal accounting operations between publishers

			Internal Accounting Operations		Total
			No	**Yes**	
Publisher	Trauner Verlag	Number	613	114	727
		Expected Number	608.5	118.5	727
		% of Publisher	84.3%	15.7%	
	Hölzel Verlag	Number	545	79	624
		Expected Number	522.3	101.7	624
		% of Publisher	87.3%	12.7%	
	Verlag Jugend & Volk	Number	516	133	649
		Expected Number	543.2	105.8	649
		% of Publisher	79.5%	20.5%	
Total		Number	1674	326	2000
		Expected Number	1674.0	326.0	2000
		% of Publisher	83.7%	16.3%	

inventory. The category of internal accounting work includes several subcategories to describe the operations to be performed more precisely. The following subcategories were defined: internal accounting bookings (e.g. opening accounts, closing accounts, setting up balancing entries, making transfers), preparation of the balance sheet, creation of the profit and loss statement, setting up a more-or-less calculation, and other internal accounting operations (e.g. maintaining an asset register, submitting a VAT return, etc.). All categories are dichotomous.

The results of the descriptive evaluations show that internal accounting activities must be carried out in 16.3% of the tasks (n = 326). In the remaining 89.4% of the tasks, no internal accounting operations are to be performed. In total, 360 internal accounting activities must be performed in the 2000 tasks. If we look at the results for the individual subcategories (Table 7.1), it becomes apparent that internal accounting bookings must be made in 10.7% (n = 213) of the tasks, a balance sheet must be created in 2.4% (n = 48) of the tasks, a profit and loss statement in 2.0% (n = 40) of the tasks, other internal accounting tasks must be performed in 2.0% (n = 39) of the tasks, and a more-or-less calculation must be set up in 1.0% (n = 20) of the tasks. The preparation of booking entries thus forms the largest group of tasks to be performed within the internal accounting operations (59.2% of all internal accounting work), followed by the preparation of balance sheets (13.3%), the creation of profit and loss statements (11.1%), other internal accounting tasks (10.8%) and the performance of more-or-less calculations (5.6%).

Examples of internal accounting activities

Table 7.17 shows examples of different internal accounting activities. In Example 1, internal accounting entries are to be set up, in which the input tax and the sales tax are to be transferred to the VAT liability account. This is a purely internal accounting task. The processes in the real world (e.g. the purchase of goods from the supplier Kolbitz) are represented by the booking of the business case. In Example 2, provisions are to be made for various occasions (= translation from the real world into the world of accounting). Subsequently, the accounts are to be closed. This is a purely accounting task with no reference to real business transactions. Example 3 represents a type of task where no bookings are to be made, but it is still a purely accounting task without translation from the business reality. An account is to be assigned a class of accounts and an account number. These and similar tasks were therefore recorded in this category. Examples 4 and 5 are example tasks for creating a balance sheet and a profit and loss statement, as a balance sheet and a profit and loss statement are to be created based on an opening balance sheet and following the booking of ongoing business transactions (Example 4) or based on an existing list of balances (Example 5). Example 6 represents a task for the category "Setting up a more-or-less calculation". Starting from the company law profit, the tax law profit is to be determined by considering various facts and applying the more-or-less calculation. This is again a purely internal accounting task. Examples 7 and 8 show example tasks for other internal accounting activities. In Example 7, an asset register is to be created (or completed), in Example 8 a VAT return is to be submitted.

Year and publisher comparisons for internal accounting operations

To identify differences for internal accounting operations between publishers, only the main category was considered again. An evaluation at the subcategory level was omitted for reasons of clarity. Therefore, a Chi-square test is used again, as the characteristic to be examined is dichotomously designed (Are internal accounting operations to be carried out or not?) For the differences between the publishers, the Chi-square test shows significant results, but with small effect sizes (χ^2 (2) = 14.627, p =.001, V =.086) (Cohen, 1988, pp. 224–225). Table 7.18 presents a cross-table in which both the observed and expected frequencies are listed. At Trauner Verlag, 15.7% of the tasks involve internal accounting activities, while at Hölzel Verlag it is 12.7% and at Verlag Jugend & Volk it is 20.5%

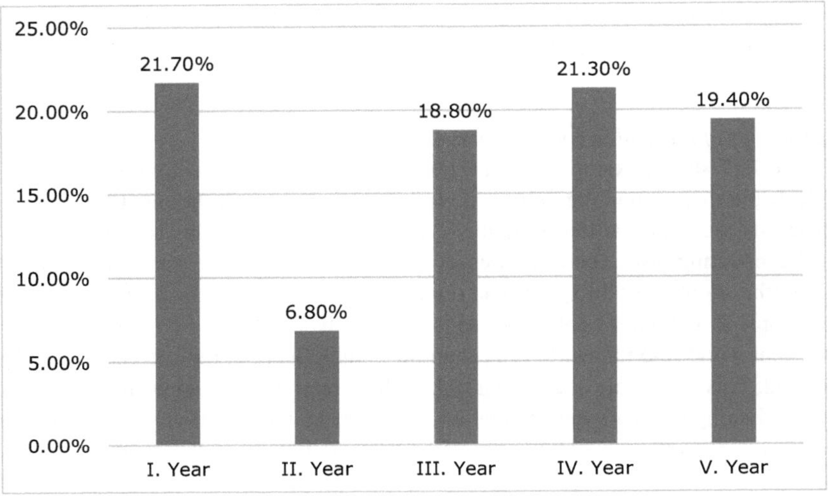

Fig. 7.21 Internal accounting operations by grade

of the tasks that involve internal accounting work. Post-hoc tests show that at Hölzel Verlag and Verlag Jugend & Volk, expected and observed values significantly differ, with the observed value at Hölzel Verlag significantly below the expected value and at Verlag Jugend & Volk significantly above it.

Significant differences are also evident at the grade level. However, the relationship between the grade and internal accounting operations can also be described as weak (χ^2 (4) = 61.388, p =.001, V =.175) (Cohen, 1988, pp. 224–225). It is noticeable that particularly in the 2nd grade (see Fig. 7.21), significantly fewer internal accounting operations are to be carried out. This, however, meets expectations, as the curriculum in the 2nd grade primarily focuses on ongoing bookkeeping. The post-hoc tests show that in the 1st and 4th grades, the observed frequencies are significantly above the expected values, and significantly below in the 2nd grade. For the 3rd and 5th grades, there are no significant deviations between observed and expected values.

Mathematical Work

Descriptive Findings on Mathematical Work

The category of mathematical work is not integrated into the cycle of accounting modeling as a separate step, but can be used in different steps of the modeling cycle. For example, mathematical work may be required when translating the real world into the world of accounting, for instance when calculations need to be made when forming booking entries (e.g., calculation of gross, net and sales tax amounts, calculation of discount amounts, etc.). Mathematical work may also be necessary for internal accounting tasks, for example when preparing profit and loss statements or balance sheets, determining account balances, filling out advance VAT returns, or making entries in the asset directory. Mathematical work may also be required for interpretation services, for example when it needs to be specified how much a business transaction affects the company's profit. Mathematical operations may also be necessary for validation (i.e., checking or justifying a solution), for example when a calculation or a performed calculation needs to be checked for mathematical correctness. The category of mathematical work is dichotomously designed, so it is differentiated whether mathematical operations (usually simple operations such as additions, subtractions, multiplications and divisions) are necessary to cope with the task or not. No distinction is made as to how complex the operations are and also not in which part of the step they occur.

The results of the descriptive evaluations (see Table 7.1) show that mathematical operations are required in 60% of the tasks (n = 1200), while in the remaining 40% of the tasks (n = 800) no mathematical work is required.

Year and publisher comparisons for mathematical work

At the publisher level, no significant differences can be identified for mathematical work (χ^2 (2) = 4150, p =.126). However, significant differences were found between the years. According to Cramer's *V*, the strength of the correlation can be described as weak (χ^2 (4) = 65.805, p =.001, V = 181) (Cohen, 1988, pp. 224–225). Fig. 7.22 shows the percentage of tasks that require mathematical activities. The post-hoc evaluations show that in the 1st and 2nd year the observed value is significantly below the expected value, while in the 4th year it is significantly above the expected value.

7.1.4.4 Results for the Step of Interpreting

Descriptive findings for the category of interpreting

In the category of interpreting, the central question is whether the task calls for interpreting a business case in terms of its impact on a particular size (e.g., liquidity, unit or period success, tax burden). Based on the "Linzer Ebenenmodell" (Neuweg, 2020), profitability, liquidity (or liquid funds), the balance sheet (or individual balance sheet items), the tax burden and external

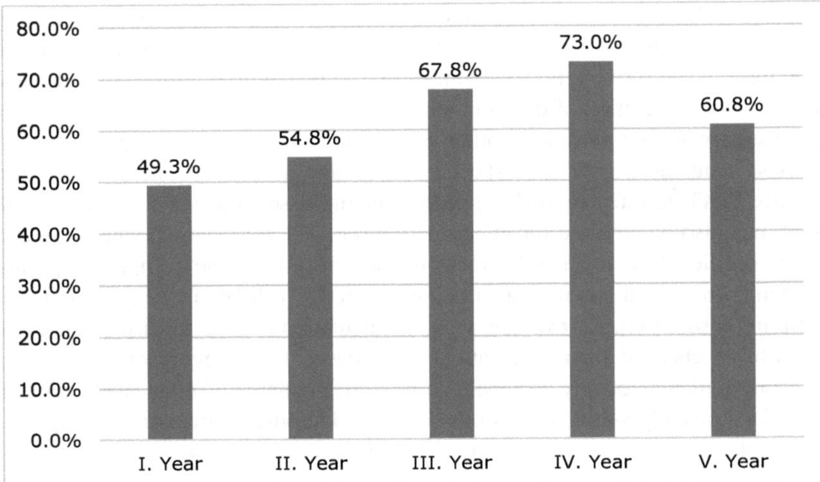

Fig. 7.22 Mathematical work by year

representation (How does a business case appear externally or when is it visible externally at all?) were defined as relevant sizes. The category "Other" was inductively included, as not all interpretation services could always be clearly assigned to one of the sizes mentioned above. This particularly affects the interpretation of key figures. The six subcategories are all dichotomous. So it is differentiated whether an interpretation service is to be provided, but not to what extent or in what quality.

The results (Table 7.1) show that in 62.4% of the tasks (n = 1248) no interpretation service is to be provided. In 37.7% of the tasks (n = 754), however, an interpretation service is to be provided (with 726 tasks interpreting a business case in terms of its impact on *one* formal goal, and 28 tasks on *two* formal goals. This results in a total of 782 interpretation services). If we look at which sizes are to be used for the interpretation, it is clear that with 88% of all interpretation services, the indication of the profit impact (the impact on the company's success) is clearly dominant. It is striking that all codings that were assigned to the area of profitability (or unit or period success) exclusively concern the indication of the impact on profit (the company's success). The area of profitability (defined as the ratio of a size to the capital employed, see Sect. 2.1) is never addressed. For this reason, the category is subsequently described as "profit impact". 7.0% of the

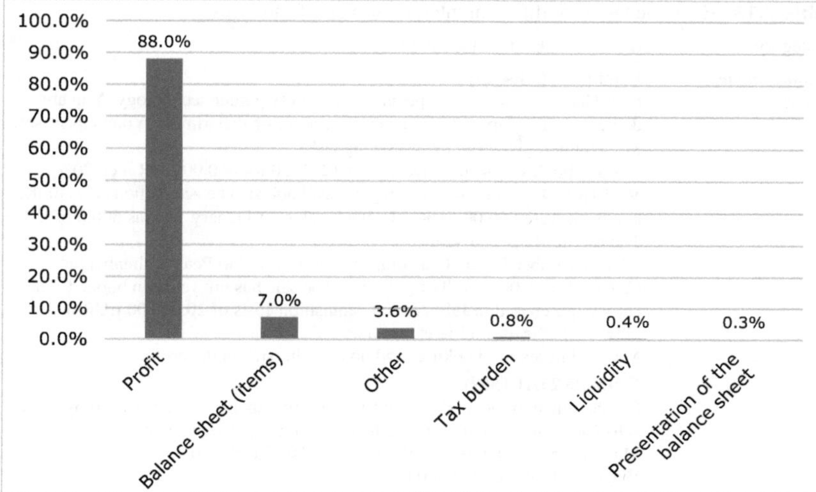

Fig. 7.23 Interpretation services according to different formal goals

interpretations concern the impact on the balance sheet (or on individual balance sheet items) and another 3.6% concern other interpretation services. The indication of the impact of a business case on the company's tax burden accounts for 0.8% of all interpretation services, the impact on liquidity 0.4% and the impact on external representation 0.3%. Fig. 7.23 visualizes the results.

Examples of different interpretation services

Table 7.19 contains tasks in which learners are asked to interpret a business case in terms of its impact on a formal goal. Example 1 represents a typical task, as it often appears in textbooks. A business case is to be booked and then the profit impact is to be indicated. The same applies to Example 2. Regarding the impact of a business case on the company's liquidity, no example could be identified that asks for the liquidity impact in a structure similar to tasks with indication of the profit impact. Example 3 represents an example for the category "Impact on liquidity", as learners have to deal with how individual business cases change the stock of liquid funds. This can be seen as an interpretation service. In examples 4 and 5, it is to be indicated how a business case affects a balance sheet item. In Example 4, the impact on equity is queried. Since equity is a balance sheet item, a coding with 1 was carried out.

Table 7.19 Example tasks for different interpretation performances

Category	Example tasks from the sample
Impact on the Profit	**Example 1 (AE415):** Eder Garten eTOOLs is a specialist for battery garden technology. You are doing an internship in the company's accounting department. Your supervisor, Mr. Wallner, gives you the following tasks: – A notebook was sold on December 12, 2020 for 460.00 EUR incl. 20% VAT (KA247). The sale has not yet been booked. The acquisition costs of the notebook were 800.00 EUR. The book value on January 1st was 600.00 EUR. The useful life is four years. – On December 18, 2020, a company car was sold to Peter Kaltenberger (20031) for 15,000.00 EUR (AR254). The sale has not yet been booked. The car was purchased in July 2018 at acquisition costs of 20,000.00 EUR incl. 20% VAT, the useful life is 8 years. Make all necessary bookings and note the impact on the profit.
	Example 2 (AE1569): For the office of the Teak carpentry, old office shelves were replaced by new, self-made ones. In this context, the following expenses were booked: Material (raw materials, auxiliary materials): € 1,250.00 Wages and salaries: € 2,360.00 Various expenses: € 900.00 The office shelves were completed on 04.02.20.. and immediately put into operation. Your task: Activate the shelves and indicate the impact on the company's profit.
Impact on the Liquidity	**Example 3 (AE1424, excerpt):** Also in the second year, the photo lamps in the Fotostudie Schwarz are resold. Purchase price: € 100.00, selling price: € 150.00, AB in the cash register: € 7,000.00. The following business cases arise: 1. Karina acquires the first 20 lamps for cash 2. Sale of 15 lamps in cash. 3. The inventory results in a final stock of five pieces 4. Conclusion account cash register 5. Conclusion account sales revenues 6. Conclusion account goods consumption 7. Conclusion account goods stock [...] Answer the following questions afterwards: [...] How much cash should be in the cash register after these business cases?

(continued)

Table 7.19 (continued)

Category	Example tasks from the sample
Impact on balance sheet (positions)	**Example 4 (AE746, excerpt):** In the Walter Luger GmbH, among other things, the following business cases arise: Bank transfer for radio advertising €4500,- (account advertising expense) a) Form the booking sentences. b) Tick next to the booking sentence whether the respective business case increases or decreases equity.
	Example 5 (AE1366, excerpt): Valerie Weber closes her fitness studio between 01.01 and 06.01 to prepare herself with new energy for the coming year. a) Tick next to the account designations on the accounts whether it is an active or passive inventory account. b) Enter the business cases on the accounts. The accounts have already been opened. Don't forget to specify the counter account next to the date. c) Tick in the margin column the type of booking. Is it a balance sheet extension, balance sheet reduction, active exchange or passive exchange? 03.01.20.. From the bank, 1,000.00 € are withdrawn and put into the cash register. 04.01.20.. The borrowed loan is increased by 1,500.00 € to pay immediately due supplier debts.
Impact on the tax burden/MWR	**Example 6 (AE596):** In the fashion boutique Clarissa GmbH, the following value is shown on account 2090 flat rate value adjustment as of 31.12.20..: 3,700.00 EUR. As part of the annual financial statements, a flat rate value adjustment of 3970 EUR results for the current financial year. How is this business case treated in the context of the tax more-less calculation?
Impact on the External representation	**Example 7 (AE1970):** Claudia Stern analyzes the annual financial statements of Sport Stern GmbH for the first time. She writes a detailed, commented report and files it. She would have expected many things, but not incredible interest from: her husband Peter; Hubert, the apprentice; Dieter Schneider, long-time tax consultant and friend of the Sterns; her personal bank advisor; Marie Bauer, the managing director of Easy Living Hotel GmbH, who asked Sport Stern for a complete set of new fitness equipment last week. All the people mentioned ask Claudia for her key figure analysis. Claudia is curious—she wants to know from everyone why they are interested in the data. a) Enter in the speech bubbles which key figure information each person is interested in and how the individual persons could explain their interest. b) Claudia is not sure whether she wants to hand over the key figures to Marie. What could be the reason for this?

(continued)

Table 7.19 (continued)

Category	Example tasks from the sample
Other interpretation services	**Example 8 (AE1983):** Calculate some of the key figures presented by Josef Manner & Comp. AG in the annual report with the formulas you have learned for the 2019 financial year. Interpret the results and compare your figures with those from the Manner annual report: – ROS (Return on Sales) – ROE (Return on Equity) – ROI – Equity Ratio

In Example 5, the encoding with 1 in the category "Impact on Balance Sheet (positions)" is less clear. However, by asking to specify what type of booking it is (balance sheet extension, balance sheet reduction, asset swap, liability swap), the learners must interpret how the business transaction changes the balance sheet (Does the balance sheet total change? Does it increase or decrease? etc.). Therefore, these and structurally similar tasks were coded with 1 in this category. In the category "Impact on Tax Burden", the majority of tasks identified were those in which learners must indicate how a business transaction should be handled in the course of the more-less calculation. This indirectly also addresses the company's income tax burden. For this reason, such tasks were coded with 1. For the category "Impact on External Representation", only two tasks could be identified, both of which could be argued that coding does not seem plausible. In Example 7, although the learners do not have to indicate how a business transaction is represented externally (i.e., to external stakeholders) (e.g., at what point does a business transaction become visible externally and in what form?), they must deal with stakeholders relevant to the company and explain what external impact the annual financial statements (or key figures) have on different stakeholder groups. From this perspective, a coding with 1 seems appropriate. Example 8 finally provides an example of another interpretation service. As part of the tasks, key figures are to be calculated and interpreted. Since no clear assignment to one (or several) other categories could be made (for example, the return on equity could most likely be assigned to the category "Impact on Balance Sheet", the return on sales to the category "Impact on Profit", but a clear assignment is not possible), a new category was introduced that covers these and similar interpretation services.

Table 7.20 Differences in interpretation performance by publisher

			Interpretation		Total
			No	Yes	
Publisher	Trauner Publishing	Number	566	161	727
		Expected Number	452.9	274.1	727
		%	77.9%	22.1%	
	Hölzel Publishing	Number	252	372	624
		Expected Number	388.8	235.2	624
		%	40.4%	59.6%	
	Publisher Jugend & Volk	Number	428	221	649
		Expected Number	404.3	244.7	649
		%	65.9%	34.1%	
Total		Number	1246	754	2000
		Expected Number	1,246.0	754.0	2000
		% of Publisher	62.3%	37.7%	

Year and publisher comparisons for the interpreting step

To determine the differences in interpretation performance, the main category is first considered again (i.e., whether an interpretation performance is to be provided or not, regardless of which formal goal the interpretation performance addresses). This is done firstly to maintain clarity, and secondly because a chi-square test cannot be performed for most subcategories due to the small number of encodings at level 1 (this applies to the categories liquidity, tax burden, external representation, and other interpretation services). Table 7.20 shows the observed and expected values separated by publishers. The chi-square test provides a significant result, with a moderate correlation according to Cramer's V (χ^2 (2) = 206.163, p =.001, V =.321) (Cohen, 1988, pp. 224–225). In the Trauner publishing house, an interpretation performance is to be provided in 22.1% of the tasks, in the Jugend & Volk publishing house in 34.1% of the tasks. In the tasks of the Hölzel publishing house, an interpretation of the result is to be made in more than half of the tasks (59.6%). Accordingly, the post-hoc evaluations show that the values of the Trauner publishing house are significantly below, the values of the Hölzel publishing house significantly above the expected value.

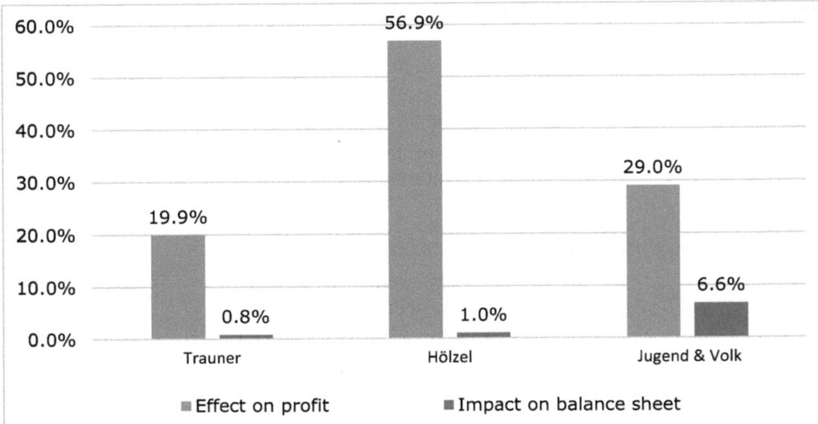

Fig. 7.24 Tasks with indication of impact on profit or balance sheet by publisher

If we now consider the results in more detail at the level of the subcategories (specifically, only the subcategories "Impact on Balance Sheet" and "Impact on Profit" can be reported here), it becomes apparent that the results vary greatly, particularly in the category "Specify Profit Impact" (Fig. 7.24). The differences are significant for both subcategories (Profit Impact: χ^2 (2) = 215.677, p =.001, V =.328; Impact on Balance Sheet: χ^2 (2) = 53.983, p =.001, V =.164).

Significant differences are also shown for the main category among the different years (χ^2 (4) = 111.217, p =.001, V =.236), with only the 2nd year being significantly above, and the 3rd year significantly below the expected value. The observed values of the other years do not deviate significantly from the expected values. Figure 7.25 again shows the percentage of tasks, separated by years, that require interpretation.

If we analyze the subcategories "Impact on Profit" and "Impact on the Balance Sheet", significant differences are also shown there (Impact on Profit: χ^2 (4) = 164.940, p =.001, V =.287; Impact on Balance Sheet: χ^2 (4) = 116.3, p =.001, V =.241). Figure 7.26 visualizes the findings.

7.1.4.5 Results on the Partial Step of Validation and Legal Norm Orientation

Descriptive Findings on the Category of Validation

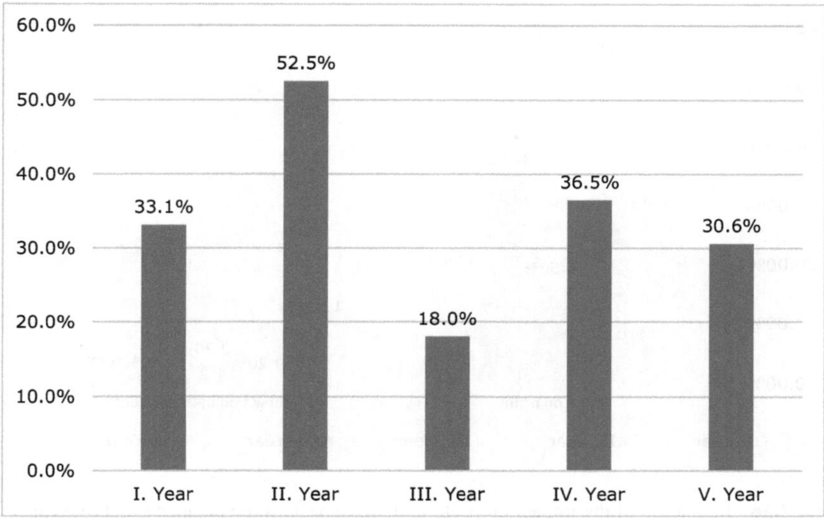

Fig. 7.25 Tasks requiring interpretation by year

The category of validation is about whether a task prompts learners to check their own solution or an existing solution for plausibility, for example by mathematical verification or by applying alternative solution paths for verification. Furthermore, this category includes cases where learners have to justify their own approach or a solution they have worked out themselves. The category is also dichotomous (0 = no validation required, 1 = validation required). So again, it was only checked whether such a performance must be provided by the learners or not. However, no further distinctions were made (e.g., to what extent must the validation happen and based on which criteria?).

The descriptive evaluations (Table 7.1) show that in 4.9% of the tasks, a validation, i.e., a review of one's own or an existing solution, is required. In the remaining 95.1% of the tasks, no review is required.

Examples of Different Validation Performances

Below, four tasks will be presented as examples, in which learners are asked to check their own solutions in one way or another, choose alternative processing paths, or check existing solutions. In Example 1, an already prepared balance sheet is to be checked for errors, in Example 3, a wrongly booked business case

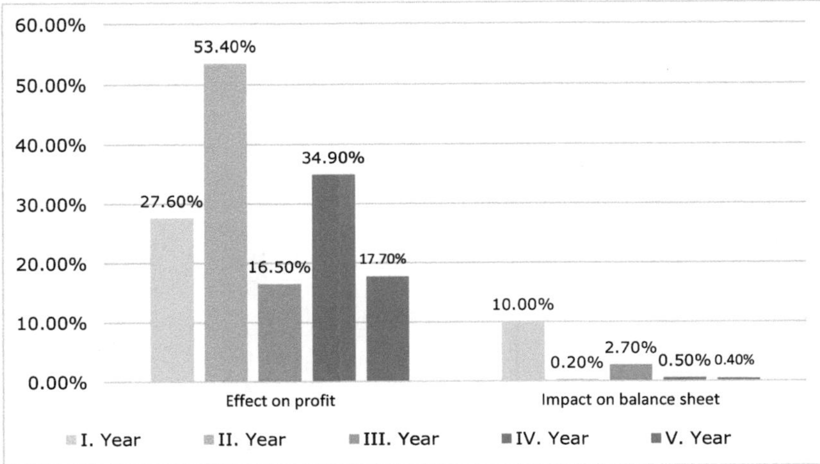

Fig. 7.26 Indication of the impact on profit and the impact on the balance sheet by year

is to be corrected. However, it should be noted for both examples that the learners are given assistance by making it clear that there are apparently errors in the solutions already worked out. Nevertheless, these and comparable tasks were coded with 1. Example 4 also requires validation, namely the verification of the mathematical and factual correctness of two cash receipts. On the other hand, Example 2 prompts learners to justify their own approach/solution (Table 7.21).

Publisher and Year Comparisons for the Partial Step of Validation

Figure 7.27 shows what percentage of tasks require the verification of a self-developed or an existing solution. In the tasks of the Trauner publishing house, 3.4% of the tasks require validation, while it is 1.4% for the tasks of the Hölzel publishing house and 9.9% for the tasks of the publishing house Jugend & Volk. In other words, of the tasks that require validation, 65.3% come from the books of the publishing house Jugend & Volk, 25.51% from the books of the Trauner publishing house and 9.18% from the books of the Hölzel publishing house. A Chi-square test was conducted to determine whether the differences are significant. This shows that there are significant differences between observed and expected values (χ^2 (2) = 53.622, p =.001, V =.164). The correlation can be described as weak. The post-hoc tests show that the observed value of the Hölzel publishing house is significantly below, the observed value of the publishing house Jugend

Table 7.21 Example tasks for validation performances

Category	Example tasks from the sample
Validate	**Example 1 (AE13):** Susanne is a commercial apprentice at Kriechbaum GmbH. For practice purposes, she was supposed to prepare a balance sheet for 31.12.20.. When her supervisor checks the result, she finds the errors. What did Susanne do wrong? Note the errors. *(faulty balance sheet given)*
	Example 2 (AE1573): Lukas and Bernd are so excited about the new monitor that they want to equip their training room with five pieces of the model. What is the booking now? Assume that a discount of 10% is granted on the original €806.00 incl. VAT per piece. Payment will not be made until next month. Briefly justify your booking. How does the booking affect the company's success?
	Example 3 (AE1383, excerpt): In the following cases, the booking was incorrect. Correct the wrong bookings. Transfer of open supplier invoice in the amount of €1,860.00. *(incorrect booking sentence given)*
	Example 4 (AE1500): Check the following receipts of the company Sport Stern for their correctness (mathematically and factually). Also check the components according to the VAT Act. *(two receipts listed)*

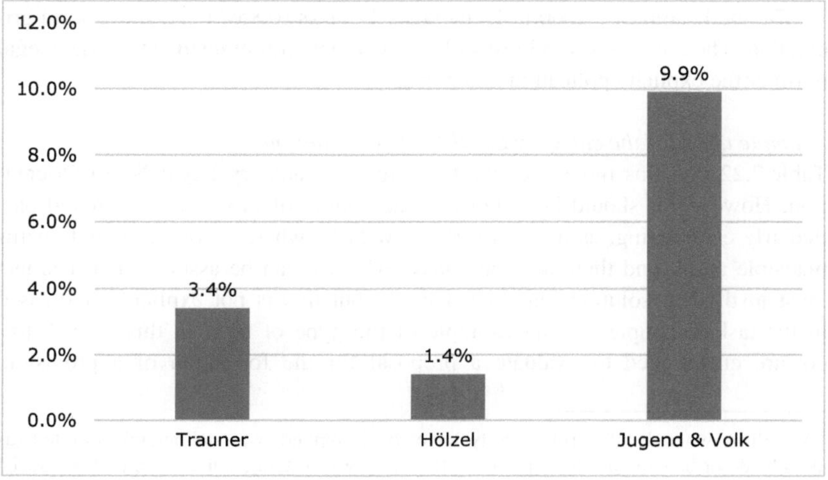

Fig. 7.27 Proportion of tasks requiring validation by publisher

& Volk significantly above the expected value. There is no significant deviation between the observed and expected value for the Trauner publishing house. On the other hand, there are no significant differences between the years (χ^2 (4) = 9.073, p =.059).

Descriptive Findings on the Category of Norm Orientation
The category of norm orientation is about whether a task calls for a task/solution/explanation to be *explicitly* justified by an existing legal norm, or whether learners are asked to work *explicitly* with a norm. This category was again derived on the basis of the Linz Levels Model (Neuweg, 2020) and is therefore not part of the modeling cycle. There are therefore points of connection to the modeling cycle at different points (e.g., during orientation, when it is first necessary to decide whether the business case in question is relevant to accounting and therefore requires translation into the world of accounting; during translation and internal accounting work, when norms must be applied, e.g., the formation of a provision according to the requirements of § 198 para 8 Z 1 to 4 UGB). However, tasks in this category are only coded if they require a solution/procedure to be *justified* explicitly by a norm, so it can be most closely associated with the validation sub-step.[3] The category is dichotomous, with tasks being coded with 0 if no justification of bookings, activities or solutions via norms is to be made, and with 1 if a booking, an activity or a solution is to be justified via a legal norm or if *explicitly* asked to apply a norm.

The total sample of 2000 tasks includes 17 tasks (0.85%) that show norm orientation. The remaining 1983 tasks (99.2%) do not require justification via a legal norm or the explicit application of a norm.

Example tasks for the category Legal Norm Orientation
Table 7.22 contains three example tasks for the category Legal Norm Orientation. However, it should be noted that the coding of this category proved particularly challenging, as there are very few tasks where a coding with 1 seems plausible at all, and there are some tasks where it can be assumed that learners must justify the solution via a legal norm, but this is not explicitly addressed in the task. Example 1 is an example of this type of task. In this case, learners are encouraged to evaluate a proposal for the formation of a provision.

[3] A coding, when legal norms merely have to be applied, was deliberately omitted (as already described in the description of the category system), since it cannot be traced whether learners really mentally refer to a specific legal norm during the processing of the task, e.g., when booking a low-value economic good according to § 13 EstG.

Table 7.22 Example tasks for the category Norm Orientation

Category	Example tasks from the sample
Legal Norm Orientation	**Example 1 (AE503):**
Justification of an activity, a solution, etc. via a legal norm	The managing director of Hinterberger GmbH plans to purchase a new production machine for the business year after next, which will cost approximately 100,000.00 EUR net. He therefore suggests to his accountant to form a provision for the planned machine purchase in the amount of 50,000.00 EUR each on December 31 of this year and on December 31 of next year. Evaluate the permissibility of implementing this proposal. Justify your answer!
explicit application of a legal norm	**Example 2 (AE1996):** Assume that the managing director would take five meters of the fabric for a private New Year's Eve party on 31.12.X26. Determine the amount with which the private withdrawal is valued for VAT purposes and justify your valuation.
	Example 3 (AE455, excerpt): Which valuation principle is violated in the Huber GmbH in the following cases? Huber GmbH sells a racing bike worth 3,900.00 EUR to a customer on December 27 of this year. The customer transfers the invoice amount on January 9 of next year, so the incoming profit is allocated to the next business year.

This refers to the *legal* permissibility (is it allowed to form a provision in this case or not?), without explicitly referring to the UGB or the EstG. For such tasks, the information part was therefore always examined. If there are also no indications of the relevant legal norm there, then the legal norm orientation was also coded with 0 (for more detailed explanations, see the category system in the appendix in the electronic supplementary material). However, for example 1, based on the information part in the book, it can be assumed that learners have to assess the permissibility of the proposal with reference to the relevant legal texts (the present example specifically refers to the formation of an expense provision, which is definitely not permissible according to § 9 EstG due to the lack of obligation to external third parties). In example 2, a legal norm is also explicitly to be applied (self-consumption according to § 3 UStG). In example 3, it is necessary to explain for different facts which valuation principle was violated, which in turn represents the application of a norm. Example 4 of the "Validate" category also provides an example for the category of norm orientation, as learners must explicitly apply the provisions of the UStG when checking the invoice (§ 11 UStG para 1 Z 3) (Table 7.21).

Comparisons by year and publisher

When comparing the tasks of different publishers regarding legal norm orientation, the picture shown in Fig. 7.28 emerges. A conducted Chi-square test confirms that there is a significant difference between the groups, with only the observed value for the publisher Jugend & Volk significantly above the expected value ($\chi^2(2) = 53.622$, $p = .001$, $V = .164$). There are no statistically significant differences between the years (χ^2 $(4) = 9073$, $p = .059$).

7.1.4.6 Results for the Decision-Making Substep

Descriptive findings for the decision-making category

The decision-making substep asks whether learners have to make a business decision in the course of task processing, which in turn influences processes in the real world. It is important to mention that this substep does *not* involve decisions

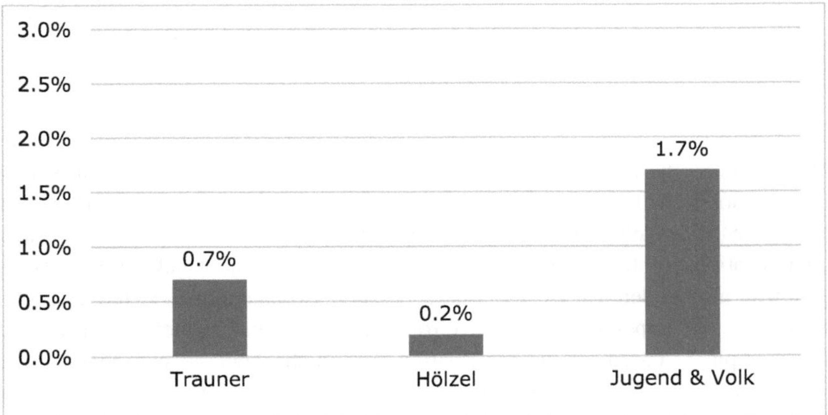

Fig. 7.28 Proportion of tasks with legal norm orientation by publisher

AE915 (excerpt):

In Klose-Plastik GmbH, the following business cases arise, among others:

[...]

E 465 Purchase of four tires for the truck including rims, balancing and mounting from Reifeprofi Rainer GmbH (22121). The invoice is € 680,- + € 136,- VAT = € 816,-. Terms of payment: Payable within 30 days without deduction, within ten days with 2% discount. In the event of late payment, 12 % p.a. interest will be charged.

a) Set up the posting records.
b) Indicate whether the respective transaction increases or decreases equity or whether it is a neutral entry.
c) Calculate the annual interest that results from the use of the cash discount when purchasing the tires for Klose-Plastik GmbH.
d) Based on this annual interest rate, would you take the cash discount or not? Explain your answer.

Fig. 7.29 Example task 1 for the category making business decisions

that need to be made at the beginning of the modeling cycle (e.g., at what depreciation rate should the machine be depreciated, how much provision should be made?), but decisions that are made at the end of the process and subsequently influence operations in the business reality (e.g., Should product A be removed from the range based on the calculations? Should the operation be closed based on the data? etc.). The category is also dichotomous, with a coding of 0 being made if no business decision had to be made and a coding of 1 being made if the task involved making a business decision.

The evaluations (Table 7.1) show that in 8 tasks (which corresponds to 0.4%) a business decision has to be made. Due to the small number of codings with 1, no statistically significant differences could be calculated.

Examples for the decision-making substep

In the textbooks, hardly any tasks could be identified in which learners have to make a business decision. Figure 7.29 and 7.30 present two tasks where the category was coded with 1. In both cases, however, strictly speaking, no decision has to be made, but rather a recommendation for an alternative action has to be given. In example 1, a recommendation for or against taking advantage of a discount is to be given by calculating the annual interest rate. In example 2, a recommendation is to be given based on the calculation of various key figures as

AE1987:
It wasn't so long ago that Melanie realized her dream of running her own car repair shop. The second annual financial statement for a complete financial year is finally available. No cars have been rented or sold in these years. This means that the turnover comes exclusively from the workshop, where repairs and tune-ups are carried out. The majority of customers are wealthy and invest in expensive spare parts, which are fitted by Melanie's workshop when required.

Your tasks:

a) Calculate the key figures according to the table at the end of the task for Melanie Maxian's company Pimp my Car GmbH. Enter all the values in the table or create your own table in the Excel template and use the data given there for your calculations. Analyze the key figure areas:
   1. The key figure itself,
   2. In comparison over time
   3. And–if possible–in comparison to the industry. Since the start of the business, the company has consistently employed three workers and one employee.

b) Carry out the quick test for the closing year and interpret the result.

c) Finally, evaluate the company in general. Which values are perfect, which values should Melanie improve in order to run her company successfully in the long term?

d) How could the figures for this year change if Melanie expands her business activities and also offers car rental and car sales from next year? Based on the data available, would you recommend or advise against it?

Balance sheet and income statement listed; various key figures to be calculated (equity ratio, asset intensity, asset coverage, liquidity ratios, return on equity, return on assets, return on sales, return on investment, cash flow as a percentage of operating performance, personnel expenses as a percentage of operating performance, personnel expenses and sales per employee, etc.).

Fig. 7.30 Example task 2 for the category making business decisions

to whether the company should expand its business activities or not. In the other examples where the value 1 was given, either a decision about taking advantage of a discount has to be made or a recommendation about the continuation of the company (Should the company be closed or not?) has to be given. In three further examples, measures to improve the business situation are to be proposed (Table 7.30).

7.1.5 Results for the Category Connections to Other Content Areas

Descriptive Findings

The category Connections asks whether a reference or connection to other content areas is established within a task or needs to be established by the learner. The relevant content areas were defined as internal accounting (covered by the subcategories cost accounting and liquidity management) on the one hand, and general business management topics on the other. Coding is done for the connection to cost accounting or liquidity management whenever a reference is established by the task (e.g., reference to data from cost accounting) or the learners have to establish a reference (e.g., booking goods purchase and calculating the selling price). For connections to business management, however, coding is only done when the learners have to provide a connection. All three subcategories are again dichotomous.

The descriptive evaluations (Table 7.1) show that in 2.1% of the tasks (n = 41) a reference to business management topics is established, in 1.0% of the tasks (n = 19) to cost accounting and in 0.8% of the tasks (n = 15) to financial accounting. In total, a connection is established in 75 tasks (3.75%) or a connection performance is to be provided by the learners.

Examples of Tasks with Connections to Other Subject Areas

Examples 1, 2 and 3 (Table 7.23) show tasks with a reference to business management content. In Example 1, the learners have to process the document (account assignment and booking). This is followed by a question about the delivery and payment conditions. These are contents that are covered in business management lessons (in the area of purchase contract including correspondence, 1st grade). The same applies to examples 2 and 3, where a business case also has to be documented in accounting terms (booking incoming invoices or credit note) and subsequently questions with a business management reference (legal components of a purchase contract, defects) have to be answered. These and similar tasks were therefore coded as tasks with a connection to business management. Isolated knowledge questions with business management content (e.g., Explain why companies grant discounts? Explain what a POS terminal is?) were not coded if these tasks were not asked in the *context* of a task from accounting, as this is not a *connection*. In examples 4 and 5 (Table 7.23), a reference to cost accounting is established by either referring to the fact that the data provided comes from cost accounting (example 5) or by determining the manufacturing

Table 7.23 Example tasks for connections with other content areas

<table>
<tr><th>Category</th><th>Example tasks from the sample</th></tr>
<tr><td rowspan="3">Connections to Business Administration</td><td>Example 1 (AE1623):
Post and book the documents and answer the questions.

3
SoftBit
SoftBit GmbH
Längenfeldgasse 12
1120 Wien
Tel: +43 1 599 18 20-0
E-Mail: office@softbit.at
www.softbit.com
Die Programmierer GmbH
Siebensterngasse 17
1070 Wien
RECHNUNG Nr.: 130 Rechnungsdatum: 21.03.20..
Menge | Bezeichnung | Einzelpreis | Gesamtpreis
1 | Sub-Entry Storage Server System | € 500,00 | € 500,00
Rechnungsbetrag € 500,00
- 10% Stammkundenrabatt € 50,00
Rechnungsbetrag netto € 450,00
+ 20% Umsatzsteuer € 90,00
Gesamtpreis € 540,00
Konto | Soll | Haben
Beleg
Lieferung: frei Haus | Fälligkeit: innerhalb von 14 Tagen ohne Abzug!
Verzugszinsen 10% ab ursprünglicher Rechnungsfälligkeit.
Die Ware bleibt bis zur vollständigen Bezahlung unser Eigentum!
Bankverbindung: Erste Bank, BIC: GIBAATWW, IBAN AT232011130143103067
UID: ATU80321198 – Handelsgericht Wien – Firmenbuch FN 334376 h
What delivery and payment terms were agreed between the buyer and the seller? Briefly explain their meaning.</td></tr>
<tr><td>Example 2 (AE1004, excerpt):
The machinery industry AG needs larger quantities of cleaning material. In this context, the following stocks and business cases arise.
E247 Purchase of various cleaning materials from Unisolv AG (33080) for € 10,494,- + € _________ VAT 20 % = € ______
2.7 Incoming invoice depicted
[…]
a) Set up the booking entries.
b) Indicate whether the respective business case increases, decreases the equity, or if it is a neutral booking.
c) […]
d) Provide the legal components of the purchase contract for the business case on July 2nd. (Who sells? Who buys? What is bought? How much is bought? At what price is it bought?)</td></tr>
<tr><td>Example 3 (AE861, excerpt):
In the Elektro Markt GmbH, a specialist dealer for electrical appliances in Klagenfurt am Wörthersee, the following business cases arise in May among others:
[…]
10.5 Invoice for the sale of a Liebherr freezer to the customer Amina Jarisch (20014) €1480,- + € 296,- VAT = € 1776,-
[…]
17.5 The customer Amina Jarisch (20014) returns the freezer due to an irreparable damage in the cooling system; credit note of € 1776,- (incl. 20 % VAT).
[…]
a) Formulate the booking entries.
b) Indicate whether the respective business case increases, decreases the equity, or if it is a neutral booking.
c) Work on the following tasks in relation to the delivery of the freezer to Amira Jarisch and its return.
• Describe how defects are identified and reported.
• Analyze what types of defects were identified by Amina Jarisch.
• Explain what legal options Amina Jarisch has.</td></tr>
</table>

(continued)

Table 7.23 (continued)

<table>
<tr><th>Category</th><th>Example tasks from the sample</th></tr>
<tr><td rowspan="2">Connections to cost accounting</td><td>Example 4 (AE398):
Ergonomica sit and walk GmbH: The company specializes in the production of office furniture. A special machine was produced in the development department for the production of an ergonomic office chair, with which wooden slats can be shaped precisely.
a) For the calculation of the manufacturing costs, you have the following data from cost accounting. Complete the table and determine the calculation rates.
<table>
<tr><th>Berechnung</th><th>Material</th><th>Fertigung</th></tr>
<tr><td>Summe Gemeinkosten laut BAB</td><td>180.000,00</td><td>125.000,00</td></tr>
<tr><td>– kalkulatorische Abschreibung laut BAB</td><td>12.000,00</td><td>35.000,00</td></tr>
<tr><td>– kalkulatorische Wagnisse laut BAB</td><td>2.500,00</td><td>3.800,00</td></tr>
<tr><td>– kalkulatorische Zinsen laut BAB</td><td>1.500,00</td><td>2.400,00</td></tr>
<tr><td>– kalkulatorischer Unternehmerlohn laut BAB</td><td>-</td><td>-</td></tr>
<tr><td>+ Abschreibung laut GuV</td><td>11.800,00</td><td>28.900,00</td></tr>
<tr><td>+ Schadensfälle laut GuV</td><td>2.400,00</td><td>2.900,00</td></tr>
<tr><td>= Summe Gemeinkosten</td><td></td><td></td></tr>
<tr><td>Bezugsbasis</td><td>Materialeinzelkosten</td><td>Fertigungseinzelkosten</td></tr>
<tr><td>Werte</td><td>265.800,00</td><td>165.800,00</td></tr>
<tr><td>GK-Kalkulationssätze</td><td></td><td></td></tr>
</table>
b) Determine and book the manufacturing costs for the machine. The machine was completed and put into operation on July 2, 20.. Material individual costs: 3,600.00 EUR, manufacturing individual costs: 1,263.00 EUR.
c) Calculate and book the depreciation for the machine. The useful life is ten years. Enter the system in the asset directory.</td></tr>
<tr><td>Example 5 (AE1089):
Starckl GmbH is the market leader in the product area of wood chipping machines and produces a stationary chipping machine with electric drive for the production of wood chips for the company's own power plant. According to the records of cost accounting, the manufacturing costs are € 45,000,-. The plant is put into operation on March 27; useful life ten years.
Task: Book the recording of the chipping machine (U5) and the declining balance depreciation (30 % of the manufacturing costs, U 28).</td></tr>
</table>

(continued)

Table 7.23 (continued)

<table>
<tr><th>Category</th><th>Example tasks from the sample</th></tr>
<tr><td rowspan="2">Connections to liquidity management</td><td>Example 6 (AE1360):
Doris Kremser, passionate golfer and graduate of the business university, turns her hobby into a profession. With her savings, she opens a trading company in which she offers various golf articles. Before the opening, she has already made first purchases and bought trading goods. At the end of the year, Doris takes stock.
Your tasks:
a) Create the final balance for Doris Kremser's trading company. The following data is available as of December 31, 20..:
<table>
<tr><td>Bankschulden</td><td>€ 40.000,00</td><td>PC</td><td>€ 480,00</td></tr>
<tr><td>Lieferforderungen</td><td>€ 2.980,00</td><td>Regale</td><td>€ 6.450,00</td></tr>
<tr><td>Büroeinrichtung</td><td>€ 3.422,00</td><td>Lieferverbindlichkeiten</td><td>€ 5.628,00</td></tr>
<tr><td>Golfartikel (laut Inventur)</td><td>€ 47.520,00</td><td>Bankguthaben</td><td>€ 7.821,00</td></tr>
<tr><td>Alarmsystem</td><td>€ 1.450,00</td><td>Drucker</td><td>€ 639,00</td></tr>
<tr><td>Bargeld in der Kassa</td><td>€ 866,00</td><td></td><td></td></tr>
</table>
b) Answer the following questions:
[…]
5. Could Doris currently repay her debts to the bank? If yes, where would she get the money from?</td></tr>
<tr><td>Example 7 (AE1362):
Susanne is desperate—her pocket money keeps running out. She decides to write down exactly what she spent how much money on. Her notes show the initial balance, expenses and income:
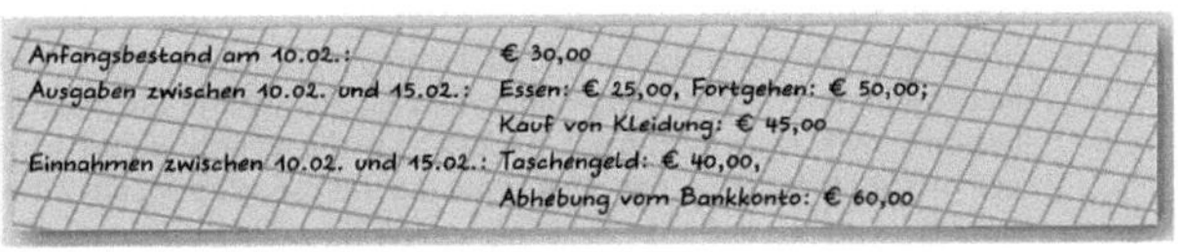

Your task:
Create the pocket money account for Susanne.</td></tr>
</table>

costs based on cost accounting data and then booking them in accounting terms (example 4). Identifying examples that show a connection to financial accounting or liquidity management proved to be very difficult. For the connection to financial accounting, tasks were also coded in which key figures related to financial accounting (e.g., liquidity 1st degree, cash flow) have to be determined. Strictly speaking, however, these are not *connection performances*, as these tasks usually only require the key figure to be determined. In example 6, a final balance sheet is to be prepared. This is followed by questions to be answered. This includes, among other things, the question of whether the company could currently pay off its existing debts and if so, where the money would come from. This establishes

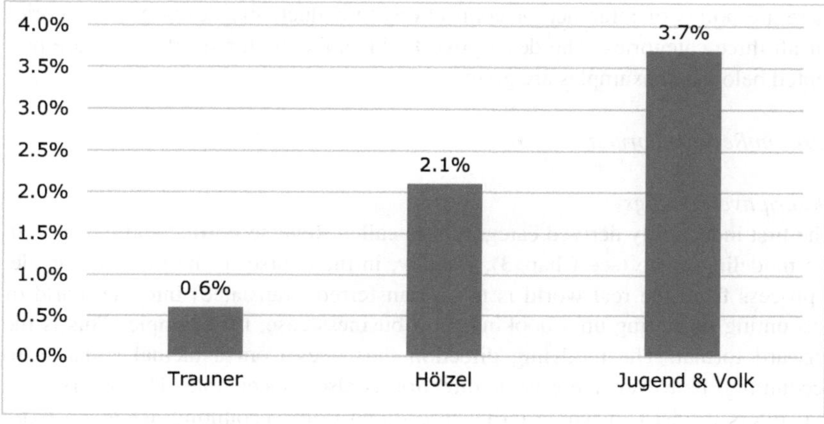

Fig. 7.31 Tasks with connection to business management topics per publisher

at least an indirect reference to financial accounting. In example 6 (Table 7.23), a reference to liquidity management is established by documenting deposits and withdrawals on a pocket money account.

Publisher and Grade Comparisons

For the connection to cost accounting and financial accounting, either no significant differences were found or an evaluation was not possible due to the small number of codings. This applies to differences between publishers as well as between grades. Significant differences between publishers, however, were found for the connection to business management topics. However, the correlation is to be considered weak (χ^2 (2) = 16.926, p =.001, V =.092) (Cohen, 1988, pp. 224–225). The post-hoc evaluations show that the observed value for the Trauner publishing house is significantly below, the value for the Jugend & Volk publishing house significantly above the expected value (Fig. 7.31). No significant differences were found at the grade level (χ^2 (4) = 6504, p =.165).

7.1.6 Results for Inductively Formed Categories

In addition to the categories developed on the basis of theoretical preliminary work (deductive), three other categories proved to be interesting in the course of the coding process. Although these were inductively derived from the material, there are points of reference or connections to deductively developed categories for all three categories. The descriptive findings for the three categories are presented below and examples are given.

Tasks in Reverse Format

Descriptive Findings
The first inductively derived category was called Reverse Format and ties in with the modeling cycle (see Chap. 3). Usually, in the course of the modeling cycle, a process from the real world is to be transferred (translated) into the world of accounting by setting up a booking for a business case, for example. This is the forward format. The modeling direction thus goes from a factual situation to accounting. However, the reverse direction is also conceivable. The reverse format refers to tasks in which terms/procedures from accounting are given (e.g., booking sentences, terms, balance sheets, etc.) and suitable real business processes are to be identified for these. Berding (2019, p. 145) also distinguishes between tasks in forward and reverse format in diagnostic tasks for determining basic ideas (see also Sect. 3.2). Figure 7.32 graphically represents the two different modeling directions. However, the distinction between forward and reverse format was initially not included in the original category system, as tasks in common textbooks are traditionally designed in the forward format. During the first coding process, a few tasks in the reverse format were identified and therefore the category was included in the category system.

In total, however, only 8 tasks (0.4%) were identified in which a real situation is to be described based on procedures and terms of accounting. Due to the small number of codings, it is not possible to determine significant differences between publishers or grades.

Examples of Tasks in Reverse Format
Figure 7.33 and 7.34 present tasks in reverse format. In both cases, learners are asked to consider what real business cases lie behind these bookings. The modeling direction therefore goes from accounting to the real world (= reverse format).

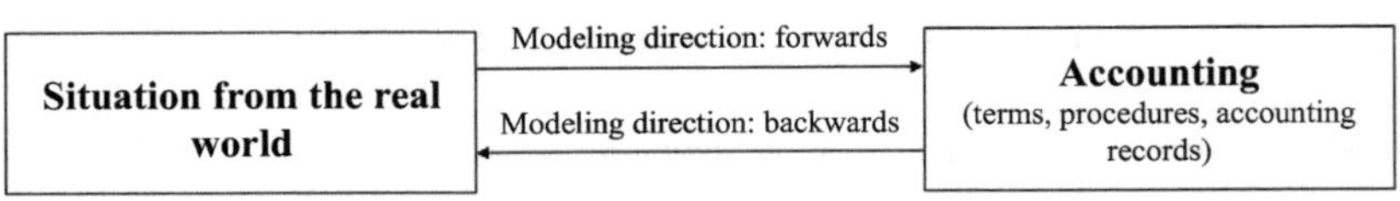

Fig. 7.32 Forward and Reverse Format of Accounting Tasks

Your task:
Think about which business case could have led to the respective posting and enter it in keywords above the accounts.

1. ______________________________

Cash desk			
Date	Contra account	Debit	Credit
02.05.	Rental income	2,000.00	

Rental income			
Date	Contra account	Debit	Credit
02.05.	Cash		2,000.00

2. ______________________________

Bank			
Date	Contra account	Debit	Credit
	Miscellaneous	15,400.00	
02.05.	Private		5,000.00

Private			
Date	Contra account	Debit	Credit
02.05.	Bank		5,000.00

Fig. 7.33 Example task 1 in reverse format

Specification of a business management formal objective

Descriptive findings
The category "specification of a formal objective" was also inductively included in the category system, with connections here to the theoretical preliminary work (especially the "Linzer Ebenenmodell" according to Neuweg, 2020) or to the deductively developed category system. The question at the center here is whether a formal objective is specified in the course of the task that the learners must take into account when mapping the business cases in accounting. This primarily concerns the utilization of balance sheet policy valuation leeway, for example to show the profit as high or as low as possible. A similar category can also be found in the category system of Wuttke et al. (2022).

Table 7.1 contains the descriptive findings for this category and shows that in 2.2% of the tasks a formal objective is given, which the learners must align their

S 2: Which business transactions are the postings based on? Explain in detail. Ⓒ

a)

2800 Bank 9610 Private taxes	/ 8071 Final taxed dividend income

b)

2800 Bank 7790 Money transfer expenses 9610 Private taxes	/ 8150 Proceeds from the disposal of other financial assets

c)

0870 Shares in corporations without equity character (shares)	/ 2800 Bank

Fig. 7.34 Example task 2 in reverse format

activities with. In 97.8% of the tasks, no formal objective is given. The tasks that contain a specification exclusively involve the specification to show the profit as low (or as high) as possible, other formal objectives are not addressed.

Example task for the category specification of a formal objective

Figure 7.35 shows an excerpt of a task that was coded with 1 in this category. The learners are asked to carry out their activities taking into account the goal of showing the profit as low as possible. The balance sheet policy valuation leeway is therefore to be used in such a way that the highest possible expense is booked, which subsequently reduces profit.

Publisher and year comparisons

In the specification of a balance sheet policy objective, significant differences are shown between the publishers and between the years (publisher: χ^2 (2) = 41.447, p =.001, V =.144; year: χ^2 (4) = 59.819, p =.001, V =.173). The results for the years are as expected due to the curriculum content, as the observed values in the 1st and 2nd year are significantly below, in the 4th and 5th year significantly

Company: Hairdressing salon Elke, Mozartgasse 3, 5020 Salzburg
In the course of the financial statements as at 31.12.2020, the hairdressing salon's business equipment is depreciated.

The aim is to achieve the lowest possible profit.

Notes: All tasks are to be solved in the form of accounting records.

S1: Give at least five reasons why the hairdressing salon's equipment will lose value over time. Give specific examples.

S2: Calculate the book values and previous depreciation up to 01.01 of the financial statements. Enter the book values in the asset register.

S3: Calculate the depreciation for the closing year.

[...]

Fig. 7.35 Example task for the specification of balance sheet policy objectives

above the expected value. When evaluating separately by publishers, it is shown that of the 44 analysis units in which a balance sheet policy objective is specified, 82% come from the Trauner publisher, 16% from the Jugend & Volk publisher and 2.3% from the Hölzel publisher. Accordingly, the post-hoc evaluations show that the observed value at the Trauner publisher is significantly above, the observed value at the Hölzel publisher significantly below the expected value.

Change of perspective

Descriptive findings on the change of perspective
The category "change of perspective" was also included as a further inductive category. This category is about the question of whether *one* task or *one* business case has to be processed from different perspectives, for example from the buyer's and the seller's point of view, or whether only one perspective has to be taken. Here too, it has been shown that individual tasks in the sample require the processing of a task from several perspectives. For this reason, the category was also included. It can be assumed that viewing a business case from several different perspectives leads to a better understanding of operational reality, which in turn means that learners are better able to connect the real world and the world of accounting. Seifried and Sembill (2004, p. 378) also formulate the "multiple

Michael Resch from the Resch bakery is planning a customer event for commercial customers. He wants to organize a raffle. While searching for suitable gift items, he comes across the game.area website, which convinces him with the following offer:

"Sims 4 – Get to Work"
Now only 34.90 euros
Gain insights into various professions. You can realize yourself as a master baker with your own bakery or get a taste of the everyday life of a surgeon ..."

Michael Resch and Stefan Pfeiffer agree on a 2% discount for payment within one week. Two days later, Michael receives the PC games with the invoice:

Your tasks:
a) Post the invoice from the game.area's point of view (account number for Michael Resch: 20999 Miscellaneous customers) and state the effect on profit. (invoice quoted)
b) Calculate the payment amount less discount, the net amount and the required tax adjustment.
c) [...]
e) Present the entries from the perspective of the Resch bakery.

Fig. 7.36 Example of a task with a change of perspective

processing of similar facts from different perspectives" as a key element for a "sustainable increase in student orientation and learning activity in class".

The frequency evaluation shows that in 2.0% of the tasks (n = 39) a change of perspective has to be made, i.e. a business case has to be processed from *more than one* perspective. This is not the case in the remaining 98.1% of the tasks. The different perspectives usually always involve the role of the buyer on the one hand and the role of the seller on the other.

Examples of tasks with a change of perspective
Figure 7.36 shows an excerpt of a task in which a change of perspective has to be made. First, the business case has to be processed from the perspective of the company game.area (booking of the outgoing invoice, receipt of the invoice amount). Subsequently, at sub-item e), the bookings from the perspective of the customer Bäckerei Resch are to be presented. A business case therefore has to be processed from two perspectives (seller and buyer).

Publisher and year comparisons
For the category, significant differences are shown both between the publishers and between the years (publisher: χ^2 (2) = 55.480, p =.001, V =.167; year: χ^2 (4) = 41.375, p =.001, V =.144). No change of perspective has to be made at the Trauner publisher, at the Hölzel publisher in 0.8% of the tasks and at the Jugend & Volk publisher a change of perspective is required in 5.2% of the tasks. Accordingly, the post-hoc tests show that the observed value at the Jugend & Volk publisher is significantly above the expected value, at the Trauner publisher significantly below the expected value. The differences between the years show that a change of perspective is particularly necessary in the 2nd year (specifically in 4.8% of the tasks, while in the years 1 and 3 to 5 it is between 0 and 1.6%).

7.2 Assessment of the Quality of the Evaluative Content Analysis

An important aspect of any research project is the assessment of the quality of the data collection and evaluation methods used. Since the material is assessed on different scales in the course of the evaluative content analysis (which in turn orient themselves on the standards of scaling when formulating the manifestations), the transfer of the classic quality criteria seems permissible for the present *evaluative* task analysis in order to assess the quality of the survey (Mayring, 2015, p. 108). These are the criteria of objectivity, reliability, and validity (Döring & Bortz, 2016, p. 107; Kuckartz & Rädiker, 2022, p. 235; Mayring, 2015, pp. 123–124; Moosbrugger & Kelava, 2012, p. 8; Neuendorf, 2017, p. 171).

The *objectivity* assesses the independence of the results from the researching individuals (Döring & Bortz, 2016, p. 184; Moosbrugger & Kelava, 2012, p. 8). Objectivity is divided into implementation objectivity, evaluation objectivity, and interpretation objectivity (Döring & Bortz, 2016, p. 443; Lamnek & Krell, 2016, p. 168; Moosbrugger & Kelava, 2012, pp. 10–11). *Implementation objectivity* is present when the results are achieved under controlled implementation conditions, which lead to the same results being achieved by different implementing individuals. This can be achieved through a high degree of standardization in the test implementation (Döring & Bortz, 2016, p. 443; Moosbrugger & Kelava, 2012, p. 9). The *evaluation objectivity*, on the other hand, is intended to ensure that the same test results are achieved, regardless of the evaluating person (Döring & Bortz, 2016, p. 443; Lamnek & Krell, 2016, p. 168). This refers to the "agreement of different test evaluators", which can also be measured in the form of agreement measures (Moosbrugger & Kelava, 2012, p. 10). A high evaluation objectivity can again be achieved through a high degree of standardization, for example by clearly formulating coding rules and providing anchor examples (Döring & Bortz, 2016, p. 443; Lamnek & Krell, 2016, p. 168). The *interpretation objectivity* is intended to ensure the "independence of the test result from the person interpreting the test value" (Döring & Bortz, 2016, p. 443). The aim is to draw the same conclusions based on the results achieved, regardless of the evaluating person (Lamnek & Krell, 2016, p. 168).

In addition to objectivity, *reliability* (consistency, dependability) is another quality criterion to be met (Mayring, 2015, p. 123; Moosbrugger & Kelava, 2012, p. 11). Reliability refers to the "stability and accuracy of the measurement" and indicates, so to speak, how reliably data collection has been carried out (Atteslander, 2010, pp. 228–229; Lamnek & Krell, 2016, p. 162).

To determine reliability, a distinction is regularly made between different methods (Döring & Bortz, 2016, p. 444; Krippendorff, 2004, pp. 215–216; Lamnek & Krell, 2016, pp. 163–164; Mayring, 2015, p. 123; Moosbrugger & Kelava, 2012, p. 12):

- Test-retest method (test repetition): In the test repetition method, the research operation (e.g., the test, the evaluation procedure, etc.) is carried out a second time and it is checked whether the same results are achieved.
- Parallel test method: In the parallel test method, a second data collection instrument is used and it is checked whether there is a match between the results. The prerequisite for this is that there are several data collection instruments for the variables to be measured.
- Split-half method (test halving): In the split-half method, the examination material or the examination instrument is divided into two parts and it is checked whether similar results are achieved.

For the present study, the test-retest method was applied by examining whether the same results are achieved at two different points in time or whether the same results are achieved when the coder is changed. In the context of reliability assessment, it is therefore necessary to distinguish between *inter* and *intra* coder reliability. Intercoder reliability provides information about the agreement of codings between several coders who independently evaluate the same material. It can therefore strictly speaking also be seen as a measure for measuring objectivity (Mayring, 2015, p. 124). Intracoder reliability, on the other hand, is a measure of the temporal stability of the evaluations. The material is assessed at two different points in time, but by the same person (Döring & Bortz, 2016, p. 558).

A variety of different indicators are available for measuring reliability, which are suitable for different types of data and are based on different assumptions.[4] These different assumptions lead to the reliability estimates of the indices varying greatly when analyzing the same data set (Hove et al., 2018). Overall, however, it can be said that each indicator has specific advantages and disadvantages and there is no clear recommendation for an indicator. In previous task analyses in the accounting domain, very different indicators were also calculated (e.g., Spearman's Rho in Bloemen (2011), the Holsti formula in Ernst (2012a), Cohen's (Weighted) Kappa in Wuttke et al. (2022)).

The best-known indicators include the percentage agreement ("Holsti formula"), Cohen's (Weighted) Kappa (Cohen's κ), Spearman's Rho (Spearman's ρ), Kendall's Tau (Kendall's τ), or Krippendorff's Alpha (Krippendorff's α). The various coefficients differ (among other things) in the scale level of the categories in the observation system for which they are applicable, for how many different coders in the coding process they can be used, and whether corrections are made for random agreements. The Holsti formula (percentage agreement) and Cohen's Kappa are most commonly used, although the percentage agreement does not correct for random agreements. This usually leads to an overestimation of the actual agreement (Döring & Bortz, 2016, pp. 346–347; Hove et al., 2018; Neuendorf, 2017, pp. 245–246; Scheufele & Engelmann, 2009, pp. 172–173). The Holsti formula and Cohen's Kappa are suitable for nominal scales. An extension of Cohen's Kappa is Cohen's Weighted Kappa. This indicator is suitable for ordinal-scaled data (Cohen, 1968).[5] Spearman's Rho and Kendall's Tau, which are also suitable for ordinal-scaled data, on the other hand, do not correct for random codings (Döring & Bortz, 2016, p. 347).

Krippendorff's Alpha is one of the most complex and strictest indicators. It takes into account not only random agreement but also the scale level of the variables and the number of coders (Mayring, 2015, p. 128). However, past evaluations have shown that Krippendorff's Alpha leads to problematic results with

[4] For a discussion on the suitability of the different indicators for measuring reliability, see the works of Berding and Pargmann (2022), Berding et al. (2022), von Hove et al. (2018), Zhao et al. (2018), Feng and Zhao (2016), and Zhao et al. (2013).

[5] The central distinguishing criterion is that Cohen's Weighted Kappa allows partial agreements or weights. It takes into account a weighting, for example, that a deviation of the codings between the values 0 and 1 (one person has coded with 0, the other with 1) is less serious than a deviation between the values 0 and 2 (one person has coded with 0, the other with 2).

unevenly distributed data and unjustifiably low reliability values (Feng, 2013; Zhao et al., 2013). This is particularly problematic in task analyses, as it has been shown in the past that the manifestations are very unevenly distributed (e.g., Bloemen (2011), Berding and Lau (2018), Davidson (2005), Wuttke et al. (2022)).

For the present study, the percentage agreement (Holsti formula) and the calculation of Cohen's (Weighted) Kappa were carried out for the following reasons:

- Although the percentage agreement does not correct for chance agreement, it simultaneously produces the fewest paradoxes. It is also an intuitive, easily understandable measure (Zhao et al., 2013, p. 423). Since it does not correct for chance agreements, it is recommended to report a second measure in addition (Neuendorf, 2017, p. 279).
- Therefore, Cohen's Kappa is reported as a second measure, which corrects for chance agreements. However, with Cohen's Kappa, all non-agreements are treated equally, which can be problematic for ordinal scales. Therefore, Cohen's Weighted Kappa is used for categories with an ordinal scale (Döring & Bortz, 2016, pp. 346–347; Neuendorf, 2017, p. 248). Although Cohen's Kappa also has some paradoxes, it has fewer than Krippendorff's Alpha. Therefore, the use of Krippendorff's Alpha is avoided, as this measure leads to problematic results with data with unequal distribution (which is expected here) (Zhao et al., 2013).
- The use of Spearman's Rho and Kendall's Tau is avoided. Although these would be suitable for ordinal scales, they do not correct for chance agreements. Strictly speaking, both measures are correlation measures (Döring & Bortz, 2016, p. 347; Tausendpfund, 2022, p. 116).

It is also necessary to ask how much material needs to be coded twice in order to carry out the reliability tests. There are different recommendations for this. One recommendation is to double-code a minimum of 30 to 50 codings per category (Scheufele & Engelmann, 2009, p. 173). Alternatively, it is often recommended to double-code approximately 10% of the material (Neuendorf, 2017, p. 263). Following these recommendations, 100 tasks were coded at two different times to calculate the intracoder reliability. This corresponds to 5% of the material. To calculate the intercoder reliability, 300 tasks were coded by two people, which corresponds to 15% of the material.

Table 7.24 Results on intercoder reliability

	Categories	Intercoder reliability (N = 300) R_H	Cohen's (Weighted) κ
Task master	Process orientation	.97	.935
	Process reference of task processing	.95	.928
	Flow of goods and services	.97	.898
	Cash flows	.97	.935
	Social processes	1.00	1.00
	Use of documents	.93	.792
Modeling cycle	Recognize activity	.97	.864
	Information research	.96	.935
	Information evaluation	.96	.904
	Translation performance through other Work	.95	.806
	Translation performance through accounting records	.96	.892
	Internal accounting postings	.96	.794
	Preparing the balance sheet	.98	.819
	Prepare income statement	.99	.854
	Set up more-less-calculation	1.00	.856
	Other work within Accounting	.99	.797
	Mathematical work	.92	.832
	Impact of success	.97	.934
	Effect on liquidity	1.00	-*
	Impact on balance sheet	1.00	1.00
	Effect on tax burden	1.00	1.00
	Impact on external image	1.00	-*
	Other interpretation services	1.00	1.00
	Validation/justification	1.00	.913
	Legal norm orientation	1.00	1.00
	Business management Decisions	1.00	1.00
Networking	Cost Accounting	1.00	.798
	Liquidity Accounting	1.00	1.00
	Business Administration	1.00	0.92

Note: * Calculation not possible due to lack of variance in the data.

Table 7.24 shows the results for intercoder reliability. The double codings were carried out as part of a diploma thesis.[6] The Holsti reliability coefficient corresponds to the percentage agreement and can take a value between 0

[6] Since the inductively formed categories were only included in the category system after the double codings, there are no values for the intercoder reliability for these.

(no agreement) and 1 (perfect agreement), with values from.80 being considered satisfactory (Krippendorff, 2004, p. 241). Since the Holsti reliability coefficient does not correct for chance agreements, Cohen's (Weighted) Kappa was also calculated in SPSS (IBM SPSS Statistics Version 28). For the calculation of Cohen's Kappa, the "cross tables" function was used for the nominally scaled categories. For Cohen's Weighted Kappa, the SPSS extension "*Stats Weighted Kappa Version 2.0*" was used.[7] Cohen's (Weighted) Kappa can take values between 0 and 1, with values between.61 and.80 being seen as "considerable, substantial agreement" and values from.81 as "(almost) complete, perfect agreement" (Neuendorf, 2017, p. 236). The Holsti reliability coefficient is above the cut-off value of.80 for all categories and can therefore be described as satisfactory. A value of 1 was achieved for 13 categories. The values of Cohen's (Weighted) Kappa can also be described as good. Only the values of four categories are below the value of.81, but still above the value of.61, which can also be rated as substantial agreement. The good values were achieved by discussing the category system in advance and testing it together on examples. During the coding process, unclear cases were also discussed and debated. In addition, the good values are due to the high number of 0-codings in some categories.

To check the temporal stability of the ratings, double codings were carried out at two different times for a subset of the analysis units. The first round of codings took place during the first coding pass in January and February 2022. For a subsample of 100 analysis units, the codings were repeated after approximately 3 months. The subsample was determined by random selection. Table 7.25 shows the results of the calculations. Overall, very good values were achieved for the Holsti reliability coefficient. All values are above the recommended cut-off value of.80. For 13 (out of 32) categories, an agreement of 1 (perfect agreement) was achieved. It should be noted again that the Holsti reliability coefficient does not correct for chance agreements. Therefore, Cohen's Kappa (or for the ordinal scaled categories Cohen's Weighted Kappa) was calculated in addition, following the procedure for calculating intercoder reliability. Here too, consistently satisfactory values are shown. 20 (out of 26) categories show values above.80, which corresponds to an almost perfect agreement. For seven categories, a perfect agreement of 1 was even achieved. For six categories, the values are just below the.80

[7] For the calculation of Cohen's Weighted Kappa using the extension "*Stats Weighted Kappa*", a recoding of the variables was necessary. The recoding (0 = 1, 1 = 2, 2 = 3) was done using the "Recoding into other variables" function.

Table 7.25 Results on intracoder reliability

	Categories	Intracoder reliability (N = 100) R_H	Cohen's (Weighted) κ
Task master	Process orientation	0.90	.845
	Process reference of task processing	0.95	.880
	Flow of goods and services	0.95	.899
	Cash flows	0.95	.896
	Social processes	0.99	.795
	Use of documents	1.00	1.00
Modeling cycle	Recognize activity	0.92	.750
	Information research	0.99	.983
	Information evaluation	0.99	.979
	Translation performance through other work	0.98	.917
	Translation performance through Posting records	0.98	.948
	Internal accounting entries	0.97	.863
	Set up balance sheet	0.99	.795
	Set up income statement	0.99	.852
	Set up more-less-calculation	1.00	1.00
	Other work within Accounting	0.99	.795
	Mathematical work	0.90	.786
	Effect of success	0.99	.975
	Effect on liquidity	1.00	-*
	Impact on balance sheet	1.00	1.00
	Effect on tax burden	1.00	-*
	Impact on external image	1.00	-*
	Other interpretation services	0.99	-*
	Validation/justification	0.99	.852
	Legal norm orientation	1.00	1.00
	Business management Making decisions	0.99	.795
Networking	Cost Accounting	1.00	-*
	Liquidity Accounting	1.00	-*
	Business Administration	1.00	1.00
inductive	Reverse format	1.00	1.00
	Specification of a relevant formal target	1.00	1.00
	Change of perspective	1.00	1.00

Note: * Calculation not possible due to lack of variance in the data.

threshold, which also corresponds to sufficient reliability. It should be noted that for some categories, no calculation could be carried out due to the lack of variance in the data.

In addition to objectivity and reliability, *validity* is a key quality criterion (Brosius et al., 2022, p. 56; Kuckartz, 2018, pp. 201–202; Rammstedt, 2010, p. 250). This refers to the "accuracy with which a procedure actually measures or predicts what it is supposed to measure or predict" (Rammstedt, 2010, p. 250). Testing the validity of a measurement instrument is very difficult (Atteslander, 2010, p. 228). Generally, three types of validity are distinguished in the context of validity: content validity, criterion validity, and construct validity (Brosius et al., 2022, pp. 56–59; Döring & Bortz, 2016, pp. 445–446; Rammstedt, 2010, pp. 250–256).

The *content validity* indicates whether the measuring instrument fully and meaningfully reflects the target construct in its aspects of meaning. Ensuring content validity already begins with the creation of the measuring instrument. To assess content validity, it must be determined whether all relevant aspects of a construct have been included and whether the individual categories or items adequately represent the theoretically predetermined meanings. Content validity cannot be expressed through a numerical validity coefficient. One method for assessing content validity is the evaluation by subject matter experts (Brosius et al., 2022, p. 57; Döring & Bortz, 2016, p. 446). Applied to the category system used here, this means that during the creation of the categories, it must be ensured that all relevant aspects of the construct have been taken into account. This already presents an initial problem, as the category system is not based on a singular construct. Rather, it is a compilation of different characteristics identified as relevant for tasks in the accounting domain through theoretical preliminary work. However, only certain theories, models or didactic approaches, which were consciously and justifiably selected, served as theoretical templates. Within the different characteristics and for the different theoretical reference concepts (e.g. Linz level model, modeling cycle), however, an attempt was made to fully cover these in the category system.

With the *construct validity*, the "appropriateness of the operational definitions is considered based on the theoretical background" (Mayring, 2015, p. 124). The construct validity, similar to content validity, is largely determined by the quality of the theoretical preliminary work (concept specification) and the operationalization of the characteristics (Döring & Bortz, 2016, p. 97). Analogous to the argumentation regarding content validity, it can be stated that the development of the category system is oriented towards the current didactic discourse and takes into account models and approaches relevant in the discipline.

The *criterion validity* as the third type of validity measures "the degree of agreement of the result obtained with the survey instrument with an external criterion [...]" (Rammstedt, 2010, p. 251). Content-corresponding characteristics that are independent of the survey instrument used serve as an external criterion.[8] The agreement is then expressed in the form of a correlation of the two characteristics. However, a prerequisite for determining criterion validity is the existence of a valid external criterion (Döring & Bortz, 2016, p. 447). Also suitable as an external criterion are "research results that are closely related to one's own research question and subject matter" (Mayring, 2015, p. 124). If we now consider existing research results on task analyses in the accounting domain, which differ in the exact evaluation criteria and the subject of investigation, it nevertheless becomes apparent that the research findings obtained in the course of this study fit very well into the previous results (see also Sect. 8.1). Overall, however, it should be noted that the demarcation of the three types of validity is difficult and that these are defined differently, sometimes overlapping or contradictory, in different works on quantitative and qualitative research methods.

7.3 Analysis of the Relationships between the Task Characteristics and Identification of Task Types

7.3.1 Inter-Correlations between the Task Characteristics

In this section, the relationships between the different characteristics of the category system are to be worked out and discussed using a correlation table in order to answer research question 9. This allows a more detailed insight into the data and the relationships between the different categories. All subcategories of the category system were included in the correlation table, but not the characteristics added inductively during the coding. Kendall's Tau (τ) is suitable for representing relationships between ordinal-scaled characteristics (Döring & Bortz, 2016, p. 681). With a positive sign, values between.10 and.30 can be interpreted as a low correlation, values between.30 and.50 as a medium correlation, values between.50 and.70 as a high correlation, and values above.70 as a very high or strong correlation. The same applies to values with negative signs. The following inter-correlation table (Table 7.26) shows the results. Significant correlations are marked with a * or ** as such (Döring & Bortz, 2016, p. 681; Renner et al., 2009, p. 91–92).

[8] For example, for the construct "religiosity", the external criterion "church visits per year" can be used for validation (Rammstedt, 2010, p. 251).

Table 7.26 Inter-correlations between the characteristics of the task analysis

Variable	1	2	3	4	5	6	7	8	9	10	11	12	13	14
1 Process Orientation	–													
2 Goods/services flows	.239 **	–												
3 Cash Flows	.171 **	.141 **	–											
4 Social Processes	.185 **	.083 **	.027	–										
5 Documents	–.005	.083 **	.001	.036	–									
6 Recognize Activity	.220 **	.212 **	.172 **	.057 **	.195 **	–								
7 Gather Information	–.026	–.001	–.053 *	.014	.543 **	.149 **	–							
8 Evaluate Information	.015	.069 **	–.045 *	–.004	.512 **	.152 **	.794 **	–						
9 Preparatory Activities	.029	.072 **	–.002	.005	–.063 **	–.115 **	–.093 **	–.060 **	–					
10 Bookings	.351 **	.371 **	.350 **	.043	.085 **	.451 **	–.092 **	–.061 **	–.097 **	–				
11 Internal Accounting Entries	–.120 **	–.149 **	–.132 **	–.047 *	.115 **	–.012	.135 **	.087 **	–.067 **	–.286 **	–			
12 Create Balance Sheet	–.110 **	–.137 **	–.086 **	–.042	.009	–.020	.141 **	.117 **	–.044	–.255 **	.009	–		
13 Create Income Statement	–.108 **	–.135 **	–.099 **	–.038	–.006	–.001	.155 **	.099 **	–.038	–.233 **	.009	.398 **	–	
14 Create More-Less-Calculation	–.068 **	–.061 **	–.046 *	.013	–.055 *	.036	–.043 *	–.046 *	–.035	–.073 **	–.035	–.016	.022	–
15 Other internal works	.017	.055 *	–.068 **	.029	.055 *	–.003	.068 **	.074 **	.022	–.019	.022	–.022	–.020	–.014
16 Mathematical works	.111 **	.031	–.009	.031	.046 *	.198 **	.015	.051 *	–.039	.091 **	.133 **	.101 **	.109 **	.051 *

(continued)

Table 7.26 (continued)

Variable	1	2	3	4	5	6	7	8	9	10	11	12	13	14
17 Interpreting: Profit	.194 **	.121 **	.145 **	.021	−.014	.142 **	−.073 **	−.054*	−.059**	.339 *	−.165 **	−.093 **	−.081 **	−.073 **
18 Interpreting: Liquidity	−.033	.012	.043 *	−.010	.015	−.023	.043	−.003	−.013	−.063 **	−.013	.163 **	−.006	−.004
19 Interpreting: Balance Sheet	−.032	.001	.037	−.033	−.006	−.021	−.056 *	−.055 *	.190**	−.041	−.038	.093 **	−.024	−.017
20 Interpret: Tax Burden	−.031	−.037	−.026	.058**	−.015	.013	−.040	−.041	−.019	−.069 **	−.019	−.009	−.008	−.006
21 Interpret: External Representation	−.027	−.032	−.025	.054*	−.030	.044 *	−.023	−.024	−.011	−.052 *	−.011	−.005	−.005	−.003
22 Interpret: Miscellaneous	−.086 **	−.102 **	−.077 **	−.015	.075 **	.036	.183 **	.148 **	−.041	−.194 **	.290 **	−.019	−.017	−.012
23 Validate	−.046 *	−.021	−.029	.023	−.015	.051 *	−.002	−.014	.027	−.120 **	.012	−.036	.083 **	−.023
24 Legal Norm Orientation	.015	.036	−.021	.018	−.022	−.035	−.021	−.015	.039	−.065 **	−.032	−.015	−.013	−.009
25 Decision Making	−.015	−.016	.011	.014	.035	.141 **	.057 **	.063 **	−.022	−.085 **	−.022	−.010	−.009	−.006
26 Connections to cost accounting	.001	.004	−.067 **	−.026	.042	−.016	.038	.033	.050*	−.055 *	.050 *	−.015	−.014	−.010
27 Connections to Liquidity Management	−.073 **	−.052 *	−.035	.000	.092 **	−.008	.113 **	.073 **	−.030	−.129 **	.195 **	.062 **	−.012	−.009
28 Connec-tions to Business Administration	.002	−.019	−.080 **	.031	.019	.152 **	.045 *	.039	−.039	−.117 **	−.016	−.023	−.021	−.015

Variable	15	16	17	18	19	20	21	22	23	24	25	26	27
1 Process Orientation													

(continued)

Table 7.26 (continued)

Variable	15	16	17	18	19	20	21	22	23	24	25	26	27
2 Goods/ Service Flows													
3 Cash Flows													
4 Social Processes													
5 Documents													
6 Recognize Activity													
7 Obtain Information													
8 Evaluate Information													
9 Preparatory Activities													
10 Bookings													
11 Internal Accounting Entries													
12 Create Balance Sheet													

(continued)

Table 7.26 (continued)

Variable	15	16	17	18	19	20	21	22	23	24	25	26	27
13 Create Profit and Loss Statement													
14 Create MWR													
15 Other internal tasks	–												
16 Mathematical tasks	.108 **	–											
17 Interpretation: Profit	–.087 **	–.068 **	–										
18 Interpretation: Liquidity	–.005	.032	–.028	–									
19 Interpretation: Balance sheet	–.024	–.031	.046*	.151 **	–								
20 Interpretation: Tax burden	–.008	.026	–.040	–.002	–.009	–							

(continued)

Table 7.26 (continued)

Variable	15	16	17	18	19	20	21	22	23	24	25	26	27
21 Interpretation: External representation	–.004	–.039	–.023	–.001	–.005	–.002	–						
22 Interpretation: Miscellaneous	–.017	.045 *	–.086 **	–.005	–.020	–.007	–.004	–					
23 Validate	.001	–.037	–.072 **	–.009	.004	–.012	.139 **	.052*	–				
24 Standards	–.013	–.036	–.056 *	–.004	.084 **	–.005	–.003	–.011	.231 **	–			
25 Decide	–.009	–.061 **	–.029	–.002	–.011	–.003	–.002	.127 **	.059 **	–.006	–		
26 KORE Networking	–.014	.038	–.028	–.004	–.016	–.005	–.003	–.012	–.022	–.009	–.006	–	
27 FINRE Networking	–.012	.035	–.063 **	.296 **	.056 *	–.005	–.003	.582 **	.034	–.008	–.006	–.009	–
28 BW Networking	–.020	–.112**	–.045*	–.006	–.024	.057*	.107 **	.043	.114 **	.025	.438 **	.059**	–.013

Note: **. The correlation is significant at the 0.01 level (2-tailed). *. The correlation is significant at the 0.05 level (2-tailed). Abbreviations: DL-Streams = Service streams; KORE = Cost accounting; FINRE = Financial accounting; BW = Business administration

The process orientation strongly correlates with the process orientation of task processing (τ =.708, p =.01; category not shown in the correlation table). This is not surprising, as the category "process orientation of task processing" is related to the process orientation in such a way that a task in this category can only be coded if a process orientation exists at all. Only if a process orientation exists within the task (i.e., reference is made to previous or subsequent business cases), is there also the possibility that the learners must process several of these sub-steps themselves (and not just be referred to in the task). A correlation of 1 would mean in this case that in every task with process orientation (e.g., at level 1), there is also a process orientation of task processing (at level 1). A missing perfect match (of 1) therefore indicates that there are tasks where a process orientation exists, but this process does not have to be processed by the learners (or not in full). This finding is also reflected in the cross-table shown in Sect. 7.1.1 (Table 7.4).

In addition, the process orientation correlates significantly (though weakly) with the representation of reality, represented by the three subcategories of goods and service flows (τ =.239, p =.01), cash flows (τ =.171, p =.01), and social processes (τ =.185, p =.01). All categories are measured on an ordinal scale with the characteristics "no representation", "abstract representation" and "detailed representation". This relationship is also as expected, as the process orientation usually refers to the reference to previous or future goods flows, cash flows or social processes. So there is a connection between the representation of a process orientation and the description of reality.

With regard to the process orientation, a number of other positive correlations can be identified, most of which are as expected. For example, there is a positive correlation of the process orientation with the subcategory "recognizing activity". This means that process-oriented task assignments are associated with an increased level of demand in terms of independently recognizing or defining the activity to be performed or the openness of the task solution (τ =.220, p =.01). Similarly, the subcategories of the main category "representation of reality" also correlate significantly positively with the subcategory "recognizing activity". The more detailed the description of goods or service flows (τ =.212, p =.01) or cash flows (τ =.172, p =.01), the more demanding is the requirement for learners to identify the activity to be performed in the task. Furthermore, a positive correlation was found between the degree of process orientation of a task and the requirement to translate a business case into the world of accounting (τ =.351, p =.01) and to interpret it in terms of its impact on profit (τ =.194, p =.01). If tasks are designed in a process-oriented way, then these processes often also have to be translated into the world of accounting and subsequently related back to the real world.

However, some negative correlations can also be identified. For example, the process orientation correlates negatively with a number of categories that primarily concern operating within the accounting system (e.g., performing intra-accounting bookings, τ =.120, p =.01; preparing a balance sheet, τ =.110, p =.01; preparing a profit and loss statement, τ =.108, p =.01). If tasks are designed in a process-oriented way, they tend not to require intra-accounting work. This suggests that tasks requiring operation within the accounting system are often designed in isolation without reference to operational processes. This is also reflected in the almost consistently negative correlations between the categories that represent operations within accounting and the subcategories representing reality (e.g., intra-accounting bookings and goods flows, τ =.149, p =.01; preparing a balance sheet and goods flows, τ =.137, p =.01).

The subcategories of the main category "representation of reality" correlate (partially) with each other, but less strongly than one might assume (e.g., goods flows with cash flows, τ =.141, p =.01; social processes with goods flows, τ =.083, p =.01). This suggests that tasks often focus on a specific area and the three aspects of reality are addressed in isolation and not together. The representation of reality (specifically goods flows and cash flows) in turn correlates positively with the translation of a business case into the world of accounting by setting up booking entries (goods flows: τ =.371, p =.01; cash flows: τ =.350, p =.01). This is also as expected. If goods flows or cash flows are addressed, they usually also have to be translated into the world of accounting. It is therefore also expected that the representation of social processes does not correlate with the setting up of bookings, as social processes usually do not result in accounting-relevant transactions. There are significant positive correlations between the representation of goods flows or cash flows and the interpretation of the impact on profit. So if goods or cash flows are represented, they often also have to be interpreted in terms of their impact on the company's profit (goods flows: τ =.121, p =.01; cash flows: τ =.145, p =.01).

The use of documents in tasks correlates with a number of other task characteristics. First, the use of documents is positively associated with the subcategory "recognizing activity". Thus, the complexity of independently identifying the underlying problem is higher when one or more documents are used in the task (τ =.195, p =.01). This seems understandable, as documents require learners to orient themselves more strongly in a first step than would be the case with the specification of a continuous text. In addition, the use of documents is associated with the need to obtain information to solve the task (τ =.543, p =.01) or to distinguish between relevant and irrelevant information (τ =.512, p =.01). This is also conceptually understandable and is also due to the construction of the categories. Thus, if documents are used in the task, information from these documents needs to be researched. At the same time, documents usually also contain information that is not relevant for the immediate task completion. Therefore, learners must filter out the information relevant to the solution of the task and thus evaluate information in terms of its relevance. If the two characteristics "obtaining information" and "evaluating information" are so strongly associated with the use of documents, then the question arises why the correlations are not even stronger. This can also be explained by the construction of the categories. Both characteristics are ordinally scaled with three levels each. In the category "obtaining information", the highest category means that information must be obtained either from more than one document or from external sources (e.g., internet or legal text). With the external sources, the use of documents (because the documents are not directly contained in the task) is coded with 0. In addition, the use of documents only distinguishes whether documents are used, not how many. In the category "evaluating information", the highest level is coded when it can be assumed that the task contains a deliberate information surplus. This is the case, for example, when different prices (e.g., cost price, selling price, replacement price) are given and the learners must recognize which price is relevant for solving the task at hand. This deliberate information surplus is usually not presented via documents, but in the continuous text. The characteristics "obtaining information" and "evaluating information" correlate as expected very strongly (τ =.794, p =.01), as the procurement of information (e.g., from a document) usually goes hand in hand with the distinction between relevant and irrelevant information. Furthermore, the use of documents correlates weakly positively with the translation of a business case into the world of accounting (= setting up booking entries) (τ =.085, p =.01) as well as with the formation of bookings within the accounting system (τ =.115, p =.01). This can mean, on the one hand, that documents need to be documented (e.g., booking of an incoming invoice) in the accounting system or that documents are to be used as a source of information (e.g., a balance list is to be consulted to check whether an amount is already shown on a corresponding account) in order to depict other processes in accounting or to work within the system.

Looking at the first sub-step of the modeling cycle, orientation, it becomes apparent that the three sub-facets correlate positively with each other and also (positively or negatively) with a number of other characteristics. The strong correlation between the characteristics "obtaining information" and "evaluating information" has already been reported. The third subcategory "recognizing activity" also correlates positively with these, but less strongly (e.g., with information procurement: τ =.149, p =.01). This is also conceptually plausible, as the procurement and/or evaluation of information usually leads to higher demands on problem recognition and makes the orientation performance of learners more complex. Or to put it another way: If the problem/activity has to be recognized by the learner himself, this often goes hand in hand with the need to research and/or evaluate information. The category "recognizing activity" correlates positively with the translation of a business case into the world of accounting (setting up bookings) (τ =.451, p =.01). From a content perspective, it can be concluded that the problems contained in the tasks are often those that can be solved by setting up bookings. The same applies to mathematical work (τ =.198, p =.01) and the interpretation of the impact on profit (τ =.142, p =.01). Interesting in this context are also the positive correlations with the sub-step of deciding (τ =.141, p =.01) and the networking with business administration content (τ =.152, p =.01). Higher demands on orientation performance (i.e., the problem has to be recognized independently or there is a problem at all) go hand in hand with the requirement to make a business decision and to establish a connection to business administration. Conversely, if learners have to make decisions or establish connections to other subject areas, this increases the demand on their orientation performance. The two other subcategories "obtaining information" and "evaluating information" correlate positively beyond the already presented correlations with a number of other task characteristics. This first concerns some characteristics of the main category "Operating within the accounting system". For example, intra-accounting booking (info procurement: τ =.135, p =.01), setting up a balance sheet (info procurement: τ =.141, p =.01; info evaluation: τ =.117, p =.01) or creating a profit and loss account (info procurement: τ =.155, p =.01) often go hand in hand with the research or evaluation of information. This is also conceptually plausible, as documents (e.g., balance lists, sum and balance sheets, etc.) are often used in this process, which in turn requires information research and evaluation. The positive correlations with the category "Interpreting: Other" (info procurement: τ =.183, p =.01; info evaluation: τ =.148, p =.01) can be explained by the type of other interpretation services (key figures).

Looking at the second sub-step of the modeling cycle, it is first necessary to mention the many negative correlations of the sub-step "setting up bookings" with other categories. While the category correlates strongly positively with the category "recognizing activity" (as one facet of orientation, τ =.451, p =.01), there is, however, a negative correlation between setting up bookings and the next sub-step of intra-accounting operation (e.g., intra-accounting bookings: τ =.286, p =.01; setting up a balance sheet: τ =.255, p =.01; creating a profit and loss account: τ =.233, p =.01), as well as with the further subsequent sub-steps, e.g., with interpreting (e.g., other interpretation services: τ =.194, p =.01), vali-

Table 7.27 Correlation table for the variables of the modeling cycle

Variable	1	2	3	4	5
1 Orientation	–				
2 Translation	.390**	–			
3 Operation	.045*	−.451**	–		
4 Interpretation	.203**	.226**	−.184**	–	
5 Validation	−.024	−.101**	.019	−.043	–
6 Decision-making	.021	−.097**	−.028	.000	.059**

Note: **. The correlation is significant at the 0.01 level (2-tailed). *. The correlation is significant at the 0.05 level (2-tailed)

dating (τ =.120, p =.01) and deciding (τ = −.085, p =.01). A negative correlation also exists with networking services (e.g., FINRE: τ = −.129, p =.01; BW: τ = −.117, p =.01). The only correlation with the indication of the impact on profit is positive (τ =.339, p =.05). The predominantly negative correlations of the sub-step Translate with the other sub-steps of the modeling cycle suggest that the tasks often address the sub-steps separately from each other (with a focus on translation), and that learners do not have to complete several sub-steps within one task.

For the sub-step of internal accounting operations, it is evident that the individual subcategories do not significantly correlate with each other, suggesting that different internal accounting operations are hardly interrelated. However, this does not apply to the preparation of balance sheets and profit and loss accounts (τ =.398, p =.01). Apart from the correlations already discussed, there are hardly any significant relationships to the other sub-steps of the modeling cycle. Exceptions are the consistently negative correlations between all sub-facets of internal accounting work and the interpretation of profit impact (e.g., internal accounting bookings: τ = −.165, p =.01). Interestingly, and not easily understandable in terms of content, is the positive correlation between the requirement to prepare a balance sheet and the indication of the impact on liquidity (τ =.163, p =.01). In the sub-step of interpretation, there are occasional positive correlations between the various subcategories, e.g., between the requirement to indicate the impact of a business case on the balance sheet and to make a statement on the impact on liquidity (τ =.151, p =.01). Overall, however, it can be concluded that business cases or developed solutions are mostly only to be interpreted from one aspect.

The last two sub-steps of the modeling cycle, validating and decision-making, correlate weakly with each other (τ =.059, p =.01), but hardly with the other sub-steps of the modeling cycle. If one looks at the relationships of the categories to the modeling cycle in aggregated form, some interesting correlations also become apparent (Table 7.27). The sub-step of orientation correlates positively with the sub-step of translation (τ =.390, p =.01), suggesting that these two sub-steps often need to be processed together. The same applies to the sub-step of interpretation (τ =.203, p =.01). Overall, the aggregated representation of the correlations reveals a kind of "task pattern". While the three sub-steps of orientation, translation, and interpretation correlate positively, for example, translation and internal accounting operations correlate strongly negatively (τ =.451, p =.01). It therefore seems to be the case that these two steps tend to exclude each other within tasks and tasks rather consist of capturing a real process, translating it into the world of accounting, and then giving it content meaning again. There is also a negative correlation between internal accounting work and the partial performance of interpretation (τ =.184, p =.01). The sub-steps of validation and decision-making, on the other hand, correlate negatively with the requirement to transfer a business case into the world of accounting (Validation: τ =.101, p =.01; Decision-making: τ =.097, p =.01).

Mathematical work correlates positively with the category "Recognizing Activity" (τ =.201, p =.01). So, if higher demands are placed on the orientation performance, this often also requires the execution of calculations. In addition, there is a positive correlation between all subcategories of internal accounting operations and mathematical work (e.g., setting up a balance sheet: τ =.101, p =.01). The same applies to the setting up of bookings (τ =.091, p =.01). Both are plausible in terms of content, as these activities often require the execution of calculations.

The category "Legal Norm Orientation" has not yet been discussed. Its aim is to assess whether an activity (a booking, etc.) needs to be explicitly justified by a legal norm or whether a norm needs to be explicitly applied (with reference in the task). Therefore, positive correlations with the sub-step of validation (because this also includes whether something needs to be justified) and the sub-step of translation would be obvious. Surprisingly, the category Norm Orientation has a negative, but weak, correlation with the requirement to set up a booking (τ = −.065, p =.01), indicating that booking entries are not to be set up under explicit application of legal regulations. Norm Orientation and the sub-step of validation, on the other hand, correlate positively as expected (τ =.231, p =.01).

Finally, the categories of networking with other content areas (specifically cost accounting, financial accounting, or business management topics) need to be addressed. In addition to the relationships already discussed, the strong correlation between the category "Networking with business content" and making business decisions should be mentioned (τ =.438, p =.01). So, if learners are required to relate a task to a business topic, this often involves making decisions. A positive correlation also exists with validation (τ =.114, p =.01). It can be concluded that tasks with business references often require a validation performance from the learners. At the same time, of course, this can also mean that when validating solutions or making decisions, references to business topics need to be established. The networking with financial accounting (i.e., liquidity management) unsurprisingly correlates with the requirement to interpret a business case from the perspective of liquidity (τ =.296, p =.01). A strong positive correlation also exists with the category "Interpreting: Other" (τ =.582, p =.01). Since this primarily involves the interpretation of key figures, which in turn often address liquidity, this correlation is also understandable.

7.3.2 Results of the Latent Class Analysis for the Identification of Task Classes

A latent class analysis was conducted to determine task classes. The exact procedure and implementation with *MPlus* is described in Sect. 6.2.2. Due to the large number of categories (and some categories with low variance in the data) and the correspondingly small sample size, only selected criteria were included in the analysis (for the problem of optimal sample size, see also Sect. 6.3.2). The variables describing the reality (document use, process orientation, and the description of goods and service flows, cash flows, and social processes) were included in the analysis. While document use is a dichotomous feature, the other variables are ordinal scaled with three manifestations each. In addition, the variables of the modeling cycle were included. Some of these variables were summarized. For example, the subcategories for internal accounting work were combined into a category "internal accounting operations" and this was made dichotomous. The same applies to interpreting and translating. In the main category of orientation, the three subcategories were retained. Mathematical work and legal norm orientation were not included in the analysis, as they are not part of the modeling cycle (but are cross-cutting) and there is hardly any variance in the data for norm orientation. The other features of the modeling cycle were included in the analysis unchanged. Originally, it was planned to calculate the latent class analysis with class solutions from one to eight classes and to compare these using absolute and relative model indices. However, only class solutions with a maximum of seven classes could be calculated, as problems with parameter estimation and local maxima have been shown with a higher number of classes. To meet the condensation claim of the latent class analysis and in the sense of model parsimony, a solution with fewer classes is sensible anyway.

The assessment of the *absolute* model fit using the likelihood ratio test and Pearson-χ^2 statistic provides satisfactory (i.e., non-significant in the sense of the tests) results for all class solutions. However, it should be noted that the values of the likelihood ratio test and the Pearson-χ^2 statistic for individual class solutions sometimes differ greatly. Therefore, the *p* values can only be interpreted with caution.[9]

Table 7.28 provides an overview of different indicators for assessing the *relative* model fit for different class solutions. The different indices do not provide a clear result as to which class solution best fits the data. The information criteria *AIC* and *aBIC* suggest a solution with seven different classes due to the lowest values, while the *BIC* recommended by Geiser (2013, p. 269) implies a solution with five classes. A significant Vuong-Lo-Mendell-Rubin test indicates that a model with G classes fits the data better than a model with G—1 classes. Consequently, this test also points to a solution with five classes. The Bootstrap-LR-Difference-Test, which also checks whether a model with G classes fits better than a model with G—1 classes, suggests a solution with more classes. The entropy, which indicates whether or to what extent the different classes are separated from each other, should be at least.80 and is therefore satisfactory for all class solutions (Celeux & Soromenho, 1996, p. 200; Geiser, 2013, p. 247). The average assignment probability (ZOW) should be at least 80% and can therefore also be considered sufficient for all classes (Geiser, 2013, p. 248).

Based solely on the absolute and relative model fits, class solutions with four (high entropy value, high assignment probabilities, and model parsimony due to the smallest number of classes), five (lowest BIC value, significant VLMRT and BLRT, satisfactory entropy and assignment probability), or seven (lowest AIC and aBIC value, significant BLRT, satisfactory entropy and assignment probability) classes are considered. However, in addition to the model quality criteria, the content interpretability of the solutions is also important. Therefore, a more detailed inspection of the evaluations and a first interpretation of the task classes were carried out for these three class solutions. After an analysis of the class sizes and task characteristics using line diagrams, it becomes apparent that a solution with five classes is most interpretable in terms of content. With a solution of four classes, individual classes are difficult to interpret in terms of content, the

[9] A parametric bootstrap method to avoid this problem is implemented in *MPlus* only for assessing the relative model fit, not for assessing the absolute model fit (Geiser, 2013, pp. 258–259).

Table 7.28 Indicators for assessing the absolute and relative model fit

Classes	Loglikelihood (LL)	AIC	BIC	aBIC	VLMRT	BLRT	Entropy	ZOW
1	−14948.984	29937.968	30049.986	29986.445	–	–	–	
2	−13537.469	27156.937	27386.574	27256.315	p =.000	p =.000	.972	.993
3	−12764.262	25652.523	25999.779	25802.082	p =.000	p =.000	.933	.971
4	−12423.349	25012.697	25477.572	25213.877	p =.000	p =.000	.932	.948
5	−12323.100	24854.201	**25436.695**	25106.281	p =.006	p =.000	.883	.830
6	−12254.630	24759.200	25459.373	25062.241	p =.938	p =.000	.910	.880
7	−12200.216	**24692.431**	25510.163	**25046.313**	p =.088	p =.000	.906	.868

Note: *AIC* Akaike Information Criterion, *BIC* Bayesian Information Criterion, *aBIC* sample-size-adjusted BIC, *VLMRT* Vuong-Lo-Mendell-Rubin-Likelihood-Ratio-Test, *BLRT* Bootstrap-Likelihood-Ratio-Test, *ZOW* average, minimum assignment probability

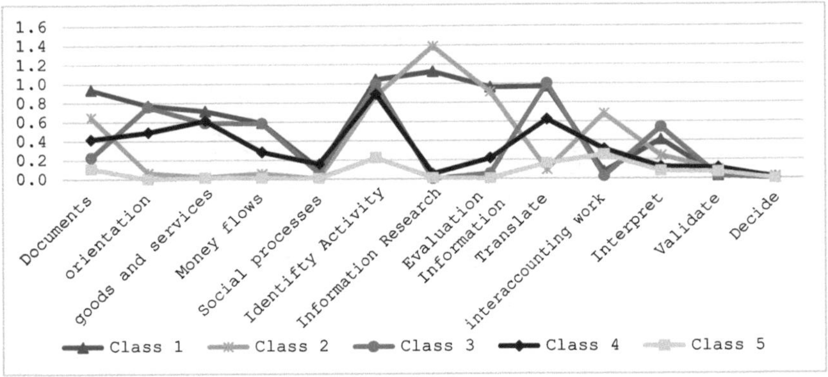

Fig. 7.37 Expected values for the 5-class solution

solution with seven classes results in two classes being very small (n = 72 and 88 respectively) and some classes being hardly distinguishable from each other in terms of content. The analysis will therefore continue with five classes.

Figure 7.37 shows the expected values for the five-class solution. The expected values are calculated by multiplying the characteristics of a feature (in this case 0, 1, or 2) by the respective probability. For the dichotomous features (use of documents, translating, operating within accounting, interpreting, validating, and deciding), the expected value simultaneously represents the assignment probability at level 1 (What is the probability in the respective class that the feature is present).

It is striking at first that the tasks differ very clearly in terms of some features, while hardly any differences can be detected for other features. For the use of documents (Are documents used or not?), there are clear differences between the different task classes. For example, the expected value (or the assignment probability) for task class 1 is almost 1 (0.939), while for task type 5 it is almost 0 (0.111). Strong differences in the expected values are therefore also evident in the categories of information research and information evaluation. There are also clear differences between individual task classes in the features of process orientation, representation of goods and service flows, representation of cash flows, translating, internal accounting work, and interpreting.

Comparatively less strong or hardly any differences, however, are found in the categories of representation of social processes as well as validating and deciding. In all three categories, it is evident that they were coded relatively rarely

Table 7.29 Overview of different task classes

Class	N	%	Designation	Short description
1	535	26.75 %	Document-oriented translation tasks	Use of documents, description of reality with focus on goods and service flows, process orientation, information research and evaluation, translation performance into the world of accounting, interpretation performance
2	199	9.95 %	Internal accounting tasks	Operating within the management accounting system, no description of the reality, no translation performance from the real world into the world of accounting, information evaluation
3	862	43.10 %	Text-based translation tasks	Text-based description of the reality, process orientation, translation performance into the world of accounting, interpretation performance
4	200	10.00 %	Mixed-type tasks	Medium assignment probabilities, polarization in the category "recognize activity", translation performance, validation performance
5	204	10.20 %	Knowledge-oriented tasks without context reference	No use of documents, no representation of the reality, low problem orientation, focus on reproduction performances

overall (e.g., the category deciding was only coded 8 times for 2000 tasks) and are therefore not well suited to determine *differences* between various tasks. It is also striking that the expected values of task class 5 are very low overall across all criteria. This shows that the tasks inadequately fulfill the criteria listed in the category system. The different task types will be described in more detail below. Table 7.29 summarizes the findings in tabular form.

Maria Aufschlager e.U. runs a specialist store for high-quality designer furniture in Kitzbühel. The following business transactions are to be recorded:

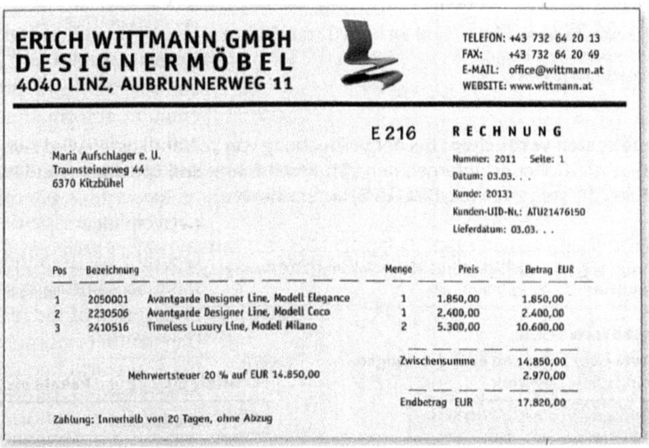

ERICH WITTMANN GMBH
DESIGNERMÖBEL
4040 LINZ, AUBRUNNERWEG 11

TELEFON: +43 732 64 20 13
FAX: +43 732 64 20 49
E-MAIL: office@wittmann.at
WEBSITE: www.wittmann.at

E 216

RECHNUNG

Maria Aufschlager e. U.
Traunsteinerweg 44
6370 Kitzbühel

Nummer: 2011 Seite: 1
Datum: 03.03. . .
Kunde: 20131
Kunden-UID-Nr.: ATU21476150
Lieferdatum: 03.03. . .

Pos		Bezeichnung	Menge	Preis	Betrag EUR
1	2050001	Avantgarde Designer Line, Modell Elegance	1	1.850,00	1.850,00
2	2230506	Avantgarde Designer Line, Modell Coco	1	2.400,00	2.400,00
3	2410516	Timeless Luxury Line, Modell Milano	2	5.300,00	10.600,00
			Zwischensumme		14.850,00
		Mehrwertsteuer 20 % auf EUR 14.850,00			2.970,00
			Endbetrag EUR		17.820,00

Zahlung: Innerhalb von 20 Tagen, ohne Abzug

5.3 E240 The leather seating sets are collected by the forwarding agent Schenker & Co AG (3315) from the distribution warehouse of Erich Wittmann GmbH, Linz, and brought to Maria Aufschlager e. U. in Kitzbühel. The delivery costs amount to € 232.20 (incl. 20 % VAT).

11.3. p 108 Credit note from Erich Wittmann GmbH for the return of a leather seat set € 5,300 + € 1,060 VAT.

18.3. B 40 Transfer to Erich Wittmann GmbH

[...]

a) Form the accounting records.

b) Indicate whether the respective transaction increases or decreases equity or whether it is an entry not affecting net income.

Fig. 7.38 Example task of task class 1

The tasks of *Class 1* (n = 535, 26.75%) are characterized primarily by a high expected value for the use of documents (0.939). Accordingly, many tasks of class 1 use documents. Corresponding to the use of documents, information research (expected value = 1.127) or information evaluation (expected value = 0.961) is often required in the tasks of this class. The tasks usually contain a problem, but it is already limited by the task and therefore not to be recognized by the learners themselves. The expected values are (with the exception of the category "social processes", where all task classes show low expected values) at a medium level, with the expected value for the representation of goods or service flows being significantly higher with a value of 0.714. Therefore, tasks of class 1 often address goods or service flows at an abstract level. Also, the expected value for process orientation is above the expected values of the other classes (0.772) in task class 1. Therefore, the tasks of class 1 can often be described as at least limited process-oriented. It can also be seen that this type of task almost always requires a translation into the world of accounting (expected value = 0.967), but almost never requires an operation within the system (expected value = 0.074). In addition, many of the tasks require an interpretation, i.e., a retranslation from the world of accounting into the real world (expected value = 0.407). The sub-steps of validating and deciding in the modeling cycle have very low expected values of 0.027 and 0.004 respectively and therefore hardly occur in this type of task. Based on the strong document orientation, the translation as a key performance, and the (at least limited) reference to the real world, this task class is classified as *"Document-oriented translation tasks"*. Figure 7.38 shows an example task for this task class. The task uses a document from which the learners have to research information. At the same time, an information evaluation (at level 1) is required. The task is process-oriented (in this case at the highest level), as it addresses not only the purchase but also the freight service, the return, and the payment. The task deals with goods and service flows (leather seat sets and the freight service) and goods flows. The task requires translating a business case into the world of accounting and interpreting the solution. However, operating in the accounting system, validating the solution, or making a business decision are not required.

The tasks of *Class 2* (n = 199, 9.95%) are referred to as *"internal accounting tasks"* because they are characterized primarily by the fact that these tasks mainly involve operating within the accounting system. The expected value for internal accounting operation is significantly higher than the expected values of the other classes with a value of 0.683. Accordingly, the reality is almost never represented in these tasks, and these tasks are also hardly designed to be process-oriented (e.g., expected value for the representation of goods and service flows: 0.02; for process orientation: 0.063). The expected value of the category "use of documents" is at a medium to higher level with a value of 0.647, indicating that many of these tasks use documents. This is also reflected in the relatively high expected values in the categories "procuring information" (1.389) and "evaluating information" (0.913). Since these tasks mainly involve internal accounting work, no translation from the real world is required (expected value = 0.094), a retranslation into the real world (interpreting) is necessary in some tasks (expected value = 0.239). The expected values of the sub-steps validating (0.093)

Create a complete balance sheet for Heidis Fashion GmbH from the determined inventory.

ASSETS	Balance sheet on 31.12. of the financial year	LIABILITIES
Total		**Total**

Fig. 7.39 Example task of task class 2

and deciding (0.019) are again low. Therefore, validating a solution or making business decisions are usually not required in these tasks.

Figure 7.39 shows a task of the type "internal accounting task". As part of the task, work is to be done within the accounting system, as a balance sheet is to be created based on a determined inventory. Accordingly, there is no direct translation of the real world into the world of accounting in this task (this has already happened in a previous step). For the task, information from the inventory needs to be researched. Subsequently (not shown here), questions about the specific balance sheet need to be answered (e.g., What is the value of the fixed assets?), which in turn requires information research and evaluation.

Task class 3 makes up the largest proportion in the sample (n = 862, 43.10%). The tasks of *class 3* are characterized by a medium to higher expected value in terms of process orientation (0.758) as well as the representation of goods or service flows (0.589) and cash flows (0.584). These tasks are therefore often designed in a process-oriented manner and describe the goods or service flows and/or cash flows occurring in the company. The expected value in the category "social processes" is again low (0.062). The tasks tend not to use documents (expected value = 0.228) and therefore do not require information research or evaluation (expected values = 0.003 and 0.056, respectively). The activities required in the course of the task are usually already defined for the learner, so the tasks can be described as limited problem-oriented (expected value = 0.997). Regarding the different sub-steps of the modeling cycle, these tasks require translation (expected value = 1) as well as the interpretation of solutions (expected value = 0.540). Operating within the accounting system (expected value = 0.024) as well as validating (expected value = 0.028) and deciding (expected value = 0) are not necessary. The tasks of class 3 can be described as *"text-based translation tasks"*.

Figure 7.40 shows an example task of this task type. The task does not use documents, but describes a goods flow (purchase of a truck) and a cash flow (payment for the truck) in abstract form. The task is also limited process-oriented (purchase and payment) and requires the translation of a real business case into the world of accounting. For the learners, the activity is clear ("Set up the booking entries!"), but still needs to be specified (Which accounts are affected? On which side of the account is to be booked? Which amounts are to be used? etc.). The task also requires an interpretation, but not the validation of the solution or the making of a business decision.

The *task class 4* (n = 200, 10%) is the most difficult to interpret in terms of content, as it is characterized by medium assignment probabilities or expected values and also has some peculiarities. For example, the expected value for the use of documents is in the medium range (0.418), while in these tasks, however, hardly any information needs to be researched and evaluated (expected values = 0.053 and 0.218, respectively). The expected values for the categories process orientation (0.492), goods and service flows (0.614), and cash flows (0.285) are in the medium range, with the tasks of this task type often focusing on social processes (expected value = 0.157). The expected value for the category "recognizing activity" is also in the medium range with a value of 0.893. However, if one looks at the assignment probabilities at the highest level, it is striking that task class 4 is characterized by the highest assignment probability at the highest level of the category "recognizing activity". Some of the tasks of class 4 therefore require the learners to independently recognize the underlying problem. At the same time, the assignment probabilities to level 0 (no problem present) are also significantly higher than in the other classes (with the exception of class 5), which in turn suggests that in some tasks there is no problem at all. Regarding problem orientation, this task class cannot be clearly characterized. While in the

Carina Holzer GmbH, a producer of packaging materials, would like to expand its vehicle fleet. This results in the following business transactions:
5.3 E 138 Purchase of a small truck from Tim Steyr OG (33159) for € 75,000 (incl. 20% VAT).
20.3. B 37 Transfer € 75,000 to Tim Steyr OG to settle E138.
a) Set up the posting records.
b) Indicate whether the respective transaction increases or decreases equity or whether it is a posting with no effect on income.

Fig. 7.40 Example task of task class 3

Explain to which account and on which account side the sales of merchandise are posted.

Fig. 7.41 Example task of task class 5

other task classes usually either a translation service or work within the accounting system is required, in the tasks of this type both sub-steps can occur (expected values = 0.624 and 0.310, respectively). In addition, this task type has the highest expected value for the sub-step of validating (0.113). Making business decisions, as in the other task types, is not provided for (expected value = 0.008). Upon closer inspection of the tasks, this task type differs from task class 3 mainly in that translation service and operation within the accounting system are often worked on together in these tasks, while in task class 3 only the translation (or the retranslation) is in the foreground. These tasks are therefore referred to as *mixed type tasks*.

The *task type 5* (n = 204, 10.2%) is characterized by low expected values in almost all categories. These are primarily *"knowledge-oriented tasks without context reference"*. These tasks hardly work with documents (expected value = 0.111). Accordingly, the research or evaluation of information is hardly required (expected values = 0.013 and 0.007, respectively). The tasks do without context reference and are also not designed in a process-oriented manner. For example, the expected value for the representation of goods and service flows is 0.014, for the representation of cash flows it is 0.012, and for the process orientation it is 0. The tasks usually contain no problem, but demand the reproduction of knowledge, for example in the form of reproducing bookings or definitions. The expected value for the category "recognizing activity" is therefore with a value of 0.223 significantly below the expected values of the other task classes. Within this class, the sub-steps of translating (0.162) and operating within accounting (0.252) have the highest expected values. Figure 7.41 shows a task of this task type.

Table 7.29 provides an overview of the different task classes and indicates the size of each class as well as the designation and a brief description.

Task types in publishers and years

It is also interesting to see how the different task types are distributed among the various publishers. It is necessary to distinguish how the classes are distributed percentage-wise among the different publishers and how the classes are distributed within the publishers (i.e., what is the proportion of the respective classes in the tasks of a publisher). Figure 7.42 first shows how the different task types are

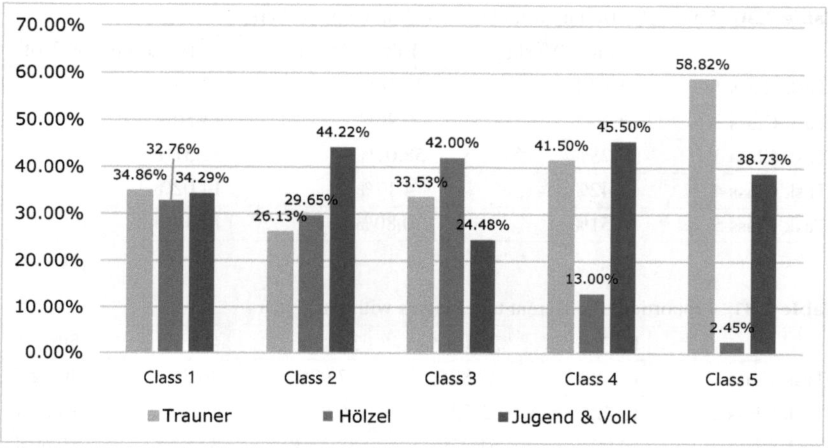

Fig. 7.42 Distribution of task classes by publisher

distributed among the publishers.[10] The evaluations show that the tasks of class 1 are evenly distributed over the three different publishers. The tasks of class 2 (internal accounting tasks) are particularly common in the Jugend & Volk publishing house. For the tasks of class 3 (text-based translation tasks), it is shown that 42 % of them come from the Hölzel publishing house and 25 % from the Jugend & Volk publishing house. A particularly strong unequal distribution is shown in task types 4 and 5. While 46 % of the tasks of type 4 come from the Jugend & Volk publishing house, only 13 % come from the Hölzel publishing house. The knowledge-oriented tasks (class 5), on the other hand, do not occur at all in the Hölzel publishing house, while 60 % of the tasks of this type come from the Trauner publishing house.

One can also consider the distribution of different types of tasks within a publishing house. Table 7.30 shows the proportional share of task types per publisher. For tasks of type 1 (document-oriented translation tasks), there are hardly any differences between the publishers. For task class 2 (internal accounting tasks), the share varies by publisher between 7.15% (Trauner Verlag) and 13.5% (Verlag Jugend & Volk). Larger differences in the distributions are shown for the

[10] It should be noted that the sample was not drawn equally from the tasks of the three publishers, but was drawn proportionally to the total population.

Table 7.30 Share of different task classes within the publishers

	Trauner Verlag	Hölzel Verlag	Verlag Jugend & Volk
Task Class 1	25.17%	27.56%	27.73%
Task Class 2	7.15%	9.46%	13.50%
Task Class 3	39.75%	58.01%	32.51%
Task Class 4	11.42%	4.17%	14.02%
Task Class 5	16.51%	0.80%	12.17%

Table 7.31 Proportion of different task classes within the years

	1st Yr	2nd Yr	3rd Yr	4th Yr	5th Yr
Task Class 1	17.58%	27.87%	27.97%	26.3%	40.52%
Task Class 2	11.42%	5.73%	6.90%	11.79%	18.53%
Task Class 3	49.09%	51.27%	38.31%	34.92%	30.60%
Task Class 4	10.27%	5.41%	16.72%	13.39%	6.90%
Task Class 5	11.64%	9.71%	9.20%	13.61%	3.45%

remaining three task classes. At Hölzel Verlag, 58% of the tasks are of type 3 (text-based translation services), while at Trauner Verlag it is about 40% and at Verlag Jugend & Volk it is 32.51%. Task class 4 (mixed-type tasks) accounts for 11.42% of the tasks of Trauner Verlag and 14.02% of the tasks of Verlag Jugend & Volk. For the tasks of Hölzel Verlag, it is only 4.17%. Knowledge-oriented tasks (class 5) can be assigned to 12.17% of the tasks of Verlag Jugend & Volk or 16.51% of Trauner Verlag, but only 0.8% of Hölzel Verlag.

In addition to the publisher, the extent to which different types of tasks are represented over the years can be evaluated. Table 7.31 shows the distribution of task classes for each year. Class 1 tasks are particularly strongly represented in the 5th year (40.52% of the tasks in the 5th year can be assigned to class 1), while they represented between 18 and 28% of the tasks in the 1st year. Approximately 19% of the tasks in the 5th year are internal accounting tasks (class 2), whereas in the 2nd year it is only about 6%. In the 2nd year, the majority of tasks (51.27%) can be assigned to the category "text-based translation tasks". The proportion of class 3 tasks is high across all years, although it is lowest in the 5th year. For class 4 tasks, the proportion varies between 5.41% (2nd year) and 16.72% (3rd year). Knowledge questions represent (with the exception of the 5th year) about 10% of the tasks over the years.

7.4 Summary of Results Along the Research Questions

After the results have been presented in great detail in the previous sections and backed up with examples, a brief summary of the findings along the research questions will be given here, before the results are discussed in Chap. 8.

RQ1: *How process-oriented are tasks from textbooks for the domain of accounting?*

- The findings show that the tasks from the textbooks for the subject of accounting can only be described as limited in their process orientation. 55% of the tasks have no reference to previous or subsequent business transactions—they are therefore not process-oriented. 32.2% of the tasks are limited in their process orientation. This means that they either refer to a previous or a subsequent business transaction. 13% of the tasks can be described as comprehensively process-oriented. These are tasks that represent a comprehensive process chain, for example by referring to several previous and/or future processes.

RQ2: *How realistically is the reality represented in the tasks?*

- The descriptive evaluations show that a large part of the tasks do not represent reality at all or only very limited and abstractly. Almost 50% of the tasks do not address goods and service flows. The values are significantly worse for cash flows and especially for social processes (60.5% and 93.3% respectively). This means that social processes are hardly addressed in the tasks. When reality is represented, these descriptions are usually not very concrete. Thus, an abstract description of goods or service flows is made in 49.4% of the tasks—for the description of cash flows this value is 35.4%, for social processes 5.8%. A detailed and realistic description of business processes is given in 0.8% of the tasks for goods and service flows, in 4.2% of the tasks for cash flows and in 0.9% of the cases for social processes.
- If you add up the values for the three subcategories (with a maximum of six if both goods and service flows as well as cash flows and social processes are detailed), it shows that the majority of tasks achieve values of one or two (about 64%) and 32.2% of the tasks achieve a value of 0. Only 4.2% of the tasks achieve values greater than three. This shows that tasks usually focus

on the representation of individual or two aspects (e.g. only goods or service flows or goods and service flows as well as cash flows each represented abstractly) and there are very few tasks that comprehensively represent business reality.

RQ3: *To what extent are documents used in the tasks and which documents are predominantly used?*

- 47.2% of the tasks use documents, while no documents are used in 52.8% of the tasks.
- If you differentiate the findings further, it shows that of the 47.2% of tasks that use documents, 81% use one type of document, 18% two types of documents and a further 1.4% of tasks use three different types of documents.
- Receipts are used most frequently (in 19% of tasks), followed by balance lists (9.2%), other documents (6.2%, e.g. invoices, open item lists, extracts from accounting programs, terms and conditions, notices, contracts, emails, notes, memos, etc.), account representations (5.7%), images (4.9%), chart of accounts (3.7%), balance sheets (3.6%), tables (2.3%), asset directories (1.5%) and profit and loss accounts (1.3%).

RQ4: *Which substeps of the modeling cycle occur in which frequency in the textbook tasks? Are there substeps that are addressed comparatively frequently or can substeps be identified that are addressed comparatively infrequently?*

- Orientation performances are required in 89.9% of tasks, translation performances in 76.9%, operations within accounting in 16.3%, interpretation performances in 37.7% and validation services in 4.9%. Business decisions must be made in 0.4% of tasks.
- 45.05% of tasks require the completion of 2 substeps, 40% of three substeps and 2.1% of tasks require the completion of four or more substeps. The combination of the substeps Orientation and Translation occurs most frequently (34.75%), followed by the substeps Orientation, Translation and Interpretation (31.7%).
- If you look at the results at the level of the subcategories of the substeps (if available), it shows for the substep of orientation that in 83% of tasks a problem is present, but already narrowed down and the solution is clear. In almost 4% of tasks, the activity and/or the solution path is open. In 32% of tasks, information research is required, in 37% an evaluation of information. For the internal accounting tasks, the requirement to set up internal accounting book-

ings (e.g. opening or closing accounts) predominates, followed by the task of preparing a balance sheet or setting up a profit and loss account. For the interpretation performances, it is evident that these primarily aim to assess the profit impact of a business case, while other formal objectives (e.g. liquidity) are addressed much less frequently.

- In summary, it can be said that the substep Translation is particularly overrepresented, while the substeps Validation and Deciding are comparatively underrepresented.

RQ5: *Do the textbook tasks have a legal norm orientation? Do learners have to explicitly justify their activity or solution via a legal norm?*

- The descriptive findings show that the tasks from the textbooks have little legal norm orientation and learners almost never have to explicitly justify their activity or the solution they have worked out via a relevant legal norm. Only 17 tasks (0.85%) require the justification of an activity via a corresponding legal norm or the explicit application of a legal norm.

RQ6: *Are connections to other subject areas, specifically to business administration, cost accounting and liquidity management, established in the textbook tasks?*

- In the tasks from the subject areas of financial accounting, hardly any connections are made to other subject areas, e.g. to business administration, cost accounting or liquidity management. In 2.1% of the tasks, there is a connection to business administration. In 19 tasks (1.0%), reference is made to topics of cost accounting or learners have to additionally complete tasks from cost accounting (e.g. calculation of a selling price). A reference to liquidity management can be found in 0.8% of the tasks. In total, a connection to other content areas is established in 3.75% of the tasks.

RQ7: *Do the tasks from different publishers differ in terms of the characteristics mentioned above?*

- The implementation of Chi-square tests or Kruskal-Wallis tests has shown that the tasks of the different publishers differ significantly from each other in many or almost all characteristics. There were no significant differences only in the categories "Document Use" and "Mathematical Work". In some categories, no tests could be carried out due to the small number of codings at level 1 (for dichotomous characteristics). A summary of the findings can be found in Table 7.2.

- In terms of the process orientation of the tasks, it is evident that the tasks from the Hölzel publishing house achieve the comparatively highest (i.e., best) values, while the tasks of the Trauner publishing house have the comparatively lowest values (e.g., no process orientation: 29.4% to 62.4%, comprehensive process orientation 17.0% to 8.1%).
- Regarding the representation of the reality (measured by a sum value between 0 and 6), it is evident that the Hölzel publishing house contains fewer tasks that do not represent reality at all (e.g., 25.3% to 35.5% from the Trauner publishing house), but also comparatively fewer tasks that represent reality very comprehensively (e.g., 0.2% to 1.5% from the Jugend & Volk publishing house).
- For the subcategories of the modeling cycle, the tests also yield significant results. For the characteristic "Recognizing Activity" (first subfacet of orientation), the tasks of the Hölzel publishing house again significantly deviate from the tasks of the other two publishers, with comparatively fewer tasks located at level 0 (no problem orientation, e.g., 3.2% to 18.5% of the tasks of the Jugend & Volk publishing house), but also fewer tasks are classified at level 2 (activity and/or solution open). In the subcategories "Obtaining Information" and "Evaluating Information", the tasks from the Jugend & Volk publishing house perform significantly better than those from the Trauner publishing house (e.g., level 2 "Obtaining Information": 11.1% to 5.1% of the tasks from the Trauner publishing house). For the translation step, it is evident that the tasks of the Hölzel publishing house require a translation performance above average, while the tasks of the Jugend & Volk publishing house require it below average. Internal accounting tasks, on the other hand, are particularly often to be carried out in the tasks of the Jugend & Volk publishing house (e.g., 20.5% to 12.7% of the tasks from the Hölzel publishing house). In the tasks of the Hölzel publishing house, interpretation performances are significantly more often required (e.g., 59.6% to 22.1% of the tasks of the Trauner publishing house), while validation performances are particularly common in the tasks of the Jugend & Volk publishing house (e.g., 9.9% to 1.4% of the tasks of the Hölzel publishing house). The tasks from the Jugend & Volk publishing house also have the highest values for legal norm orientation and connections to business topics. Overall, it is evident that the tasks from the Trauner publishing house are comparatively the worst rated, those from the Jugend & Volk publishing house are comparatively the best.

RQ8: Do the tasks differ at different grade levels in terms of the various characteristics?

- Significant differences between the tasks of different grades could also be determined using Chi-square tests or Kruskal-Wallis tests. There are no significant differences between the school years for the characteristics "Validate", "Legal Norm Orientation" and "Connections to Business Administration". For some characteristics, no examination of the differences could be carried out again. A summary of the findings can be found in Table 7.2.
- In terms of the process orientation of the tasks, it is evident that especially the tasks from the 1st grade significantly differ from the tasks of the other grades, with comparatively many tasks in the 1st grade showing no process orientation at all (e.g., 72.6% to 39.8% from the 3rd grade) or comparatively few tasks are comprehensively process-oriented (3.7% to 22.1% in the 2nd grade). The tasks from the 2nd and 3rd grades achieve the best values.
- In terms of the representation of reality, it can be determined that the tasks of the 4th and 5th grades significantly differ from the tasks of the other grades, with the tasks in these two grades achieving the worst values (e.g., 55.1% of the tasks from the 4th grade do not represent the reality at all, while it is only about 20% of the tasks in the 2nd grade). The tasks thus describe the real operational processes much less detailed than tasks from the other grades. However, this is largely due to the content focus of the curriculum, as the preparation of the annual financial statements (including more-less calculation) and the annual financial statement analysis are defined as topics in the 4th and 5th grades.
- Documents are used significantly more often in the 5th grade, while they are significantly below the expected value in the 2nd grade. At least the intensive use of documents in the 5th grade is plausible, as the topic of annual financial statement analysis almost always involves working with balance sheets, profit and loss accounts, and other documents.
- For the different steps of the modeling cycle, significant differences between the tasks of the different grades could also be determined (but not for the step of validating). For the first subfacet, orientation, it is evident that for all three subcategories (recognizing activity, obtaining information, evaluating information) the tasks from the 5th grade significantly differ from the tasks of the other grades, with the tasks from the 5th grade achieving higher (i.e., better) values in all three facets (except for the conscious information surplus). Translation performances occur significantly more often in the 2nd grade (e.g., 82.5% to 73.2% in the 4th grade), which can also be justified by the curricu-

lar content determination (BMBF, 2014, p. 57). In internal accounting work, the tasks of the 2nd and 4th grades significantly differ from the others, with increased internal accounting activities required in these two grades. At least for the 4th grade, this finding seems to be curricularly conditioned (BMBF, 2014, pp. 60–61). In the interpreting step, it is evident that in the tasks from the 2nd grade, an interpretation performance is often required (52.5%), whereas in the 3rd grade it is significantly less often (18.0%).

RQ9: *How are the different task characteristics related to each other? Are certain characteristics often associated with each other?*

- The cross-table shown in Table 7.26 shows that there are significant correlations between many task characteristics. For example, the process orientation correlates as expected with the variables representing reality. The process orientation also correlates significantly positively with the features "recognizing activity", "setting up bookings" and "indicating profit impact". The subcategories of the representation of reality (representation of goods and service flows as well as cash flows) correlate positively with the requirement to set up a booking. This is also as expected. Therefore, if goods or service flows or cash flows are represented in the task, they are usually also to be translated into accounting.
- Interesting are the almost exclusively negative correlations between the features that concern internal accounting operations (e.g., setting up internal accounting bookings, creating balance sheets) and most other features. This suggests that internal accounting tasks are often to be performed in isolation from other tasks and there is no connection to real, operational processes.
- As expected, there are high correlations between the features "use of documents" and "obtaining information" and "evaluating information". As for the other features of the modeling cycle, the three subfacets of the first step (orienting) correlate positively with each other. It is again striking that internal accounting work does not correlate (or negatively correlate) with the other steps, for example with translating and interpreting. There is only a positive relationship with the first step. It is also interesting that the steps of validating and deciding correlate weakly positively with each other, but negatively with the step of translating. Translation and interpretation performances correlate positively with each other (see also Table 7.27).

RQ10: Can different types of tasks or task classes be identified?

- The execution of a latent class analysis has shown that a model with five task classes fits the data best and can also be interpreted most sensibly in terms of content.
- The first type of task comprises 26.75% of all tasks and was classified as *"document-oriented translation tasks"*. In these tasks, documents are usually used, which are generally to be transferred into the world of accounting through a translation. Interpretation performances also occur more frequently in this type than in most other task classes. The tasks of the second class are referred to as *"internal accounting tasks"*. They comprise 9.95% of all tasks and are characterized by the fact that these tasks usually involve operating within the accounting system, but no translation from the real world into the world of accounting is required. Accordingly, the reality is usually not represented in these tasks. However, information research and evaluation is often required. Task class 3, with 43.10% of all tasks, is the largest class. These are " *text-based translation services"*. This task class has a similar profile to the first class, with the difference that in task class 3, documents are almost never used, but the description of the reality is contained in text form. Accordingly, no information research or evaluation is required for these tasks. A retranslation from the world of accounting into the real world is, however, often required. The fourth task class (10% of all tasks) is the most difficult to interpret in terms of content, as it is characterized by medium expectation values for almost all categories. This type of task was therefore referred to as *"mixed-type tasks"*. Task class five, on the other hand, is characterized by low expectation values for almost all categories. This type of task comprises 10.2% of all tasks and can be described as *"knowledge-oriented tasks without context reference"*. These tasks focus on the reproduction of knowledge, for example, the reproduction of definitions or of (standardized) booking sentences.

Discussion of the Results and Implications for the Design of Curricula and Tasks in Accounting

8

8.1 Discussion of the Results in Light of Previous Research Findings

The results of the empirical study largely fit into the picture drawn by previous findings on task quality in the domain of accounting and related domains, although other criteria (e.g., professional action competence, business process orientation, cognitive level, relevance to life, etc.) were used for evaluation and other tasks were analyzed (see Sect. 4.3). The results of the empirical study are subsequently compared with the existing research results based on criteria. Since there are no studies in which identical criteria were used (an exception is partly the study by Stütz et al. (2022)), results are reported in which similar or comparable criteria were used.

The results of the study show that the reality in the tasks is represented rather abstractly and the tasks are not very process-oriented. Thus, 13% of the tasks are formulated comprehensively process-oriented, about 32% of the tasks can be described as limited process-oriented. Goods or service flows, cash flows, and social processes are also usually represented abstractly, a detailed and realistic representation is found in only a few tasks. Thus, in almost 50% of the tasks, goods or service flows are at least abstractly represented, cash flows in 35.4% of the tasks, and social processes in 5.8% of the tasks. A detailed description is given in only about 1% of the tasks (goods and service flows as well as social processes) or in 4.2% of the tasks (cash flows). It is positive to note that almost half of the tasks use documents (e.g., receipts, balance lists, emails, etc.) to make the described business cases more realistic. Looking at the results of the study by Stütz et al. (2022, p. 19), a similar picture emerges, with some

S. Reindl-Stütz, *Characteristics of Tasks in the Domain of Accounting*,
https://doi.org/10.1007/978-3-658-48958-8_8

exceptions. The examined accounting tasks from various German textbooks for different vocational training professions are also not very process-oriented. Thus, 27% of the tasks can be classified as limited process-oriented and 16% as comprehensively process-oriented. However, a somewhat different picture emerges in the representation of the real world. In about 82% of the tasks, no goods and service flows, cash flows, or social processes are represented at all, in about 17% of the tasks there is at least an abstract representation. It is also striking that documents are used in only 3% of the tasks, while in the tasks examined here it is about half. Also in the analysis conducted by Ernst (2012a, p. 107) of German and American accounting textbooks, it is shown that 2.7% of the tasks use receipts, although there only booking receipts or invoices were included. This shows that the tasks evaluated here use documents much more frequently and also represent reality comparatively better. The reasons for this strong deviation can only be speculated. For example, it is possible that in dual training, the reference to reality is given anyway through work in the company and therefore less emphasis is placed on the representation of entrepreneurial processes in the books. Trainees also come into contact with documents much more frequently in their everyday professional life than full-time students. This may particularly create a need to train working with documents. The study by Stock et al. (2011, p. 17) shows again that documents are used much more frequently in final exams. An evaluation of the business exams of one year showed that 88% of the tasks work with receipts. However, this is also partly due to the guidelines, which state that final exams should pay attention to an appropriate practical reference, for example through the use of documents (BMBWF, 2018, p. 36).

In a similar direction goes also the criterion of relevance to life, as used for example by Thoma and Schumacher (2018) and Ernst (2012a). Thus, Thoma and Schumacher (2018, p. 10) define authentic tasks as follows: "The task setting takes very clear, realistic references to operational practice, for example through a representation of authentically appearing receipts." The evaluations of the tasks from textbooks for the subject of accounting show that only 11.5% of the tasks were classified as authentic. 24.2% of the tasks have a constructed relevance to life (abstract situational references) and 64.3% are "completely context-free and thus without embedding and reference to situational circumstances". Comparing these findings with the findings on the criteria of process orientation and the representation of reality, a coherent picture emerges. The findings of Ernst (2012a, p. 106) also show similar results for the relevance to life. There, too, only 13% of the tasks have a high relevance to life. There is also a similarity to the criterion of authenticity. Thus, Wuttke et al. (2022, p. 35) define that tasks are to be assessed as authentic "if the requirement formulated in the task could also be posed in a similar way in professional practice." Here too, the findings show that a large part of the tasks can be assessed as not very authentic (Wuttke et al., 2022, p. 43).

An aspect at least similar to the process orientation is captured by the criterion of business process orientation (Bloemen, 2011; Kombacher, 2016). The criterion captures whether individual activities are considered in isolation within a task setting or whether references are made to cross-interface business processes. Tasks with comprehensive business process orientation are those that include upstream and downstream business processes and "encourage the modeling of internal and external networking" (Bloemen, 2011, p. 106). Here too, a similar picture emerges as in the present results on the process orientation of the tasks. 5.7% of the tasks have a complete business process orientation, while 57.7% of the tasks only look at isolated activities. In the tasks with ERP reference from different subjects examined by Kombacher (2016, p. 201), about 10% of the tasks are designed to be comprehensively process-oriented.

There are numerous points of connection, however, to the sub-steps of the modeling cycle that were recorded in this study. Thus, connections can be made to the criteria of openness, differentiated by the openness of the problem, the openness of the solution path, and the openness of the result (Bloemen, 2011; Kombacher, 2016; Thoma & Schumacher, 2018; Zhou, 2022), to the steps of the problem-solving process (Wuttke et al., 2022) or to the criteria for determining the levels in the processing of subject-specific problem situations collected by Zhou (2022) based on the model by Seifried et al. (2010).

The first sub-step of the modeling cycle, orientation, was differentiated in this work into three subcategories, which determine how specifically the task to be performed is given, whether the solution can be clearly determined, and whether information needs to be researched and evaluated for the solution of the task. For comparison, studies that have evaluated the openness of tasks are initially suitable, as it is also about whether the task contains a problem, whether this is to be identified by the learners themselves, and how narrow or open solution paths and results are outlined. The evaluations of the present study have shown that in 3.9% of the tasks the problem is openly formulated and therefore the task is to be recognized by the learners themselves or the solution is not clearly given. In 13.15% of the tasks, the problem is exactly given. In the remaining 83% of the tasks, an initial limitation takes place and further concretizations by the learners are necessary. If we now compare these results with existing findings, a consistent picture emerges again, although differences can be identified in detail and in nuances. Thus, the results of Bloemen (2011, p. 135) show that in only 3.5% of the tasks the problem description is incomplete and must be determined independently by the learners. In Kombacher (2016, p. 190), on the other hand, the problem description is incomplete in about 20% of the tasks. Thoma and Schumacher (2018, p. 10) used the category system developed by Maier et al. (2010) to determine the openness of a task. For the tasks from the accounting books of the commercial college, it turns out that almost all tasks (92.6%) have a clear and concrete task, each allowing a correct solution. Only 6.4% of the tasks allow different solutions. No completely open tasks with high degrees of freedom and different solution paths could be identified. This finding is also comparable with the results obtained in this study. In contrast, the evaluations of Zhou (2022, p. 101) show that the tasks from Chinese accounting books allow different solutions much more frequently and provide an open and unclearly formulated starting situation (19.1%), while 30% of the tasks also exactly specify both the task and the solution. The findings of Stütz et al. (2022) can be compared well with the results of this study, as partly identical or very similar criteria were used. Here it is shown that the tasks from the German textbooks perform significantly worse, as in 68% of the tasks there is no problem or the problem is clearly defined (compared to 13.2%), while in only 0.3% tasks an independent identification of the activity by the learners is required (compared to 3.9%). The results of Wuttke et al. (2022, p. 41) also fit well into this picture, as only 1.5% of the tasks were classified as open to solution and in about 80% of the tasks the initial situation (status quo) is clearly defined. The problem contained is therefore not to be recognized by the learners themselves.

For the comparison of the other two subcategories, information research and information evaluation, the results of the study by Stütz et al. (2022) and Wuttke et al. (2022) are also suitable. In the present study, it was determined that information research (from one or more sources) is required in about 38% of the tasks. Furthermore, a distinction between relevant and irrelevant information is required in about 37% of the tasks. The evaluations of Wuttke et al. (2022, p. 41) show that only in about 0.7% of the tasks "information from several (extensive) appendices must be matched and evaluated", but irrelevant information could be identified in about 21% of the tasks. Thus, the tasks of the present study perform somewhat better in this area, although it should be noted that in the study by Wuttke et al. (2022) examination tasks were evaluated, in which at least information procurement from external sources is not possible. In the study by Stütz et al. (2022, p. 19), the research of additional information is required in 44% of the tasks, which corresponds to a similar value of the findings collected here. The category of information evaluation is not comparable due to the different design.

For the sub-step of interpreting, the results of the study by Stütz et al. (2022, p. 19) can be used again. While in 34.4% of the tasks from the Austrian textbooks an interpretation performance with regard to the profit of a company is to be made, an interpretation of the results is required in about 22% of the tasks from the German textbooks. In 0.15% of the tasks, an interpretation in the light of liquidity is to be made. In the tasks from the books for different commercial vocational training professions in Germany, such an interpretation performance is required in 5% of the tasks. Thus, interpretation performances are more frequently required in the tasks from the Austrian textbooks, although the effects on liquidity are less frequently addressed. For the sub-step of validating, it was determined in the present study that 4.9% of all tasks require the verification or justification of a solution. In the study by Wuttke et al. (2022, p. 42), a very similar picture emerges. There too, only 4.8% of the tasks require action control or reflection. In the empirical study by Stütz et al. (2022, p. 19), however, only two tasks (out of 3,361) could be identified that require such validation.

For the remaining categories (e.g., connections to other content areas, orientation to legal norms, etc.), no suitable categories from existing studies could be identified for comparison. In addition, the comparisons are based only on the descriptive findings, as in the available studies so far, purely descriptive evaluations have usually been prioritized and no systematic differences have been identified, for example, between books, years, or publishers. In the studies by Stütz et al. (2022) and Zhou (2022), latent class analyses or a cluster analysis were conducted to identify task types. While no task types could be identified in the study by Stütz et al. (2022, p. 21), three task types were identified in the study by Zhou (2022, pp. 102–112) using a cluster analysis. However, due to the difference in the evaluation categories, a meaningful comparison is not possible.

In summary, it can be said that the findings fit well into the existing research results on the quality of tasks in accounting and related domains. The present findings do not systematically deviate from previous findings, although the tasks achieve better values in individual aspects (e.g., use of documents, interpretation performances). However, for an exact comparison, the identical categories for analysis and evaluation would have to be used.

8.2 Discussion of the Results in the Light of the Subject-Didactic Discussion

The discussion, evaluation, and classification of the results in the light of the subject-didactic discussion is of central importance. For only a classification of the results in the state of subject-didactic discussion allows a critical appreciation of the findings, an interpretation of the results, and subsequently the derivation of implications. If we now look at the results not in detail, but from a slightly higher altitude, then some findings, especially in the light of the subject-didactic discussion, are particularly interesting and worthy of discussion.

Firstly, it can be noted as a major criticism that the tasks systematically place too much emphasis on practicing booking techniques. While the proportion of tasks requiring a translation performance varies significantly depending on the publisher between 67.2% and almost 90% or depending on the years between 73% and 82%, setting up a booking is the dominant activity in the task assignments. Now, of course, it can be noted that the documentation and depiction of operational processes in accounting should be exactly the goal and content of accounting instruction. However, three aspects seem particularly problematic in this context, which will be addressed below.

Firstly, the tasks almost exclusively require the manual preparation of booking entries, while a systematic integration of booking software does not take place. This finding is also consistent with the statements of students that Seifried (2004b, p. 43) collected in a study. The learners indicate that they practice calculation skills and bookkeeping skills in most lessons, but never or almost never "use software to solve tasks and exercises". However, this circumstance is also due to the curricular design in the current curriculum (at least at the commercial colleges), as the topic "Computer-supported accounting" is explicitly only provided in the 2nd year (4th semester) (BMBF, 2014, p. 57). At the same time, however, the didactic principles for the subject of accounting state that "the use of modern IT techniques" should be part of learning arrangements (BMBF, 2014, p. 55). For the development of a basic understanding, it initially seems appropriate that booking entries are set up manually in order to understand the booking logic (and because software often deviates from this logic), but this intensity is certainly not necessary. Klein and Küst (2020, p. 94) also emphasize that the "training of the previously necessary routine can be reduced". If one considers the explanations in Sect. 2.2.2 on the changes in the professional field in the course of digitization and especially the use of RPA and AI-systems (e.g. Hmyzo & Muzzu, 2020; Jordanski, 2020), the strong focus on the manual preparation of booking entries seems particularly outdated. It is more than questionable how the relevance of these content and activity areas can be legitimized and whether the goal of employability, as stated in the curriculum, can be achieved.

A second aspect that appears particularly problematic is that other essential activities or skills that will continue to gain importance in the future, such as validating and plausibility checking of solutions, making business decisions based on data, and an independent problem detection and solution, are hardly or significantly less frequently addressed (see, for example, Jordanski, 2020; Neuweg, 2020; Preiß, 2015). For example, a validation performance is required in less than 5% of the tasks, a decision has to be made in 0.4% of the tasks, which in turn has effects on real operational processes. In 4% of the tasks, the learners have to independently recognize the problem contained in the task. However, significant differences can again be found between publishers or years. For example, the proportion of tasks requiring a validation of the solution varies between 1.4% (Hölzel Verlag) and 9.9% (Verlag Jugend & Volk) depending on the publisher. The proportion of tasks requiring independent problem recognition also varies by publisher between 2.6% and 5.2%, while it varies by year between 1.9% (3rd year) and 11.6% (5th year).

Thirdly, it seems problematic that the documentation function of accounting is overemphasized due to the strong focus on booking activities, while the important functions of control, planning, and monitoring are neglected. This has also been noted several times in the past in the didactic discussion and is also reflected in the findings presented here (e.g. Neuweg, 2020, p. 137; Preiß, 2015, p. 190). However, it should be noted that the sample only includes tasks from the areas of regular accounting and balance sheet accounting—two areas where the documentation of operational processes is certainly in focus. Other areas, such as cost accounting, controlling, or financial planning, which are primarily about planning, control, and monitoring, were not considered here. This naturally also leads to a distortion of the results and therefore does not allow any statement about the intensity with which the documentation, control, planning, and monitoring functions of accounting are addressed in class. However, due to the clear dominance of external accounting in the currently valid curriculum, it can be assumed that the documentation function of accounting is at the center of classroom activities, while internal accounting and the associated functions of controlling, planning, and monitoring of operational processes are neglected.

In this context, it is particularly critical to that the task assignments hardly make any references to the sub-areas of internal accounting (e.g. cost accounting or liquidity management) or to business content areas. For example, references to cost accounting are made in 0.95% of the tasks, to liquidity management in 0.75% of the tasks, and to business content in 2.05% of the tasks. Here too, at least for the connections to business administration, significant differences between the publishers could be found. For example, a connection is to be established in 0.6% of the tasks of the Trauner Verlag, while it is 3.7% in the tasks of the Verlag Jugend & Volk. However, it can again be said that although statistically significant results are available, the tasks overall establish too few references and connections to other relevant content areas. The missing references, especially to business topics, initially seem questionable from a curricular point of view, as networking of the different business vocational subjects is explicitly stated as a goal in the general didactic principles in the curriculum (BMBF, 2014, p. 4). This should also be reflected in the task assignments. From a didactic point of view, a stronger connection between internal and external accounting on the one hand, and between accounting and business administration on the other hand, would be desirable. Preiß (2015, p. 190) criticizes that in class it is still pretended "as if it were mainly about documentation, billing and control (past orientation) and not about operative planning (future orientation) and control (present orientation) of the processes" and "as if traditional accounting were the most important component and not the numerous subsidiary books [...] as well as cost accounting and liquidity management". For Sloane (1996, p. 26), the subject of accounting is a catalyst for the expansion of business competence and the importance of connections to other content areas is also emphasized in the "Linzer Ebenenmodell" and in the economic instrumental accounting (Neuweg, 2020; Preiß & Tramm, 1996). Thus, Preiß and Tramm (1996, p. 222) already demanded in 1996 that accounting teaching "is to be designed and legitimized in the overall context of a commercial curriculum" and that accounting activities "are necessary in connection with business decisions and evaluations" in order to "build cognitive structures for economically accentuated life contexts." However, for the development of these cognitive structures, networking and references between accounting and business administration or the systems of internal accounting must first be established and established in the task assignments.

On a positive note, in almost 38% of the tasks a solution or a business case has to be interpreted, i.e. for example how the booking of a provision affects the company's profit. Here too, significant differences can be seen again between the tasks of different publishers. For example, the proportion of tasks in which a business case or a booking has to be interpreted with regard to the impact on the company's profit varies between 20% (Trauner Verlag) and almost 57% (Hölzel Verlag). The proportion also varies significantly between tasks of different years, between 18% (3rd year) and 53% (2nd year). In this way, a connection is made between the real world and the world of accounting in the sense of the modeling cycle, and a connection is made between the factual field of action and the formal goal level in the sense of the "Linzer Ebenenmodell". If you look at the results in detail, however, it becomes apparent that the interpretation performances almost exclusively cover the aspect of profit impact, while other formal goals are hardly or not addressed at all. Thus, about 88% of all interpretation performances concern the aspect of profit impact, while only 0.4% of the interpretations aim at liquidity. The lack of consideration of liquidity as a central size for ensuring the company's survival ability is particularly problematic. Schneider and Schneider (2019, p. 13) also note that the question is particularly important whether a company can manage with the funds available, as one can "survive losses according to accounting", but "not insolvency". Preiß (2015, p. 190) and Neuweg (2020, p. 138) also emphasize the importance of considering liquidity aspects.

The empirical findings on working with standards and laws are particularly dramatic. In only 0.85% of the tasks, a procedure or a developed solution has to be explicitly justified on a legal basis. This finding is particularly surprising, especially considering the topics of double-entry bookkeeping and especially accounting considered in the analysis. External accounting is largely regulated by corporate and tax law requirements (Denk et al., 2016, p. 2). By ignoring the legal foundations, essential aspects are not made clear to the students, e.g. 1) that accounting processes are largely based on legal requirements and therefore the reality is only distortedly represented, that 2) laws, e.g. corporate law and income tax law, pursue different objectives and are therefore designed differently and 3) that accounting processes do not primarily or only result from the logic of double-entry bookkeeping, but are largely determined by standards (see also Neuweg, 2020, pp. 140–141). Of course, it cannot be answered here to what extent the legal norms and principles are discussed in the lessons themselves, but they play no role in the task assignments of the textbooks.

Referring to the previous statements, from the aspect of the modeling cycle or modeling ability, it is also questionable whether the tasks are suitable to sufficiently promote the modeling ability of the learners. This refers to the ability to "model real economic phenomena with accounting" (Berding, Beckmann & Kürten, 2019, p. 567), i.e. to use accounting as a "tool for solving commercial problems" (Berding, 2019, p. 93). While the translation of a real phenomenon into the world of accounting (by setting up booking entries) is promoted, other sub-steps such as operating within accounting and the retranslation into the real world (e.g. by interpreting or making decisions) are addressed much less frequently. At the same time, an evaluation shows how many different sub-steps have to be completed within *one* task, that learners hardly get the opportunity to go through the entire modeling cycle within one task assignment. If the six-step cycle developed in this work based on the "Linzer Ebenenmodell" and modeling cycles from mathematics didactics is used as a basis (composed of the sub-steps of orientation, translation, internal accounting operation, interpretation, validation, and decision-making), then the empirical findings show that in 85% of the tasks only two or three sub-steps have to be completed within one task. These are predominantly the combinations of orientation and translation as well as orientation, translation, and interpretation. These findings are also reflected in the correlation matrix (Table 7.27), which shows partly negative correlations between the different sub-steps (e.g. translation and internal accounting work or translation and decision-making).

The didactic discussion has also repeatedly criticized that too little reference is made in accounting teaching to the processes and procedures in the real world and therefore the learners lack insight into the processes behind the accounting representations. Therefore, the reality should be depicted more detailed and realistic in teaching and accordingly also in the tasks. In the language of the "Linzer Ebenenmodell", references between the reference field of action and the actual field of action must be established (Neuweg, 2020, p. 136; Pargmann et al., 2022, p. 20; Preiß & Tramm, 1996, p. 246; Seifried, 2004b, p. 291). The abstractness of the content and the lack of reference to reality are regularly cited as causes for learning difficulties, as it is difficult for learners to "gain a vivid idea of the underlying operational processes from the numbers of accounting" (Tramm et al., 1996, p. 205). Documents are given special importance in this context, as they on the one hand form the "bridge between the reference field of action and the actual field of action" (Neuweg, 2020, p. 140) and on the other hand abstract and real operational processes form the starting point for further abstraction processes (Berding, Beckmann & Kürten, 2019, p. 573). It is positive to note for the present results that documents of various kinds are used in 47.20% of the tasks. Predominantly used are receipts (in 19% of the tasks), balance lists (9.2%), other documents (6.2%), account representations (5.7%) as well as pictures (4.9%). This finding is certainly to be assessed as positive, even though many documents are used in excerpts. But this is of course due to the limitation of the number of pages of the textbooks. How the different documents are represented in any additional material cannot be assessed.

In addition to the use of documents in the task assignments, it should also be noted that the reality is depicted rather abstractly and in little detail in the majority of the tasks. Thus, detailed descriptions of goods and service flows (0.8%), cash flows (4.2%) or social processes (0.9%) can be found in 0.8% to 4.2% of the tasks. In many tasks, no goods or service flows (49.8%), cash flows (60.45%) or social processes (93.3%) are addressed at all. The abstract representation of the content is in line with the findings of Seifried (2009a, p. 246) and Berding and Jahncke (2020, p. 240), who show that teachers particularly often emphasize the formalism and schema aspect. While the results appear understandable and plausible at least for the representation of social processes, as they have no immediate accounting relevance, the representation of goods and service flows as well as cash flows seems central. Here, potential for improvement can be identified, although it is understandable that a very detailed representation of the real processes and procedures within task assignments in a textbook is difficult to implement. By reducing the content, by a stronger intertwining with the subject of Business Administration and especially also by a stronger intertwining with the practice firm as well as by the use of other task formats (e.g. case studies, project work or company visits), a stronger integration of the accounting teaching with the operational practice could also succeed. This could reduce the abstractness of the content and give the students better insight into why the content is needed at all. Some studies show that it often does not become clear to the learners why accounting is needed at all (e.g. Stütz, 2021, p. 12; Türling, 2014, p. 162).

Of course, it can generally be noted that tasks from textbooks fail to meet the requirements of the category system for pragmatic reasons alone due to the limited availability of page numbers, because the text volumes of the tasks would increase significantly. However, it should be noted that it is neither sensible nor possible for *all* tasks to fully meet the requirements formulated by the category system. Rather, it is obvious that the full complexity is only exemplified in some tasks over the respective semesters. At this point, the multifunctionality of both the "Linzer Ebenenmodell" (Neuweg, 2020) and the developed category system should also be pointed out. Both tools are not only suitable for analyzing and evaluating existing textbook tasks, but are also useful in the course of lesson planning, e.g. in the development, expansion or adaptation of learning tasks. An example of this is given in the following Sect. 8.3. At the same time, a reduction of the content or the tasks that focus on practicing booking skills means that more space (and by the way also more time for processing in class) is available for other tasks.

Briefly, it should now be discussed whether a recommendation can be made for tasks from a specific publisher. It is striking that the tasks from the books of the publisher Jugend & Volk perform statistically significantly better in central categories than the tasks of the other two publishers. Thus, the tasks of the books of the publisher Jugend & Volk achieve better values with regard to the criteria of detailed representation of operational reality, information procurement, networking with business content, norm orientation, and the required validation performance. This would suggest the preferability of the tasks of this publisher. However, it should be noted that, although these are statistically significant results, the effect sizes are in some cases very small and no particularly noticeable and strong differences can be identified. Therefore, the criticism expressed in the discussion section applies, albeit more or less strongly, to the tasks of all three publishers. Since the information parts of the books were not systematically reviewed and evaluated, no recommendation can be made for the textbooks of a specific publisher. It is also interesting in connection with the tasks of different years that statistically significant differences can be identified there as well, but the effect sizes are also small and it is not apparent that the level of demand is increasing over the years. This is surprising insofar as the "curriculum is conceived as a spiral curriculum in which central contents are repeated over the course of the five years with increasing degree of detail and ascending level of complexity" (BMBF, 2014, p. 4).

If one now tries to classify the findings of the task analysis in terms of whether the objectives of accounting instruction discussed in the didactic discussion are achieved, this seems more than questionable. Thus, Achtenhagen (1996, pp. 27–28) sees the development of economic competence as the primary goal of accounting instruction. For Tramm and Preiß (1996, p. 5), the guiding objective of accounting instruction is the "understanding of economic interrelationships through the penetration and mastery of commercial techniques". Dubs (1996, p. 136) sees as a key goal of instruction that learners "can analyze and interpret the financial data of a company in order to understand the planning and control of financial events in a company and to analyze financial transactions." For this, the "emphasis of instruction is on understanding the larger context [...]" (Dubs, 1996, p. 127). For Schneider (2010, p. 66), the primary goal is also to promote system understanding. This addresses the objectives of both the "practical" and the "thinking accountant". If one now has to judge whether the tasks promote the "practical accountant" or rather the "thinking accountant", it can be discussed on the basis of the present results that both models are not adequately considered and also the objectives of employability and study ability outlined in the curriculum are not adequately promoted. Initially, the focus for both models is too strongly on practicing manual booking skills. If one had to characterize a "typical" task for the subject of corporate accounting, it usually consists of a brief assignment with information about the company and the role of the learners (e.g., "You work in a company and are responsible for the accounting"), with some briefly presented business cases that the learners have to book in the further course. In many tasks, the profit impact of the booking is also to be indicated. This description is similar to the finding already presented in 1996 by Tramm et al. (1996, p. 199), in which they characterize tasks as a "business process with initial stocks, 10 lifeless business transactions and some even less exciting closing statements." At this point, however, it should be pointed out once again that both the division into "practical accountants", who are competent in "practice" but do not understand things, and "thinking accountants", who have understanding but may not be able to act competently, as well as the term "accountant" in general, are to be seen critically. The remarks on digitization in accounting in Sect. 2.2.2 have made it clear that on the one hand, understanding is required for competent action in accounting due to technology, and on the other hand, typical tasks performed by the "practical accountant" are automated. In this sense, in the future, one could much rather speak of the "thinking controller".

The strong dominance of booking activities is also evident in the results of the latent class analysis. Thus, about 70% of all tasks can be assigned to two task classes ("document-oriented translation tasks" and "text-based translation tasks"). Both types of tasks are characterized, among other things, by the fact that they abstractly represent the reality with or without the use of documents and the given business cases are to be translated into the world of accounting by setting up a booking. For a stronger emphasis on the "practical accountant", the tasks would have to focus on the consistent use of booking software and integrate business practice more strongly into the teaching, for example through project work, case study work and company visits. For the promotion of the "thinking accountant", the tasks would have to encourage the interpretation and analysis of data more than before, encourage the answering of why-questions, consider the legal bases and the underlying intentions of the legislator more strongly and overall promote the understanding of the interrelationships between the systems of accounting.

In view of the previous discussion, however, it also becomes clear that a sole focus on improving the tasks in accounting instruction is not sufficient. On a higher and preliminary level, adaptations and further developments of the curriculum are probably also necessary. Thus, in light of the results presented here, the question arises as to what objectives should be pursued with accounting instruction. If the main aim is to prepare students for the world of work, then the teaching (and subsequently also the teaching materials) must be oriented much more strongly towards the realities of business practice than has been the case so far. This would, analogous to the changes in the task assignments, mean in any case to work more intensively with (different) booking software and ERP systems, to massively reduce the intensity of manual booking activity and probably also to focus more on topics such as cost accounting and liquidity management.[1]

[1] However, whether a predominant orientation towards professional practice is goal-oriented can be doubted considering the transition rates into the higher education system. On average, about 60% of graduates from commercial academies enter the higher education system within three years of leaving school (Statistik Austria, 2022, p. 63). Schneider (2010, p. 56) also argues against too strong an orientation towards employability, noting that "only about 10–20% of graduates find their first job in the field of accounting and thus need immediate operational security."

It therefore seems essential that a basic understanding of the functions and purpose of internal and external accounting is built up in accounting instruction. However, this would also require curricular changes, for example to treat the instruments of internal and external accounting in parallel and to establish connections, rather than to discuss them one after the other and without references, or to deal with topics such as controlling or annual financial statement analysis much earlier and more intensively. Further recommendations for a possible redesign of the curriculum are discussed in Sect. 8.3.

8.3 Implications for Curriculum Development and Task Design

The evaluations of the empirical findings have shown that there is significant potential for improvement in the textbook tasks for the subject of corporate accounting and a change in task culture is necessary. It can be asserted that the textbook tasks in their current design do not adequately prepare for either the professional everyday life in accounting or an economic university study. In light of the current didactic discussion, the model of the "thinking accountant" is given too little consideration, although the "practical accountant" is also not sufficiently promoted due to the lack of systematic orientation towards professional requirements.

Overall, the tasks focus too much on practicing booking skills and too little on building a comprehensive and networked economic understanding. The real operational processes are only fragmentarily represented, which in turn leads to learners being able to connect the real world and the systems of accounting only inadequately. The tasks demand too little interpretation and validation of data as well as the making of business decisions. While the documentation function of accounting is intensively discussed, the functions of control, planning, and monitoring are given too little attention.

From the empirical findings and the current didactic discussion, some implications for the design of tasks in accounting and accordingly for teaching in the subject of business accounting can be derived. Firstly, regardless of or prior to the concrete design of textbook tasks, a curricular redesign of accounting teaching seems inevitable.

If one looks at the curriculum of the commercial academy (BMBF, 2014) from a content perspective, some peculiarities become apparent, especially with regard to the content focus and the arrangement of the content. Firstly, it is noticeable that a large part of the content deals with financial accounting and the annual financial statements, while for example cost accounting is taught as an "insert" in the 3rd year for one semester. Financial accounting is not explicitly dealt with in the subject of business accounting (if at all, then most likely in the area of controlling in the 5th year), but in the subject of business administration. Moreover, there seems to be little connection between the areas. It is also striking that content that primarily concerns the planning and control function of accounting and focuses more on the analysis and interpretation of data is dealt with later in time. Thus, the contents of annual financial statement analysis and controlling are located in the 5th year. The curriculum is also characterized by a high degree of detail, especially in the area of booking knowledge.[2] However, it is interesting in this context that working with software is only explicitly planned for one semester. The focus on detailed booking knowledge without systematic and continuous use of booking software seems particularly surprising and problematic in light of the explanations in Sect. 2.2.2. If one now asks whether the curriculum is aimed more at the "practical accountant" or more at the "thinking accountant", then there are indications in the document for the promotion of both models (see also Riebenbauer, 2021, pp. 150–151). So an attempt is made to target both professional action competence and understanding. The high degree of detail in setting up bookings, the use of software (although not consistently) and the reference to as practical as possible task settings are however aspects that primarily focus on the "practical accountant". In the current design of the curriculum, however, it is questionable whether either *one* of the two models is satisfactorily targeted. For the promotion of the model of the "practical accountant", the content is probably too little oriented towards practice, for the promotion of the "thinking accountant" too much focus is placed on booking knowledge, while the understanding of the purpose and purpose of accounting, of legal bases and of balance sheet policy considerations is given too little consideration. In any case, for the promotion of *both* models or an integrative model (e.g. in the sense of a "thinking controller", see Sect. 2.2.2), the proportion of content that involves the mere booking of facts would have to be significantly reduced, as these are taken over by the software in the light of the "practical accountant" and are not necessary to this extent in the light of the "thinking accountant" for an understanding of the connections.

[2] Thus, students learn how to book subsequent discounts, how to record packaging or how to depict a cash discount in accounting. So the documentation function of accounting is strongly emphasized.

For the further development of the curriculum, the following aspects seem essential (see also Neuweg, 2020; Preiß, 2015):

- Firstly, there is a need to clarify the objectives of accounting teaching. Here, an initial orientation towards the objectives of employability and studiability given in the curriculum and towards the models of the "practical" and "thinking accountant" discussed in the didactic discourse is advisable. In light of all previous statements and especially with regard to digitalization and the increasing use of AI (e.g. *large language models*, see Sect. 2.2.2), it is advocated to abandon the contrasting dichotomization of action security ("practical accountant") and understanding ("thinking accountant") in favor of an integrative model in the sense of a "thinking controller" and to develop the curricula more in this direction.
- Furthermore, a stronger interlinking and connection of accounting teaching with other business subjects, especially with business administration teaching (up to a possible merger of these two subjects in the sense of the learning field approach) and in this context a better connection between operational processes and the systems of accounting is indicated.
- Greater emphasis should be placed on internal accounting, especially cost accounting and liquidity management, if necessary at the expense of double-entry bookkeeping and accounting. In addition, the control, planning and control functions of accounting should be emphasized more in teaching and a better connection between the systems of internal and external accounting should be ensured.
- There also seems to be a need to reduce the content and competences that focus on the routine practice of booking skills, in favor of promoting the abilities for plausibility checks, interpretation, validation and decision-making, as well as a stronger consideration of the legal bases.

The curricular developments are then to be transferred in a next step to the textbooks and subsequently to the tasks contained in the textbooks.

Finally, tools or didactic models will be presented that can facilitate or support the adaptation of teaching or the tasks used in teaching. The *Learning Cockpit* developed by Pargmann et al. (2022, p. 21) and the planning grid proposed by Berding (2019, p. 289) for planning teaching in accounting appear particularly promising as development aids for designing teaching in accounting and for developing and adapting tasks. The *Learning Cockpit* is a software that allows the simulation of activities and extends them by the use of digital technologies and didactic functions. Figure 8.1 shows an example of a *Learning Cockpit*. The

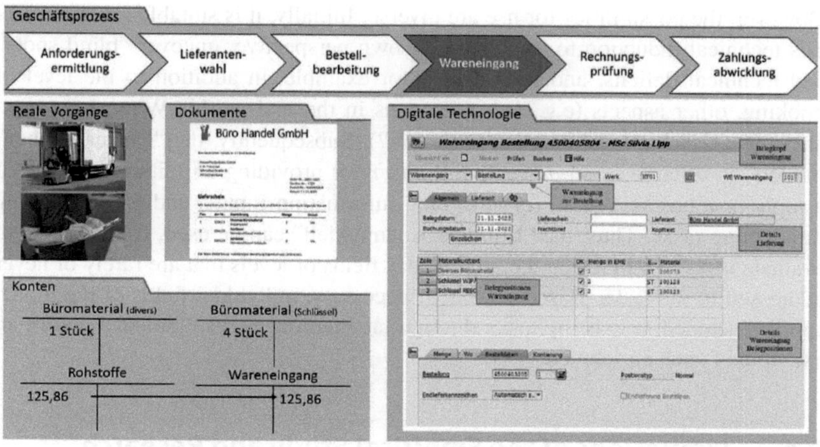

Fig. 8.1 Learning Cockpit according to Pargmann et al. (2022, p. 21)

"business process" field shows that the relevant business case is embedded in an event chain, which in turn ensures an overview of the process. The "real events" field shows which real operational processes are "behind" the accounting processes, while the documents represent the bridge between the real processes and the representation in accounting. The representation in accounting becomes visible in the "Digital Technology" field, as the booking mask is depicted there. The "Accounts" field visualizes the account movements, which in turn can promote the understanding of the learners (Pargmann et al., 2022, pp. 20–21).

Also interesting is the planning grid for teaching developed by Berding (2019, pp. 288–289) based on the model of basic ideas. This allows for "conscious planning of the connection between economic phenomena and abstractions in accounting" (Berding, 2019, p. 288), by providing in the planning grid the description of reality (real processes in the company), the mediators (receipts and documents), and accounting (booking entries, key figures, accounts, etc.). Both presented tools can be connected to other concepts, especially the "Linzer Ebenenmodell", and can help to overcome the one-sided focus on the (manual) booking of business transactions and to more closely interlink operational reality and its representation in accounting. While the planning grid is particularly useful in lesson preparation, the *Learning Cockpit* can be used directly in the classroom.

In the present research project, the "Linzer Ebenenmodell" was primarily used as a basis for developing a category system for analyzing and evaluating tasks.

However, the possibilities for use are diverse. Initially, it is suitable for the teacher's technical induction to broaden their own perspective, uncover "blind spots" and technical deficits, and to consider, for example, in addition to the level of booking, other aspects (e.g., What happens in the real world? What documents are created? What legal bases are relevant?). Subsequently, the "Linzer Ebenenmodell" is suitable as an *advance organizer* for providing an initial overview of a topic or a business case, for designing information inputs, and for developing or adapting tasks. Thus, the "Linzer Ebenenmodell" can be used, for example, to evaluate tasks in a first step, i.e., to identify fields or levels that are rarely or never addressed in the tasks. Based on this, if necessary, individual fields of the model can be included in existing tasks through targeted questions. Table 8.1 shows an example of such enrichment.

8.4 Limitations of the Empirical Study and Research Desiderata

As with any scientific study, a number of limitations can be identified for the present empirical survey, which in turn provide starting points for further research efforts and are discussed below.

A first limitation concerns initially *the definition and selection of tasks*. Initially, only accounting teaching at Austrian commercial colleges was considered. The commercial college was chosen because it is the "most important vocational training track in the full-time school sector" (Aff & Greimel-Fuhrmann, 2018, p. 205) and there is hardly any research findings for the Austrian area. It is therefore initially questionable to what extent the findings can be transferred to accounting teaching at other types of schools, to teaching in the dual system, and to accounting teaching in Germany or Switzerland. While the transferability to the dual system and to teaching in Germany and Switzerland is certainly more questionable, a transferability of the findings to other full-time school types in Austria is quite plausible. If one looks, for example, at the curriculum for the HLW (BMBF, 2015) and the textbooks available for the HLW, there are strong similarities with the curriculum and textbooks for the commercial academy. The existing research findings on the quality of tasks in accounting, which mainly come from Germany and particularly focus on the dual system, speak for a transferability beyond the HLW. As shown in Sect. 8.1, the results of the present study fit well into the existing findings, which in turn suggests that the findings are transferable and accordingly represent an example for "the" accounting teaching.

Table 8.1 The "Linzer Ebenenmodell" as a tool for enriching textbook tasks

<u>**Exemplary task from a textbook:**</u>
GBB Garden Center GmbH: The GBB Garden Center GmbH estimates the amount of tax consulting costs for the closing year at 4,800.00 EUR incl. 20% VAT. So far, no provisions have been made in this regard
a) Form a provision for tax consulting expenses and set up the necessary booking entry
b) How does this booking affect the company's success?

<u>**Levels addressed in the "Linzer Ebenenmodell":**</u>
Factual field of action, booking level (5b): "Form a provision for tax consulting expenses and set up the necessary booking entry."
Commercial target field, field piece and period success/profitability (9): "How does this booking affect the company's success?"

<u>**Exemplary questions for enriching the tasks using the "Linzer Ebenenmodell":**</u>

Goods and service flows (1)	• What services does a tax consultant offer? • For which services could the GBB Garden Center GmbH have used the tax consultant? • What are the advantages of using a tax consultant?
Cash flows (2)	• Does money flow through the present business case? If yes, to whom, in what amount and when? If no, why not?
Social processes (3)	• In what form does the GBB Garden Center GmbH communicate with the tax consultant? How are documents transmitted to the tax consultant?
Receipts and documents (4)	• Enrichment of the learning task with fee notes from previous years to estimate the amount for the provision.
Standards (5a)	• On what legal basis can/must/should the provision be formed? • What type of provision is it? • Is the provision also permissible under the Income Tax Act?
Balance sheet, P&L, tax disclosure (5c)	• Is the provision visible in the balance sheet? If yes, where? If no, why not? • Is the provision visible in the income statement? If yes, where? If no, why not? • Is a line item in the more-less calculation necessary due to the formation of the provision?
Cost accounting (7)	• Are provisions also considered in cost accounting in any form?
Liquidity (8)	• Does the present business case affect the company's liquidity? If yes, how? If no, why not?

Another limitation is the focus on the content areas of double-entry bookkeeping and accounting, and thus on external accounting. This is critical considering that internal accounting is of central importance (see Sect. 2.1) and dealing with internal accounting represents a didactic desideratum (e.g., Jungwirth, 2015; Preiß, 2015). It should also be mentioned that a stratified, proportional random selection of 2,000 analysis units was drawn to determine the sample, which represents 27.6% of the total population. The criteria for stratification were the publisher and the year of publication, although other meaningful stratification characteristics could be discussed (e.g., task type). However, stratified, proportional random selection is preferable to simple random selection. Included were *all* textbooks approved for the subject of accounting at commercial colleges (3 publishers, 15 textbooks) in the most recent edition at the time of evaluation, but not any exercise books. Only tasks included in the print version of the respective textbook were considered. Online materials were not taken into account. It cannot be ruled out that the tasks in the exercise books and in the online materials differ from those in the print textbooks. The basis for the selection of textbooks was the 2021/22 textbook list for Higher Commercial Schools (Code: 4600) of the BMBWF. From these books, tasks were taken proportionally to the total number of tasks from the respective textbook. Therefore, the distribution of the respective textbooks in the schools and the actual use in class were not taken into account. Therefore, only the quality and characteristics of the potentially available textbook tasks can be assessed. No statement can be made about the actual selection and use of textbook tasks in accounting classes.

This leads to another limitation of the present study. Only *textbook* tasks were analyzed, not tasks created by teachers themselves or exam tasks. Attempts to gain access to tasks developed by teachers have unfortunately failed despite multiple inquiries through different channels. Therefore, it cannot be ruled out that a) textbooks and subsequently textbook tasks are rarely used in accounting classes or the extent and intensity of their use vary depending on the school or teacher and b) the quality of self-created tasks is significantly better than that of textbook tasks.

Based on these limitations, some research desiderata can already be derived. First, it would be desirable to expand the sample to other subject areas (e.g., cost accounting, financial accounting), which would require an adaptation of the category system. An expansion of the sample to include exercise books and online materials would also be desirable. However, research efforts to spread different textbooks from various publishers and to use textbooks in the subject of business accounting and in this context to use textbook tasks in class seem particularly important. In addition, it is necessary to focus more on self-created tasks and exam tasks, although obtaining these tasks poses a great challenge and the risk of distortion is likely to be high, especially for tasks created by teachers, as it can be assumed that particularly committed and competent teachers provide tasks.

Another limitation of the study is that each task was included in the analysis with equal weighting. The *time effort* required to complete the tasks was not taken into account. For example, students usually need significantly less time to answer a knowledge question than to work on a case study or an exercise task. Therefore, for future studies, it may be considered to take into account the time effort of task processing. Suggestions for implementing this proposal are provided by Janovec (2014), who included the processing time of tasks as a weighting factor in the analysis of the cognitive stimulation content of textbook tasks on the subject of marketing.

Another limitation is the design of the *category system*. The category system was developed based on the current didactic discussion status, focusing on the "Linzer Ebenenmodell" and the modeling cycle. However, there are also other, especially general didactic, criteria that could be used for the analysis and evaluation of tasks, e.g., the cognitive stimulation content in the sense of the taxonomy matrix according to Anderson and Krathwohl. This would also allow a comparison of evaluations according to different criteria (e.g., modeling cycle and taxonomy matrix). For all categories, either a dichotomous scale (present or not present) or an ordinal scale with three expressions was chosen as the level of differentiation. To get even more detailed insights into the task characteristics, a more differentiated level of differentiation would be desirable, although this could again cause problems with the exact delimitation of the levels and subsequently with the comparability (reliability) of the codings. The research desiderata thus include the analysis and evaluation of the existing sample with additional criteria relevant to accounting didactics, as well as the further development and, if necessary, differentiation of the existing category system.

A final, but significant limitation of the present study is that the analysis and evaluation of textbook tasks do not allow any statements about which *cognitivethinking processes* occur in learners during task processing and whether the intentions pursued with the tasks are actually achieved by the learners. Therefore, only the *potential of the tasks* can be assessed. This problem is particularly evident in categories that (at least indirectly) address activities on the part of learners. For example, the indication of the liquidity effect of a business case is about whether a task prompts learners to interpret a business case in terms of its impact on the company's liquid assets. So if the question is included "How does the business case affect the company's liquidity?", the category is rated with 1 (present). However, no statement can be made about the level of detail in which the answer should be given, how the learners proceed in processing the task, and especially how they would justify their answer. It is conceivable, for example, that they justify the impact on liquid assets via the position of the accounts in debit or credit (e.g., "The bank account is in debit, so the liquid assets increase.") or via the processes taking place in the real world (e.g., "We paid the fuel bill in cash, so money is leaving the company and liquidity is decreasing."). However, a systematic analysis of these thought processes would be necessary to uncover learning and understanding difficulties and erroneous basic ideas (see Berding, 2019) and to counteract them. Helm (2016d) and Nobiling et al. (2020) have already dealt with the cognitive thought processes of learners when processing tasks (see Sect. 2.3.3) and thus provided initial valuable insights, although further research efforts are indicated here.

8.5 Final Considerations

The aim of the dissertation project was initially to develop a didactic category system for the analysis and evaluation of tasks from the domain of accounting. To this end, the didactic discussion status was worked out in a first step. Based on this, requirements for "successful" accounting tasks were formulated and developed into a comprehensive classification scheme. Reference concepts were the "Linzer Ebenenmodell" (Neuweg, 2020) and other didactic approaches (e.g., the economic-instrumental accounting, Preiß & Tramm, 1990), existing competence models (Guggemos, 2016; Guggemos & Schönlein, 2015; Preiß, 2005a), models for describing thinking steps when processing accounting tasks (Helm, 2016d; Seifried et al., 2010; Wuttke & Seifried, 2012), the role models of the "practical" and the "thinking accountant" (Reinisch, 1996, 2005), research on learning difficulties in accounting (Pawlik, 1979, 1980; Tramm et al., 1996; Türling, 2014; Türling et al., 2011) as well as the modeling cycle transferred from mathematics didactics to accounting (Berding, 2019; Berding, Beckmann & Kürten, 2019; Blum, 1985, 2011).

The category system is therefore suitable for analyzing and evaluating existing tasks from accounting. At the same time, it can also be used to develop new tasks or adapt or expand existing tasks. It is multifunctional and serves textbook authors and teachers alike as a guide in designing teaching elements, especially in the development of tasks. At the same time, it can be assumed that individual features of the category system can also be used profitably for task analyses in other domains. Thus, the category system contributes to task research in general, and of course specifically to task research in accounting didactics.

With the first trial of the category system on 2,000 textbook tasks for the subject of business accounting at Austrian commercial academies, the level of knowledge about the quality of tasks in accounting is substantially expanded. With a focus on tasks from Austrian textbooks, an area is analyzed that has so far been largely overlooked.

Finally, the question should be pursued as to how the findings, which are problematic on the one hand, but not surprising in the light of the state of didactic discussion on the other hand, can be explained.

Firstly, it can be noted that the results fit well into the existing findings on the quality of accounting tasks (see Sect. 4.3 and 8.1). This suggests firstly that accounting tasks for different target groups (e.g., tasks for learners in the dual system or tasks for learners in the full-time school system), from different countries (e.g., Austria, Germany, USA) and for different purposes (learning tasks and examination tasks) are similarly (problematically) assessed and secondly that no substantial improvements or further developments in task culture have taken place over the years.

Only assumptions can be made about the reasons for the lack of progress in the area of task design in accounting education. The fact that accounting education has not substantially evolved in recent years and decades, also on a curricular, content and methodological level, is often discussed in the didactic discourse (e.g., Jahn, 2020, p. 29; Reinisch, 1996, p. 66, 2005, p. 28; Seifried, 2004b, p. 277; Stütz, 2021, p. 2). Reinisch and Struve (2002, p. 108) describe accounting education as resistant to change and reform. As an example, Reinisch (1996, pp. 64–67) cites the discussion that has been ongoing for several decades about the curricular location of accounting, as an independent subject or in connection with other content areas. He sees the reasons for the lack of further development of teaching in favor of a concentration and integration of subjects to a large extent in "school organizational inertia in connection with teachers' efforts to facilitate their teaching activities [...] through specialization" (Reinisch, 1996, p. 66).

The inertia and resistance to reform are probably related to a phenomenon that Lortie (2007) refers to as *apprenticeship of observation*. Unlike other professional candidates, such as lawyers or doctors, prospective teachers gather diverse experiences in the field of school during their own school years in thousands of school hours. Through these experiences, "subjective theories" (Dann, 2000; Groeben & Scheele, 2010), "views" (Seifried, 2009a) or "beliefs" (*teacher's beliefs*) (Nespor, 1987; Reusser & Pauli, 2014) are developed. Prospective teachers therefore already have precise ideas *before* entering training about how "successful" teaching is designed, what content is covered, with which methods and in which social forms learning takes place. These beliefs usually prove to be resistant to change and guide action (Neuweg, 2022; Reusser & Pauli, 2014, pp. 644–646; Seifried, 2009a, pp. 42–43). That the beliefs internalized by teachers impact the concrete design of teaching has already been shown by many research results (for the commercial area e.g., Berding & Jahncke, 2020; Holtsch, 2018; Holtsch & Sticca, 2018; Neuweg & Mayr, 2018; Seifried, 2009a). "Because it makes a difference whether a teacher primarily sees bookkeeping as a tool for controlling the company or whether they believe that bookkeeping primarily depends on the exact use of terms and the application of solution algorithms" (Seifried, 2009a, pp. 42–43). For the domain of accounting, it is shown that teachers particularly emphasize the formalism and schema aspect and therefore believe that the domain of accounting is primarily determined by logic, order and precision and is oriented towards the processing of procedures and schemas (Seifried, 2009a, pp. 246–249). If teachers adhere to these beliefs, then it is likely that the design of teaching and subsequently the tasks will also be oriented towards this. The beliefs lead to the "traditional" accounting teaching being continued and important reforms being omitted.

During university education, therefore, dealing with one's own subjective theories, the critical juxtaposition of subjective and objective theories and, if necessary, the adaptation and reworking of one's own beliefs seems central (Neuweg, 2022, pp. 89–90; Seifried, 2009a, p. 347). "For the training and further education of teachers, this means that it is primarily necessary to address the beliefs of the teachers. It must be shown that bookkeeping teaching does not only consist of a logic inherent in the content, but is an important tool for solving practical problems" (Berding & Jahncke, 2020, p. 253).

Regardless of this, however, a curricular further development of teaching is in any case inevitable (see Sect. 8.3). These changes must then be consistently reflected in the textbooks and the tasks contained in the textbooks must be adapted accordingly.

University education and further training of teachers can also start with the critical discussion of "traditional" accounting teaching, by systematically working up the didactic discussion status and discussing development perspectives. In addition, it is necessary to convey didactic concepts that can help to further develop teaching and improve the tasks used. The Linz level model (Neuweg, 2020), the *Learning Cockpit* (Pargmann et al., 2022) and the planning grid for planning teaching on the basis of the model of basic ideas (Berding, 2019) seem particularly suitable. Further concrete starting points for further development of teaching are the cooperative development of *best practice* examples and the introduction of a teacher exchange platform for teaching materials.

In addition to the didactic concepts, the category system developed in the course of this work can also be used profitably in the training and further education of teachers and in professional practice. It reflects the current didactic discussion status on the requirements for tasks in accounting in a condensed form and is therefore suitable for pointing out deficits and concrete development options in teaching and task design.

References

Achtenhagen, F. (1996). Entwicklung ökonomischer Kompetenz als Zielkategorie des Rechnungswesenunterrichts. In P. Preiß & T. Tramm (Hrsg.), *Rechnungswesenunterricht und ökonomisches Denken: Didaktische Innovationen für die kaufmännische Ausbildung* (S. 22–44). Gabler.

Aff, J. & Greimel-Fuhrmann, B. (2018). Wirtschaftsberufliche Bildung in Österreich – quo vadis? In M. Pilz (Hrsg.), *Berufsbildung zwischen Tradition und Moderne: Festschrift für Thomas Deißinger Zum 60. Geburtstag* (S. 205–226). Springer.

Anderson, L. W. & Krathwohl, D. R. (2001). *A taxonomy for learning, teaching, and assessing: A revision of Bloom's taxonomy of educational objectives*. Longman.

Arek-Bawa, O. & Dhunpath, R. (2017). Assessment and Cognitive Demand in Higher Education Accounting Textbooks. *Alternation Interdisciplinary Journal for the Study of the Arts and Humanities in Southern Africa, 24*(2), 140–166.

Arndt, H. (2013). Fachdidaktische Analyse von Aufgaben im Wirtschaftsunterricht. In M. Kleinknecht, T. Bohl, U. Maier & K. Metz (Hrsg.), *Lern- und Leistungsaufgaben im Unterricht: Fächerübergreifende Kriterien zur Auswahl und Analyse* (S. 193–206). Julius Klinkhardt.

Arndt, H. (2014). Bedeutung und Klassifikation von Aufgaben im Wirtschaftsunterricht. In *Ökonomische Allgemeinbildung in der Sekundarstufe I und Primarstufe: Konzepte, Analysen, Studien und empirische Befunde* (S. 221–238). Wochenschau Verlag.

Atteslander, P. (2010). *Methoden der empirischen Sozialforschung* (13., neu bearbeitete und erweiterte Auflage). Erich Schmidt Verlag.

Bacher, J. & Vermunt, J. K. (2010). Analyse latenter Klassen. In C. Wolf & H. Best (Hrsg.), *Handbuch der sozialwissenschaftlichen Datenanalyse* (S. 553–574). VS Verlag für Sozialwissenschaften.

Backhaus, K., Erichson, B., Gensler, S., Weiber, R. & Weiber, T. (2021). *Multivariate Analysemethoden: Eine anwendungsorientierte Einführung* (16., vollständig überarbeitete und erweiterte Auflage). Springer Gabler.

Beasley, T. M. (1995). Multiple regression approach to analyzing contingency tables: Post hoc and planned comparison procedures. *The Journal of Experimental Education, 64*(1), 79–93.

S. Reindl-Stütz, *Characteristics of Tasks in the Domain of Accounting*,
https://doi.org/10.1007/978-3-658-48958-8

Beck, K., Landenberger, M. & Oser, F. (Hrsg.). (2016). *Technologiebasierte Kompetenzmessung in der beruflichen Bildung: Ergebnisse aus der BMBF-Förderinitiative ASCOT*. wbv.

Bensch, J. (2009). Welchen Sinn hat die Finanzbuchhaltung? – Über Irrungen und Wirrungen im Rechnungswesenunterricht und unterrichtsimmanente Lernhemmnisse. *Wirtschaft und Erziehung*(6), 198–205 (Teil 1), 226–230 (Teil 2), 267–270 (Teil 3).

Berding, F. (2015). Entwicklung eines Modells zur Beschreibung des Einflusses der epistemischen Überzeugungen von Lehrkräften auf den Aufgabeneinsatz im kaufmännischen Unterricht. *bwp@ Berufs-und Wirtschaftspädagogik online*(28), 1–30.

Berding, F. (2016a). Welche Bedeutung haben epistemische Überzeugungen für Lernende in der beruflichen Bildung? *Zeitschrift für Berufs- und Wirtschaftspädagogik, 112*(1), 80–107.

Berding, F. (2016b). Wie stellen sich Auszubildende und Studierende Wissen und Wissenserwerb im Rechnungswesen vor? *Zeitschrift für Berufs- und Wirtschaftspädagogik, 112*(2), 211–242.

Berding, F. (2018). Auf die Vorstellungen kommt es an. Grundvorstellungen im Rechnungswesen am Beispiel des Begriffs „Aufwand". *Bildung und Beruf, 1*, 6–11.

Berding, F. (2019). *Rechnungswesenunterricht: Grundvorstellungen und ihre Diagnose. Schriften zur Berufs- und Wirtschaftspädagogik: Band 14*. Rainer Hampp.

Berding, F. (2020). Ausarbeitung und Vergleich verschiedener Typen von Grundvorstellungsnetzen über erfolgswirksame Vorgänge. In F. Berding, H. Jahncke & A. Slopinski (Hrsg.), *Moderner Rechnungswesenunterricht 2020: Status quo und Entwicklungen aus wissenschaftlicher und praktischer Perspektive* (S. 125–178). Springer.

Berding, F., Beckmann, A. & Kürten, V. (2019). Modellieren mit dem Rechnungswesen: Entwicklung eines rasch-konformen Messverfahrens für erfolgswirksame Vorgänge und didaktische Implikationen. *Zeitschrift für Berufs- und Wirtschaftspädagogik, 115*(4), 567–602.

Berding, F., Irmscher, M., Vossmann, M. & Gores, A. (2018). Eine Frage des Stils? Individuelle Sicht- und Vorgehensweisen von kaufmännischen Auszubildenden bei der Konstruktion von Wissen im Kontext der Digitalisierung. *Zeitschrift für Berufs- und Wirtschaftspädagogik, 114*(2), 213–246.

Berding, F. & Jahncke, H. (2020). Die Rolle von Grundvorstellungen in Lehr-Lern-Prozessen im Rechnungswesenunterricht – eine Mehr-Ebenen-Analyse zu den Überzeugungen von Lehrkräften und Grundvorstellungen, Motivation, Modellierungsfähigkeit und Noten von Lernenden. In F. Berding, H. Jahncke & A. Slopinski (Hrsg.), *Moderner Rechnungswesenunterricht 2020: Status quo und Entwicklungen aus wissenschaftlicher und praktischer Perspektive* (S. 227–258). Springer.

Berding, F. & Lamping, C. (2014). *Epistemologische Überzeugungen als Bestandteil der professionellen Kompetenz von Lehrkräften und ihre Bedeutung für die Auswahl und Bewertung von Lernaufgaben aus Schulbüchern des Wirtschaftslehreunterrichts: Eine explorative Studie. Schriften zur Berufs- und Wirtschaftspädagogik: Band 12*. Rainer Hampp.

Berding, F. & Lau, I. (2018). Epistemic Messages in Textbooks for Vocational Education and Training. *Journal of Educational Media, Memory, and Society, 10*(2), 39–63.

Berding, F. & Pargmann, J. (2022). *Iota Reliability Concept of the Second Generation*. Logos Verlag Berlin. https://doi.org/10.30819/5581

Berding, F., Riebenbauer, E. & Slepcevic-Zach, P. (2019). Grundvorstellungen angehender Wirtschaftspädagog(inn)en im Rechnungswesen: Verknüpfungen mit Lernprozessen und Unterricht im Vergleich zwischen Deutschland und Österreich. *Zeitschrift für Berufs- und Wirtschaftspädagogik, 115*(3), 363–369.

Berding, F., Riebenbauer, E., Stütz, S., Jahncke, H., Slopinski, A. & Rebmann, K. (2022). Performance and Configuration of Artificial Intelligence in Educational Settings. Introducing a New Reliability Concept Based on Content Analysis. *Frontiers in Education, 7*, Artikel 818365. https://doi.org/10.3389/feduc.2022.818365

Berding, F., Rolf-Wittlake, K. & Buschenlange, J. (2017). Impact of Different Levels of Epistemic Beliefs on Learning Processes and Outcomes in Vocational Education and Training. *World Journal of Education, 7*(3), 103–114.

Berding, F., Stütz, S., Jahncke, H., Holt, K., Deters, C. & Schnieders, M.-T. (2021). Kosten und Leistungen, Eigenkapital und Fremdkapital. *Zeitschrift für Berufs- und Wirtschaftspädagogik, 117*(4), 560–629.

Berger, S. (2015). Fachwissen und fachdidaktisches Wissen im wirtschaftspädagogischen Studium – Entwicklung eines Testinstruments und erste empirische Befunde. In B. Koch-Priewe, A. Köker, J. Seifried & E. Wuttke (Hrsg.), *Kompetenzerwerb an Hochschulen: Modellierung und Messung: Zur Professionalisierung angehender Lehrerinnen und Lehrer sowie frühpädagogischer Fachkräfte* (S. 105–125). Julius Klinkhardt.

Bertl, R., Deutsch-Goldoni, E. & Hirschler, K. (2022). *Buchhaltungs- und Bilanzierungshandbuch* (12., neu bearbeitete Auflage, bearbeitete Ausgabe). LexisNexis.

Bieker, M. (2019). Inhaltliche Neuausrichtung des Rechnungswesens durch Digitalisierung. In T. Kümpel, K. Schlenkrich & T. Heupel (Hrsg.), *Controlling & Innovation 2019: Digitalisierung* (S. 23–38). Springer Gabler.

Bley, S. & George, A. C. (2017). Kognitive Diagnosemodelle zur Begleitung individualisierter Lehr- und Lernprozesse: Neue Möglichkeiten aus einem alternativen Ansatz? *Zeitschrift für Berufs- und Wirtschaftspädagogik, 113*(1), 56–85.

Blix, L. H., Edmonds, M. A. & Sorensen, K. B. (2021). How well do audit textbooks currently integrate data analytics? *Journal of Accounting Education, 55*, 100717. https://doi.org/10.1016/j.jaccedu.2021.100717

Bloemen, A. (2011). *Lernaufgaben in Schulbüchern der Wirtschaftslehre: Analyse, Konstruktion und Evaluation von Lernaufgaben für die Lernfelder industrieller Geschäftsprozesse. Schriften zur Berufs- und Wirtschaftspädagogik: Band 7*. Rainer Hampp.

Blömeke, S., Risse, J., Müller, C., Eichler, D. & Schulz, W. (2006). Analyse der Qualität von Aufgaben aus didaktischer und fachlicher Sicht: Ein allgemeines Modell und seine exemplarische Umsetzung im Unterrichtsfach Mathematik. *Unterrichtswissenschaft, 34*(4), 330–357.

Blum, W. (1978). Einkommensteuern als Thema des Analysisunterrichts in der beruflichen Oberstufe. *Die berufsbildende Schule, 30*(11), 642–651.

Blum, W. (1985). Anwendungsorientierter Mathematikunterricht in der didaktischen Diskussion. *Mathematische Semesterberichte, 32*, 195–232.

Blum, W. (2011). Can Modelling Be Taught and Learnt? Some Answers from Empirical Research. In G. Kaiser, W. Blum, R. Borromeo Ferri & G. Stillman (Hrsg.), *Trends in Teaching and Learning of Mathematical Modelling* (S. 15–30). Springer Netherlands.

BMBF. (2014). *Lehrplan Handelsakademie: BGBl. II Nr. 209/2014*. https://www.hak.cc/unterricht/lehrplaene/handelsakademie-lehrplan-2014

BMBF. (2015). *Lehrplan Höhere Lehranstalt für wirtschaftliche Berufe: BGBl.II Nr.340/2015*. https://www.ris.bka.gv.at/eli/bgbl/II/2015/340

BMBWF. (2018). *Leitfaden zur Umsetzung der teilzentralen, standardisierten Reife- und Diplomprüfung (sRDP)*. https://www.hak.cc/pruefungen_abschluss/rdp.

BMBWF. (2021). *Schulbücher im Schuljahr 2021/22: 4600. Höhere kaufmännische Lehranstalten*. https://www.schulbuchaktion.at/sba_downloads/sba2021/Schulbuchliste_4600_2021_2022.pdf.

Böhm, U. (2013). *Modellierungskompetenzen langfristig und kumulativ fördern*. Springer Spektrum.

Bortz, J. & Schuster, C. (2010). *Statistik für Human- und Sozialwissenschaftler* (7., vollständig überarbeitete und erweiterte Auflage). Springer.

Bouley, F. (2016). Bilanzmethode und Wirtschaftsinstrumentelles Rechnungswesen aus Expertensicht. *Wirtschaft und Erziehung*, *68*(5), 167–174.

Bouley, F. (2017). *Kompetenzerwerb im Rechnungswesen-Unterricht. Eine Untersuchung in einer bilanzmethodischen und wirtschaftsinstrumentellen Lehr-Lern-Umgebung*. Springer.

Bouley, F., Berger, S., Fritsch, S., Wuttke, E., Seifried, J., Schnick-Vollmer, K. & Schmitz, B. (2015). Der Einfluss von universitären und außeruniversitären Lerngelegenheiten auf das Fachwissen und fachdidaktische Wissen von angehenden Lehrkräften an kaufmännisch-berufsbildenden Schulen. In S. Blömeke & O. Zlatkin-Troitschanskaia (Hrsg.), *Kompetenzen von Studierenden* (S. 100–115). Beltz Juventa.

Brand, S. (2020). Erfassung unterschiedlicher Dimensionen von Modellierungskompetenzen im Rahmen eines vergleichenden Interventionsprojekts. In G. Greefrath & K. Maaß (Hrsg.), *Realitätsbezüge im Mathematikunterricht. Modellierungskompetenzen – Diagnose und Bewertung* (S. 45–64). Springer Spektrum.

Brosius, H.-B., Haas, A. & Unkel, J. (2022). *Methoden der empirischen Kommunikationsforschung: Eine Einführung* (8. Aufl.). *Studienbücher zur Kommunikations- und Medienwissenschaft*. VS Verlag für Sozialwissenschaften.

Brötz, R., Kock, A., Annen, S. & Schaal, T. (2015). Gemeinsamkeiten und Unterschiede der kaufmännischen Ausbildungsberufe. In R. Brötz & F. Kaiser (Hrsg.), *Kaufmännische Berufe: Charakteristik, Vielfalt und Perspektiven* (S. 91–106). Bertelsmann.

Bruhn, J. (1986). *Statistische Verfahren: Datenanalyse mit BASIC-Programmen. Technisch-naturwissenschaftliche Anwendungen*. Vieweg.

Buchholz, L. & Gerhards, R. (2016). *Internes Rechnungswesen: Kosten- und Leistungsrechnung, Betriebsstatistik und Planungsrechnung*. Springer Gabler.

Büchter, A. & Leuders, T. (2006). Ein Aufgabenmodell für die Praxis. *Praxis der Naturwissenschaften – Chemie in der Schule*, *55*(8), 16–20.

Burkhardt, F., Hinsch, H., Kostede, W. & Wesseloh, H. (2014). Neues Rechnungswesen: süßes Nervengift oder ernst zu nehmender didaktischer Ansatz für den Rechnungswesenunterricht – eine Antwort auf Axel Stommel. *Wirtschaft und Erziehung*, *66*(6), 233–235.

Butze, F. (1936). *Der Wert der Buchhaltung als Bildungsgut der wirtschaftsberuflichen Schulung*. Handelshochschule, Leipzig.

Butze, F. & Butze, A. (1932). *Leichtfaßliche Einführung in die Buchhaltung mit methodisch aufgebauten Übungsgängen. 1. Teil: Einführung in die Buchhaltung mit vielen Beispielen, Aufgaben und bildlichen Darstellungen*. Dr. Max Gehlen.

Celeux, G. & Soromenho, G. (1996). An entropy criterion for assessing the number of clusters in a mixture model. *Journal of Classification, 13*(2), 195–212. https://doi.org/10.1007/BF01246098

Cohen, J. (1968). Weighted Kappa: Nominal Scale Agreement with Provision for Scaled Disagreement or Partial Credit. *Psychological Bulletin, 70*(4), 213–220.

Cohen, J. (1988). *Statistical power analysis for the behavioral sciences*. Psychology Press.

Dann, H.-D. (2000). Lehrerkognitionen und Handlungsentscheidungen. In M. K. Schweer (Hrsg.), *Lehrer-Schüler-Interaktion: Pädagogisch-psychologische Aspekte des Lehrens und Lernens in der Schule* (S. 79–108). VS Verlag für Sozialwissenschaften.

Dauenhauer, E. (1977). *Der Anfangsunterricht im Rahmen der beruflichen Grundbildung*. Merkur Lehrmittel.

Davidson, R. A. (2005). Analysis of the complexity of writing used in accounting textbooks over the past 100 years. *Accounting Education: an international journal, 14*(1), 53–74. https://doi.org/10.1080/0963928041000169524l

Davidson, R. A. & Baldwin, B. A. (2005). Cognitive skills objectives in intermediate accounting textbooks: Evidence from end-of-chapter material. *Journal of Accounting Education, 23*(2), 79–95. https://doi.org/10.1016/j.jaccedu.2005.05.001

Dengler, K. & Matthes, B. (2015). *Folgen der Digitalisierung für die Arbeitswelt: Substituierbarkeitspotenziale von Berufen in Deutschland*. IAB-Forschungsbericht.

Dengler, K. & Matthes, B. (2018). Wenige Berufe halten mit der Digitalisierung Schritt. *IAB Kurzbericht*(4), 1–11.

Dengler, K. & Matthes, B. (2021). *Folgen des technologischen Wandels für den Arbeitsmarkt: Auch komplexere Tätigkeiten könnten zunehmend automatisiert werden*. IAB-Kurzbericht.

Denk, C., Fritz-Schmied, G., Mitter, C., Wohlschlager, T. & Wolfsgruber, H. (2016). *Externe Unternehmensrechnung: Handbuch für Studium und Bilanzierungspraxis* (5. Auflage). Linde.

Deppe, M. (2017). *Fehler als Stationen im Lernprozess: Eine kognitionswissenschaftliche Untersuchung am Beispiel Rechnungswesen*. Bertelsmann Verlag.

Diehm, J. & Benzinger, L. (2018). Digital Finance: Digitale Rechnungsverarbeitung und Workflows als Basis für ein Rechnungswesen 4.0. *Der Betrieb, 71*(15), 841–847.

Dolzsanksi, C. (2013a). Fachwissenschaft und Fachdidaktik als konzeptionelle Bausteine zur Weiterentwicklung der Fachdidaktik Rechnungswesen: Teil 2. *Erziehungswissenschaft und Beruf, 61*(3), 347–375.

Dolzsanksi, C. (2013b). Fachwissenschaft und Fachdidaktik als konzeptionelle Bausteine zur Weiterentwicklung der Fachdidaktik Rechnungswesen. *Erziehungswissenschaft und Beruf, 61*(2), 231–240.

Dolzsanksi, C. (2014). Wie kann die Diskussion über die Weiterentwicklungen der Didaktik des Rechnungswesens vorangebracht werden? *Erziehungswissenschaft und Beruf, 62*(2), 213–228.

Döring, N. & Bortz, J. (2016). *Forschungsmethoden und Evaluation in den Sozial- und Humanwissenschaften*. Springer Berlin Heidelberg. https://doi.org/10.1007/978-3-642-41089-5

Drüke-Noe, C. & Merk, S. (2013). Fachdidaktische Analyse von Aufgaben in Mathematik. In T. Bohl, M. Kleinknecht, U. Maier & K. Metz (Hrsg.), *Lern- und Leistungsaufgaben im Unterricht: Fächerübergreifende Kriterien zur Auswahl und Analyse* (S. 75–100). Julius Klinkhardt.

Dubs, R. (1996). Historische und systematische Entwicklungslinien einer Didaktik des Rechnungswesens in der Schweiz. In P. Preiß & T. Tramm (Hrsg.), *Rechnungswesenunterricht und ökonomisches Denken: Didaktische Innovationen für die kaufmännische Ausbildung* (S. 118–138). Gabler.

Eberle, F., Schumann, S., Kaufmann, E., Jüttler, A. & Ackermann, N. (2016). Modellierung und Messung wirtschaftsbürgerlicher Kompetenz von kaufmännischen Auszubildenden in der Schweiz und in Deutschland (CoBALIT). In K. Beck, M. Landenberger & F. Oser (Hrsg.), *Technologiebasierte Kompetenzmessung in der beruflichen Bildung: Ergebnisse aus der BMBF-Förderinitiative ASCOT* (S. 93–117). wbv.

Eigenmann, R., Siegfried, C., Kögler, K. & Egloffstein, M. (2015). Aufgaben angehender Industriekaufleute im Controlling: Ansätze zur Modellierung des Gegenstandsbereichs. *Zeitschrift für Berufs- und Wirtschaftspädagogik, 111*(3), 417–436.

Eloundou, T., Manning, S., Mishkin, P. & Rock, D. (2023). GPTs are GPTs: An Early Look at the Labor Market Impact Potential of Large Language Models. *Working Paper*. http://arxiv.org/pdf/2303.10130v4

Ernst, F. (2011). Lesbarkeit von Rechnungswesenbüchern an kaufmännischen Berufsschulen. *Zeitschrift für Berufs- und Wirtschaftspädagogik, 107*(3), 408–423.

Ernst, F. (2012a). *Fachdidaktische Analyse von Lehrbüchern für den Rechnungswesenunterricht in Deutschland und den USA.*

Ernst, F. (2012b). Illustrationen in Rechnungswesenbüchern. *Zeitschrift für Berufs- und Wirtschaftspädagogik, 108*(1), 63–81.

Ernst, F. (2012c). Vergleich von deutschen und US-amerikanischen Rechnungswesenbüchern. Teil 1: Anordnung der Buchführungsinhalte; Teil 2: Auswahl der Buchführungsinhalte. *Wirtschaft und Erziehung, 64*(1–3), 23 – 27;60 – 65.

Ernst, F. (2014). Bilanzmethode oder Wirtschaftsinstrumentelles Rechnungswesen. Welche Methode ist die Beste? *Wirtschaft und Erziehung, 66*(1), 16–18.

Feng, G. (2013). Factors affecting intercoder reliability: a Monte Carlo experiment. *Quality and Quantity, 47*(5), 2959–2982. https://doi.org/10.1007/s11135-012-9745-9

Feng, G. & Zhao, X. (2016). Do Not Force Agreement. *Methodology, 12*(4), 145–148. https://doi.org/10.1027/1614-2241/a000120

Field, A. (2017). *Discovering statistics using IBM SPSS statistics* (5th edition). SAGE Publications.

Findeisen, S. (2017). *Fachdidaktische Kompetenzen angehender Lehrpersonen. Eine Untersuchung zum Erklären im Rechnungswesen.* Springer.

Fischer, A. & Gerdsmeier, G. (2007). Lernaufgaben nachhaltig gedacht. Wie sind Lernaufgaben für eine zukunftsorientierte wirtschaftsberufliche Bildung zu konzipieren? In A. Fischer & K. Hahne (Hrsg.), *Strategien und Umsetzungspotentiale einer Berufsbildung für nachhaltige Entwicklung* (S. 184–191). Bertelsmann.

Fischer, H. E. & Draxler, D. (2006). Konstruktion und Bewertung von Physikaufgaben. In E. Kircher, R. Girwidz & P. Häussler (Hrsg.), *Physikdidaktik. Theorie und Praxis* (S. 639–655). Springer.

Flechsig, K. H. (2008). Komplexe Lernaufgaben in der beruflichen Aus- und Weiterbildung. In J. Thonhauser (Hrsg.), *Aufgaben als Katalysator von Lernprozessen* (S. 241–256). Waxmann.

Fortmüller, R. (2012). Eine österreichweite Vergleichsstudie zu den Rechnungswesenkenntnissen der Schüler/innen von COOL- und herkömmlichen Klassen. *wissenplus*(5), 15–18.

Fortmüller, R. & Grabowski, J. (2013). Die Rolle des Fachwissens. Eine empirische Studie zum Zusammenhang zwischen dem Fachwissen aus Rechnungswesen und den fachdidaktischen Fähigkeiten von Studienanfänger/-anfängerinnen des Masterstudiums Wirtschaftspädagogik. *wissenplus*(2), 1–8.

Fritsch, S. & Kopf, C. (2014). Identifizierung und Einschätzung des kognitiven Potenzials von Lernaufgaben: Skizze zweier Forschungsprojekte aus dem Fach Wirtschaftspädagogik. In S. Prediger, B. Ralle, M. Rothgangel & M. Hammann (Hrsg.), *Lernaufgaben entwickeln, bearbeiten und überprüfen: Ergebnisse und Perspektiven fachdidaktischer Forschung* (S. 233–235). Waxmann.

Fuchs, E., Niehaus, I. & Stoletzki, A. (2014). *Das Schulbuch in der Forschung: Analysen und Empfehlungen für die Bildungspraxis*. V&R Unipress.

Geiser, C. (2010). *Datenanalyse mit Mplus: Eine anwendungsorientierte Einführung. Springer eBook Collection Humanities, Social Science*. VS Verlag für Sozialwissenschaften.

Geiser, C. (2013). *Data analysis with Mplus*. Guilford Press.

Geissler, G. (2021). Schulbuchaufgaben und Schulbuchwahl: Evaluation und Diskussion. In B. Greimel-Fuhrmann (Hrsg.), *Das Lernen in der Wirtschaftspädagogik: Festschrift für Richard Fortmüller* (S. 67–80). Facultas.

Gerdsmeier, G. (2004). Lernaufgaben für ein selbstgesteuertes Lernen im Wirtschaftsunterricht. *Journal of Social Science Education, 3*(2), 21–63.

Goldbach, A. (2010). Vorteilhafte Buchungsregel des instrumentellen Ansatzes einer Rechnungswesendidaktik – auch für die kommunale Doppik. *Wirtschaft und Erziehung, 62*(10), 325–328.

Goldbach, A. (2012). Abschließende Stellungnahme zu den Plinke-Beiträgen in WuE 6/2010 und WuE 1–2/2011 sowie 4/2011. *Wirtschaft und Erziehung, 64*(1–2), 28–31.

Gollwitzer, M. (2012). Latent-Class-Analysis. In H. Moosbrugger & A. Kelava (Hrsg.), *Springer-Lehrbuch. Testtheorie und Fragebogenkonstruktion* (2. Aufl., S. 296–323). Springer.

Gössling, B., Hagemeier, D. & Sloane, P. F. E. (2019). Berufsbildung 4.0 als didaktische Herausforderung. *Zeitschrift für Berufs- und Wirtschaftspädagogik, 115*(4), 546–566.

Götzl, M. & Jahn, R. W. (2014). Unterrichtsmuster sichtbar machen – Zur Variabilität von Unterrichtsrhythmen und Sozialformen im kaufmännischen Unterricht. *Zeitschrift für Berufs- und Wirtschaftspädagogik, 110*(1), 57–78.

Götzl, M., Jahn, R. W. & Held, G. (2013). Bleibt alles anders!? Sozialformen, Unterrichtsphasen und echte Lernzeit im kaufmännischen Unterricht. *bwp@ Berufs- und Wirtschaftspädagogik online, Ausgabe 24*, 1–22.

Greefrath, G., Kaiser, G., Blum, W. & Ferri, R. B. (2013). Mathematisches Modellieren – Eine Einführung in theoretische und didaktische Hintergründe. In R. B. Ferri, G. Greefrath & G. Kaiser (Hrsg.), *Mathematisches Modellieren für Schule und Hochschule: Theoretische und didaktische Hintergründe* (S. 11–38). Springer.

Greefrath, G. & Maaß, K. (2020). Diagnose und Bewertung beim mathematischen Modellieren. In G. Greefrath & K. Maaß (Hrsg.), *Realitätsbezüge im Mathematikunterricht. Modellierungskompetenzen – Diagnose und Bewertung* (S. 1–20). Springer Spektrum.

Greimel-Fuhrmann, B. (2008). Interesse und Lernmotivation für Rechnungswesen – Untersuchung ihrer Struktur, Entwicklung und Förderung im kaufmännischen Unterricht. *ibw Mitteilungen*, 1–21.

Greimel-Fuhrmann, B. (2011). Kausalattribuierungen von Prüfungsleistungen im Fach Rechnungswesen. *Zeitschrift für Berufs- und Wirtschaftspädagogik, 107*(2), 239–255.

Groeben, N. & Scheele, B. (2010). Das Forschungsprogramm Subjektive Theorien. In G. Mey & K. Mruck (Hrsg.), *Handbuch qualitative Forschung in der Psychologie* (S. 151–165). VS Verlag für Sozialwissenschaften.

Gross, H. F. (1990). Die neue (pagatorische) Didaktik des Rechnungswesens. In F. Achtenhagen (Hrsg.), *Didaktik des Rechnungswesens: Programm und Kritik eines wirtschaftsinstrumentellen Ansatzes* (S. 195–218). Gabler.

Guggemos, J. (2016). *Modellierung und Messung von Kompetenz im externen Rechnungswesen*. Dr. Hut.

Guggemos, J. & Schönlein, M. (2015). Modellierung von Kompetenzen in der beruflichen Bildung: Entwicklung und Validierung eines Kompetenzniveaumodells für das externe Rechnungswesen. *Zeitschrift für Berufs- und Wirtschaftspädagogik, 111*(4), 524–551.

Hankeln, C. (2019). *Mathematisches Modellieren mit dynamischer Geometrie-Software: Ergebnisse einer Interventionsstudie*. Springer Spektrum.

Hankeln, C. & Beckschulte, C. (2020). Teilkompetenzen des Modellierens und ihre Erfassung – Darstellung einer Testentwicklung. In G. Greefrath & K. Maaß (Hrsg.), *Realitätsbezüge im Mathematikunterricht. Modellierungskompetenzen – Diagnose und Bewertung* (S. 65–86). Springer Spektrum.

Hartmann, F. G., Kopp, J. & Lois, D. (2022). *Sozialwissenschaftliche Datenanalyse: Eine Einführung* (3. Auflage). Springer VS.

Helm, C. (2015). Determinants of competence development in accounting in upper secondary education. *Empirical Research in Vocational Education and Training, 7*(10), 1–36.

Helm, C. (2016a). Berufsbildungsstandards und Kompetenzmodellierung im Fach Rechnungswesen. In A. Dietzen, R. Nickolaus, B. Rammstedt & R. Weiß (Hrsg.), *Kompetenzorientierung: Berufliche Kompetenzen entwickeln, messen und anerkennen* (S. 149–168). Bertelsmann.

Helm, C. (2016b). Empirische Unterrichtsforschung im Fach Rechnungswesen – ein Überblick zum Publikationsstand. *bwp@ Spezial 11 Unterrichtsforschung im Fach Rechnungswesen*, 1–21.

Helm, C. (2016c). *Lernen in Offenen und Traditionellen UnterrichtsSettings (LOTUS): Empirische Analysen zur Kompetenzentwicklung im Fach Rechnungswesen sowie zum kooperativen, offenen Lernen*. Waxmann.

Helm, C. (2016d). Welche Denkschritte durchlaufen Schüler/innen beim Erstellen von Buchungssätzen? *wissenplus, 16/17*(1), 38–41.

Helm, C. (2016e). Zentrale Qualitätsdimensionen von Unterricht und ihre Effekte auf Schüleroutcomes im Fach Rechnungswesen. *Zeitschrift für Bildungsforschung, 6*(2), 101–119.

Helm, C. (2019). Lehrermotivation, Autonomieerleben und die Entwicklung der intrinsischen Motivation der Schülerinnen und Schüler im kaufmännischen Unterricht. In N. McElvany, W. Bos & H. G. Holtappels (Hrsg.), *Bedingungen und Effekte von Lehrerbildung, Lehrkraftkompetenzen und Lehrkrafthandeln* (S. 151–162). Waxmann.

Helm, C. & Mayer, S. A. (2016). Pedagogical Content Knowledge von Rechnungswesenlehrkräften – Explorative Befunde einer Onlinebefragung aus Österreich. In J. Seifried, S. Seeber & B. Ziegler (Hrsg.), *Jahrbuch der wirtschaftspädagogischen Forschung 2016* (S. 171–188). Verlag Barbara Budrich.

Helm, C. & Stütz, S. (2020). Die Rolle individueller Schülermerkmale für das Lernen im Rechnungswesen – Ein psychologischer Blick auf die „Natur" des Rechnungswesenunterrichts. In F. Berding, H. Jahncke & A. Slopinski (Hrsg.), *Moderner Rechnungswesenunterricht 2020: Status quo und Entwicklungen aus wissenschaftlicher und praktischer Perspektive* (S. 35–58). Springer.

Helm, C., Warwas, J. & Schirmer, H. (2022). Cognitive diagnosis models of students' skill profiles as a basis for adaptive teaching: an example from introductory accounting classes. *Empirical Research in Vocational Education and Training, 14*(1). https://doi.org/10.1186/s40461-022-00137-3

Helm, C. & Wimmer, B. (2012). Wie lässt sich der Lernerfolg von Schülerinnen/Schülern im Fach Rechnungswesen messen? *wissenplus*(5), 24–29.

Hmyzo, E. & Muzzu, A. (2020). Technologie im Rechnungswesen – Wenn die Maschine besser und schneller bucht. In F. Berding, H. Jahncke & A. Slopinski (Hrsg.), *Moderner Rechnungswesenunterricht 2020: Status quo und Entwicklungen aus wissenschaftlicher und praktischer Perspektive* (S. 99–116). Springer.

Holtsch, D. (2018). Zur professionellen Kompetenz von Lehrpersonen. In D. Holtsch & F. Eberle (Hrsg.), *Untersuchungen zu Lehr-Lernprozessen im kaufmännischen Bereich: Ergebnisse aus dem Leading House LINCA und Schlussfolgerungen für die Praxis* (S. 129–160). Waxmann.

Holtsch, D. & Eberle, F. (Hrsg.). (2018). *Untersuchungen zu Lehr-Lernprozessen im kaufmännischen Bereich: Ergebnisse aus dem Leading House LINCA und Schlussfolgerungen für die Praxis*. Waxmann.

Holtsch, D. & Sticca, F. (2018). Zusammenhänge zwischen der professionellen Kompetenz der Lehrpersonen und subjektiver Unterrichtswahrnehmung von kaufmännischen Lernenden. In D. Holtsch & F. Eberle (Hrsg.), *Untersuchungen zu Lehr-Lernprozessen im kaufmännischen Bereich: Ergebnisse aus dem Leading House LINCA und Schlussfolgerungen für die Praxis* (S. 171–178). Waxmann.

Hove, D., Jorgensen, T. D. & van der Ark, L. A. (2018). On the Usefulness of Interrater Reliability Coefficients. In M. Wiberg, S. Culpepper, R. Janssen, J. González & D. Molenaar (Hrsg.), *Springer Proceedings in Mathematics & Statistics. Quantitative Psychology* (Bd. 233, S. 67–75). Springer International Publishing. https://doi.org/10.1007/978-3-319-77249-3_6

Imhof, U. (1993). Auswahl und Einsatz von Schulbüchern im Arbeits- und Wirtschaftslehreunterricht. *arbeiten+lernen/Wirtschaft, 3*(3), 22–25.

Jahn, R. W. (2020). Noch mal anders?! Analyse unterrichtlicher Sichtstrukturen im Rechnungswesenunterricht. In F. Berding, H. Jahncke & A. Slopinski (Hrsg.), *Moderner Rechnungswesenunterricht 2020: Status quo und Entwicklungen aus wissenschaftlicher und praktischer Perspektive* (S. 11–34). Springer.

Janovec, D. (2014). *Der kognitive Anregungsgehalt österreichischer BWL-Schulbücher: eine Teilanalyse am Beispiel des Kapitel „Marketing"*. Johannes Kepler Universität, Linz.

Joost, D., Kripke, G. & Tramm, T. (2007). *Wirtschaftsinstrumentelles Rechnungswesen* (3. Auflage). Bildungsverlag EINS.

Jordan, A., Krauss, S., Löwen, K., Blum, W., Neubrand, M., Brunner, M., Kunter, M. & Baumert, J. (2008). Aufgaben im COACTIV-Projekt: Zeugnisse des kognitiven Aktivierungspotentials im deutschen Mathematikunterricht. *Journal für Mathematik-Didaktik, 29*(2), 83–107. https://doi.org/10.1007/BF03339055

Jordan, A., Ross, N., Krauss, S., Baumert, J., Blum, W., Neubrand, M., Löwen, K., Brunner, M. & Kunter, M. (2006). *Klassifikationsschema für Mathematikaufgaben: Dokumentation der Aufgabenkategorisierung im COACTIV-Projekt. Materialien aus der Bildungsforschung: Nr. 81*. Max-Planck-Inst. für Bildungsforschung.

Jordanski, G. (2020). Kaufmännische Steuerung und Kontrolle im 4.0 Arbeitsumfeld – Anforderungen an duale Ausbildungsberufe. In F. Berding, H. Jahncke & A. Slopinski (Hrsg.), *Moderner Rechnungswesenunterricht 2020: Status quo und Entwicklungen aus wissenschaftlicher und praktischer Perspektive* (S. 59–82). Springer.

Jungwirth, N. (2015). Modellieren im Kostenrechnungsunterricht: Funktionsweise von prozessbezogenen Kompetenzen der Angewandten Mathematik im Kostenrechnungsunterricht am Beispiel der Break-Even-Point-Analyse. *wissenplus*(1), 34–37.

Kaiser, G. (1995). Realitätsbezüge im Mathematikunterricht – Ein Überblick über die aktuelle und historische Diskussion. In G. Graumann, T. Jahnke, G. Kaiser & J. Meyer (Hrsg.), *Materialien für einen realitätsbezogenen Mathematikunterricht: Band 2* (S. 66–84). Franzbecker.

Kaiser, G., Blum, W., Borromeo Ferri, R. & Greefrath, G. (2015). Anwendungen und Modellieren. In R. Bruder, L. Hefendehl-Hebeker, B. Schmidt-Thieme & H.-G. Weigand (Hrsg.), *Handbuch der Mathematikdidaktik* (357–285). Springer Spektrum.

Kauermann, G. & Küchenhoff, H. (2011). *Stichproben: Methoden und praktische Umsetzung mit R*. Springer.

Kefer, I. (2013). Die Lesbarkeit von Schulbüchern für den Betriebswirtschaftslehreunterricht: Befunde und forschungsmethodische Grundprobleme. *Zeitschrift für Berufs- und Wirtschaftspädagogik, 109*(1), 94–107.

Klafki, W. (1963). *Studien zur Bildungstheorie und Didaktik*. Beltz.

Klein, J. & Küst, C. (2020). Wie die Digitalisierung im Rechnungswesen die Aufgaben und Anforderungen an die Mitarbeiter/-innen verändert. In F. Berding, H. Jahncke & A. Slopinski (Hrsg.), *Moderner Rechnungswesenunterricht 2020: Status quo und Entwicklungen aus wissenschaftlicher und praktischer Perspektive* (S. 83–98). Springer.

Kleinknecht, M., Bohl, T., Maier, U. & Metz, K. (Hrsg.). (2013). *Lern- und Leistungsaufgaben im Unterricht: Fächerübergreifende Kriterien zur Auswahl und Analyse*. Julius Klinkhardt.

Kleinknecht, M., Maier, U., Metz, K. & Bohl, T. (2011). Analyse des kognitiven Aufgabenpotenzials: Entwicklung und Erprobung eines allgemeindidaktischen Auswertungsmanuals. *Unterrichtswissenschaft, 39*, 328–344.

Kleinknecht, M. & Schmid-Kühn, S. M. (2020). Lern- und Leistungsaufgaben in der Schule: Eine Bilanz nach zwei Jahrzehnten Forschung und Entwicklung. In U. Greiner, F. Hofmann, C. Schreiner & C. Wiesner (Hrsg.), *Bildungsstandards: Kompetenzorientierung, Aufgabenkultur und Qualitätsentwicklung im Schulsystem* (S. 410–421). Waxmann.

Klotz, V. & Winther, E. (2012). Kompetenzmessung in der kaufmännischen Berufsausbildung. Zwischen Prozessorientierung und Fachbezug: Eine Analyse der aktuellen Prüfungspraxis. *bwp@ Berufs-und Wirtschaftspädagogik online*(22), 1–16.

Kögler, K. (2015). *Langeweile in kaufmännischen Unterrichtsprozessen: Entstehung und Wirkung emotionalen Erlebens ungenutzter Zeitpotentiale*. Peter Lang.

Kögler, K. & Wuttke, E. (2012). Unterrichtliche Monotonie als Bedingungsfaktor für Schülerlangeweile im Fach Rechnungswesen. In U. Faßhauser & B. Fürstenau (Hrsg.),

Berufs- und wirtschaftspädagogische Analysen – aktuelle Forschungen zur beruflichen Bildung (S. 75–87). Verlag Barbara Budrich.

Kombacher, D. M. (2016). *ERP-Integration in Schulbüchern für den kaufmännischen Unterricht an berufsbildenden Schulen: Analyse und Design von Lernaufgaben für den Einsatz kaufmännischer Standardsoftware – gezeigt am Beispiel der Handelsakademie*. Peter Lang Edition.

Krippendorff, K. (2004). *Content analysis: An introduction to its methodology*. SAGE.

Kuckartz, U. (2010). Typenbildung. In G. Mey & K. Mruck (Hrsg.), *Handbuch qualitative Forschung in der Psychologie* (S. 553–568). VS Verlag für Sozialwissenschaften.

Kuckartz, U. (2018). *Qualitative Inhaltsanalyse: Methoden, Praxis, Computerunterstützung*. Beltz Juventa.

Kuckartz, U. & Rädiker, S. (2022). *Qualitative Inhaltsanalyse: Methoden, Praxis, Computerunterstützung* (5. Aufl.). *Grundlagentexte Methoden*. Beltz Juventa.

Kuckartz, U., Rädiker, S., Ebert, T. & Schehl, J. (2013). *Statistik: Eine verständliche Einführung* (2., überarbeitete Auflage). Springer VS.

Lamnek, S. & Krell, C. (2016). *Qualitative Sozialforschung: Mit Online-Materialien* (6., überarbeitete Auflage). Beltz.

Langmann, C. (2020). Robotic Process Automation als Wegbereiter eines modernen Rechnungswesens. *Rethinking Finance*(3), 4–8.

Lehmann, R. & Seeber, S. (2007). *Untersuchungen von Leistungen, Motivation und Einstellungen der Schülerinnen und Schüler in den Abschlussklassen der Berufsschlussklassen der Berufsschulen (ULME III)*. Behörde für Bildung und Sport.

Leuders, T. (2014). Aufgaben in Forschung und Praxis: Aufgabenklassifikationen und Aufgabenforschung aus fachdidaktischer Perspektive. In S. Prediger, B. Ralle, M. Rothgangel & M. Hammann (Hrsg.), *Lernaufgaben entwickeln, bearbeiten und überprüfen: Ergebnisse und Perspektiven fachdidaktischer Forschung* (S. 33–50). Waxmann.

Leutner, D., Fischer, H., Kauertz, A., Schabram, N. & Fleischer, J. (2008). Instruktionspsychologische und fachdidaktische Aspekte der Qualität von Lernaufgaben und Testaufgaben im Physikunterricht. In J. Thonhauser (Hrsg.), *Aufgaben als Katalysator von Lernprozessen* (S. 169–182). Waxmann.

Lortie, D. C. (2007). *Schoolteacher: A sociological study*. University of Chicago Press.

Luthinger, H., Wilhelm, M. & Wespi, C. (2014). Entwicklung von kompetenzorientierten Aufgabensets. *Journal für Lehrerinnen- und Lehrerbildung, 13*(3), 56–66.

Maaß, K. (2005). Modellieren im Mathematikunterricht der Sekundarstufe I. *Journal für Mathematik-Didaktik, 26*(2), 114–142.

Maaß, K. (2010). Classification Scheme for Modelling Tasks. *Journal for Mathematik-Didaktik, 31*(2), 285–311. https://doi.org/10.1007/s13138-010-0010-2

Maier, U., Bohl, T., Kleinknecht, M. & Metz, K. (2013). Allgemeindidaktische Kriterien für die Analyse von Aufgaben. In M. Kleinknecht, T. Bohl, U. Maier & K. Metz (Hrsg.), *Lern- und Leistungsaufgaben im Unterricht: Fächerübergreifende Kriterien zur Auswahl und Analyse* (S. 9–46). Julius Klinkhardt.

Maier, U., Kleinknecht, M., Metz, K. & Bohl, T. (2010). Ein allgemeindidaktisches Kategoriensystem zur Analyse des kognitiven Potenzials von Aufgaben. *Beiträge zur Lehrerinnen- und Lehrerbildung, 28*(1), 84–96.

Mathes, C. (2006). *Wirtschaft unterrichten: Methodik und Didaktik der Wirtschaftslehre* (4. aktualisierte Auflage). Verlag Europa-Lehrmittel.

Mathes, C. (2008). Ist die Bilanzmethode am Ende? *Wirtschaft und Erziehung*(4), 115–116.

Mayring, P. (2015). *Qualitative Inhaltsanalyse: Grundlagen und Techniken* (12., überarb. Aufl.). Beltz.

McCutcheon, A. L. (1987). *Latent class analysis. Quantitative Applications in the Social Sciences: Bd. 64*. SAGE Publications.

McCutcheon, A. L. (2002). Basic Concepts and Procedures in Single- and Multiple-Group Latent Class Analysis. In J. A. Hagenaars & A. L. McCutcheon (Hrsg.), *Applied latent class analysis* (S. 56–88).

McKinney, E., Yoos, C. J. & Snead, K. (2017). The need for 'skeptical' accountants in the era of Big Data. *Journal of Accounting Education, 38*, 63–80. https://doi.org/10.1016/j.jaccedu.2016.12.007

Mindnich, A., Berger, S. & Fritsch, S. (2013). Modellierung des fachlichen und fachdidaktischen Wissens von Lehrkräften im Rechnungswesen – Überlegungen zur Konstruktion eines Testinstruments. In U. Faßhauer, B. Fürstenau & E. Wuttke (Hrsg.), *Jahrbuch der berufs- und wirtschaftspädagogischen Forschung 2013* (S. 61–72). Verlag Barbara Budrich.

Minnameier, G. & Link, M. (2010). Jenseits des wirtschaftsinstrumentellen Rechnungswesens. Ein kognitiv-struktureller und inferentieller Ansatz. In J. Seifried (Hrsg.), *Lehr-Lern-Forschung in der kaufmännischen Berufsbildung: Ergebnisse und Gestaltungsaufgaben* (S. 107–121). Steiner Verlag.

Moosbrugger, H. & Kelava, A. (2012). Qualitätsanforderungen an einen psychologischen Test (Testgütekriterien). In H. Moosbrugger & A. Kelava (Hrsg.), *Springer-Lehrbuch. Testtheorie und Fragebogenkonstruktion* (2. Aufl., S. 8–25). Springer.

Mullis, I. V. S., Martin, M. O., Foy, P. & Arora, A. (2012). *Timss 2011 international results in mathematics*. TIMSS & PIRLS International Study Center.

Muthén, L. K. & Muthén, B. O. (2017). *Mplus User's Guide* (Eighth Edition). Muthén & Muthén.

Najderek, A. (2020). Auswirkungen der Digitalisierung im Rechnungswesen – ein Überblick. In A. Müller, M. Graumann & H.-J. Weiß (Hrsg.), *Innovationen für eine digitale Wirtschaft: Wie Unternehmen den Wandel meistern* (S. 127–145). Springer Gabler.

Nespor, J. (1987). The role of beliefs in the practice of teaching. *Journal of Curriculum Studies, 19*(4), 317–328.

Neubrand, J. (2002). *Eine Klassifikation mathematischer Aufgaben zur Analyse von Unterrichtssituationen: Selbsttätiges Arbeiten in Schülerarbeitsphasen in den Stunden der TIMSS-Video-Studie*. Franzbecker.

Neubrand, M., Jordan, A., Krauss, S., Blum, W. & Löwen, K. (2013). Task Analysis in COACTIV: Examining the Potential for Cognitive Activation in German Mathematics Classrooms. In M. Kunter, J. Baumert, W. Blum, U. Klusmann, S. Krauss & M. Neubrand (Hrsg.), *Mathematics Teacher Education: Bd. 8. Cognitive Activation in the Mathematics Classroom and Professional Competence of Teachers: Results from the COACTIV Project* (S. 125–146). Springer.

Neuendorf, K. A. (2017). *The content analysis guidebook*. SAGE Publications.

Neuweg, G. H. (2018). Was ist „betriebswirtschaftliche Kompetenz"? In J. Schlicht & U. Moschner (Hrsg.), *Berufliche Bildung an der Grenze zwischen Wirtschaft und Pädagogik: Reflexionen aus Theorie und Praxis* (S. 239–253). Springer.

Neuweg, G. H. (2019). *Kompetenzorientierte Leistungsbeurteilung: Pädagogische und rechtliche Hilfestellungen für die Schulpraxis*. Trauner Verlag.

Neuweg, G. H. (2020). Das Linzer Ebenen-Modell als Instrument zur Ausbildung des denkenden Buchhalters. In B. Greimel-Fuhrmann & R. Fortmüller (Hrsg.), *Wirtschaftsdidaktik – den Bildungshorizont durch Berufs- und Allgemeinbildung erweitern: Festschrift für Josef Aff* (S. 135–144). Facultas.

Neuweg, G. H. (2022). *Lehrerbildung: Zwölf Denkfiguren im Spannungsfeld von Wissen und Können*. Waxmann.

Neuweg, G. H. & Mayr, J. (2018). Die unterrichtsmethodische Grundeinstellung kaufmännischer Lehrpersonen im Spannungsfeld von Instruktivismus und Konstruktivismus. *bwp@ Spezial AT-1*, 1–14.

Neuweg, G. H. & Pfatschbacher, A. (2013). Was wir aus Schulzeugnissen über den Charakter der Übungsfirmenarbeit lernen können: Eine empirische Untersuchung zur Leistungsbeurteilung im Übungsfirmenunterricht an kaufmännischen Vollzeitschulen in Österreich. *wissenplus*(5–12/13), 21–25.

Nickolaus, R. (2008). Modellierungen zur beruflichen Fachkompetenz und ihre empirische Prüfung. *Zeitschrift für Berufs- und Wirtschaftspädagogik*, *104*(1), 1–6.

Nobiling, M., Seifried, J., Wuttke, E. & Kögler, K. (2020). Kognitive Prozesse von Lernenden beim Bearbeiten von Rechnungswesenaufgaben – eine Think-Aloud Studie. In F. Berding, H. Jahncke & A. Slopinski (Hrsg.), *Moderner Rechnungswesenunterricht 2020: Status quo und Entwicklungen aus wissenschaftlicher und praktischer Perspektive* (S. 117–134). Springer.

Oberle, M. & Tatje, C. (2017). Schulbuchnutzung im Politikunterricht – eine empirische Studie. In S. Manzel & C. Schelle (Hrsg.), *Empirische Forschung zur schulischen Politischen Bildung* (S. 113–126). Springer VS.

Ortlieb, C. P. (2004). Mathematische Modelle und Naturerkenntnis. *math.did.*, *27*(1), 23–40.

Pahl, J.-P. (1998). Berufsdidaktische Perspektiven der Lern- und Arbeitsaufgaben. In H. Holz, J. Koch, D. Schemme & E. Witzgall (Hrsg.), *Lern- und Arbeitsaufgabenkonzepte in Theorie und Praxis* (S. 13–30). Bertelsmann.

Pargmann, J., Berding, F., Riebenbauer, E. & Flick-Holtsch, D. (2022). Implikationen der Digitalisierung für die Didaktik des Rechnungswesens – konzeptionelle Überlegungen und Vorstellung eines Learning Cockpits. *bwp@ Berufs-und Wirtschaftspädagogik online*(43), 1–30.

Pargmann, J., Riebenbauer, E., Flick-Holtsch, D. & Berding, F. (2023). Digitalisation in accounting: a systematic literature review of activities and implications for competences. *Empirical Research in Vocational Education and Training*, *15*(1), 1. https://doi.org/10.1186/s40461-023-00141-1

Pawlik, W. (1979). Ansätze zu einer empirischen Analyse didaktischer Problemfelder im Fach Rechnungswesen. *Wirtschaft und Erziehung*, *31*(9), 249–254.

Pawlik, W. (1980). Fachdidaktik des Unterrichts in Rechnungswesen. Empirische Untersuchung zur schülerbezogenen Abgrenzung von Problemfeldern. *Zeitschrift für Berufs- und Wirtschaftspädagogik*, *76*(1), 33–43.

Perridon, L., Steiner, M. & Rathgeber, A. W. (2022). *Finanzwirtschaft der Unternehmung* (18. Aufl.). *Vahlens Handbücher der Wirtschafts- und Sozialwissenschaften*. Verlag Franz Vahlen.

Plinke, W. (2010). Inakzeptable Buchungsregel des wirtschaftsinstrumentellen Ansatzes, des Werte- und Geldflussmodells sowie des Modells des doppischen Rechnungs- und Haushaltswesens für Kommunen in Deutschland. *Wirtschaft und Erziehung*, *62*(10), 171–173.

Plinke, W. (2011a). Gravierende Mängel in der wirtschaftsinstrumentellen Rechnungswesendidaktik: Wenn der Ausnahmebegriff „negatives Wirtschaftsgut" zur Argumentationsbasis wird. *Wirtschaft und Erziehung*, *64*(3), 66–71.

Plinke, W. (2011b). Mangelhafte Terminologie, Aussagen und Junktoren in der wirtschaftsinstrumentellen Rechnungswesendidaktik. *Wirtschaft und Erziehung*, *63*(1–2), 21–27.

Plinke, W. (2012). Mikrokosmos der wirtschaftsinstrumentellen Rechnungswesendidaktik erfordern ein Umdenken. *Wirtschaft und Erziehung*, *63*(4), 98–104.

Plinke, W. (2013). Plädoyer für eine funktions- und nutzenorientierte Rechnungswesendidaktik. *Erziehungswissenschaft und Beruf*, *61*(1), 14–31.

Plinke, W. (2014a). Essay zur Kakophonie in der (wirtschaftsinstrumentellen) Rechnungswesendidaktik, der die langersehnte Euphonie nicht gelingen will. *Wirtschaft und Erziehung*, *66*(8), 306–311.

Plinke, W. (2014b). Kann die Rechnungswesendidaktik mithilfe der Übertragung von didaktischen Konstruktionsmerkmalen aus der Fachdidaktik Betriebswirtschaftslehre weiterentwickelt werden? *Erziehungswissenschaft und Beruf*, *62*(1), 101–113.

Plinke, W. (2014c). Wie kann die Diskussion über die Weiterentwicklungen der Didaktik des Rechnungswesens vorangebracht werden? *Erziehungswissenschaft und Beruf*, *62*(4), 477–492.

Plinke, W. (2015). Buchführung im digitalen Zeitalter: Sicherstellung der Ordnungsmäßigkeit mithilfe der GoB und der GoBD. *Wirtschaft und Erziehung*, *67*(5), 177–182.

Preiß, P. (1999). *Didaktik des wirtschaftsinstrumentellen Rechnungswesens*. De Gruyter.

Preiß, P. (2000). Der Rechnungswesenunterricht als Beitrag zum Verständnis ökonomischer Zusammenhänge und wirtschaftlicher Entscheidungen. In Bundesverband der Lehrer an Wirtschaftsschulen e.V. (Hrsg.), *Funktionswandel des Rechnungswesens. Von der Dokumentation zur Steuerung* (S. 7–29). Heckner.

Preiß, P. (2005a). Entwurf eines Kompetenzmodells für den Inhaltsbereich Rechnungswesen/Controlling. In P. Gonon, F. Klauser, R. Nickolaus & R. Huisinga (Hrsg.), *Kompetenz, Kognition und neue Konzepte der beruflichen Bildung* (S. 67–85). VS Verlag für Sozialwissenschaften.

Preiß, P. (2005b). Förderung kaufmännischer Kompetenzen mit Hilfe des wirtschaftsinstrumentellen Rechnungswesens – aus fachlich-curricularer Perspektive. In D. Sembill & J. Seifried (Hrsg.), *Rechnungswesenunterricht am Scheideweg: Lehren, lernen und prüfen* (S. 53–97). Deutscher Universitätsverlag.

Preiß, P. (2008). Bilanzgleichung und Buchungsregeln auf der Basis von Beträgen oder Werten? *Wirtschaft und Erziehung*(1–2), 16–24.

Preiß, P. (2011). Symmetrie von Wert und Gegenwert als Grundlage der Doppik – Eine Entgegnung zu den Aufsätzen von W. Plinke in WuE 6/2010 und 1–2/2011. *Wirtschaft und Erziehung*, 284–291; 328–333.

Preiß, P. (2015). Kaufmännische Steuerung und Kontrolle als Kernqualifikation kaufmännischer Ausbildung – von der Dokumentation zur Steuerung der Geschäftsvorfälle als Arbeitsprozesse im Rahmen von Geschäftsprozessen. In R. Brötz & F. Kaiser (Hrsg.), *Kaufmännische Berufe: Charakteristik, Vielfalt und Perspektiven* (S. 189–205). Bertelsmann.

Preiß, P. & Tramm, T. (1988). Grundlagen und Grundzüge eines Konzepts der wirtschaftsinstrumentellen Buchführung. *Wirtschaft und Erziehung*, *42*, 83–90.

Preiß, P. & Tramm, T. (1990). Wirtschaftsinstrumentelle Buchführung – Grundzüge eines Konzepts der beruflichen Grundqualifikation im Umgang mit Informationen über Mengen und Werte. In F. Achtenhagen (Hrsg.), *Didaktik des Rechnungswesens: Programm und Kritik eines wirtschaftsinstrumentellen Ansatzes* (S. 13–94). Gabler.

Preiß, P. & Tramm, T. (1996). Die Göttinger Unterrichtskonzeption des wirtschaftsinstrumentellen Rechnungswesens. In P. Preiß & T. Tramm (Hrsg.), *Rechnungswesenunterricht und ökonomisches Denken: Didaktische Innovationen für die kaufmännische Ausbildung* (S. 222–323). Gabler.

Prell-Leopoldseder, S. (2021). *Einführung in die Budgetierung und integrierte Planungsrechnung: Lehr- und Arbeitsbuch* (3. Auflage). Linde Verlag.

Quatember, A. (2019). *Datenqualität in Stichprobenerhebungen: Eine verständnisorientierte Einführung in die Survey-Statistik* (3. Aufl.). *Statistik und ihre Anwendungen*. Springer Spektrum.

Rammstedt, B. (2010). Reliabilität, Validität, Objektivität. In C. Wolf & H. Best (Hrsg.), *Handbuch der sozialwissenschaftlichen Datenanalyse* (S. 239–258). VS Verlag für Sozialwissenschaften.

Rasch, B., Friese, M., Hofmann, W. & Naumann, E. (2010). *Quantitative Methoden Band 2: Einführung in die Statistik für Psychologen und Sozialwissenschaftler* (3., erweiterte Auflage). Springer.

Rausch, A., Seifried, J., Wuttke, E., Kögler, K. & Brandt, S. (2016). Reliability and validity of a computer-based assessment of cognitive and non-cognitive facets of problem-solving competence in the business domain. *Empirical Research in Vocational Education and Training*, *8*(1). https://doi.org/10.1186/s40461-016-0035-y

Rausch, A. & Wuttke, E. (2016). Development of a multi-faceted model of domain-specific problem-solving competence and its acceptance by different stakeholders in the business domain. *Unterrichtswissenschaft*, *44*(2), 169–184.

Rebmann, K. & Tenfelde, W. (2008). *Betriebliches Lernen: Explorationen zur theoriegeleiteten Begründung, Modellierung und praktischen Gestaltung arbeitsbezogenen Lernens*. *Schriften zur Berufs- und Wirtschaftspädagogik: Band 2*. Rainer Hampp Verlag.

Reetz, L. & Witt, R. (1974). *Berufsausbildung in der Kritik: Curriuculumanalyse Wirtschaftslehre*. Hoffmann und Campe.

Reinisch, H. (1994). Luca Pacioli und wirtschaftsethische Dimensionen des Rechnungswesenunterrichts heute. *Zeitschrift für Berufs- und Wirtschaftspädagogik*, *90*(6), 559–585.

Reinisch, H. (1996). „Leitbilder“, Argumentationsmuster und curriculare Konstruktionen in der Didaktik des Rechnungswesenunterrichts – eine historisch-systematische Analyse. In P. Preiß & T. Tramm (Hrsg.), *Rechnungswesenunterricht und ökonomisches Denken: Didaktische Innovationen für die kaufmännische Ausbildung* (S. 45–84). Gabler.

Reinisch, H. (2005). Gibt es aus historischer Perspektive konstante Leitlinien der Diskussion um das Rechnungswesen? In D. Sembill & J. Seifried (Hrsg.), *Rechnungswesenunterricht am Scheideweg: Lehren, lernen und prüfen* (S. 15–31). Deutscher Universitätsverlag.

Reinisch, H. & Struve, K. (2002). Was können wir aus der Geschichte beruflicher Arbeit und berufsbezogener Didaktik lernen? Zur Bedeutung einer historischen Analyse/

Synthese der gegenständlichen Dimension ökonomischer und gewerblich-technischer Bildung. In M. Eckert (Hrsg.), *Bilanzierungen: Schulentwicklung, Lehrerbildung und Wissenschaftsgeschichte im Feld der Wirtschafts- und Berufspädagogik* (S. 99–150). Verl. der Ges. zur Förderung Arbeitsorientierter Forschung und Bildung.

Renner, K.-H., Ströhlein, G. & Heydasch, T. (2009). *Forschungsmethoden der Psychologie: Von der Fragestellung zur Präsentation. Basiswissen Psychologie.* VS Verlag für Sozialwissenschaften.

Resch, M. (1988). *Die Handlungsregulation geistiger Arbeit. Bestimmung und Analyse geistiger Arbeitstätigkeiten in der industriellen Produktion.* Huber.

Reusser, K. (2014). Aufgaben – Träger von Lerngelegenheiten und Lernprozesse im kompetenzorientierten Unterricht. *Seminar – Lehrerbildung und Schule*(4), 77–101.

Reusser, K. & Pauli, C. (2014). Berufsbezogene Überzeugungen von Lehrerinnen und Lehrern. In E. Terhart, H. Bennewitz & M. Rothland (Hrsg.), *Handbuch der Forschung zum Lehrerberuf* (S. 642–661). Waxmann Verlag.

Riebenbauer, E. (2015). Analyse von Einflussfaktoren auf das Rechnungswesenwissen von Studierenden der Wirtschaftspädagogik. *wissenplus*(5), 42–45.

Riebenbauer, E. (2020). Wie entwickelt sich die Fähigkeit zur Planung von Rechnungswesenunterricht bei angehenden Lehrenden? Ausgewählte Ergebnisse einer österreichweiten Längsschnittstudie mit Masterstudierenden der Wirtschaftspädagogik. In F. Berding, H. Jahncke & A. Slopinski (Hrsg.), *Moderner Rechnungswesenunterricht 2020: Status quo und Entwicklungen aus wissenschaftlicher und praktischer Perspektive* (S. 207–226). Springer.

Riebenbauer, E. (2021). *Kompetenzentwicklung im Masterstudium Wirtschaftspädagogik: Längsschnittstudie zur Unterrichtsplanung im Rechnungswesen. Wirtschaft – Beruf – Ethik: Band 40.* wbv.

Riebenbauer, E., Berding, F. & Holtsch, D. (2022). Fachwissenschaftliche Implikationen für die Aus- und Fortbildung von Lehrkräften zur Digitalisierung im Rechnungswesen. In K.-H. Gerholz, P. Schlottmann, P. Slepcevic-Zach & M. Stock (Hrsg.), *Berufsbildung, Arbeit und Innovation: Band 68. Digital Literacy in der beruflichen Lehrer:innenbildung: Didaktik, Empirie und Innovation* (S. 199–212). wbv Media GmbH & Co. KG.

Rohr-Mentele, S. (2022). *Modellierung und Messung von Kompetenzen Kaufmännisch Lernender in der Schweiz.* Universität Zürich. https://doi.org/10.5167/UZH-219237

Rost, J. (2004). *Lehrbuch Testtheorie – Testkonstruktion* (2., vollst. überarb. und erw. Aufl.). Huber.

Rost, J. (2006). Latent-Class-Analyse. In F. Petermann & M. Eid (Hrsg.), *Handbuch der Psychologischen Diagnostik* (S. 275–287). Hogrefe.

Rückwart, W. (2009). Die didaktische Ausrichtung des Rechnungswesens auf der betriebswirtschaftlichen Grundlage von Werte- und Geldflüssen. *Flügelstift*(2), 38–61.

Rückwart, W. (2010). Und sie bewegt sich doch: Buchführungsdidaktik im Umbruch. *Wirtschaft und Erziehung*, *64*(11), 359–364.

Schalek, Y. (2007). *Die Integration handlungsorientierter Gestaltungsmerkmale in Schulbüchern.* Kovac.

Scheufele, B. & Engelmann, I. (2009). *Empirische Kommunikationsforschung. UTB basics: Bd. 3211.* UVK-Verlagsgesellschaft.

Schierenbeck, H. & Wöhle, C. B. (2016). *Grundzüge der Betriebswirtschaftslehre* (19. aktualisierte Auflage). De Gruyter.

Schiller, G. (2004). Lernschwierigkeiten im Fach Rechnungswesen. *Erziehungswissenschaft und Beruf, 52*(3), 335–364.

Schneider, W. (2000). Didaktik des Rechnungswesens im Konflikt zwischen Fachwissenschaft, komplexer Realität und subjektiver Fasslichkeit. In D. Euler, H.-C. Jongebloed & P. F. E. Sloane (Hrsg.), *Sozialökonomische Theorie – sozialökonomisches Handeln: Konturen und Perspektiven der Wirtschafts- und Sozialpädagogik: Festschrift für Martin Twardy zum 60. Geburtstag* (S. 191–210). bajOsch-Hein.

Schneider, W. (2005). Didaktik des Rechnungswesens zwischen Situationsorientierung und Fachsystematik. In D. Sembill & J. Seifried (Hrsg.), *Rechnungswesenunterricht am Scheideweg: Lehren, lernen und prüfen* (S. 33–52). Deutscher Universitätsverlag.

Schneider, W. (2010). Didaktische Entscheidungen im Rechnungswesen. Theoretischer Hintergrund und exemplarische Beispiele. In R. Fortmüller (Hrsg.), *Wirtschaftsdidaktik – eine Tour d'Horizon von den theoretischen Grundlagen bis zur praktischen Anwendung: Festschrift für Josef Aff zum 60. Geburtstag* (S. 55–69). Manz.

Schneider, W., Dobrovits, I. & Schneider, D. (2022). *Einführung in die Buchhaltung im Selbststudium* (24., aktualisierte und ergänzte Auflage). Facultas.

Schneider, W. & Schneider, D. (2019). *Einführung in die Systeme des Rechnungswesens: Finanzplanung, Doppelte Buchhaltung, Kostenrechnung; Aufbau und Fehlerquellen.* Facultas.

Schopf, C., Dobrovits, I., Lorenz, M. & Schmid, P. (2018). Was bringt Stationenlernen im RW-Unterricht? Eine experimentelle Studie zu Lernmotivation und Lernerfolg. *bwp@ Spezial AT-1*, 1–23.

Schopf, C. & Zwischenbrugger, A. (2015). Wie gut erklären Studienanfänger/innen und welche Rolle spielt dabei ihr Fachwissen? Eine quantitative Untersuchung im Masterstudium Wirtschaftspädagogik an der Wirtschaftsuniversität Wien. *wissenplus*(5), 45–49.

Schröder, J. (2020). Folgen der Digitalisierung für die kaufmännische Ausbildung bei der Palfinger Tail Lifts GmbH. In F. Berding, H. Jahncke & A. Slopinski (Hrsg.), *Moderner Rechnungswesenunterricht 2020: Status quo und Entwicklungen aus wissenschaftlicher und praktischer Perspektive* (S. 321–326). Springer.

Schukajlow, S. (2011). *Mathematisches Modellieren: Schwierigkeiten und Strategien von Lernenden als Bausteine einer lernprozessorientierten Didaktik der neuen Aufgabenkultur. Empirische Studien zur Didaktik der Mathematik: Band 6.* Waxmann.

Schupp, H. (1988). Anwendungsorientierter Mathematikunterricht in der Sekundarstufe I zwischen Tradition und neuen Impulsen. *Der Mathematikunterricht, 34*(6), 5–16.

Seifried, J. (2004a). Der Einfluss didaktischer Schwerpunktsetzungen auf das motivationale Erleben des Rechnungswesenunterrichts in einer selbstorganisationsoffenen Lernumgebung. *Zeitschrift für Berufs- und Wirtschaftspädagogik, 100*(2), 242–255.

Seifried, J. (2004b). *Fachdidaktische Variationen in einer selbstorganisationsoffenen Lernumgebung: Eine empirische Untersuchung im Rechnungswesenunterricht.* Deutscher Universitätsverlag.

Seifried, J. (2004c). Rechnungswesenunterricht aus Schülersicht. *Erziehungswissenschaft und Beruf, 52*(3), 327–334.

Seifried, J. (2004d). Schüleraktivitäten beim selbstorganisierten Lernen und deren Auswirkungen auf den Lernerfolg. *Zeitschrift für Erziehungswissenschaft, 7*(4), 569–584.

Seifried, J. (2006a). Sichtweisen auf die methodische Gestaltung von Unterricht. *Zeitschrift für Berufs- und Wirtschaftspädagogik, 102*(4), 578–596.

Seifried, J. (2006b). Überzeugungen von (angehenden) Handelslehrern. In J. Seifried & J. Abel (Hrsg.), *Empirische Lehrerbildungsforschung. Stand und Perspektiven* (S. 109–128). Waxmann Verlag.

Seifried, J. (2008). Methodische Gestaltung des Unterrichts an kaufmännischen Schulen. *Wirtschaft und Erziehung, 60*(1–2), 364–370.

Seifried, J. (2009a). *Unterricht aus der Sicht von Handelslehrern. Konzepte des Lehrens und Lernens: Bd. 16*. Lang.

Seifried, J. (2009b). Unterrichtsplanung von (angehenden) Lehrkräften an kaufmännischen Schulen. *Zeitschrift für Berufs- und Wirtschaftspädagogik, 105*(2), 179–197.

Seifried, J. (2010). Sichtweisen von Lehrkräften an kaufmännischen Schulen. *Zeitschrift für Berufs- und Wirtschaftspädagogik, 106*(2), 199–219.

Seifried, J., Grill, L. & Wagner, M. (2006). Unterrichtsmethoden in der kaufmännischen Unterrichtspraxis. *Wirtschaft und Erziehung, 58*(7–8), 234–241.

Seifried, J. & Klüber, C. (2006). Unterrichtserleben in schüler- und lehrerzentrierten Unterrichtsphasen. *Unterrichtswissenschaft, 34*(1), 2–21.

Seifried, J., Rausch, A., Kögler, K., Brandt, S., Eigenmann, R., Schley, T. & Wolf, K. D. (2016). Problemlösekompetenz angehender Industriekaufleute: Konzeption des Messinstruments und ausgewählte empirische Befunde. In K. Beck, M. Landenberger & F. Oser (Hrsg.), *Technologiebasierte Kompetenzmessung in der beruflichen Bildung: Ergebnisse aus der BMBF-Förderinitiative ASCOT* (S. 119–138). wbv.

Seifried, J. & Sembill, D. (2004). Rechnungswesenunterricht neu gestalten – Empirische Befunde aus einem Kooperationsprojekt zwischen Schule und Hochschule. *Wirtschaft und Erziehung, 56*(11), 371–379.

Seifried, J. & Sembill, D. (2005a). Rechnungswesenunterricht am Scheideweg? – Einführung in den Sammelband. In D. Sembill & J. Seifried (Hrsg.), *Rechnungswesenunterricht am Scheideweg: Lehren, lernen und prüfen* (S. 1–14). Deutscher Universitätsverlag.

Seifried, J. & Sembill, D. (2005b). Schülerfragen – ein brach liegendes didaktisches Feld. *Zeitschrift für Berufs- und Wirtschaftspädagogik, 101*(2), 229–245.

Seifried, J., Türling, J. & Wuttke, E. (2010). Professionelles Lehrerhandeln – Schülerfehler erkennen und für Lernprozesse nutzen. In J. Warwas & D. Sembill (Hrsg.), *Schule zwischen Effizienzkriterien und Sinnfragen* (S. 137–155). Schneider Hohengehren.

Seifried, J. & Wuttke, E. (2010). Potenziale des Lernens aus Fehlern in Abhängigkeit von methodischen Grundentscheidungen. In J. Seifried, E. Wuttke, R. Nickolaus & P. F. Sloane (Hrsg.), *Lehr-Lern-Forschung in der kaufmännischen Berufsbildung. Ergebnisse und Gestaltungsaufgaben* (S. 155–171). Steiner Verlag.

Sharpe, D. (2015). Chi-Square Test is Statistically Significant: Now What? *Practical Assessment, Research, and Evaluation, 20*. https://doi.org/10.7275/tbfa-x148

Sloane, P. F. (1996). *Didaktik des Rechnungswesens*. Centaurus.

Stachowiak, H. (1973). *Allgemeine Modelltheorie*. Springer.

Statistik Austria. (2022). *Bildung in Zahlen 2020/21*.

Stock, M., Slepcevic-Zach, P., Fernandez, K. & Bodi, O. (2011). Prüft die BDA vernetztes Wissen? Zentrale Ergebnisse aus der Evaluation der Reife- und Diplomprüfung an österreichischen Handelsakademien. *wissenplus, 5*(10–11), 14–20.

Stommel, A. (2014a). Bilanzmethode oder „Neues Rechnungswesen": Welche Methode fördert das ökonomische Denken? *Wirtschaft und Erziehung, 66*(4), 148–154.

Stommel, A. (2014b). Die schöne, neue Welt des „Neuen Rechnungswesens". *Erziehungswissenschaft und Beruf, 62*(1), 229–239.

Stütz, S. (2021). Der Rechnungswesenunterricht im retrospektiven Erleben von Studierenden der Wirtschaftspädagogik. *Bwp@ Österreich spezial AT-3*(1–22). http://www.bwpat.de/wipaed-at3/stuetz_wipaed-at_2021.pdf

Stütz, S., Berding, F., Reincke, S. & Scheper, L. (2022). Characteristics of learning tasks in accounting textbooks: an AI assisted analysis. *Empirical Research in Vocational Education and Training, 14*(1). https://doi.org/10.1186/s40461-022-00138-2

Svatopluk, A., Haisermann, A., Schabicki, T. & Frank, S. (2018). Robotic Process Automation (RPA) im Rechnungswesen und Controlling – welche Chancen ergeben sich? *Controlling, 30*(3), 11–19. https://doi.org/10.15358/0935-0381-2018-3-11

Tausendpfund, M. (2022). *Quantitative Datenanalyse: Eine Einführung mit SPSS* (2. Aufl.). *Studientexte zur Soziologie*. Springer VS.

Thoma, M. & Schumacher, V. (2018). Lernaufgaben in Schulbüchern – Empirische Befunde zum kognitiven Aktivierungspotenzial im Fach Rechnungswesen. *bwp@ Österreich Spezial AT-1*, 1–18. http://www.bwpat.de/wipaed-at1/thoma_schumacher_wipaed-at_2018.pdf

Thonhauser, J. (2008). Warum (neues) Interesse am Thema „Aufgaben"? In J. Thonhauser (Hrsg.), *Aufgaben als Katalysator von Lernprozessen* (S. 13–27). Waxmann.

Thonhauser, J. (2020). Aufgaben als Katalysatoren von Lernprozessen. In U. Greiner, F. Hofmann, C. Schreiner & C. Wiesner (Hrsg.), *Bildungsstandards: Kompetenzorientierung, Aufgabenkultur und Qualitätsentwicklung im Schulsystem* (S. 464–481). Waxmann.

Töpfer, A. (2007). *Betriebswirtschaftslehre: Anwendungs- und prozessorientierte Grundlagen* (2., überarb. Aufl.). Springer.

Tramm, T. (2003). Wirtschaftsinstrumentelles Rechnungswesen und die Modellierungsmethode – eine fachdidaktische Einführung. In D. Joost, G. Kripke & T. Tramm (Hrsg.), *Wirtschaftsinstrumentelles Rechnungswesen – Materialienband* (S. 4–10). Bildungsverlag EINS.

Tramm, T. (2005). Wirtschaftsinstrumentelles Rechnungswesen konkrekt. In D. Sembill & J. Seifried (Hrsg.), *Rechnungswesenunterricht am Scheideweg: Lehren, lernen und prüfen* (S. 99–122). Deutscher Universitätsverlag.

Tramm, T. (2009). Von der Geschäftsprozess- zur Lernprozessperspektive: Das Zusammenspiel von Prozessorientierung, systemischer Perspektive und prozessübergreifender Kompetenzentwicklung im lernfeldstrukturierten Berufsschulunterricht. In H. Pongratz (Hrsg.), *Prozessorientierte Wirtschaftsdidaktik und Einsatz von ERP-Systemen im kaufmännischen Unterricht* (S. 77–101). Shaker.

Tramm, T. (2010). Berufliche Kompetenzentwicklung im Kontext kaufmännischer Arbeits- und Geschäftsprozesse. In F. Schapfel-Kaiser (Hrsg.), *Anforderungen an kaufmännisch-betriebswirtschaftliche Berufe: Berichte zur beruflichen Bildung* (S. 65–88). Bertelsmann.

Tramm, T. (2014). Ökonomisches Systemverständnis und systemisches Denken als Dimensionen kaufmännischer Bildung. In H. H. Kremer, T. Tramm & K. Wilbers (Hrsg.), *Kaufmännische Bildung? Sondierungen zu einer vernachlässigten Sinndimension* (S. 95–116). epubli.

Tramm, T. & Goldbach, A. (2005). Gestaltungsprinzipien und theoretische Grundlagen innovativer Schulbücher zur ökonomischen Berufsbildung – am Beispiel der „prozessorientierten Wirtschaftslehre". *Wirtschaft und Erziehung*(6), 203–213.

Tramm, T., Hinrichs, K. & Langenheim, H. (1996). Lernschwierigkeiten im Buchführungsunterricht. In P. Preiß & T. Tramm (Hrsg.), *Rechnungswesenunterricht und ökonomisches Denken: Didaktische Innovationen für die kaufmännische Ausbildung* (S. 158–221). Gabler.

Tramm, T. & Preiß, P. (1996). Rechnungswesenunterricht und ökonomisches Denken. In P. Preiß & T. Tramm (Hrsg.), *Rechnungswesenunterricht und ökonomisches Denken: Didaktische Innovationen für die kaufmännische Ausbildung* (S. 1–21). Gabler.

Tramm, T. & Seeber, S. (2006). Überlegungen und Analysen zur Spezifizität kaufmännischer Kompetenz. In G. Minnameier (Hrsg.), *Berufs- und wirtschaftspädagogische Grundlagenforschung. Lehr-Lern-Prozesse und Kompetenzdiagnostik: Festschrift für Klaus Beck* (S. 273–288). Lang.

Troßmann, E. & Baumeister, A. (2015). *Internes Rechnungswesen: Kostenrechnung als Standardinstrument im Controlling*. Vahlen.

Türling, J. (2014). *Die professionelle Fehlerkompetenz von (angehenden) Lehrkräften: Eine empirische Untersuchung im Rechnungswesenunterricht*. Springer.

Türling, J., Seifried, J. & Wuttke, E. (2012). Teachers' Knowledge about Domain Specific Student Errors. In E. Wuttke & J. Seifried (Hrsg.), *Learning from errors at school and at work* (S. 95–110). Verlag Barbara Budrich.

Türling, J., Seifried, J., Wuttke, E., Gewiese, A. & Kästner, R. (2011). „Typische" Schülerfehler im Rechnungswesenunterricht: empirische Befunde einer Interviewstudie. *Zeitschrift für Berufs- und Wirtschaftspädagogik*, *107*(3), 390–407.

Vahs, D. (2019). *Organisation: Ein Lehr- und Managementbuch* (10., überarbeitete Auflage). Schäffer-Poeschel.

vom Hofe, R. (1995). *Grundvorstellungen mathematischer Inhalte. Texte zur Didaktik der Mathematik*. Spektrum.

Waltermann, A. (1976). Neustrukturierung des Anfangsunterrichts in Buchführung. *Wirtschaft und Erziehung*(7), 189–202.

Weber, S., Draxler, C., Achtenhagen, F., Bley, S., Wiethe-Körprich, M. & Kreuzer, C. (2021). Measuring Apprentices' Intrapreneurship Competence in Vocational Education and Traning (VET): An Interdisciplinary Model-Based Assessment. In E. Kuusisto, M. Ubani, P. Nokelainen & A. Toom (Hrsg.), *Moral development and citizenship education: Bd. 16. Good Teachers for Tomorrow´s Schools. Purpose, Values, and Talents in Education*. Brill.

Weber, S., Draxler, C., Bley, S., Wiethe-Körprich, M., Weiß, C. & Gürer, C. (2016). Large scale assessments in der kaufmännischen Berufsbildung – Intrapreneurship (CoBALIT). In K. Beck, M. Landenberger & F. Oser (Hrsg.), *Technologiebasierte Kompetenzmessung in der beruflichen Bildung: Ergebnisse aus der BMBF-Förderinitiative ASCOT* (S. 75–92). wbv.

Weber, S., Wiethe-Körprich, M., Bley, S., Weiß, C., Draxler, C. & Gürer, C. (2016). Modellierung und Validierung eines Intrapreneurship-Kompetenz-Modells bei Industriekaufleuten. *Unterrichtswissenschaft*, *44*(2), 149–168.

Weller, H. & Fischer, H. (1998). Überwindung von Schwachstellen des traditionellen Rechnungswesen-Unterrichts: Teil 1 – 6. *Wirtschaft und Erziehung*, *50*(2–11).

Wilbers, K. (2019). Veränderungen im Zusammenspiel von gewerblich-technischem und kaufmännischem Handeln durch Industrie 4.0 als Chance für die Berufsausbildung. In G. Spöttl & L. Windelband (Hrsg.), *Berufsbildung, Arbeit und Innovation. Industrie 4.0: Risiken und Chancen für die Berufsbildung* (S. 273–289).

Winther, E. (2010). *Kompetenzmessung in der beruflichen Bildung*. Bertelsmann.

Winther, E. & Achtenhagen, F. (2008). Kompetenzstrukturmodell für die kaufmännische Bildung. *Zeitschrift für Berufs- und Wirtschaftspädagogik*, *104*(4), 511–538.

Winther, E. & Achtenhagen, F. (2009). Skalen und Stufen kaufmännischer Kompetenz. *Zeitschrift für Berufs- und Wirtschaftspädagogik*, *105*(4), 521–556.

Winther, E., Festner, D., Sangmeister, J. & Klotz, V. (2016). Facing commercial competence: Modeling domain-linked and domain-specific competence as key elements of vocational development. In E. Wuttke (Hrsg.), *Research in Vocational Education Series: Band 3. Economic Competence and Financial Literacy of Young Adults: Status and Challenges* (S. 149–163). Verlag Barbara Budrich.

Winther, E., Seeber, S., Festner, D., Sangmeister, J. & Liedtke, M. (2016). Large scale assessments in der kaufmännischen Berufsbildung – Das Unternehmensassessment ALUSIM (CoBALIT). In K. Beck, M. Landenberger & F. Oser (Hrsg.), *Technologiebasierte Kompetenzmessung in der beruflichen Bildung: Ergebnisse aus der BMBF-Förderinitiative ASCOT* (S. 55–74). wbv.

Wöhe, G., Döring, U. & Brösel, G. (2020). *Einführung in die allgemeine Betriebswirtschaftslehre* (27., überarbeitete und aktualisierte Auflage). Verlag Franz Vahlen.

Wuttke, E. (1999). *Motivation und Lernstrategien in einer selbstorganisationsoffenen Lernumgebung: Eine empirische Untersuchung bei Industriekaufleuten*. Lang.

Wuttke, E., Seeber, S., Geiser, C. & Turhan, L. (2022). Zur Problemhaltigkeit von Aufgaben in kaufmännischem Abschlussund Zwischenprüfungen – Ergebnisse aus Aufgabenanalysen. *Zeitschrift für Berufs- und Wirtschaftspädagogik*, *118*(1), 25. https://doi.org/10.25162/zbw-2022-0002

Wuttke, E. & Seifried, J. (2012). Ansätze der Identifikation typischer Schülerfehler – Ergebnisse aus Studien in kaufmännischen Schulen. *Unterrichtswissenschaft*, *40*(2), 174–192.

Wuttke, E., Seifried, J., Brandt, S., Rausch, A., Sembill, D., Martens, T. & Wolf, K. (2015). Modellierung und Messung domänenspezifischer Problemlösekompetenz bei angehenden Industriekaufleuten. *Zeitschrift für Berufs- und Wirtschaftspädagogik*, *111*(2), 189–207.

Zhao, X., Feng, G., Liu, J. & Deng, K. (2018). We agreed to measure agreement – Redefining reliability de-justifies Krippendorff's alpha. *China Media Research*, *14*(2), 1–15.

Zhao, X., Liu, J. S. & Deng, K. (2013). Assumptions behind Intercoder Reliability Indices. *Annals of the International Communication Association*, *36*(1), 419–480. https://doi.org/10.1080/23808985.2013.11679142

Zhou, Y. (2022). *Cognitive Requirement of Accounting Tasks: A Task Analysis in Chinese Vocational School Textbooks. Berufsbildung, Arbeit und Innovation – Dissertationen und Habilitationen*. wbv.

Zurstrassen, B. (2009). Das Lernfeldkonzept an Berufsschulen: Von der Chance, berufliche und politische Bildung zu vereinen. *Gesellschaft, Wirtschaft, Politik*(3), 437–448.

MIX
Papier aus verantwortungsvollen Quellen
Paper from responsible sources
FSC® C105338

If you have any concerns about our products,
you can contact us on
ProductSafety@springernature.com

In case Publisher is established outside the EU,
the EU authorized representative is:
Springer Nature Customer Service Center GmbH
Europaplatz 3, 69115 Heidelberg, Germany

Printed by Libri Plureos GmbH
in Hamburg, Germany